THE COMPLETE GUIDE TO TRAINING DELIVERY

A COMPETENCY-BASED APPROACH

Stephen B. King

Marsha King

William J. Rothwell

With a Foreword by

William C. Byham, Ph.D.
President and Chief Executive Officer
Development Dimensions International, Inc. (DDI)

AMACOM

American Management Association

New York • Atlanta • Boston • Chicago • Kansas City • San Francisco • Washington, D.C.
Brussels • Mexico City • Tokyo • Toronto

This publication is designed to provide accurate and authoritative information in regard to the subject matter covered. It is sold with the understanding that the publisher is not engaged in rendering legal, accounting, or other professional service. If legal advice or other expert assistance is required, the services of a competent professional person should be sought.

Library of Congress Cataloging-in-Publication Data

King, Stephen B.
    The complete guide to training delivery: a competency-based approach / Stephen B. King, Marsha King, William J. Rothwell ; with a foreword by William C. Byham.
        p. cm.
    Includes index.
    ISBN 0-8144-0490-1
    1. Training—Handbooks, manuals, etc. 2. Employees—Training of—Handbooks, manuals, etc. 3. Competency based education—Handbooks, manuals, etc.
    I. King, Marsha, Ph. D. II. Rothwell, William J., 1951 - III. Title.

    LB1027.47 .K49 2000
    658.3'124—dc21   00-038580

Printing number

10 9 8 7 6 5 4

CONTENTS

FOREWORD

Continuous learning is a necessity of the twenty-first century. Changing technologies, new organizational structures, frequent horizontal and vertical job movement, numerous task force and committee assignments, plus increasingly complicated responsibilities at home and as part of civic and religious activities will provide a learning challenge never before seen. There will be a tremendous amount to learn and the amount will increase every year.

Continuous learning is the responsibility of each individual. However, organizations have the responsibility to help individuals assess their skills and knowledge so they can define their development needs and provide them with access to learning opportunities that meet their unique and changing needs. Organizations have traditionally provided learning opportunities through on-the-job or short-term assignments and through appropriate training programs.

In the twenty-first century, learning needs will increasingly be met in a variety of high-tech ways, such as computer-based interactive training delivered by CD-ROM or the World Wide Web. But a significant amount of learning will continue to come through a classroom experience. Classroom training still is the most effective means of delivering certain content. Many people want to learn in groups and learn best by interacting with others. Others need the motivation provided by an organized classroom experience, where participants can compare themselves with the achievements of others. The secret of effective twenty-first-century delivery of learning will be in the mix of high-tech and live classroom experiences (often being intermediated through videoconferencing and other technologies).

Providing classroom training in the twenty-first century will not be easy! Effectiveness (quality) will be increasingly important. Organizations will see training as a strategic advantage. There will be increased competition for the learner's time. There certainly will be no time to waste. Learners will select training programs that are as short and as efficient as possible—programs that will be delivered just in time for application. Organizations won't want to waste the time and effort of their valuable human resources on something that doesn't work. Keeping the audience's attention will be an increasing challenge. A generation reared on TV and computer games, with short attention spans, will present unique challenges to the instructor. Also, audience characteristics will vary widely. Programs will need to be more tailored to the specific motivations, learning styles, and social backgrounds of the learners.

The Complete Guide to Training Delivery: A Competency-Based Approach is a book for the twenty-first-century classroom trainer who wants to be the best he or she can be in providing the most beneficial experience possible for the learner. The book focuses on the competencies defined by the International Board of Standards for Training, Performance, and Instruction and provides the flesh around the bones shown by the IBSTPI research. Each competency is defined, illustrated, and thoroughly discussed.

Excellent examples and expansions of concepts are provided for the trainer. *The Complete Guide to Training Delivery* provides what is necessary for a trainer to achieve the competencies that are required for success.

William C. Byham, Ph.D.
President and CEO
Development Dimensions International, Inc.

PREFACE

For many years training has been considered by some people to be a low-profile and thankless job. Often trainers resided in the "low-rent" district of the organization, isolated from the top management team and key decision-makers. They had to fight for conference room space to deliver a training session that was attended by only half the people who signed up for it. These problems persist even today in some organizations. If you find that hard to believe, then consider the following situation recently described to us by one trainer. The tone of this description underscores the trainer's frustration.

No Room at the Inn

" The most typical problem is finding training space for both classroom and laboratory (hands-on) training. We do not have our own space and have to rely on other areas/departments to get space. The result of this is a lot of wasted time related to finding rooms, changing rooms when we are tossed out for a higher priority meeting, and moving equipment around. "

But the last decade ushered in an era of unparalleled focus on people, which has changed the role of training in organizations. This new focus is apparent from the many slogans that you might hear used by senior executives, such as "People are our most important asset" and "Human resources are our company's only truly sustainable competitive advantage." The top managers who make these statements want to emphasize the importance they place on intellectual and human capital. With this increased emphasis on human resources, the training and development field has gained attention as one important way to improve individual, as well as organizational, performance.

According to the 1999 *State of the Industry Report* published by the American Society for Training and Development (ASTD), U.S. organizations invested an average of $649 per employee on training each year. Vice presidents and directors of training and human resources today frequently occupy a highly visible role on the top management team. Training is incorporated into, and integrated with, the strategic planning process. In fact, training is now considered to be one important way to implement, and even lead, organizational change efforts.

The focus of this book is on *training delivery*. Many different people undertake training delivery. Just think about it: The person who conducts a course on how to use a word processing software package is a trainer. The individual who delivers a three-day teambuilding workshop to a department of ten is a trainer. The executive who steps in to kick off a half-day basic supervisory skills seminar for new supervisors is a trainer, albeit on a part-time basis. The technical specialist who instructs a customer group on the proper use of the organization's product is a trainer. The vendor who delivers a program on basic welding skills in a manufacturing organization is a trainer. Regardless of the subject matter that is presented, trainers are those who build the work-related skills of learners through workshops, courses, classes, presentations, seminars, or sessions. While electronically assisted delivery methods such as computer-based training or Web-based training are on the rise, organizations still rely heavily on classroom training that is led by instructors. This book focuses on improving the effectiveness of anyone who conducts training in group or classroom settings. It is therefore centered on improving what are sometimes also called *platform presentation skills*.

FOUNDATION FOR THE BOOK

Most books on training delivery are based on the opinions of seasoned training practitioners. While insightful and interesting, these books sometimes lack sound, research-based foundations and organizing principles. But *The Complete Guide to Training Delivery: A Competency-Based Approach* stands in stark contrast to those books. It is based on research about instructor competencies found in Hutchison, Stein, and Shepherd's *Instructor Competencies, Volume 1: The Standards*. This research study, sponsored by the International Board of Standards for Training, Performance, and Instruction (IBSTPI), pinpointed the competencies essential to successful training delivery. The IBSTPI researchers used literature searches, observations, peer reviews, corporate documentation, expert judgment, and other methods to isolate the *competencies*—a term defined here to mean knowledge, skills, and attitudes—essential to success in delivering group training. Throughout this book we refer to the IBSTPI-sponsored competency study as simply the IBSTPI Standards.

The Complete Guide to Training Delivery builds on the IBSTPI Standards by providing practical strategies that can be *applied* by trainers when they deliver training. In addition to relying on the research results found in the IBSTPI Standards, we also conducted survey research among training practitioners to gain additional insight into their opinions of instructor competencies derived from their experience. This research is described in Chapter One and in Appendix A.

Throughout the book we have placed *critical incidents* (difficult situations) in training delivery encountered by our survey respondents. Further, we have also included excerpts in this book from interviews we conducted with such well-known training practitioners as Bob Pike and Sivasailam Thiagarajan ("Thiagi"), both well known for their outstanding presentation skills.

The IBSTPI Standards were written in general terms so that they could be applied across many organizations. *The Complete Guide to Training Delivery* translates these competencies into practical applications for trainers involved in instructor-led, group training delivery. The competencies listed in the IBSTPI Standards and described more completely in this book provide you with a solid foundation of the fundamental skills essential to effective training delivery. *The Complete Guide to Training Delivery* gives you practical guidance on how to build your training delivery competence. Further, at the end of each chapter we provide *Strategy Lists* with actionable strategies for improving your training effectiveness.

INTENDED AUDIENCE

A wide audience exists for *The Complete Guide to Training Delivery*. You can benefit from this book if you are a teacher, educator, manager, part-time instructor, or public speaker. If you are a new or part-time trainer, you should find the book valuable because it introduces the fundamentals of training delivery. By practicing the skills and incorporating the strategies covered in this book, you can develop the skills leading to successful training delivery. Even if you are an experienced trainer, you will find competencies in this book that you may need to refine. You will learn from the many practical training delivery strategies that we describe throughout the book.

OVERVIEW OF THE CONTENTS

In the first three chapters we present a "big picture" view of how and where training contributes to improving organizational performance. Chapter One summarizes each of the fourteen delivery competencies that are identified in the IBSTPI Standards and which serve as the basis for subsequent chapters in the book. Chapter Two matches training content (the subject matter) to the targeted learners (the audience) and discusses key learner styles and characteristics. Chapter Three deals with preparing the training site and laying out the room and the equipment that you will need to deliver training. It also gives you some pointers on how to handle logistical arrangements.

In Chapters Four and Five, we make suggestions for establishing and maintaining your credibility and for managing the learning environment. Chapter Four deals with establishing credibility by demonstrating acceptable conduct, content expertise, and flexibility. In Chapter Five we cover the *psychological* climate or the atmosphere of the learning environment. We outline several time management techniques that are designed to ensure that you cover all the material in a manner that facilitates learner understanding, and we give you effective ways to deal with the bane of any good training instructor—disruptive, resistant, or silent learners.

Chapters Six through Ten describe effective communication and presentation skills that will help you capture and maintain learners' attention and will ensure that they grasp your meaning. In Chapter Six we discuss how to use verbal and nonverbal language and adapt your messages to learner needs. Chapter Seven focuses on developing effective presentation skills by making effective use of your voice, eye contact, gestures, movement, and other visible actions to seize and hold learner attention. Effective questioning skills and techniques are covered in Chapter Eight, where we emphasize how to ask questions, how to use active listening during the questioning process, and how to follow up effectively on questions. In Chapter Nine we focus on responding to learner questions or comments during training, providing you with specific strategies for identifying when learners need clarification or feedback, planning an appropriate response, and delivering the response effectively. In Chapter Ten you will learn how to provide positive reinforcement and motivational incentives to learners.

Chapter Eleven introduces *training methods*, defined as specific techniques and processes used to facilitate learning and achieve the objectives. We explain how to use such methods as case studies, role playing, lectures, group discussions, and small or large group activities.

Chapter Twelve covers *training media*, including overhead transparencies, printed material, flipcharts, computer-related presentations, and video. We discuss what strategies you can use to transition from one medium to another and how to troubleshoot media-related problems you may encounter during delivery.

Chapter Thirteen reviews ways you can compare learners' achievements to training objectives. We review tested approaches you can use to accomplish this task both during and following training, and we discuss Donald Kirkpatrick's well-known "four levels of evaluation" framework.

The primary focus of Chapter Fourteen is on assessing your ability to help learners achieve the objectives. In addition, we discuss evaluation of the instructional design, including modifying the design during training. Chapter Fifteen discusses how best to provide an evaluation report to the appropriate stakeholders, including the supervisors of training participants, top managers, and instructional designers. The purpose of the evaluation report is to provide key people with relevant summary information concerning instructional and organizational outcomes stemming from the training effort.

Chapter Sixteen looks at three increasingly relevant topics in training delivery. First we discuss training in international settings. We then turn attention to the subject of co-training, including when and how to use multiple trainers during delivery. The third topic addressed in this chapter is the transfer of training from classroom to workplace. *Training transfer*—which refers to how what is learned in training is applied in the workplace—has been the focus of growing interest in recent years as decision makers demand to know whether training makes a difference in worker job performance and organizational productivity.

As mentioned above, the first of the three appendixes contains the details of our survey, which was the source for the "critical incidents" and many of the statistics used throughout the book. Appendix B contains critical incidents from our survey respondents that do not appear elsewhere in the book. You might find it useful to use them as an exercise to stimulate your own thinking about how to deal with the challenges facing trainers. Appendix C contains an annotated list of the resources that are mentioned in the text, with contact information that will allow you to explore these sources in more detail.

The Complete Guide to Training Delivery: A Competency-Based Approach is about improving the effectiveness of training delivery. The fourteen instructor competencies identified by the International Board of Standards for Training, Performance, and Instruction provide the foundation for most of the book. We bring these competencies to life by providing descriptions, explanations, and discussions about what those competencies mean for you as you deliver training. More important, we provide examples, job aids, worksheets, case studies, and sample dialogs throughout the book to help you become a more effective trainer. The book also contains actual experiences and critical incidents faced by trainers who participated in our survey study.

The Complete Guide to Training Delivery is intended to provide you with the tools and techniques you need to be more effective when you deliver training. Whether you are a new trainer or a seasoned veteran, the information and tools in this book will help you improve your skills. It will be your responsibility to apply the competencies to your training delivery. That is where you will realize the true benefits.

Each training delivery experience is truly an adventure. Good luck as you embark on your adventures.

ACKNOWLEDGMENTS

We wish to thank the International Board of Standards for Training, Performance, and Instruction (IBSTPI) for allowing us to use the fourteen instructor competencies, which serve as the foundation for *The Complete Guide to Training Delivery*. We also thank the 107 training practitioners who participated in our survey study on training delivery issues. Their willingness to share their "critical incident" experiences helped to ground the book by providing real-world examples. We express our deep appreciation to William C. Byham, Sivasailam Thiagarajan, and Bob Pike for making gracious contributions to this book. We thank the entire staff at AMACOM Books, especially Jacquie Flynn, Christina McLaughlin, and Adrienne Hickey. We also appreciate the contributions made by Ray Keresky, Pam Loughner, and Doug Harvey. We appreciate the support, encouragement, and prodding that our families gave us as we saw this work through to completion. Last but not least, we give thanks to God for the countless blessings.

CHAPTER 1

INTRODUCING TRAINING AND TRAINING DELIVERY

Each time you prepare to deliver training it is like embarking on an incredible journey. You make plans, chart your course, assemble your equipment, and then you begin. Professional trainers who make a career of presenting instruction cite what they love most about the job—its constant variety, the joy of watching learners grow and develop, and the thrill of standing before a group of learners. Sometimes, however, there can be bumps in the road on the training journey: stage fright experienced by novice trainers; resistant, disruptive, and even hostile learners; and organizational problems that fall outside the instructor's ability to control. Trainers learn to take the good with the bad. In the end, they regard their unpleasant experiences as battle scars marking their own growth.

This chapter provides some important background information for you as you prepare for your journey. It covers the following topics:

- Definitions of key terms.

- How to determine when training is the appropriate solution to problems.

- How training is related to effective performance improvement.

- Summary of the fourteen competencies that are essential to effective training delivery (instruction).

You will find that each competency is like an important tool that you will need on your journey. By building these competencies systematically, as this book permits you to do, you can improve your effectiveness as a trainer and avoid common mistakes made by novice instructors.

DEFINING KEY TERMS

Many terms are used to describe activities associated with delivering classroom training. *Training,* for our purposes, focuses on enhancing learners' knowledge and skills. *Knowledge* is what people know or understand. *Skills* are what they can do. Training usually focuses on improving knowledge or skills related to an individual's current job performance. The immediacy of training can be contrasted with the longer-term focus of *development,* which prepares individuals for future responsibilities.

The people who conduct classroom training—who are called trainers or instructors—engage in such varied activities as presenting information, leading small and large group discussions, facilitating group processes, asking questions, and guiding learners through structured activities such as role plays or games. While training can be undertaken in many settings and through the use of many methods or media, in this book we will use the terms *training* or *training delivery* to refer specifically to classroom training delivery. The term *instruction* will be used synonymously with training delivery.

What are trainers expected to do? To answer that question, you might find it helpful to review the following—and typical—advertisement for a trainer that appeared in the International Society for Performance Improvement's (ISPI) monthly newsletter entitled *News & Notes*:

TRAINER POSITION: As a trainer you will conduct training sessions covering specific areas such as new employee orientation, on-the-job training, use of computers and software, sales techniques, systems training, new product information, and leadership development. You will participate on Curriculum Advisory Committees and confer with management to gain knowledge of work situations that require training in policy changes, procedures, and technologies. This position requires excellent communication (oral and written), stand-up training skills, and the ability to solve problems creatively. Qualified candidates must be customer-service oriented and show strong ability to form business partnerships with associates in the field, with the operations department, and within the training team.[1]

This advertisement provides an encapsulated position description of a trainer. It emphasizes the topics, such as new employee orientation and sales techniques, that the trainer will be expected to present. It also emphasizes key competencies required of an effective trainer, such as "excellent communication (oral and written)," "stand-up training skills," and "the ability to solve problems creatively."

Throughout this book we refer to instructional designers and make a clear distinction between trainers and instructional designers. *Instructional designers*, sometimes referred to simply as designers or *instructional design experts* (IDEs), are individuals who are trained in how to create instruction. They follow a rigorous, systematic process called the Instructional Systems Design (ISD) model to design and develop effective training programs. You may wish to consult Rothwell and Kazanas, *Mastering the Instructional Design Process*, an excellent text on instructional design.

Designers work with subject matter experts to create programs that improve learners' knowledge, skills, or attitudes. Instructional designers, unlike instructors or trainers who deliver instruction, perform such activities as writing training objectives, preparing tests that cover the training material, deciding which training methods are appropriate, preparing instructional materials such as participant guides, instructor guides, and class activities, and much more. Trainers then deliver the materials prepared by instructional designers. In practice, trainers sometimes play both the role of instructional designer and that of instructor/trainer. But, in this book, we distinguish between the two roles to emphasize that effective training delivery must be based on a sound instructional design.

THE IMPORTANCE OF TRADITIONAL TRAINING DELIVERY

Classroom presentation skills remain important to success in the training field.

For instance, the 2000 ASTD State of the Industry Report identified instructor-led classroom training as the most frequently used instructional delivery method. The survey results revealed that over 70 percent of organizations considered to be training investment leaders used classroom training.

The results of this ASTD survey predict a rise in interest in technology-based training delivery methods, such as Web-based training or CD-ROM-based training. Some people believe that classroom training is becoming obsolete and is being supplanted by training delivered by personal computers, the Internet, or other technology-based platforms.

While interest in technology-based delivery is obvious, it is unlikely that classroom training will ever become obsolete. One reason is that training participants want a "human touch," which cannot be easily given by technology-based training delivery media. A second reason is that classroom training methods are generally more effective than technology-based methods for teaching people how to interact with other people. A third reason is that people in groups are more creative than they are as individuals, which makes group settings like classrooms ideal places to pool the knowledge of people to solve problems and discover new knowledge. In this book, we focus on how technology can augment training delivery rather than replace it.

TRAINING IS NOT ALWAYS THE APPROPRIATE SOLUTION

To be effective as a trainer, you need to know when training is an appropriate means for solving problems—and when it is not appropriate.

To give you a chance to think about this, listen in on several conversations. The first is between an operations manager in a manufacturing organization and a trainer:

MANAGER: *The work-teams down in the finishing department have really been having some trouble working together. The supervisors are at a loss to figure out what is wrong. They say they have tried everything—talking to the groups, individual counseling, and even taking disciplinary action such as writing people up. I can't figure out what is wrong down there.*

TRAINER: *Well, it sounds pretty serious to me. I'm not sure if you are aware of this, but we have a two-day team building program that might help. We cover things like communication styles, getting to know others, and working together. This might be the answer.*

MANAGER: *Yes, that sounds good. Let's run all fifty people through that, and down the road we might send the whole plant.*

TRAINER: *Great! I'll get right on it and we'll get this thing rolled out.*

The next conversation takes place between the general manager of a large business unit and a trainer in a financial services organization:

GENERAL MANAGER: *The reason I wanted to see you was that I recently had a conversation with a good colleague of mine. Her organization recently installed a TQM program that people are really excited about. I also read an article about TQM in the flight magazine on a recent trip to Cambridge branch.*

TRAINER: *Yes, I'm familiar with TQM.*

GENERAL MANAGER: *What I want you to do is pull together a three-day workshop on TQM.*

TRAINER: *No problem. How soon do we want to run it?*

GENERAL MANAGER: *Well, Sarah, the colleague I mentioned, already has a jump on us, so I'd like to see it ready to go as soon as possible.*

TRAINER: *We'll give it top priority.*

These conversations reveal a trap that trainers can sometimes fall into. Trainers, by the nature of their work, may view too many problems as requiring a training solution. Likewise, trainers may sometimes accept, without question, requests for training from others in the organization.

If you find this hard to believe, then consider the following critical incidents (difficult situations) provided by two respondents in our survey of training practitioners. (Our survey is described in more detail at the end of this chapter and in Appendix A.) These two stories, told in the actual words of trainers, demonstrate the valuable lessons that these trainers learned by acting on inappropriate requests for training when other solutions might have been more effective in solving problems.

Mismatch between Objectives and Needs

" I was hired by technical college to present an introductory Total Quality Management class to machine operators in a manufacturing company. I met with their human resource/training person and a site engineer to get the course objectives established. It seemed that they knew what they wanted, so I developed the course and delivered it. On the evaluations the response was so-so, but the HR person said the participants didn't like it much since they weren't going to use the information in their jobs. The coordinator from the technical college wasn't very happy either. I asked them to review what they had asked for, and it was apparent that what they asked for and what was needed were definitely different. "

No Training Required

" Management decided to inundate employees (plant operations) with fundamentals of the process they were already working on. To this end, I spend about 75 percent of my time gathering information about the manufacturing process and 25 percent of my time delivering the "information" to people that already had a sound background on the subject matter. This was a very frustrating situation that I have little control over. "

Trainers, when confronted with a performance problem or a request for training, sometimes accept the request at face value or assume that training is the best or only solution. But what if training is not the best or only solution? What if the person making the request is inaccurate? What if other solutions to the problem are more appropriate or cost-effective? The perception of training as a panacea for all performance problems may prevent you from troubleshooting the issues or discovering the root causes of problems. If training is not the best solution, using it will at best address symptoms rather than root causes. At worst, the desired results will not be achieved, and you will lose time, money, effort, and credibility.

The Relationship between Training and Performance Improvement

Before you can use instructional delivery or training delivery skills effectively, you must first possess a good understanding of the difference between training and performance improvement. In recent years, there has been a surge of interest in Human Performance Improvement (HPI). Training is not synonymous with HPI, but is rather a subset of it because training is only one of many solutions to performance problems. Joe Harless, a pioneer of HPI, defines it as "the process of analysis, design, development, testing, implementation, and evaluation of relevant and cost-effective interventions." The four steps of the Human Performance Improvement process (see Exhibit 1–1 on next page) include analysis of the situation, selection of the appropriate intervention, implementation of that intervention, and evaluation of the results. The possible appropriate interventions include the workshops and programs traditionally viewed as training.

However, HPI is much larger than that and can encompass hundreds of specific interventions that can be brought together to solve performance problems or seize performance improvement opportunities. Training solutions (sometimes called instructional or learning solutions) are just one of a multitude of strategies and tactics that can be used. Other, nontraining solutions (sometimes called nonlearning or management solutions) may include taking action to improve feedback, implementing reward systems, offering individualized coaching, and developing job aids. It is important for you to recognize that training is an appropriate solution to a performance problem only when the root cause of the problem is, in whole or part, attributable to deficiencies in individual knowledge, skill, or attitude. When the root causes of the problem are attributable to other factors, then training is not the right solution.

What is also apparent from these scenarios is that a great deal of information was missing. To make a sound decision about whether training is an appropriate solution, you must dig deeper to gain a more thorough understanding of each problem through accurate analysis and diagnosis. This is accomplished by interviewing key stakeholders, observing people performing their jobs, and collecting and analyzing performance data.

Results-Based Training

When training is an appropriate intervention because the problem is caused by a deficiency in individual knowledge, skill, or attitude, then it

Exhibit 1–1
Human performance improvement process model.

Analyze the Situation

**Choose the Appropriate
Intervention**

Implement the Intervention

Evaluate the Results

should be results-oriented. Results are measurable accomplishments or outputs that focus on improved performance. Dana Gaines-Robinson and James Robinson, coauthors of the book *Training for Impact*, contrast *results-based training* with *activity-based training*. In activity-based training the success of the effort is measured by the number of participants in attendance (referred to as "butts in seats"), learner ratings on end-of-course evaluation forms, and the thickness of the training course catalog. These measures are based on activities related to coordinating and conducting training. But these measures are not necessarily related to the real impact of the training program in addressing the root causes of performance problems. The purpose of training is to bring about individualized change in the performance of the learners. It can be measured by comparing what they can do more effectively or efficiently after the training with what they could do before the training.

Training programs should not be designed or delivered based on what is "nice to know." Instead, training should be time-efficient and focused carefully on what people must know or do to perform their work successfully. How often have learners in a training program on word processing been bored by a two-hour lecture on the history of computers that the trainer found interesting and therefore included in the training program? In such situations, fundamental questions to ask include: "How will this information help the learner meet the training objectives?" and "How will this information help the learner improve on-the-job performance?" If it will not, then it should not be included. Similar errors include incorporating games or activities into the training simply because they are fun. While entertaining activities can energize a group, they should not be overused, or used solely because they are entertaining. Always ask yourself, "How does the game or activity lead to improved learner knowledge, skill, or attitude that is essential to successful job performance?"

TRAINING THAT IS INSTRUCTIONALLY SOUND

Sound instructional design is the backbone of effective training. *Instructional design* is the term used to denote the process of preparing effective training. It should, of course, precede delivery of that training.

We make the assumption in this book that the training to be delivered by a classroom trainer has been designed using an *instructional systems design* (ISD) approach. Such an approach ensures that needs were properly assessed and clarified, instructional objectives were correctly written, evaluation strategies were incorporated in the training, and the content, activities, and methods were identified and developed with attainment of the training objectives uppermost in mind. Training that was not developed using an instructional systems design approach is much less likely to lead to the training objectives.

In 1986 the International Board of Standards for Training, Performance, and Instruction (IBSTPI) sponsored a study that identified sixteen competencies associated with instructional design, which is a different study from the training delivery competencies but also described by IBSTPI. The basic instructional design model calls for five basic steps: *a*nalysis, *d*esign, *d*evelopment, *i*mplementation, and *e*valuation. This model is commonly referred to as the "ADDIE" model. The *implementation* step in the ADDIE model encompasses the main focus of this book, because it deals with classroom training delivery. Exhibit 1–2 illustrates an expanded version of the instructional design process derived from the IBSTPI instructional design study.

If you are the trainer, you must view the training design and content with a critical, honest eye. When the requirements of the instructional systems design model are not met, then you must initiate corrective action to modify the design, reassess the training needs and purposes of the course, and possibly even recommend the cancellation of outmoded, ineffective, poorly designed, or obsolete programs. You may find it difficult to cancel a program that you enjoy presenting. But even a good program will not endure forever. When the training no longer meets work-related needs, you may have to change it or drop it. If you ignore the need for course redesign when it is necessary, you will soon see problems such as dissatisfied learners, lack of results, or questions from management about its value. It is best to avoid this by taking action to ensure that the training is of top quality and is continually improved. Only in that way can you preserve your credibility and that of the training department.

TRAINING DELIVERY COMPETENCIES

The International Board of Standards for Training, Performance and Instruction (IBSTPI) has developed a set of standards that uses a straightforward definition of the term *competency* as "an essential skill without which an individual is not a qualified practitioner." This definition of *competency* emphasizes the practical nature of the fourteen competencies identified in the IBSTPI study, which we will refer to throughout this book as the IBSTPI Standards. These competencies are focused on the job skills and behaviors of anyone who delivers training.

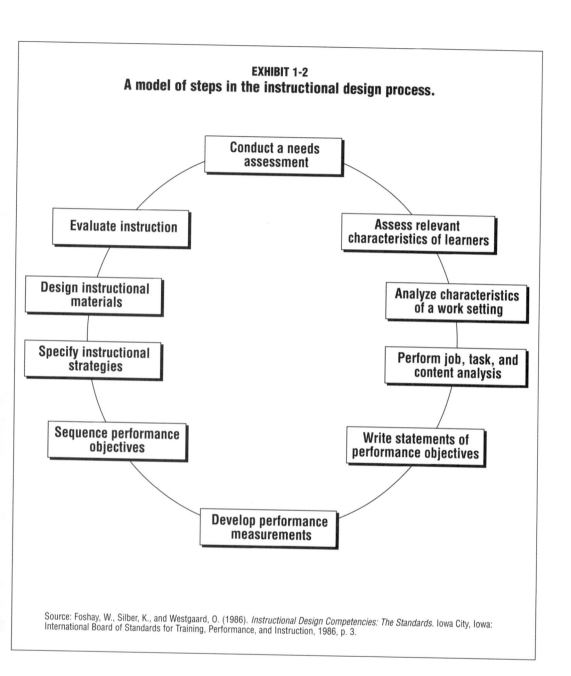

EXHIBIT 1-2
A model of steps in the instructional design process.

Conduct a needs assessment

Assess relevant characteristics of learners

Analyze characteristics of a work setting

Perform job, task, and content analysis

Write statements of performance objectives

Develop performance measurements

Sequence performance objectives

Specify instructional strategies

Design instructional materials

Evaluate instruction

Source: Foshay, W., Silber, K., and Westgaard, O. (1986). *Instructional Design Competencies: The Standards.* Iowa City, Iowa: International Board of Standards for Training, Performance, and Instruction, 1986, p. 3.

To be a competent trainer, you should be able to demonstrate the fourteen training delivery competencies found in the IBSTPI Standards. They are:

1. Analyze course material and learner information.

2. Assure preparation of the training site.

3. Establish and maintain instructor credibility.

4. Manage the learning environment.

5. Demonstrate effective communication skills.

6. Demonstrate effective presentation skills.

7. Demonstrate effective questioning skills and techniques.

8. Respond appropriately to learners' needs for clarification or feedback.

9. Provide positive reinforcement and motivational incentives.

10. Use training methods appropriately.

11. Use media effectively.

12. Evaluate learner performance.

13. Evaluate the delivery of training.

14. Report evaluation information.

The competencies can also be divided into three segments: those usually demonstrated *before* actual training delivery, those usually enacted *during* training delivery, and those exhibited *after* training delivery (see Exhibit 1–3). The competencies enacted during training delivery are organized into a circular pattern in the exhibit because there is no established sequence in which the competencies are exhibited. Rather, in practice, you should demonstrate the competencies as the situation demands.

RESEARCH STUDY

Although this book is based on the competencies appearing in the IBSTPI Standards, we also conducted our own survey to assess

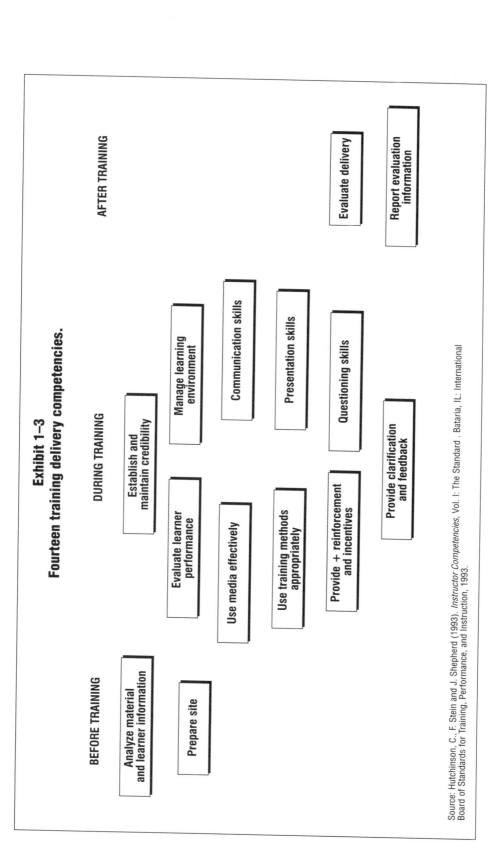

Exhibit 1–3
Fourteen training delivery competencies.

BEFORE TRAINING

Analyze material and learner information

Prepare site

DURING TRAINING

Establish and maintain credibility

Manage learning environment

Communication skills

Presentation skills

Questioning skills

Evaluate learner performance

Use media effectively

Use training methods appropriately

Provide + reinforcement and incentives

Provide clarification and feedback

AFTER TRAINING

Evaluate delivery

Report evaluation information

Source: Hutchinson, C., F. Stein and J. Shepherd (1993). *Instructor Competencies*, Vol. I: The Standard . Bataria, IL: International Board of Standards for Training, Performance, and Instruction, 1993.

how trainers apply the delivery competencies. We also wanted to discover what common problems trainers face and how they overcome them.

We prepared and mailed out a survey that addressed the following four questions:

1. How important to success in delivery do trainers perceive the fourteen competencies to be?

2. How difficult to demonstrate do trainers perceive each competency to be?

3. What are the most difficult training delivery problems that trainers encounter, and how do they solve those problems?

4. What are the most common training delivery problems that trainers encounter, and how do they solve those problems?

Selected survey results are presented in appropriate places throughout the book. They are meant to dramatize the competencies by introducing the perceptions and experiences of practitioners as they deliver training. We refer to these experiences as critical incidents. These critical incidents are difficult situations occurring in the lives of trainers that can shed light on what problems they face and what they do to solve them. Appendix A provides a more detailed description of the research methodology we used and the results we obtained.

SUMMARY

This chapter set the stage for the book and covered the following:

- When training is (and is not) appropriate to solve performance problems.

- How training delivery relates to training design.

- The fourteen competencies tied to effective training delivery.

- How our research will be used throughout the remainder of this book.

STRATEGY LIST

Actionable Strategies to Improve Training Effectiveness:

Training Is Not Always the Appropriate Solution

❑ Remember that training cannot solve all human performance problems.

❑ Always analyze performance problems before recommending a solution. Analysis helps to ensure that the appropriate solution is applied.

❑ Nontraining solutions that can be applied to human performance problems include feedback, incentive systems, tools and equipment, performance standards, and hundreds of other interventions.

❑ Recognize that training is only appropriate for improving people's knowledge, skills, or attitudes.

❑ Avoid accepting requests for training, unless you know that training is appropriate.

Results-Based Training

❑ Recognize the difference between results-based training (training that makes an impact and leads to improved learner performance) and activity-based training (training that is conducted merely for the sake of training).

❑ Avoid training that is based on what is "nice to know" and focus on what learners must know and do on the job.

❑ Ensure that the training you deliver is instructionally sound and based on an instructional systems design (ISD) approach.

❑ Discontinue programs that no longer meet work-related needs.

CHAPTER 2

ANALYZING COURSE MATERIAL AND LEARNER INFORMATION

SKILLS ASSESSMENT

Take a moment to review the competency and associated performances that will be covered in this chapter. Consider your current level of proficiency in the competency as a whole as well as each performance and check the items where you feel you need to improve. As you read the chapter, concentrate on those areas most in need of development.

Competency:

❒ Analyze course material and learner information.

Associated Performances:

❒ Review materials and audience information and identify areas where adjustments may be needed.

❒ Make minor adjustments to learning materials.

❒ Judge the appropriateness and adequacy of adjustments.

Analyzing course material and learner information is the first training delivery competency identified by the IBSTPI Standards. By using this competency, you can ensure that an appropriate match exists between the training you deliver and the people who attend the training. You should usually demonstrate it *before* you deliver training; however, depending on the situation and time constraints, you may have to demonstrate this competency *during* training delivery.

This chapter covers the following topics:

■ Learner characteristics you should consider before delivery, including individual learning styles and the learners' prior knowledge, skills, experience, job positions, and physical characteristics.

■ Practical advice about how to gather information about the learners' characteristics.

■ Making changes to training before and during delivery.

Achieving this competency is important because it ensures that alignment exists between instructional materials and participants in a training program. Just how important is it to analyze course material and learner information? To reflect on that question, think about the following critical incident supplied by one trainer in our survey.

From the Top Down

" I was teaching a civil treatment class to management. "All levels," from first-line supervisors to vice presidents, were present. I was doing an exercise with the class when one of the vice presidents got bored. This VP is very gruff and tries to be "one of the guys" and he loves to intimidate people. He asked in front of everyone "why are we wasting our time with this nonsense." He wanted to rile me and he did. I still have flashbacks of this moment. I, as calmly as I could, explained to him that he may be very experienced in this area but other people in the class may not be as knowledgeable and that is the reason for the exercise. "

This critical incident emphasizes how important it is to have the right people in the right place for the right training at the right time. The vice president in this incident was probably someone who should not have been attending this course. The fact that many trainers in our survey provided critical incidents related to this competency seems to indicate that it is a common problem for trainers to find mismatches between the training they deliver and the people to whom they are delivering it.

Generally speaking, it is easier to present training to *homogeneous* groups (where people share common knowledge, skills, and attitudes) than to *heterogeneous* groups (where people are dramatically different). Most of the time, training is designed with the aim of meeting the needs of a targeted learner group. But that does not mean that the people who sign up for, or attend, a training course have the characteristics for which the training was designed. This difference can lead to big problems.

Too Many Differences

"*I am involved with new employee orientation, cross-training, presenter training, management development, and other types of training. One of the most typical "problems" I have is participant diversity. Having a variety of communication systems, skill levels, and education levels in a training room at the same time, and attempting to meet all their needs and maintain course energy is very trying.*"

While each learner is unique and possesses his or her own background, experience, knowledge, skills, and attitudes, you will usually find that group training delivered in classroom settings is designed based on general assumptions about the kind of person who will attend it. One key advantage of classroom or group training is that it can lead to *synergy*, a state in which the pooled experiences of a group can be more powerful than the individual experience of one learner. However, a key disadvantage of classroom training is that it makes assumptions about what most people in the group already know or can do.

LEARNER CHARACTERISTICS

Learner characteristics include the knowledge, skills, and attitudes of the learners. For example, learner characteristics may include knowledge about various problem-solving techniques, skill with certain sales tactics, or the possession of a negative attitude. Other learner characteristics include the educational level, the job position, and the gender of the learner.

Learner characteristics are important for several reasons. The focus of training and learning is on individual change and on building the knowledge, skills, and attitudes of learners. It is imperative that you recognize and consider characteristics before and during training delivery because they can dramatically affect learning. For example, if most learners in a training program are elderly, then steps should be taken to accommodate potential problems with poor vision (a learner characteristic) that some of the participants might have. An appropriate step to take might be to enlarge the text in participant guides or on overhead transparencies. Exhibit 2–1 provides a brief synopsis of learner characteristics and questions you should ask about the training participants before you deliver training.

It just makes sense that you should try to know as much as you can about your participants before you deliver a course. If you know what kind of people will attend training, you have a better chance of building rapport and trust with them. That awareness may also give you clues about what kind of examples or stories might be particularly relevant to your audience.

As an example, you might say the following:

> I realize that this group has attended training on teamwork in the past. However, this session is going to cover some important things that relate to the new organizational structure. As you have heard, in roughly three months this department will be transitioning into self-directed work teams. This means that there will be some significant changes in store for you. For example, you will no longer have an immediate supervisor that you will be reporting to.

A statement like this shows that you understand the learners and the organizational setting in which they perform. It also shows that you are aware of pending changes in the organization that make the training topic of particular importance to this group. By making this statement, you emphasize the relevance of the training topic to the learners and build their confidence in your ability to help them acquire useful knowledge and skills they will need to be successful.

LEARNING STYLES

Each person learns in a uniquely individualized way. An individual's preferred learning style is one important learner characteristic to identify before or during training.

Learning style refers to how people learn best. Some individuals learn most effectively by hearing information (referred to as "auditory learners"). Others learn better by reading words, or by seeing visual images,

Exhibit 2–1
Learner characteristics and key questions to consider before and during delivery.

Category of Learner Characteristics:	Examples:	Questions to Ask:
Physical	• Eyesight • Hearing • Strength • Gender • Age	• Do learners have any physical needs to consider? • Are there any limitations to their ability?
Knowledge	• Experience • Level of education • Position in the organization	• Do the learners have the prerequisite knowledge or skills necessary to be in the training?
Other	• Learning styles • Personality types	• Will learners enjoy the training? • Will they learn from the training?

graphics, or pictures (called "visual learners"). Many people learn by doing (called "kinesthetic learners" or "experiential learners"). In addition to these three preferred modes of learning, other factors—environmental, emotional, and sociological—also influence learning. It is important to note that these learning styles can all be effective and that most people learn through a combination of methods. Many presentation experts stress the importance of maintaining variations to accommodate different styles. Thomas Crum of Aiki Works, Inc., of Aspen, Colorado, suggests that trainers "keep the learning alive with a continual flow of visual, auditory, and kinesthetic learning."[1] He also notes that trainers should be sure to have fun because "learning and laughter go hand in hand."

Understanding learning style is important for you as a trainer so that you can accommodate the learning preferences found in a group. You should avoid favoring your own style, and you can't assume that others have learning style preferences like yours.

Many learning style inventories or questionnaires are available to help individuals determine their preferred personal learning styles. Some are commercially available in print, while others are computer- or Internet-based. Learning style inventories vary widely from simple, self-scoring questionnaires to complex, multi-rater instruments that cover many learning dimensions. Exhibit 2–2 shows twelve items from a free sample learning style inventory available over the Internet from the Merex Corporation.

The Merex inventory covers three predominant learning styles—visual, auditory, and kinesthetic. A user of the Merex online inventory is prompted to click the items applying to his or her behaviors and preferences. Based on the items chosen, a learning style profile is automatically generated—along with suggestions for fully maximizing that style. Exhibit 2–3 shows these profiles and sample tips.

SIVASAILAM THIAGARAJAN

In an interview we conducted for this book, we asked training expert Sivasailam Thiagarajan ("Thiagi") this question: *What are the most common difficulties you face in instructing groups and how do you resolve them?"* He answered: "Individual differences in learning preferences. I handle this by acknowledging that different participants may prefer to learn in different modes. I encourage participants to ask for a change in the way I am conducting the session if it does not suit their style of learning. At the same time, I point out that I should strive to accommodate most of the participants most of the time. I use training techniques that take into account as many different learning styles as possible. For example, I use transparencies for visual iconic learners, handouts for visual digital learners, activities for kinesthetic learners, and presentations for auditory learners."

Exhibit 2–2
Sample items from the Merex learning styles inventory.

1. When I'm concentrating, I fidget or tap my feet or move around a lot.

2. To learn something best, I need to take notes and review them.

3. The best way I learn something new is by "doing it."

4. I will try to understand visual handouts in a meeting even if they are not very good.

5. When I tell someone something, I expect they will remember it, because I usually do.

6. I usually enjoy fixing things.

7. I like to take part in discussions.

8. If someone wants me to remember to do something they should write it down.

9. When I have trouble understanding something it may help if I say it out loud or talk about it.

10. Usually, I don't like it when it is "too quiet" at work or at home.

11. I tend to keep things organized and orderly at work and at home.

12. I like to have several tasks to do at once.

Source: Merex Corporation (1999). http://www.merex.com/. 1270 E. Broadway Rd., Ste. 103, Tempe, Ariz. 85282 (800-383-5636). ("Items from Learning Style Inventory" and "Learning Style Profiles and Suggestions for Maximizing").

But we offer these words of caution about using learning style inventories: They are not all the same. They vary in what they measure, how they measure it, and what definitions they use. For this reason, you should thoroughly understand a learning style inventory before you use it. Inventories are helpful in giving people a place to start in exploring their learning style preferences, but they should not be regarded as absolutes or as objective portrayals of reality.

PREVIOUS KNOWLEDGE, EXPERIENCE, AND SKILL

A key principle of adult education is that learner experience is valuable. Tapping into this vast well of experience helps bring your subject to life.

Exhibit 2–3
Learning style profiles and suggestions.

Visual Learners

Some people learn best by *seeing* something. When they ask somebody for directions, they like to see it on a map. When they sit in on a meeting, they like to see the main points written on the board. These are **visual learners**.

We use all three learning modalities (visual, auditory, tactile-kinesthetic) at different times, for different tasks. Your score is *one indication* of your learning preference. For the next few days, see what else you notice about your learning style. Try using the following learning suggestion.

A Tip for Visual Learners

Always have pen and paper handy. Use them—doodle, take notes, draw the idea in pictures, write key words. Make an info-map. Use colored markers and highlighters to mark up text. Give your eyes a way to see the information you're taking in.

Auditory Learners

Other people learn best by *hearing* something. They can learn well from hearing somebody talk about a new idea, or from discussing it with another person. These people are **auditory learners**.

We use all three learning modalities (visual, auditory, tactile-kinesthetic) at different times, for different tasks. Your score is *one indication* of your learning preference. For the next few days, see what else you notice about your learning style. Try using the following learning suggestion.

A Tip for Auditory Learners

Reduce outside interference when you read or study, or when you're discussing something. Maybe you need to shut off the radio...unplug the phone...or go into a quieter room. Or, maybe you don't. Notice what level of noise works best for you, and set up your learning environment that way.

Tactile-Kinesthetic Learners

Then there are people who learn best by doing something. They really "get it" when they can use their hands or their body. They are **tactile-kinesthetic learners**.

We use all three learning modalities (visual, auditory, tactile-kinesthetic) at different times, for different tasks. Your score is *one indication* of your learning preference. For the next few days, see what else you notice about your learning style. Try using the following learning suggestion.

A Tip for Tactile-Kinesthetic Learners

Be as physical as you can when you learn. Use your body in unusual ways. Sit up on the desk or table. Stand up and pace back and forth. Draw pictures in the air to fix concepts in your mind.

Source: Merex Corporation (1999). http://www.merex.com/. 1270 E. Broadway Rd., Ste. 103, Tempe, Ariz. 85282 (800-383-5636). ("Items from Learning Style Inventory" and "Learning Style Profiles and Suggestions for Maximizing").

If you draw on the life and work experiences of the participants in the training, you can usually discover examples to reinforce the importance of the topic and illustrate practical applications of it.

Experience is a filter that influences how people perceive and interpret information. Tapping into learner experience helps to activate these existing filters and increases what people remember and how much they remember. Relating new information to previous experiences (a process sometimes called "scaffolding") also makes it easier for learners to acquire new knowledge. That is why, whenever possible, you should base training on the work tasks, situations, and problems faced by the learners. When delivering a customer service training program, one of the authors was able to tap into participants' experiences by asking them to relate the worst treatment they had received as a customer. A number of vivid horror stories were recalled. The author was able to refer to these actual experiences throughout the program to enhance understanding, introduce new concepts, and reinforce skills being learned.

The following critical incident illustrates the dilemma of a new trainer who was unable to relate training content to work situations as well as a strategy used by the trainer to avoid this problem in the future.

Know Thy Audience

 "When I started in my current job, I was assigned the task of delivering a three-day supervision session (three days in a row). I had been doing training for a few years and had good platform skills, but knew very little about my audience and their day-to-day concerns. I didn't have appropriate examples, and the group was big enough (thirty-five people) that I wasn't getting much participation. I knew that what I was saying applied to their jobs, but I couldn't apply it to their work situations. It was an awful feeling, because I knew I wasn't connecting. After the first day, I asked even more questions, and would not go on until someone answered. Then I used that example for all it was worth until I got another one. After the session was over, I spent a lot of time at the client companies, watching the supervisors work and observing the operation so I would understand it better. That helped tremendously the next time I did training, and each session gave me more material. "

Exhibit 2–4
Strategies for contextualizing training before and during delivery.

Before Delivery	During Delivery
• Plan ahead to use titles, jargon, examples, and jobs with which learners are familiar.	• Ask learners to provide examples and analogies from their own work or experiences.
• Talk to learners and their coworkers to develop concepts, principles, and examples that learners can relate to during training.	• Use company letterhead and other stationery items with the organization's logo when possible.
• Shadow several people from the target audience for several days to get a good sense of the realities of the job.	• Arrange to conduct part or all of the training in or near the learners' work area.
• Refer to job- or organization-specific examples or experiences that will resonate with learners.	• Incorporate tools or other equipment that learners are familiar with into the training.
• Consult with subject matter experts when developing training.	• Ask learners how they might apply the new skills to their jobs and encourage them to do so.
• When introducing unfamiliar jargon to learners, define it and how it relates to their jobs.	• Plan to teach skills that learners are currently using or will use in the near future.

Designing and conducting training in a job context makes abstract principles more concrete. Realistic training of this kind also increases the transfer of training from the classroom to the workplace. Exhibit 2–4 lists specific strategies you can use to ground training in a relevant context. Some strategies can be planned before the training is delivered. Others must be incorporated during delivery.

In any classroom training course, the learners' experience levels can vary—sometimes dramatically. While learner experience is dynamic, several issues associated with it should be considered when you evaluate learner characteristics. For instance, new hires with low amounts of job knowledge are likely to be highly motivated to learn because they want to adjust successfully to a new organization or job. Job-related experience is particularly important. Further, those learners who possess limited work experience usually require more explanations and examples than those with more experience. For example, newly promoted supervisors who are learning about disciplinary procedures may require step-by-step instruction because they have never had to apply these procedures. In contrast, experienced supervisors who have dealt with disciplinary issues may need only minor skill enhancement or sophisticated treatments of the topic.

What are some strategies you can use to determine learners' experience levels? During the course you can ask learners questions about themselves to learn more. For example, you could ask a group of customer service representatives attending training, "How many people here have been in their current position for more than three years?" as a way to identify those who are likely to have attained some level of competence. Alternatively, sometimes the course registration forms will include information such as years in position or years of service. You can also consult the human resources department to obtain this information.

The learners' knowledge or skill level with the training topic is also an important learner characteristic that warrants attention. When learners possess widely varying levels of knowledge or skill, you may find yourself struggling in a training course to adapt your coverage of the topic so that all learners can understand it. Some trainers face this difficult problem all the time, as illustrated by the following critical incident that also describes how a trainer handled that problem.

Divide and Conquer

" *A typical problem for me is that, in a given class, the participants will have different knowledge levels of our software. Some move around different features quickly, while others can't find the [return] key. During the introductions, I ask for experience, job title, and other information. Then, during the early activities I watch them to identify those who need help. I try to be near those people during activities and help them without calling attention. If majority of class (instead of a couple) show lack of knowledge, I give keystroke-by-keystroke instruction. (Experienced users don't need to be told to press the Enter key, F1, etc.)* "

Individuals possessing more job-related experience or higher skill levels can solve more complex or abstract problems and understand more elaborate concepts and examples during training. In contrast, learners with limited experience are only frustrated by complex problems and elaborate examples. Imagine that Catherine is a new supervisor who is attending a training program on coaching skills. Catherine struggles during practice sessions because she has no experience with coaching. Her inexperience makes it difficult for her to see the importance of coaching or relate to coaching examples. But Jill, another participant in the same training program, is an experienced supervisor. During training, she readily grasps coaching concepts because she appreciates their importance and has had some experience with them.

Sometimes prerequisite knowledge, skill, or experience is required before a learner is qualified to participate in training. If these prerequisites are identified and communicated properly, they can help ensure that the participants in a training program will not be so widely diverse as to make it difficult for the trainer to meet their needs. One way to identify prerequisites is to ask the question, "What should learners already know or be able to do before they attend the training?" Answering that question may require a careful examination of the training objectives and the training material.

You should identify prerequisite skill and knowledge requirements and then ensure that the participants have met those prerequisites. For example, typing ability might be a prerequisite skill for a computer course on word processing. By ensuring that all participants can type to some established proficiency level before they attend training, such as by administering a brief test before the participants attend the course, you reduce the chance that some learners will fail—or will impede the progress of other learners—simply because they lack essential prerequisite knowledge or skill. If just one learner is unable to type, the whole group might be prevented from achieving the learning objectives.

Overcoming Differences in Skill Level

" *The typical problem I have is personal attention when my class does not possess the prerequisite skills. We do not send the unprepared students home, so much of the first day of class is lost to bringing participants to the correct level.* "

Exhibit 2–5
Sample questions to gauge learners' level of skill,
knowledge, or experience.

- Who here is able to write a proposal? Please raise your hand if you have this skill.

- Who knows the five steps involved in lock-out, tag-out? Please raise your hands if you possess this knowledge.

- Let's have a show of hands. Who has been in the position of supervisor for six months or less? Who has been a supervisor for less than three years? Who has been a supervisor for more than ten years?

Note that wasted time is one important consequence of permitting learners to attend training when they do not meet essential prerequisites or when those prerequisites are not enforced.

Asking key questions at the start of training is another strategy you can use to assess the learners' knowledge, skill, and experience levels. Use the questions appearing in Exhibit 2–5 to obtain information about the learners' knowledge, skill, or experience levels with a topic. The answers to these questions can help you meet the learners' key needs and ensure that the training content is better matched to the learners' experience levels.

PHYSICAL CHARACTERISTICS

The physical characteristics of the learners are another issue to be considered. Examples of physical characteristics include manual dexterity, grip strength, lifting ability, visual and hearing ability, tolerance of extreme conditions, height, weight, sense of balance, and sensitivity to chemicals or other substances. Once again, you should work to ensure that a match exists between the training and the presence or absence of these traits among the participants in training.

As one example of matching physical characteristics with course material and content, assume that training involves working in a laboratory where learners will be exposed to trace elements of nontoxic substances. While that may be a rare example, remember that some learners may have allergic reactions to these chemicals. For this reason, you may want to prescreen learners for medical conditions, including allergies that might trigger a reaction from exposure. In addition, going a step beyond screening, double-check safety equipment to be sure that it works and is available at the training site. Conduct emergency planning as well by having Material Safety Data Sheets (MSDS) handy, so that you know exactly what to do in the event of a chemical spill or other problem.

Visual ability is a physical characteristic that will have to be considered more often than safety issues in most settings. If learners in a circuit-board assembly training program have problems with eyesight, for instance, then they may encounter difficulties working on small, intricate circuit boards. Take steps to solve that problem by installing magnifying devices or create a large model of the circuit board so that visually impaired learners can more easily see the enlarged components. Of course, if these learners will eventually be working on small circuit boards in their work settings, then training might not adequately prepare them for that. In such cases you are well positioned to note the mismatch between the work requirements and individual abilities. That can lead to improvements in the workplace and steps to make reasonable accommodations, or it can indicate the need to move individuals to positions where their skills better match the work requirements.

JOB POSITION OR CATEGORY

Always be aware of the job position or job category of the targeted training group. Often training is designed and delivered for individuals possessing unique job positions, job titles, or categories because training is meant to help them meet their work requirements. For example, an organization may design and deliver a training program called *Effective Selling* for outside salespersons. If the training is, in fact, designed with the outside salesperson in mind, then participants should be from that targeted group. Such a training program would be inappropriate for inside salespersons (people who receive inbound telephone calls from customers). If inside salespersons attend the *Effective Selling* program, it will create a mismatch between the work requirements of the learners and the course material. Corrective action will be needed, such as rerouting the learners to appropriate training or making adjustments to the existing training so that it matches the work requirements of the participants.

If, for some reason, learners are routed to the wrong course, you can always redirect them to the correct course. But remember that the costs associated with doing that rise dramatically if learners traveled to attend the course. If you discover the mismatch only after training begins, your best course of action is to explain that the learner is in the wrong class and probably should not stay. If for some reason the learner chooses to stay, then you can attempt to use activities and examples that are not specifically tied to the work requirements of one group. In essence, if the concepts are general to all learners, each person can customize the training to fit it to his or her unique needs by applying the concepts to a work-related project. A danger in making content too general is that other learners may struggle with recognizing how it is relevant and applicable to them. You should try to strike a balance between providing job-specific information tied to work positions and general information that can be used and understood by anyone. The best approach, however, remains targeting training to specific learner characteristics, communicating what those characteristics are before the training, and screening participants to ensure that they match up to those characteristics before they arrive in a training course.

You can match the training requirements and the learners by collecting advance information about the participants' job positions, job categories, or other relevant characteristics. One way to do this is to obtain information about people as they sign up for training. Another way is to seek information from the human resources department. A third way is to ask prospective participants by contacting them before training by personal interview, e-mail, or other means. A fourth way is to ask their supervisors or managers so as to uncover subtle differences about people that may not otherwise be apparent. For example, an organization may have the job position of maintenance technician. However, upon exploration, you may find several classifications within this position, such as electrical technician and mechanical technician. These differences in work responsibilities may be significant enough to have an impact on training. You may find that you have to run different programs for each group. Or, if there are other reasons to have these employees attend the same course, you will need to make adjustments to ensure that examples, stories, and material are applicable to all participants.

GENDER AND RACE

Be aware of the racial and gender composition of a training group. In most training programs, it is rare to see a homogenous group, but it can happen. Some industries or occupations attract more than their fair share of males or females, for instance, which might lead to a homogenous group of learners.

Ensure that course materials and classroom examples are geared to the targeted audience. Sports examples—or sewing examples—may not communicate well to some groups, and they can produce misunderstanding or even resentment if used unthinkingly. You can avoid this problem by using examples that will appeal to everyone, or by using multiple examples that will each appeal to different learner groups.

LIFE AND CAREER STAGES

When learners enter a group training situation, they often represent many different career and life stages. You should understand what these stages mean to be effective as a trainer because they affect learner interests and motivations. Some developmental stages for learners are relatively stable, while others are marked by change and conflict. Critical events in an individual's life define and direct that person's development. The first day on a new job is an example of a critical event that is the culmination of a process that may have begun long before the start date. Other examples of transitioning events include promotions, layoffs, and retirements.

As a trainer, you will find career development models important. Greenhaus and Callahan's five-stage career development model is displayed in Exhibit 2–6. This career development model is divided into five stages that represent major classifications of a person's normal career progression, such as preparing for the working world and entering into an organization. Each career stage has an age range associated with it. Note that, while most of these ranges are discrete, individuals will experience slight, and sometimes significant, deviations from those ranges. Another useful section of the career development model identifies major tasks. Major tasks represent primary needs, conflicts, and goals confronting an individual in that stage. This information can be very helpful to you as you attempt to gear the training to the learners.

You can use the career development model shown in Exhibit 2–6 to consider the occupational characteristics of individuals. While making broad generalizations can be misleading and should not lead you to make assumptions about individuals, generalizations about learners can also be useful. By assessing a group and forecasting the issues, needs, and goals the majority of them may have, you can improve the match between learner interests and training materials or methods. For example, assume that you are working with a group of recent college graduates (most of whom are in their early to mid-twenties). By using the career development framework, you can predict the issues that confront many of them. They will be struggling to develop a niche in the company and their field of practice. You can expect that they may not yet have much loyalty or commitment to the

Exhibit 2–6
Five-stage model of career development.

1. Occupational Choice: Preparation for Work

Typical Age Range: Initially 0–25; then variable

Major Tasks: Develop occupational self-image, assess alternative occupations, develop initial occupational choice, pursue necessary education.

2. Organizational Entry

Typical Age Range: Initially 18–25; then variable

Major Tasks: Obtain job offer(s) from desired organization(s), select appropriate job based on accurate information.

3. Early Career: Establishment and Achievement

Typical Age Range: 25–40

Major Tasks: Learn job, learn organizational rules and norms, fit into chosen occupation and organization, increase competence, pursue The Dream.

4. Midcareer

Typical Age Range: 40–55

Major Tasks: Reappraise early career and early adulthood, reaffirm or modify The Dream, make choices appropriate to middle adult years, remain productive in work.

5. Late Career

Typical Age Range: 55–retirement

Major Tasks: Remain productive in work, maintain self-esteem, prepare for effective retirement.

Source: Table from *Career Management*, Second Edition by Jeffery H. Greenhaus and Gerard Callanan, copyright © 1993 by Harcourt, Inc., reprinted by permission of the publisher.

organization or the occupation. They are not yet deeply rooted in the corporate culture and are more likely to be asking themselves, "Is this an organization that I like, or am I about ready to move on?" You can also expect that some of these learners will be highly motivated to advance. That is especially true if the learners believe that the training in which they participate will help them adjust to the corporate culture or advance in their occupations.

Understanding career and life stages can be important because there is often a connection between learning and transitioning successfully through life events. Adults are most ready and willing to learn when they are confronting problems or when they are striving to realize professional or personal goals. The implication should be apparent: people are most willing to learn when they have a reason to do it. That underscores the importance of ensuring that the right person is in the right training program at the right time and for the right reasons. The reverse is also true. People are less willing to learn or change when they see no reason to do so. Imagine that a group of nurses is sent to supervisory skills training, but their jobs involve no management responsibilities. They operate as individual contributors. Would you expect a readiness to learn to be present? The answer is that it would probably not be.

You should gather information about life and/or career development stages whenever possible. Simply remaining aware that these stages exist will help you pinpoint the barriers that learners may be facing in their skills development. By helping learners relate the content of training to their work problems, you can help learners recognize how their learning will help them address their issues and achieve their goals. You can, for instance, explain to managers attending a professional development seminar how the course content will help them to gain a deeper understanding of the organization's culture, politics, and systems. Many are likely to be in the "early career" stage of the career development model shown in Exhibit 2–6. They are therefore likely to be concerned about deepening their awareness of how and where they fit in the organization. They are also likely to be interested in upward potential. For this reason, if you can show the link between the training content and the learners' goals for advancement, you are likely to find the learners to be highly receptive.

ADDITIONAL CHARACTERISTICS

Many additional learner characteristics exist. For a targeted group, they might include geographical location, health status, age, language skills, citizenship standing, motivation, value systems, disabilities, areas of interest, and socioeconomic position. Because each characteristic can affect their learning, assess each in relation to the training material to ensure that an appropriate match exists. Details on how to perform such an assessment as well as details on how to implement revisions are discussed later in this chapter.

STRATEGIES FOR GATHERING LEARNER INFORMATION

This section discusses where information on learner characteristics can be found and how you can collect it. There are two basic categories of such information. One category is information about the *intended* audience. It includes the learner profile and the instructor guide. The second category is information about the *actual* audience. It includes registration information, information from the client, and data gathered from the learners themselves before or during the program.

PROFILING THE INTENDED LEARNERS

The material for a well-designed training program should have a description of the intended learner. This is called a *learner profile*. Regardless of length, the learner profile communicates what assumptions were made during the instructional design phase. A learner profile can include learning styles, work experiences, or educational level. This information is useful because it details key ideas and the learner characteristics upon which the program was initially developed. It serves as your frame of reference as you review the course material and as you assess the characteristics of the attendees.

The sample learner profile shown in Exhibit 2–7 is from a training program on advanced word processing, and it contains important information about the intended audience. It lists prerequisite courses, which can serve to guide both you and the learners by giving a clear indication of how learners should be qualified to enter a training program. Prerequisite courses also assist you by providing you with guidelines about who should—and should not—be in the training. You can ask yourself, "Has this person taken the prerequisite course, or can he or she demonstrate the skills and knowledge required in that course?" If the answer is "no," then the learner may need to be screened or required to develop and demonstrate the appropriate prerequisite skills before attending the course.

The learner profile also highlights the *required* skills and *additional* skills. *Required* skills are mandatory for learners to enter training

---

Exhibit 2–7
Sample learner profile.

Advanced Word Processing 3.0

Prerequisite Training Programs:

- Introduction to Word Processing 1.0

- Intermediate Word Processing 2.0

Required Skills:

This training program was designed for those who are currently using word processing as part of their job. The learner must have the ability to use a computer and must possess basic computing skills such as using a keyboard and a mouse.

Additional Skills:

During the training program, students will be required to sit for long periods of time in front of a computer terminal and read information.

---

situations. If the learner does not possess these abilities, success is unlikely. Required skills are generally identified during the instructional design phase and should be spelled out in the instructor guide. Another way to determine skills required by learners is to review the course material and ask, "What must learners know or do to be ready for the training content?" For example, assume that a training program on chemical processing covers the mixing of chemicals for testing purposes. When reviewing this material, you may ask, "What must learners know or do before mixing chemicals?" The answer to this question might be that, "In order to mix chemicals, learners must know how to take the temperature of the liquids." Taking temperatures should then be mentioned in the learner profile as a required skill.

The section entitled *additional* skills in the sample learner profile contains valuable information. It contains assumptions about the learners that are sometimes taken for granted. In keeping with the profile presented, most people either already possess the skills under the required skills section or can acquire them within a reasonable time. However, the ability to sit for long periods may be a problem for some people, depending on physical capacity, stamina, or job requirements.

An example might be seen in a computer class geared toward senior citizens. Some older people may only be able to sit at a computer terminal for a short time before becoming uncomfortable, which will hamper their ability to learn. Analyzing course material and learner information in a situation such as this might lead you to change the course by taking frequent breaks or scheduling the training in shorter time increments than you might use for a different group.

INSTRUCTOR GUIDE

Information about the intended audience for a training program is also frequently contained in an important document called an *instructor guide* (IG) or an *instructor manual* (IM). This document, which is one component of a complete instructional package, is a collection of written material that is meant to provide information, instructions, guidelines, and material to training instructors on all aspects of the course— including sequencing, activities, tests, answer keys, optional exercises, key questions, important points, and other material. An instructor guide facilitates training delivery by providing structure and an explanation of the assumptions, goals, and rationale for the training program. Instructor guides may range from a few brief pages to a detailed outline or complete manual. The learner profile is generally included in introductory sections of the instructor guide.

In addition to using the instructor guide to gain a clear understanding of the target audience for the training, you should use it to review the proposed program content and gain important information about the training. Consider the questions shown in Exhibit 2–8 as you work to become intimately familiar with the content of a training course.

These (and similar) probing questions can help you get a clear picture of what the program will look like as it is delivered. Having this clear picture of the course flow, structure, and content is useful because it helps to ensure that alignment exists between the material and the learners.

STRATEGIES TO GATHER ACTUAL LEARNER INFORMATION

The learner profile and instructor guides are important sources of information to describe the intended learner. Several additional sources are important for gathering information about learners who are scheduled to attend training.

Typically, most participants must go through a registration process to attend training. Registration forms usually ask prospective trainees to supply basic information, such as name, geographic location, current

Exhibit 2–8
Key questions for reviewing course content and learner information.

Questions about the training material:

☐ Who is the intended audience?

☐ Are the objectives clear, specific, and obtainable?

☐ What instructional activities are included?

☐ What purpose(s) do these activities serve?

☐ How much time is devoted to each?

☐ What is the balance among various training methods such as lecture, skill practice, and demonstration?

☐ What content points are emphasized in the training?

☐ What examples are provided to reinforce key points?

☐ What questions or areas of confusion might arise?

☐ Do aspects of the material seem obsolete?

☐ Does any part of the material appear to be inaccurate or incorrect?

☐ How will the training lead to achievement of the objectives?

☐ How is the training evaluated?

Questions about the prospective learners:

☐ What is the demographic makeup of the group?
  - Job titles?
  - Education?
  - Years with organization?
  - Gender?
  - Age?
  - Experience?

☐ Where might resistance arise?

☐ Do the learners know one another?

☐ What common interests might they have?

☐ What style of learning do the participants prefer? (i.e. Lecture, Hands-on, Visual)

☐ What is their current skill level in the training topic?

☐ What expectations do learners have about the training?

☐ What are some potential barriers to training transfer?

☐ Are the learners required to attend or did they volunteer?

☐ Who sponsored the learners and what expectations do they have?

☐ What issues might be raised during training?

☐ Are the learners peers or are there supervisors and subordinates present?

Exhibit 2–9
Sample course registration information.

Name	Location	Position	Contact #	Sponsor	Comments
E. Lacy	Miami	Supervisor-II	702-485-0060	P. Gillenwatt	
J. Trava	Chicago	Operator-IV	412-451-6600		Will miss day 3
G. Herold	Chicago	Operator-III	412-451-6434		Will miss day 3
G. Hall	Boston	Mechanic	617-494-1803	J. King	New employee
M. Smith	Toronto	Supervisor-I		K. Carey	
C. Sanchez	South Bend	Operator-V	505-242-1358	J. Browning	Did not complete prereq. V
D. Harten	Toledo	Operator-III	211-649-1357	S. Valezquez	

job title, and supervisor or sponsor's name. Exhibit 2–9 displays a spreadsheet used to capture sample course registration information.

While this information can provide you with basic information about the learners, it is rarely detailed enough to build a complete learner profile. Take a moment to think about the insights you can gain about participants from the sample course registration spreadsheet appearing in Exhibit 2–9. As you review this registration form, note that participants are attending from multiple geographic locations and that they represent a mix of job categories or positions. Depending on what the training program is, you may find some pieces of information about learners more important than others. For example, if the training is a customer service skills program, you want to know whether the participants are currently in customer service positions. Think about other information that can be collected from the sample registration form. Consider whether there are questions that should be added to the registration form as a way to capture more information and provide a more complete picture. For example, you could ask prospective learners the following questions:

1. What is your current role and what are your current responsibilities?

2. What is your employment history?

3. Have you had any previous experience with [training topic]?

4. Do you have any special needs?

5. What concerns, if any, do you have about the upcoming training?

In addition to registration information, you may also obtain valuable data about participants from the HR department or managers. The following critical incident demonstrates how frustrating it can be to gather accurate learner information and a way that one trainer did that.

Do Your Research

" *The most typical problem I have is relying on someone else to tell me the skill level of my audience. When I train our sales force, the marketing center tries to tell me how much experience or education the audience has in relation to my product. Most of the time, they are wrong. To get around this, I have made contacts in the field whom I speak with to assess their knowledge ahead of time.* "

It can be very helpful for you to schedule a short meeting to gather information from people who are familiar with the learners, such as sponsors and managers. Sample questions you could ask during a meeting might include:

- What is the demographic makeup of the group?

- What is the educational background of these learners?

- What knowledge and skills do they possess?

- What knowledge and skills are they lacking?

- What job experience do they have?

- What training have they received in the past three years?

- What are the biggest barriers to job performance that these learners face?

- What else should I know about this group of learners?

Another strategy for gathering information is meeting with learners themselves. Often such conversations can provide valuable insights about individual learners. The previous questions could be posed directly to learners. Such discussions are also valuable because they can reveal goals and expectations that the sponsor, client, or learners might have about the training.

Another way to collect information about the participants is to poll them at the beginning of a training program. You can collect some information—such as the gender composition of the group—simply by observing who attends. For less obvious characteristics, you can simply ask the learners specific questions to gather pertinent information directly from the group. Examples of such questions might include "What is your familiarity with this software package?" and "How long have you been in the position of supervisor?" Asking such questions serves to gather relevant learner characteristics and demonstrates that you are the trainer and are concerned about customizing the training to meet learners' needs.

MAKING ADJUSTMENTS BEFORE TRAINING

If you detect a mismatch between the course material and the people signed up to attend a training course, you have several options. First, you can direct the learners into other programs to which they are better suited. If a novice computer user inadvertently attends an advanced programming class, for example, this person can be directed to a more appropriate course. The ability to reroute learners means you must possess, or have access to, information about the range of classes that you can suggest as alternatives.

Second, you can adjust the course material so that it is better tailored to the training participants. For example, assume that a trainer named Nathaniel is preparing to deliver a problem-solving and decision-making training program to a public, open-enrollment audience. He reviews the course roster and notices that, of the twenty-five participants enrolled in the course, six are from manufacturers, five are from retailers, seven are from academic institutions, four are from banks, and three are from food services organizations. Having delivered the two-day workshop many times in the past, Nathaniel quickly realizes that most examples in the course are drawn from manufacturing situations. Since he has several weeks before the program starts, Nathaniel works with an instructional designer and several subject matter experts to find and develop examples from each industry represented by the registrants for the course.

This example may appear to be an effective approach for modifying course material to meet learner needs. However, Nathaniel had the advantage of being familiar with the course material, which helped him to recognize the need for examples from the diverse industries represented by the participants. But you should not rely on the chance that you will always detect a mismatch between the course material and the prospective participants. Often, mismatches can occur that are more subtle. Asking the questions in Exhibit 2–8 is a more systematic approach which is more likely to detect gaps. It can serve as a checklist of key questions that you can ask about both the targeted audience and the existing course material to determine whether congruence exists between them.

Another approach you can take to head off potential problems is to incorporate training materials or methods that will account for these differences in all your courses.

Addressing Different Learning Styles

" The most typical problem I face is dealing with the wide range of abilities and backgrounds of trainees. Some learn rapidly, some slowly, and others in between. My challenge is to educate all to the minimum required skill level and to keep everyone interested and challenged. I handle this problem by using a wide variety of training techniques. I try to provide activities for all types of learning styles. Some of the techniques that I use include highly colorful flipcharts, small group presentations, colorful examples, games, manipulatives, analogies, and skits. I openly invite a wide variety of questions. I spend extra time with those that are struggling and provide extra exercises. I also encourage the quick learners to work with those that are progressing more slowly. Generally the results are positive and everyone learns the material, although some groups are more of a challenge than others. "

MAKING QUICK ADJUSTMENTS DURING TRAINING

As stated earlier, if training is designed properly, there should be a match between the training material and the intended group of learners. You should familiarize yourself with the program content and with the program delivery methods. You should also review the information you have about the learners before delivery. However, even if the course material and learner information are reviewed before delivery, you may detect discrepancies between the materials and the audience *during* the delivery of the program, which may require spur-of-the-moment adjustments. The subject of adapting delivery to account for learner characteristics will be treated in more depth in Chapter Five, where managing the learning environment is covered.

The focus of adjustments that might be made during training delivery is on minor modifications. Examine the following critical incident that was provided by one trainer in our study. Note the nature of the problem this person experienced and the added constraints surrounding the situation. This critical incident and the approach used highlight the importance of making adjustments.

Adjusting to Differing Needs

" The most typical problem is adjusting the material to the class needs. I train several courses to different work groups (i.e., technicians, customer service reps, sales staff). Many of my classes do have several different groups. We have considered offering different versions, but this presents scheduling and class size problems. Usually, I have been successful in addressing specific learner needs, without losing the others in the class. I do this by covering individual needs briefly or by spending time off-line (breaks or over lunch) with learners. "

Evidence of the need for major adjustments may point to fundamental problems with the design of the program. In such cases, it is a judgment call on whether to even proceed with the training. Knowing that the intended results are not likely to be achieved raises ethical questions with potentially deep consequences. If there are problems with the training design and there is time to make major revisions based on sound instructional design principles, then this should be done. However, if there is not sufficient time to make the necessary alterations, then the best option may be to postpone the training until the instructional designers can make the appropriate changes. This is a better choice than proceeding with the training and failing to achieve the desired results, which could lead to other unintended negative consequences, such as giving the learners false expectations, creating confusion, or even raising safety issues.

REPORTING ADJUSTMENTS AND RATIONALE

Changes that are made during training delivery, such as the minor adjustments we described, should be reported to the appropriate people either in writing or verbally. Most of the time you should document the revisions you make immediately—or at least soon after they are made. You can make the changes physically on the training material itself, such as by adding handwritten notes on the instructor guide. You can also take time at the end of a program or during breaks in the program to reflect on changes or to discuss the changes with learners. Some means should be established to document such changes and the rationale behind them so that they can be communicated to managers, designers, or other appropriate people. Exhibit 2–10 displays a worksheet that you can use to record changes you make before or during training delivery. This form can be kept close at hand so that changes can be documented as they occur or it can be used after training is complete.

Be sure to include the rationale for any changes, because training that is instructionally sound was designed with certain assumptions and decisions. If you make changes to the training, then revisit the original design considerations to see if the revisions could possibly lead to problems due to inconsistency with the theory or practice upon which it was originally based. Further, adjustments that are used should be logical and appropriate to the situation at hand.

Another useful piece of information that should be documented is the result of changes that were made during delivery. For example, the addition of a new analogy or metaphor to describe a particular concept could facilitate the learning of a concept that is presented later in the program. This unintended positive result should be noted because it can help future trainers to see the impact and subsequently use this new analogy or metaphor.

When formal or informal processes are in place to document, report, and communicate minor revisions to the training, they often correspond to the size and complexity of the training function or the organization. Some organizations have a large staff of instructional

Exhibit 2–10
Worksheet to document adjustments to training.

1. What was the change that was made? (Describe the adjustment)	2. Why was the change made? (Rationale for adjustment)	3. What effect did the change have? (Impact of adjustment)

designers and may require that you fill out forms concerning any changes made during delivery. Alternatively, designers may verbally communicate with you on a regular basis, so your revisions can be communicated directly to them during these exchanges. In other situations, you may play a dual role as trainer and designer and can thus make necessary changes yourself.

As important as documenting revisions to the content or delivery processes in a training course is the imperative of communicating those changes and accompanying rationale. The training competency *report evaluation information*, which will be discussed later in this book, describes reporting skills to communicate changes that were made during training to the appropriate designers, managers, or other stakeholders.

JUDGING THE APPROPRIATENESS OF ADJUSTMENTS

An important part of making revisions to training material to ensure a better match with the learner characteristics is judging the appropriateness and adequacy of those changes. The most important consideration in passing judgment on the appropriateness and adequacy of adjustments is whether the integrity of the original design has been preserved. When training is designed properly, objectives are established first, and the program content, activities, and delivery processes are then developed in order to ensure that those objectives can be achieved by learners. Any changes made to the original design can jeopardize its soundness and could mean that objectives are not fully met or are not being met at all. For this reason, you must make sure that any changes you make to training material do not have a negative impact.

You should ask a series of questions about the adjustments. As mentioned, the most fundamental question is "Are the instructional objectives still being met?" Another question is "Are the revisions negatively affecting the learners?" A question that might also be important when an adjustment involves adding an activity or revising an existing activity is "Is this change appropriate to the training site?" For example, you might want to add group activities to a course, but the training site has chairs that are bolted to the floor. Working in groups typically requires that the chairs can be moved around. Another question that can be asked when making changes is "Are there any unintended consequences that might arise from these adjustments?"

Finally, ask yourself whether the revisions are based on necessity or on your own preferences. Sometimes you may enjoy conducting certain activities, telling certain stories, or presenting certain information. This can become a problem if the activity, story, or information does not lead to achievement of the objectives, but is included solely for your enjoyment. Such changes are not appropriate and are typically not justifiable. You should ask yourself, "Does this activity/ story/information help achieve the objectives?" and "Are learners performing better as a result of this activity/story/information?" and "Is this activity/story/information teaching 'nice to know' or 'need to know' information?" If the answer to any of these questions is "no," or if the information is simply "nice to know" then chances are that the changes should probably not be made. Look at Exhibit 2–11 for some additional questions you should ask when making adjustments to training.

Exhibit 2–11
Questions trainers should ask themselves after making adjustments to training.

❑ Are the objectives still being met?

❑ Did the adjustments solve the problem or improve the training?

❑ Are the adjustments positively or negatively affecting learners?

❑ Is there still a match with the training site?

❑ Do learners approve of the adjustments?

❑ Are the adjustments affecting any other areas of the training?

❑ What are the consequences of the adjustments?

❑ Will the adjustments interfere with the training schedule?

❑ Should the adjustments be permanent?

❑ Can the adjustments be re-created?

❑ How will the adjustments be conveyed?

❑ Who needs to know about the adjustments?

SUMMARY

Analyzing course material and learner information is an important competency that is most effective when you enact it before training. However, this competency, which ensures a match between the training materials and the learners, must sometimes be demonstrated during delivery. Achieving this match is a common problem for trainers, as we found from the large number of critical incidents provided by trainers in our survey. This chapter covered the following topics:

- Examining specific learner characteristics—including learning styles and the learners' prior knowledge, experience, job positions, and physical characteristics—as a basis for gearing training to better meet the needs of your audience.

- Gathering information about the learners' characteristics.

- Making changes to training before and during delivery.

STRATEGY LIST

Actionable Strategies to Improve Training Effectiveness:

Learner Characteristics

❏ Recognize that every learner is unique and that many learner characteristics will be represented in any given training session.

❏ Learn as much as you can about various learner characteristics prior to training such as knowledge and skill levels, education level, job position, learning styles, gender, race, years of experience, and age.

Learning Styles

❏ Recognize that people typically have a preferred learning style including visual (learn best by seeing), auditory (learn best by hearing), or kinesthetic (learn best by doing or experiencing), but often use a combination of these.

❏ Activate as many learning styles as possible during delivery by using various instructional methods.

❏ Identify your own preferred learning style by taking a learning styles inventory.

Learner Knowledge, Skill, and Experience

❏ Tap into learners' previous knowledge, skill, and experience during training. Doing this helps to reinforce understanding and relates new information to what learners already know.

❏ Design and conduct training in a job context to make abstract principles more concrete.

❏ Determine and communicate prerequisite knowledge and skill necessary for learners to participate in training to avoid learner failure or impeding the progress of others.

❏ Recognize the life or career stage that different learners may be in and the major goals or tasks they might be facing. Then try to relate the content of the training to these goals, tasks, and work problems.

Strategies for Gathering Learner Information

❏ Recognize that the *intended audience* (who the training is designed for) may not be the same as the *actual audience* (who actually shows up).

❏ Review the *learner profile*, typically contained in the instructor guide, to determine the characteristics of the intended audience.

❏ Consult the instructor guide to gain important information and insight about the training and determine if there appears to be a match between the training and the intended audience.

❏ Collect as much information about the actual learners as possible prior to training by reviewing registration records, asking human resources, contacting learners prior to training, and asking their supervisor or manager.

❏ Ask the learners questions at the beginning of the training program to learn more about them and their relevant characteristics.

Making Adjustments before Training

❏ Make reasonable accommodations in advance of training to ensure that potential problems for learners with disabilities are prevented or minimized.

☐ Reroute learners to other training if there is a mismatch between the person and the training.

☐ Ensure that course materials and classroom examples are geared to the targeted audience.

Making Adjustments during Training

☐ Assess learner characteristics during training by asking them questions and making quick adjustments and accommodations if possible.

☐ Postpone training if major problems exist and adjustments are not possible.

☐ Report (verbally or in writing) adjustments made during training to the appropriate people (managers, designers, other trainers). Include rationale for adjustments and the positive and negative results that stemmed from these changes.

Judging the Appropriateness of Adjustments

☐ Determine if the original integrity of the training design was preserved in light of changes that were made (Were objectives still met? Did the changes have any negative impact on learners? Were revisions based on necessity or preference?).

CHAPTER 3

ASSURING PREPARATION OF THE TRAINING SITE

SKILLS ASSESSMENT

Take a moment to review the competency and associated performances that will be covered in this chapter. Consider your current level of proficiency in the competency as a whole as well as each performance and check the items where you feel you need to improve. As you read the chapter, concentrate on those areas most in need of development.

Competency:

❐ Assure preparation of the training site

Associated Performances:

❐ Confirm logistical arrangements.

❐ Confirm the physical arrangement of the instructional site, materials, equipment, and furniture.

❐ Control the physical environment.

❐ Plan ways to minimize distractions.

❐ Assure proper disposition of equipment, materials, and furniture.

❐ Judge how well logistical and physical arrangements support the training.

Assuring preparation of the training site is the second training delivery competency found in the IBSTPI Standards. By mastering this competency, you can ensure that the physical environment for training matches the learners' needs and that it will make the setting conducive to learning. This competency is the focus of this chapter. If you forget to apply this competency—or if you apply it improperly—you will find that the consequences can seriously hamper learning. Frequently, even when you are not able to control the physical setting for training, you will be blamed for it—and your participant evaluation results will suffer.

The *training site* is the physical location where training is delivered. This chapter will discuss different issues related to the training site as well as methods and techniques for making certain that it is ready for, and conducive to, a positive learning experience. Key issues examined in this chapter include logistics, room layout, equipment, and supplies. The chapter also provides advice about how to control the physical environment and minimize distractions.

In most situations the training site is a classroom at the job location, but it could also be a computer lab, conference room, office, or technical work area. Preparation of the site includes consideration of its physical aspects, such as furniture, as well as its environmental conditions, such as noise and lighting. Some large organizations have people who are responsible for preparing and maintaining the instructional facility. These may include building or property management staff, maintenance people, and even janitors. More often, however, trainers are responsible for at least some of these duties. Even if others are involved in some ways with preparing the training site, you will ultimately be held responsible for matching the setting to learner needs. This chapter covers the following topics:

- Logistical arrangements that you should consider when preparing for training delivery.

- Physical arrangements for the site, including the characteristics and layout of the training room and breakout rooms, and the needs for equipment and supplies.

- Management of the various components of the physical environment.

- Strategies for minimizing distractions.

CONFIRMING LOGISTICAL ARRANGEMENTS

Logistics refers to the movement of people, materials, and equipment. Logistical arrangements involve preparing the training site and ensuring that people are notified about it, that equipment is in place when and where it is needed, that food and other refreshments arrive as ordered, and that handouts and other materials arrive on schedule. You must make all logistical arrangements well in advance, then double-check, and sometimes even triple-check, them to ensure that everything runs smoothly. Think of this process as comparable to a theatrical production in which the stage manager must make sure that key elements are timed properly and carried out in a smooth, seamless flow.

What Else Can Go Wrong?

" *I was teaching two half-day classes. One was from 9:00 A.M. to noon and the other was from 1:00 P.M. to 5:00 P.M. After one of the sessions, at about 5 P.M., I checked enrollment for the following day and found that the morning participants would also be attending the afternoon session. The participants arrived at 8:45 A.M., so I started immediately in order to give them plenty of time for lunch. At 9:30, three more came. They had signed up for class at 6 P.M. the night before. I quickly got material for them and got them signed on to the computer, using resources planned for the afternoon class. I pushed and finished at 11:45. I had planned to use the lunch hour to set up new resources for the afternoon class. Also, the three late arrivals didn't realize there was an afternoon class available, and they asked if they could attend this also. As I was setting up, the fire alarm went off and everyone had to evacuate the building for twenty minutes (they were installing a new water heater, and every time solder connected, it set off the alarm). In the middle of the afternoon, we were interrupted as a participant's BMW had rolled out of its parking space and hit another car. I leveled with the participants on how the fire alarms had affected my preparation and kept my sense of humor—it was sure easier to laugh at all this later than it was at the time it happened. Also, I now always recheck the enrollment list the morning of class, to catch those last-minute additions.* "

Note in this incident that the trainer had to cope with many unexpected events—such as late arrivals, unscheduled fire alarms, and malfunctioning automobiles. These events posed distractions that could have easily derailed the training experience. Only the quick-witted actions of the trainer saved the day.

Other problems associated with dealing with logistical arrangements center around managing noisy training locations, handling setup difficulties, coping with renovations to the facility, dealing with widely dispersed training sites, and ensuring learners' access to restricted sites.

No Control Over Setup and Logistics

" *The most typical problem I face has to do with creating a proper classroom learning environment. Due to the fact that I often train at remote locations, I don't always have control over setup and logistics. Sometimes I have to use rooms with long conference tables when I would prefer a U-shaped room or small tables for groups. I often have to rely on others to obtain audiovisual equipment and set it up. Sometimes they can only get a flimsy flipchart stand, an old broken-down overhead projector, or a TV/VCR that works poorly.* "

Although logistical problems ranked high in the number of critical incidents described in our survey of trainers, survey respondents also rated it as the least difficult competency to master of the fourteen competencies identified in the IBSTPI Standards. This competency seems easy to achieve at first glance, but it also can be too easily taken for granted. Furthermore, many issues associated with logistical arrangements are often beyond the immediate control of trainers, though they may be blamed when the training site is not appropriate or when things go wrong.

Another interesting finding from our survey was that men and women rated the competency differently. Men rated assuring preparation of the training site as the most important competency of the fourteen. They placed a mean importance rating of 4.96 on this competency (where a rating of 5 indicated extremely important). But women, on the other hand, rated assuring preparation of the training site number eleven in terms of importance to effective delivery. What conclusions can you draw from this wide discrepancy between men and women trainers? Perhaps men believe that the quality of the physical dimensions of training is paramount to a successful delivery experience. Women in our survey, on the other hand, placed much greater emphasis on the learners themselves than on the physical aspects of the environment.

You will find that many issues must be considered when managing logistics. Slight problems, if ignored or forgotten, can produce dramatic disruptions.

> Chris was training a small group of electrical and computer systems engineers in the area of graphical user interfaces (GUIs). The morning session was smooth, and he planned to break for lunch at noon and then resume by taking the learners into the plant to see examples of GUIs being used. Following lunch the group was supposed to be transported to the plant site in the company van. After waiting for the van for fifteen minutes, Chris had the learners pile into his and another learner's car and drive to the facility. Upon arrival at the site, they discovered that the GUI equipment they planned to observe was out of commission for preventative maintenance and upgrade.

This incident illustrates several logistical problems. First, scheduled transportation did not arrive. This problem was handled effectively, and delayed the group by only fifteen minutes. More serious, however, was the problem that the trainer was unaware of scheduled downtime in the plant. That wasted the learners' time, and recovering credibility after that experience would pose a challenge for any trainer.

GERI MCARDLE

Logistical problems related to sending material to a remote training site even happen to seasoned training pros like Geri McArdle of the Training Group located in Reston, Virginia. Here is how Geri dealt with a logistical problem through a little advanced preparation and a lot of flexibility: Geri McArdle once walked into a five-day, overhead transparency–driven seminar to discover that none of the sixty or so overheads due from another location had arrived. The slides contained lots of theory and activities, but luckily for McArdle she had done her homework the night before by reviewing the materials, creating storyboards, and drawing pictures to remember key points. She says, "I stepped from behind the projector and made instant contact with the audience. Who needs overheads?"[1]

Scheduling or other logistical problems may appear to pose minor inconveniences. But the impact on the effectiveness of the training and on the trainer's credibility can be tremendous—especially when scheduling is tight and learners are difficult to assemble. When unexpected problems arise, you have to be resourceful to work around them—preferably without the learners realizing it. However, logistical problems are undesirable and, for this reason, you should become obsessive about checking schedules, details, and room arrangements.

Communication Breakdown

" New hires begin Monday morning and spend 8:00 A.M. to noon in human resources and then 1:00 to 5:00 P.M. with me. Well, no one told them about the afternoon training (or even the two weeks of new-hire training scheduled to be delivered) and the group of new hires had to make other arrangements in order to stay for the session. One person couldn't stay, one stayed until 3:00 P.M., one until 4:00 P.M., and two until 5:00. My manager told me I was unable to use the lab, so I was searching for a room at 10:00 A.M. Then the manager of the department sent someone for refresher training without telling me, but we only covered the basics during the first day, so she was bored. I sent her back and then ended at 4:00 since I was down to two people. I don't think the new hires were impressed that day. "

Before each training session, use a checklist that identifies the most important logistical considerations. Such a checklist appears in Exhibit 3–1. Even if you think you can remember all these items without a checklist, remember that veteran combat and airline pilots always use a checklist before takeoff to make sure they do not forget anything essential to a safe flight.

The questions in Exhibit 3–1 are organized into several categories. Some questions deal with the arrangements you need to make. Other questions relate to scheduling. Still other questions fix responsibility for action or for the process by which an activity will be carried out. Taken together, these questions can help you plan effectively. Of course, you may need to add, subtract, or modify items to tailor the checklist to your needs and to the requirements of unique training experiences.

Exhibit 3-1
Logistical considerations checklist.

- [ ] When will the training take place? (i.e. time of day, number of days, time between sessions)
- [ ] Who will be involved in delivery of the training? (i.e. trainer, subject matter expert, guest speaker, executives, others)
- [ ] Where will the training be delivered? (site location, room assignments)
- [ ] Will additional space be needed? (breakout rooms, lab, lunch area)
- [ ] When will the learners arrive?
- [ ] What lodging arrangements, if any, need to be made?
- [ ] How will registration take place?
- [ ] What prework, if any, was assigned?
- [ ] What equipment will be needed during the training? (e.g. VCR, television, overhead projector, flipchart, supplies, other)
- [ ] How will equipment be delivered to the training site?
- [ ] What material will be needed during training?
- [ ] How will material be delivered to the training site?
- [ ] What transportation arrangements, if any, need to be made? (e.g. plant visits, air-port/hotel taxis, shuttle service)
- [ ] What testing services, if any, are needed?

- [ ] What food service arrangements, if any, need to be made?
- [ ] How will announcements or messages be relayed to learners? (e.g. central bulletin board, hallway monitors, notes delivered to trainer, notes delivered to learners, posted on door)
- [ ] How many breaks, if any, are scheduled?
- [ ] Are emergency procedures posted?
- [ ] Is the training site free of potential safety hazards?
- [ ] Is the training site clean and tidy?
- [ ] What room configuration is needed?
- [ ] Who will set up and disassemble the room configuration?
- [ ] Do learners have access to the building and room?
- [ ] Were directions, if required, sent to the learners?
- [ ] Is the location of the training room clearly identified?
- [ ] Have seating assignments, if needed, been made?
- [ ] Is sound equipment in working order?
- [ ] Have special hardware and media been properly set up and tested?
- [ ] What unanticipated problems might arise?

CONFIRMING THE
PHYSICAL ARRANGEMENTS

The term *physical arrangements* refers to the furniture, room configuration, supplies, materials, and equipment that will be used during training delivery. Some organizations employ a cadre of people specifically for handling these accommodations. But it still remains your responsibility as a trainer to ensure that the physical arrangements are organized for a training experience.

As just one example of an organization that employs people to help with physical arrangements, the Fairlane Training and Development Center at Ford Motor Company costs $10 million annually to operate and employs a full-time staff of 160.[2] Some staff members devote all their work time to managing physical arrangements. Nevertheless, the final responsibility for organizing physical arrangements at Ford rests with the trainers. This section describes the management of accessibility, room layout, equipment, and supplies.

ACCESSIBILITY AND PARTICIPANTS WITH DISABILITIES

Reasonable accommodations must be made so that the training site is accessible to all learners, regardless of physical or other disabilities. The Americans with Disabilities Act (ADA) of 1990, which went into effect in July 1992, requires employers to make reasonable accommodation, including modification of physical structures, materials, and jobs, to encourage access and permit success for all people in the United States. Training facilities must comply with this legislation so that learners with hearing, vision, and other disabilities have equal access to facilities and receive equal treatment in training. Training facilities may require such accommodations as wheelchair ramps, enlarged restroom stalls, training material in Braille or large print, sign language or interpretation services, and special voice amplifiers. In some cases, the organization may need to supply one-on-one coaches to ensure that reasonable accommodation is provided. Sometimes, you may not even be aware of the changes that need to be made to accommodate those with disabilities.

Not a Laughing Matter

" *The worst experience I ever had involved an individual in my new hire train-ing class. This individual was suffering from a disability, which limited her physical and mental abilities. At times, she would become verbally abusive to myself and to her classmates. She said her outbursts were due to her illness. The class was three weeks in length and on a daily basis she would interrupt the material I was delivering or make loud and sarcastic outbursts. I imme-diately contacted my HR representative and began documenting all of her occurrences. I spoke with her on an individual basis numerous times and started bringing others into our conferences to serve as witnesses. Her behavior frazzled me, especially being a new trainer. I remained positive and focused and got through the entire three weeks by ignoring her outbursts.* "

Of course, this trainer was experiencing an individual who suf-fered from Tourette's syndrome, a disability. However, the trainer did not realize it, and ended up enduring a very challenging training expe-rience. Had the trainer been aware of the participant's disability in advance, special accommodations could have been made. Further, since the training lasted for three weeks, the trainer, as well as the HR department, had ample time to learn about this illness and take steps to accommodate the learner. This approach would have been better than ignoring the learner, because it would demonstrate respect and sensi-tivity to all of the learners. However, this incident certainly shows the difficult predicaments that trainers sometimes encounter.

What are some specific ways that you can monitor the need for making reasonable accommodations? Three ways are described below.

COLLECTING INFORMATION THROUGH REGISTRATION FORMS

One way you can monitor the need for making reasonable accommo-dations is to ask specific questions on the course registration forms. Many course registration forms are, of course, designed to collect infor-mation from learners regarding specific requests for assistance. Consider including a simple statement such as "Please circle 'Y' if you require assistance before, during, or after training," or "In the space below, please indicate any special assistance or needs that you may have." This is a simple approach that will give you an early warning system for monitoring special needs so that they can be accommodated before the training begins.

> Claudia was conducting a one-day time management course for administrative assistants. As part of the course, participants were asked to fill out a computerized logbook of their time spent on the job. The logbook was to be completed during the first part of the training session and then referred to during the rest of the course. Being proactive, Claudia sent out a short questionnaire one week prior to the course to identify any special needs that the participants might have. One participant sent back the questionnaire describing a visual impairment he had, as well as a simple solution—an attachment to his computer that enabled him to see the screen as well as the other participants. Claudia arranged to have the proper equipment ready for him and thus avoided a potentially negative situation.

INVOLVING LEARNERS WITH DISABILITIES IN PLANNING

A second way you can monitor the need for making reasonable accommodations is to involve learners with disabilities when planning the training. In that way, you can gain their valuable insights and expertise in crafting an accommodation strategy. Learners can be asked what difficulties or problems they generally encounter before or during training and how those difficulties or problems might be avoided or minimized. A related approach is to invite learners with disabilities to explore the training facility or sit through a pilot program to identify areas that might be problematic for them. That approach can help them detect issues associated with discomfort, learning impediments, mobility, visibility, and other problems before the training begins. It also allows time to take action to minimize the effects of these problems.

ENSURING ACCESSIBILITY TO THE FACILITY

Training sites should be accessible to *all learners*. The following critical incident, provided by a trainer who responded to our survey, illustrates this point dramatically.

Check the Details

" *Learners at a particular organization were to attend training that was being provided by an external vendor. This training was to be conducted at the vendor's newly established office, which was located on the fifth floor of an office building. Maps and directions were provided, and the participants were instructed to arrive by 7:30 A.M. for the training that was scheduled to begin at 7:45 A.M. Trainees arrived at the site to find the door to the office complex locked. While the trainers had special access keys, the building did not officially open until 8:00 A.M. Fortunately in this case, the trainers realized the problem, rushed downstairs, and found the trainees waiting at the front door—still in good spirits.* "

As this critical incident shows, you should give participants instructions if they may find it difficult to enter the training facility. Further, you should post clearly visible signs or assign a chaperone for sight-impaired learners to guide them to the appropriate location. A learner profile, completed during the registration process, can help you detect the need for signs, chaperones, maps, directions, or other accommodations that might be necessary.

ROOM LAYOUT

Many people associate the layout of a training room with the layout of classrooms they attended while in school. Desks and chairs are arranged in neat rows and columns, all pointed toward the front of the room. But training situations are different. Many room configurations are possible, and the choice of what configuration to select depends on such issues as the type of training, the activities that will be used, the level of formality desired, and the number of people attending. Room configurations—that is, how seats are arranged—can influence training results either positively or negatively. Of course, it is always possible to rearrange room configuration at different points in a training experience to match desired results. Exhibit 3–2 depicts some sample room configurations that you can use.

Room configurations should be deliberately chosen based on program objectives, available resources, and facility limitations. Exhibit 3–3 suggests designs based upon different situations that you might encounter. Keep in mind, however, that room size and shape will also

Exhibit 3–2
Sample room configurations.

a. U-shaped

b. Conference table

c. Theater-style

d. Traditional classroom

e. V-shaped

f. Cluster- or team-style

Exhibit 3–3
Matching room layouts with training situations.

Training Situation	Recommended Room Design
The material being used requires a large amount of group work. Students will work in groups of 4 to 5 and discuss issues and solve problems.	Because learners will be working in groups, they should be mobile. Ideally, each group works around one table (cluster-style) large enough to accommodate all the group members and their materials such as books and paper. If large tables are not available, students will need movable desks and chairs (traditional classroom) so that they can form a group. An alternative is to use separate breakout rooms.
Students will work individually on a project and then make a presentation to the rest of the class.	This room needs to be conducive to public speaking (theater-style, traditional classroom, V-shaped, U-shaped). Before class begins, someone should stand in the front of the room and speak in a normal tone. By standing in the back of the room, the trainer can determine whether or not the acoustics will help or hinder the training program.
The class involves interactive discussions between the trainer and the learners.	While the traditional "desks in rows" can work in this situation, a U-shaped or conference table design will promote discussion among the students. If the goal is to get students talking to one another and interacting during class, setting the room up so that everyone can see the others is recommended.
Part of the lesson involves a video or movie that will be displayed on a screen in the front of the class.	All students either must be able to see and hear the video from their seats (theater-style, V-shaped, U-shaped) or they will need to be able to move their desks/chairs to a place where they can (traditional-style). Ideally, students should not have to move around, because it is disruptive and time consuming.

play an important role in determining room layout. Many more seats can fit in a room if tables are not used, but not having tables may make it difficult for learners to take notes or spread out their materials. Fewer learners can be seated in a U-shaped arrangement, and fewer still at a large conference table.

When making a decision about appropriate room layout, you should consider at least the following questions:

- What will be happening around the training facility during the session? Will there be external noise due to other training courses, lawn mowing, snow blowing, or construction?

- What is the weather? Will learners be entering the training room with bulky coats, umbrellas, or boots? Where will they store these items?

- Will students be entering and exiting the facility frequently? (For instance, if the building prohibits smoking, where will the smokers go, and will they need to go through elaborate security measures every time they enter or leave the building?) Is access easy or difficult?

- What training activities will be conducted? What room layout will most closely match learners' needs?

- Where are restrooms, breakout rooms, equipment storage, supplies, light switches, power outlets, and other important locations?

- Do learners know how to evacuate the facility in case of a fire, storm, or other emergency situations?

- Where will messages for learners be posted?

Facility design plays an important role in the learning process and has an important effect on learner attitudes. Learning can be positively or negatively influenced by the design or location of a training environment. If learners are uncomfortable, have difficulty seeing or hearing, or are distracted by seating arrangements, then the probability of a successful training event is reduced. A poor physical facility can render your instruction ineffective even if you are an outstanding presenter.

Unexpected Trainees

" *I had a big problem when our Human Resource department overbooked trainees. I only had room for four to five trainees at one time. They had seven come in. I was only aware of five that were coming. Luckily, I was able to make up extra training booklets so each person had a book. However, not everyone had room at the worktable. I provided them with clipboards for writing purposes. When it came time for hands-on training on the computers, I rotated them in pairs with one on the computer and the other observing.* "

Unless incidents such as these are well managed, the trainer will usually get the blame for the poor room layout. One of the authors experienced a problem related to the location of the training room itself. He was delivering a low-budget train-the-trainer program in a small company that did not have a room dedicated to training; instead, the company lunchroom was used. Several times throughout the day, the session was disrupted by people walking through the room to reach the vending machines. Conversations would inevitably ensue and the trainer found it easier to take a short break when this happened rather than stand between the hungry workers and the sandwich machines.

AVOIDING DISTRACTIONS IN THE PHYSICAL ENVIRONMENT

A good trainer will pay close attention to distractions that may be posed by the physical environment. While these can be attractive to sightseers, they may not be conducive to effective learning. For example, hotels or conference centers may have elegant flowing drapes, elaborate tapestries, huge windows, or eye-catching artwork. Casinos, amusement parks, and cruise ships—while exotic—may have features that distract learners, posing special challenges to trainers. Even though it may be impossible for you to change permanent fixtures or arrangements, be aware that they can distract learners. If such locations can be avoided in favor of more modest, neutral surroundings, then by all means do so. In fact, the more the training location resembles the learners' typical workplace surroundings, the better. For example, trapping upper managers in a dark basement training room or factory workers in a first-class, upscale facility may cause them discomfort because they feel outside their typical surroundings.

> Bud had nearly twenty years of experience in the training field. He started as an associate relations trainer out of college and had worked his way up to the position of senior trainer for a large firm. He was out to dinner one night with his wife when a man approached him and told him that he had attended one of Bud's training courses about a year or so ago. Bud was thrilled, but slightly embarrassed because he couldn't remember the man, so he asked him several questions about the course he had attended, thinking that it might trigger some vague memory of him. To Bud's dismay, the man could not recall anything about the actual training course, but he could describe the room and even the building in great detail. The man went on and on about the technology and the elaborate decor. Bud eventually gave up, wondering how much the man had learned in his course.

BREAKOUT ROOMS

Many training facilities are equipped with *breakout rooms*, separate rooms located close to the main training location, where small learner groups can work in privacy. Often breakout rooms are fully stocked with flipcharts, tables, chairs, media, phones, computers, and other supplies that may be needed. Breakout rooms are ideal for many of the training methods that will be introduced and described in detail in Chapter Eleven, on using training methods effectively. Most notably, breakout rooms facilitate small group discussions and activities, case studies, and other project-based activities. Ideally, breakout rooms have the following characteristics:

- The rooms are private, with doors that can be shut.

- There are minimal distractions near the rooms, such as people walking by, a window overlooking a busy street, or a frequently used phone.

- The breakout rooms are close to the main training room.

- Nothing between the training room and the breakout rooms will distract the learners, such as a bank of phones, a door to the outside, colleagues' offices, or the lunchroom.

- The breakout rooms are stocked with the appropriate material and equipment that learners will need, such as flipcharts, markers, paper, and other supplies.

- The layout of the table and chairs in the breakout rooms should be appropriate for the type of activity planned for the breakout session.

Once you have decided to use breakout rooms in your program, you need to answer the following questions to make sure you will have the appropriate arrangements in place for your session:

- How many breakout rooms are required during training?

- How many breakout rooms are available at the facility you plan to use?

- Must the breakout rooms be scheduled in advance?

- How many people can use the breakout room comfortably, and what is the capacity?

- Will learners with disabilities have any problems using the breakout room?

Many questions that you ask of the main training room apply to breakout rooms as well. However, as can be seen in the questions above, there are differences. You should attempt to answer these (and other) questions about the breakout rooms before the course begins so that changes can be made and so that problems can be avoided.

EQUIPMENT AND SUPPLIES

When planning the physical environment, check the equipment and supplies before you begin delivering training. *Equipment* refers to overhead projectors, computers, and projection units. *Supplies* include items such as markers, masking tape, paper, or chalk. Training events can be unsuccessful if necessary equipment is not available (or does not work) and if necessary supplies are not available when needed.

A Clear Disconnect

" *I was training a group of seventy on a new software application that our company purchased. The software was not connected to the rest of the network, and the training was a nightmare. None of the processes being covered worked correctly from start to finish. This was extremely frustrating.* "

Equipment Woes

" *My job is to train skill trades safety classes. One time while using an overhead projector, the bulb went out and no one knew how to replace it. Everyone was somewhat anxious because I was uncomfortable with the presentation, since it was so dependent on the use of overhead materials. I made sure next time to acquaint myself with the equipment before beginning class.* "

Planning how to avoid these problems is the mark of an experienced trainer. It is especially important to do that when equipment and supplies must be shipped to a remote training site, as the next critical incident portrays.

Technology Backup Planning

" *The resources I needed to teach my class were mistakenly sent to Utah, instead of Pennsylvania. Only half of the shipment arrived. It was very difficult to teach the class, due to having to break my routine to work with what I had available. I did the best I could under the circumstances but on the third day I had to let the class go early due to not having the right equipment to use. Later, I had to make up time during the remaining two days to complete the course on time. This made me and our company look bad. It was a shipping company error, but it reflected badly on us regardless of who was to blame.* "

If you are to be successful in having the right equipment and supplies available at the right time and place, you will need to organize for that, prepare for it, and follow up. Just as you need to assume responsibility for checking the training site before you meet there, you must also check that the equipment and materials will be on hand. The checklist appearing in Exhibit 3–4 includes equipment and materials. You may modify it to meet any special requirements you may have. For example, if manufacturing employees are being trained to use a special X-ray measurement gauge, then you may need to have that device at the training site.

Failure of Technology

" *I sometimes have a problem with the computers I'm planning to use because students from prior classes have added, deleted, or changed software.* "

In this case, a statement such as "check software" or "erase practice files" could be added to the checklist to ensure this task is completed prior to delivery.

ORGANIZING EQUIPMENT AND SUPPLIES

It is just as important to organize equipment and supplies as it is to ensure that the right equipment and supplies are on hand when needed. When equipment and supplies appear disorganized, they can pose distractions to learners, detract from your credibility, and even (on occasion) pose safety hazards. Some training facilities are equipped with storage bins, shelves, file cabinets, racks, and organizing devices. Follow the simple rule of "a place for everything and everything in its place." Avoid frantic searches for equipment and supplies by putting everything where it belongs. You can also use labels to create permanent storage locations for specific items so that anyone, including new trainers and learners themselves, can retrieve supplies quickly and easily.

BACKUP PLANS

Remember that, no matter what you do and no matter how carefully you plan, technology can still fail, materials can get lost during transportation, and equipment can break. For that reason, develop backup plans that will allow the training to proceed even without the planned

Exhibit 3–4
Checksheet of equipment and supplies.

Potential equipment/supplies	Is it at the training site? If not, how will it be delivered?	Is it in proper working order?	Date checked
Computer equipped with correct software			
Projection unit for computer			
Flipcharts			
Laser pointer			
Markers			
Masking tape			
Note pads			
Writing instruments			
Participant guides			
Facilitator guide			
Computer disks			
Props			
TV/VCR			
Videos for instruction			
Blank videos			
Video camera			
Transparencies			
Overhead projector			
Extra overhead projector bulbs			
Other?			
Other?			

equipment and materials. For example, if you plan to use presentation software, make backup transparencies in case the computer-based presentation fails. Further, print a paper copy of the slides for handouts so that you have something to use in case the overhead transparency unit will not work. Make decisions about when and how far to go with contingency planning based on the situation, the level of risk, the resources available, and the time required.

CONTROLLING THE PHYSICAL ENVIRONMENT

Control the physical environment of the training facility whenever possible. The physical environment influences the learning process. It includes such factors as room temperature, air circulation, air quality, lighting, and sound. It also includes factors associated with safety and sanitation. These factors converge to create a pleasant or unpleasant environment for you and the learners. When the physical environment is too hot or too cold, learners may become tense, depressed, and disconnected. On the other hand, when the physical environment is friendly, informal, and nonthreatening, then learners feel relaxed, comfortable, and cheerful.

Too Hot to Learn

" *The classroom was full with fifteen people at fifteen computers, and it was very warm (no air conditioner). People were falling asleep and irritable. I gave several breaks, acknowledged the problem, sped up the class, tried to get the group more involved, avoided "lecturing," and added some fun topics. The results were okay. I wasn't happy with the class but the students, fortunately, were not as critical.* "

Your challenge as a trainer is to establish a climate that encourages learning, and the physical environment can either help or hinder that. You want to establish a setting in which learners are comfortable, distractions are minimized, and learning is facilitated. The checklist appearing in Exhibit 3–5 will help you do that.

ADJUSTING TEMPERATURE AND LIGHTING

Set the physical elements of the physical environment for optimal conditions, whenever possible, before the start of a program. For example, if a training room is somewhat cool early on a winter morning, turn up the heat so the temperature is comfortable by the time the learners arrive and the session begins. You may also need to adjust the temperature during training. (Recognize that it can be tough to satisfy all people, since some individuals will be too cold or too hot no matter what you do.) For this reason, seek periodic feedback from participants to identify when a change is needed. You should also be aware of air circulation and air quality so that it remains fresh and well ventilated. A sure symptom of a ventilation problem is that people begin to doze off.

Lighting is another key area that sometimes requires adjustment throughout training. For example, when showing a videotape or using an overhead projector, you may need to adjust the lights so that learners can see the screen as well as take notes. In such situations, dim the lights but do not turn them off. Seek a balance in lighting so that people have just the right amount to see the videotape or projector and take notes but not so little that they become drowsy.

PREVENTING SAFETY PROBLEMS

You should also consider safety issues that may arise during training. When possible, take steps to eliminate or minimize safety problems before they occur. For example, keep learners from tripping over electrical cords by using masking tape or duct tape to fasten cords to the floor.

```
┌─────────────────────────────────────────────────────────────────┐
│                          Exhibit 3–6                              │
│                    Sample safety guidelines.                      │
│                                                                   │
│                                                                   │
│                        COMPANY NAME                               │
│                                                                   │
│                    Trainee Safety Guidelines                      │
│          Industrial Training Center or Manufacturing Plant        │
│                                                                   │
│  All Trainees Must:                                               │
│                                                                   │
│    1. Sign in and out in the Visitor Log Book.                    │
│                                                                   │
│    2. Wear safety glasses with side shield, safety shoes, and any │
│       other safety equipment as directed by your trainer or host  │
│       in all working areas of the plant or training center.       │
│                                                                   │
│    3. Obey all safety rules and posted instructions.              │
│                                                                   │
│    4. Remain in the company of your host or trainer, or in the    │
│       assigned area of training.                                  │
│                                                                   │
│                                                                   │
│  In Case of Emergency:                                            │
│                                                                   │
│    5. The Plant and Training Center have a fire/plant evacuation  │
│       alarm system. Upon hearing the alarm, leave the plant or    │
│       training center immediately.                                │
│                                                                   │
│    6. Go to the employee lunch/locker room or alternate location  │
│       as directed by your host in the event of a tornado or       │
│       severe storm.                                               │
│                                                                   │
│                        TRAIN SAFELY!                              │
│                                                                   │
└─────────────────────────────────────────────────────────────────┘
```

You may want to distribute and review with learners a card like the one shown in Exhibit 3–6. It summarizes key safety guidelines that should be observed in certain training or plant facilities, on site visits, or in on-the-job training. Modify the card to tailor it to important issues in one organization or for use in one kind of training. Use the opportunity of discussing the cards to alert learners to what they should do if an accident occurs.

ENSURING CLEANLINESS

Finally, always examine the physical environment to ensure cleanliness, tidiness, and general neatness. Make sure that desks are clean and properly arranged, trash has been removed, and equipment and props are clean and positioned appropriately. Remember that your credibility is at stake if trash is found in the training room or chairs are in disarray at the beginning of a training session.

MINIMIZING DISTRACTIONS

Distractions are any disruptions during training that adversely affect delivery. Whenever possible, plan how to minimize or prevent distractions from occurring. Think for a minute about a training program that you were involved in recently. Develop a mental list of the distractions that arose during delivery. Did the caterers bring lunch early? Or did they make too much noise when setting up? Could hammers be heard pounding in a nearby part of the building that was under construction? Did an open window allow traffic noises and fumes to enter? Were messages delivered to learners while they were in the middle of training? Did supervisors walk into sessions to pull people out to deal with work problems? Did cellular phones ring in class, prompting learners to answer them with a whisper and slowly make their way out of the room? These distractions can create impediments to learning.

As you consider the distractions mentioned above and the mental list of distractions you created, think about how many could have been minimized or eliminated. Could caterers set up in another room? Could training have been scheduled around construction, or could construction have been delayed? Could messages have been posted outside the training room? Could cell phones have been banned or turned to silent mode? The answer to these questions is probably "yes." Thinking about them will focus your attention on how to plan for managing those distractions.

BRAINSTORM POTENTIAL DISTRACTIONS AND ALERT LEARNERS

One way you can minimize potential distractions is to brainstorm the potential problems, issues, or disruptions that might arise during training. When you have identified distractions, you can make adjustments. One way is to make changes to the training environment. Another is to alert the learners to the problem in advance so they are prepared. For example, if a heater in a training room has been on the blink and could not be repaired before a scheduled training session, alert participants to the problem and suggest they wear warm clothing. While that does not eliminate the problem, it reduces its impact.

INFORMING LEARNERS OF KEY ISSUES

Before training begins, or early in the training session, you should inform the learners of important issues affecting them. For instance, tell them what the schedule will be and when breaks will be taken. You can establish and communicate policies regarding how messages will be received and distributed. Also, alert learners to unavoidable distractions and explain why they are present.

Keep in mind that when advanced technology (such as compressed video conferencing) is introduced, you should minimize distractions. You can use various strategies to do that. Minimize exterior and interior sources of noise as much as possible. Take steps to buffer noise from nearby traffic, ringing phones, and loud ventilation systems—which some call the worst interior noise problem. Try to get a mix of fluorescent and incandescent lighting when you can. Halogen lighting has become more popular in some training sites recently.

Preventing problems is always a better approach than trying to solve them after they become apparent. You can prevent problems in some cases simply by moving locations, changing course materials, or requesting building maintenance. Once the training begins, you may find that your options are limited. However, a backup plan is always a good idea. Prepare an additional room if that is necessary and a room is available.

DEALING WITH UNEXPECTED EVENTS

Unexpected events will occur during training delivery no matter what preventative steps you take. Many critical incidents provided by trainers in our survey were centered on dealing with unexpected events occurring during delivery. While it is difficult to say whether these problems could have been prevented through better planning, you have to be flexible and inventive to deal with unexpected problems. However, when distractions do arise during delivery you must manage the situation as it happens. Competency four, *managing the learning environment,* is very important for managing distractions during delivery and will be discussed in Chapter Five. But, as a summary, review the list of common distractions and the strategies for dealing with them that appears in Exhibit 3–7.

FENG SHUI

Some U.S. organizations in recent years have adopted the Chinese philosophy and practice of *feng shui.* Feng shui seeks balance and harmony between physical structures and nature. Advocates of feng shui

Exhibit 3–7
Common distractions during delivery and suggestions for handling them.

Distractions	Suggestions for Handling
External noise such as nearby traffic or construction	Try to prevent this from happening before the training begins by selecting a location away from the noise. If it occurs during training, close windows and doors to reduce the noise. If it persists, consider moving to another site as soon as it is convenient.
Loud ventilation system	Seek help from the maintenance or technical department to eliminate or minimize the noise. If not, see if a sound system with a microphone is available. Also, if possible, move to another site.
Cellular phones and beepers	Before the training begins, ask learners to refrain from bringing their phones and beepers to training. If they are brought into the training, request that learners turn them off.
Temperature fluctuations	Adjust the temperature as necessary. If the weather is forecast to be cold, warn the learners to bring extra clothes to wear such as sweaters.
Talkative learners	Several techniques can be used such as standing close to the talkative learners, asking them questions, starting an activity, or taking a break. If the talking persists, discreetly ask the chatty learners to refrain from talking until the break or lunch.
Poor lighting	Make sure light adjustment is available before the training. If not, arrange to have supplemental lighting or add a dimmer switch if necessary.
Poor room layout	Consider the training activities that will be incorporated and plan the room layout accordingly. Make sure the room is flexible enough to move furniture around during training.
Short attention spans	Plan regular breaks, a variety of activities, and use multiple teaching methods.

believe that people are sensitive to physical orientations, surroundings, and sunlight. They use indoor plants, rooms positioned to maximize natural lighting, wind chimes, mirrors, and other artifacts to create an environment conducive to people. Their goal is to help people become more balanced, centered, focused, and productive. Realize that feng shui and other philosophies are not without skeptics. Some people regard the idea as about as useful as astrology, tarot cards, and palm reading. Not much research supports feng shui.

SUMMARY

Chapter Three has focused on *assuring preparation of the training site.* Trainers who master this competency should be able to do the following:

- Make appropriate logistical arrangements, and coordinate people, materials, and equipment.

- Plan the physical arrangements for training, and ensure that the right equipment and materials are available when needed.

- Control the physical environment to make it conducive to learning.

- Minimize distractions during training.

The emphasis throughout the chapter was on establishing optimal conditions before training, but you cannot escape the need to make some adjustments during training. From a learner's perspective, most— if not all—items covered in this chapter should remain hidden from view.

STRATEGY LIST

Actionable Strategies to Improve Training Effectiveness:

Confirm Logistical Arrangements

❏ Check, double-check, and sometimes triple-check logistical arrangements to ensure everything runs smoothly.

❏ Examine schedules, details, and room assignments.

❏ Create a checklist that includes the most important logistical considerations. Use it to ensure nothing is overlooked. Do *not* attempt to keep this information in your head.

❑ Visit the training site in advance to inspect.

Confirm the Physical Arrangements

❑ Match the physical arrangement of the facility to the training program you're delivering.

❑ Identify optimal room setup in advance and make arrangements to ensure that the room is properly configured.

❑ Identify special needs among learners and provide reasonable accommodation if necessary.

Control the Physical Environment and Minimize Distractions

❑ Anticipate and plan for environmental distractions and problems (bad weather or construction).

❑ Create a plan to minimize or prevent such distractions.

❑ Ensure that the training facility closely resembles the learners' work environment.

❑ Make a checklist of equipment and supplies needed during delivery.

❑ Create a backup plan to handle broken equipment or lost supplies.

❑ Organize material, equipment, and supplies so they are easy to locate and inventory.

❑ Determine how to control the physical environment prior to training (temperature, lights, sound).

❑ Scan the room before training to identify and remove potential safety hazards.

CHAPTER 4

ESTABLISHING AND MAINTAINING CREDIBILITY

SKILLS ASSESSMENT

Take a moment to review the competency and associated performances that will be covered in this chapter. Consider your current level of proficiency in the competency as a whole as well as each performance and check the items where you feel you need to improve. As you read the chapter, concentrate on those areas most in need of development.

Competency:

❏ Establish and maintain credibility.

Associated Performances:

❏ Demonstrate acceptable personal conduct.

❏ Demonstrate acceptable social practices.

❏ Demonstrate content expertise.

❏ Provide a model for professional and interpersonal behavior.

❏ Demonstrate flexibility in response to learner needs and interests.

❏ Judge the degree to which credibility is an issue or distraction at any time during training.

Establishing and maintaining credibility is the third training delivery competency found in the IBSTPI Standards. It is also the first that is typically exhibited *during* training delivery. This competency is the focus of this chapter.

79

Establishing and maintaining credibility has to do with the trainer's ability to leverage personal conduct, social practices, professionalism, and content expertise to command attention and respect from learners and other stakeholders (such as the learners' immediate supervisors). When you possess credibility, you build learner interest. When you lack credibility, learners may experience unmet expectations, disillusionment, and an unwillingness to apply what they learned.

To appreciate just how important credibility can be to success in training, consider the following situation in which the trainer loses credibility through misconduct:

> Imagine that you are attending a computer software training class. You arrive early and are waiting for the class to begin. The starting time passes. Five minutes go by, then ten. Still no trainer. Finally, fifteen minutes after the scheduled start time, the trainer rushes in with hair and clothing in shambles. He proceeds to explain in great detail how bad his morning has been and how he just did not have the time to learn the particular software program that was the topic of that day's session. Finally, realizing that things are getting tense, the trainer proceeds to tell an ethnic joke in an attempt to lighten the mood....

While this example may be extreme, it demonstrates how you may gain or lose credibility through your behavior. Now, read the critical incident below that describes a situation in which a trainer gained credibility through her conduct.

How Do I Gain Credibility?

" My most typical problem is establishing credibility. I'm 27 and generally speak to audiences who are 40 to 50 years old; upper-level management types. I know my material and field questions well so I generally am able to gain credibility soon after the presentation begins. "

Credibility, a somewhat elusive term, is the ability to inspire belief and trust, an image of believability and reliability, and an intuitive sense of confidence. From this definition, it is easy to see how the trainer in the opening scenario destroyed his credibility with the learners and also how the trainer in the critical incident established credibility. One purpose of this chapter is to explain further what credibility means and how you can establish and maintain it when you deliver training. Your credibility is extremely important because it reinforces the importance of the training to the learners.

The respondents in our survey rated the importance of the fourteen delivery competencies. Establishing and maintaining credibility was rated as the third most important instructor or training delivery competency. If you do not possess credibility, learners will not take the training seriously. But you can take action to establish, maintain, and build credibility with learners. That is accomplished by what you say and what you do.

This chapter covers the steps you need to take to build credibility, including:

- Demonstrating appropriate personal conduct, including visual appearance and personality characteristics.

- Applying good social practices and avoiding unacceptable behavior and inappropriate humor.

- Maintaining subject matter expertise.

- Demonstrating flexibility and making necessary adjustments.

Taken together, these dimensions lead to trainer credibility, as shown graphically in Exhibit 4–1. This chapter covers each category (personal conduct, social practices, content expertise) and also addresses how to restore credibility when it is lost or damaged.

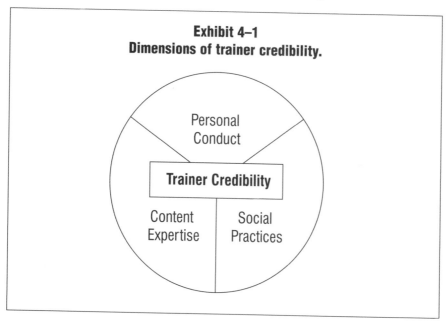

Exhibit 4–1
Dimensions of trainer credibility.

DEMONSTRATING ACCEPTABLE PERSONAL CONDUCT

To help you understand the importance of personal conduct, reflect on the following critical incident provided by one trainer in our survey. This trainer was working with a subject matter expert (SME) who did not exhibit acceptable personal conduct. Note the impact on the learners as you read:

SME Runs Wild!

" This happened when I was a very new trainer working for a department store chain. I was facilitating a trainee seminar for newly hired assistant buyer trainees. The seminar topic was "Reading and Interpreting Selling Reports." I had a buyer working with me as a subject matter expert. I had not worked with her at all prior to this seminar. I only used her as a subject matter expert on a recommendation from someone else in my department. The problem was that when she started explaining how an assistant buyer needs to work with department managers in the stores to go over selling, she kept saying things like, "All our managers are idiots and you have to treat them that way." "They are too stupid to get the job done by themselves so you have to call them and berate them all the time." "It is best to threaten to cut their stock levels to get them to do what you want." This is just a sample of some of the things she said.

I did nothing about it. I was new to my position and this person was senior to me. I was shocked and appalled about the things she was saying, but I did not know what to do about it. So I just let this go on. If this situation were to occur now, I would call a 15-minute break to stop it. During the break, I would explain to the buyer that it is inappropriate to speak of the department managers in this manner and ask her to stick to the reading and interpreting of the report.

The result here was that I had a pretty shocked group of trainees. Their perspective of how to get along with managers in the stores was tainted. Some of them actually took the advice to heart and started using it! I don't think there were any lasting long-term effects from this, but there was increased tension and anxiety among trainees about the job and about what to expect from their buyers. Needless to say, this buyer was dropped from our list of SMEs. "

Personal conduct involves your actions and your appearance. It creates the image you project to a group of learners and influences how they perceive you. The learners' image of you is affected by your personal appearance as well as your personality. Your goal should be to project an image of professionalism that will establish and maintain your credibility with the learners. In essence, you should serve as a role model for learners to show them the right way to conduct themselves and the right way to present an image of polished professionalism. Learners may model their own conduct after yours. If you interrupt others while they are talking, learners may regard this as acceptable behavior. In contrast, you also model by the behaviors you do not exhibit. If you do not create an environment where learners feel free to share their opinions and ideas, then learners will probably not share their thoughts and suggestions.

VISUAL APPEARANCE

Your visual appearance includes the physical characteristics seen by others. The clothes you wear, your grooming, and your posture contribute to your visual appearance.

CLOTHING

Match your clothing to that of the learners; otherwise your clothing may create an invisible barrier between you and the learners. For example, if you are an electrical engineer training a group of plant maintenance workers on programmable logic controllers, a three-piece suit would not be appropriate if the learners are wearing company uniforms. If you wore a suit to this training, the participants might be distracted, intimidated, or put off. It might even create negative perceptions that would interfere with learning. These learners might get the impression that you are unable to relate to a manufacturing environment. In this situation, you would be better off to dress in casual or business casual attire—preferably without a tie.

GROOMING

Grooming is as important as clothing in projecting a professional image. If you are not groomed properly, it can be distracting to learners. Grooming includes hair length and style, cleanliness, and other aspects of personal hygiene. While we do not advocate specific grooming practices, a safe rule of thumb is to match your attire and grooming to the situation, the organization's norms, and the learners' characteristics. When in doubt, ask someone—or else err by being conservative rather than opting for the latest hairstyle and hottest fashion statement.

POSTURE AND MOVEMENT

Posture refers to how you sit or stand. *Movement* refers to how you move. A slouched posture may give learners the impression that you lack confidence. An overly stiff posture, on the other hand, can encourage the perception that you are distant, awkward, or arrogant. Acceptable posture is generally relaxed and comfortable—but not overly so.

Movement is also important. If you carry yourself with smooth movements, you exude confidence. Inappropriate movement such as hair twisting, finger wagging, or the jingling of loose change in pants pockets can shift the learners' attention from the training to the distracting behavior. One of the authors recalls attending a training session where the presenter used his middle finger to push his glasses up on his nose about every ten minutes or so. At first, this gesture was shocking, then it became humorous, and finally hilarious to the learners. It was so distracting that it even became the topic of breaks and lunches. The trainer, however, never knew!

PERSONALITY CHARACTERISTICS

Some personality characteristics are absolutely essential to building and preserving credibility. Examples include your willingness to admit mistakes, accept responsibility, and remain open to feedback.

ADMITTING MISTAKES OR LACK OF KNOWLEDGE

You cannot know everything, and you cannot expect to avoid making mistakes. How you handle such situations, however, can have a direct impact on your credibility. Consider the critical incident (on page 85) provided by one trainer in our survey.

When you refuse to admit that you do not know the answer to a question or that you have made a mistake, the learners can usually detect that. Beware also of placing blame on others, which will only diminish your credibility with learners.

There are several good ways to deal with mistakes and with situations in which you do not know the answers to questions. First, admit mistakes or your own lack of knowledge and apologize if necessary. Second, accept responsibility for correcting the mistake or getting the right answer. Third, if you do not know the answer to a question, check to see if others do by redirecting the question to other participants to see if anyone knows the answer. Another way to deal with lack of knowledge is, like the trainer in the critical incident, to inform the learners that you do not know the answer but will track it down and

Delivering Training after an "All Nighter"

"I was into the second round of interviewing for my current position and I had to give a fifteen-minute training session on OSHA 19190.120 (HazCom). I had worked the night before at the same company from 6 p.m. to 6 a.m. and my presentation was at 8 a.m. I was so tired I was in a coma. The room was filled with ten people, all of whom were in the training department. The department manager was there and also her boss. I was well prepared, I knew the subject well, and I had been involved with teaching it for over five years. I was the only candidate who had color overheads. Despite my tiredness, I gave an excellent presentation. One of the members in the audience asked a simple question which I knew the answer to, but could not communicate the answer. What I told him was that I would take his name and number and get back to him within the day with the right answer. That was all they needed to hear. They hired me."

report back. If all learners, and not just one, need to know the answer to a question, find a way to follow up with everyone through mail, fax, e-mail, follow-up meetings, or other approaches. Look at the following dialogue to see how a trainer effectively handled a question she did not have answers to. Observe how she initially attempted to get the answer from the other participants but in the end, she promised to find the answer and get back to the learners. Although she did not know the answer, she did not damage her credibility. In fact, she may have gained credibility by proactively getting the answer for the other participants as well. Also notice how she asked the learner with the question if her solution was acceptable in an attempt to gain his buy-in.

TRAINER: *"Before we move on, what are your questions?"*

SIMEON: *"How will this new policy change the way we manage our departmental budgets?"*

TRAINER: *"That's a good question. I suspect that each department will handle this new policy differently, but I'm not completely sure about that. Can anyone here answer Simeon's question?"*

SEAN: *"My department is going to treat it the same as the old policy, therefore, nothing will change regarding the way we manage our budgets."*

TRAINER: *"That sounds like an effective approach. I'll check with the other departments to see if they are using the same strategy and let you know before the end of the class. Simeon, is that acceptable to you?"*

SIMEON: *"That sounds good. Thanks!"*

KEEPING PROMISES

During training delivery, learners sometimes make requests that you cannot immediately meet. For example, learners may request a copy of a transparency they found to be particularly interesting. Or you may promise to find the answer to a question and relay it to the learners. Or, learners may require information or knowledge that you are unable to supply. In each situation, you must follow through. Keep all explicit or implicit promises you make, and do not forget. Imagine if the trainer in the previous dialogue did not provide her learners with an answer to their question. The learners may have felt that she was absentminded and forgot, that she didn't care enough to follow through, or even that she was unable to get the answer. In any case, not getting the answer to them, as promised, would have damaged her relationship to them and could have caused her to lose credibility.

The importance of keeping promises is illustrated in the following critical incident from our survey:

Don't Shoot the Messenger

" This experience concerns the change in a site policy for safety. It was written by a contract individual and had no input from the people it would affect. When it was presented, the groups went ballistic. I stated that I was the messenger, but would record their concerns and forward them to safety management. The first response from the group was that it would be a waste of time, due to the fact the change had been already made. I stated that I would get back to them with some answers to their concerns. To the group's surprise, the policy was amended and the group stated that this was a first in trying to get the problem/concerns heard and having answers given back to them. "

SEEKING LEARNER FEEDBACK

Another way to enhance your credibility with learners is to show your willingness to receive feedback about yourself. When you actively seek input from the learners about your delivery skills as well as about the content of the training program, you show learners that you want to improve and perform to the best of your ability. Seek such feedback by asking questions of the learners as a group or by talking offline to individual learners during lunch or break time.

Always be sincere when you make such requests for feedback so that you convey a sense of concern and a willingness to improve yourself.

PERSONAL CONDUCT

Your personal appearance and behavior can strongly influence your credibility with a group of learners. It is vital for you to have an ongoing awareness of your personal conduct, because this awareness can lead you to correct inappropriate actions or words. Codes of conduct, like the American Society for Training and Development's National Code of Ethics (ASTD Code), can provide you with general standards for personal and professional conduct. The eleven key elements of the ASTD Code are presented in Exhibit 4–2. A code of conduct or a code of ethics serves as a compass to help you stay on course and provides an objective basis by which to judge your own actions and behaviors.

DEMONSTRATING ACCEPTABLE SOCIAL PRACTICES

While the previous section discussed the importance of personal conduct, this section describes appropriate social practices about how you should interact with others. When you demonstrate acceptable social practices, you foster an environment characterized by trust and mutual respect. On the other hand, if learners question your integrity, honesty, or character, they will be less likely to believe in the training and thus will make less effort to learn and apply it.

UNACCEPTABLE MANNERS AND BEHAVIOR

If you demonstrate such unacceptable manners and behaviors as rudeness or arrogance, you will note that it has a very negative impact on learners. Consider a trainer who interrupts a learner who is talking or a trainer who is obnoxiously loud and overbearing when interacting with others. Respect for, as well as trust in, the trainer can be greatly diminished.

Exhibit 4–2
The ASTD code of ethics.

Members of ASTD will strive to:

■ Recognize the rights and dignities of each individual.

■ Develop human potential.

■ Provide employers, clients, and learners with the highest level of quality education, training, and development.

■ Comply with all copyright laws and the laws and regulations governing the profession.

■ Keep informed of pertinent knowledge and competence in the human resource field.

■ Maintain confidentiality and integrity in the practice of the profession.

■ Support peers and avoid conduct that impedes their practicing of the profession.

■ Conduct oneself in an ethical and honest manner.

■ Improve the public understanding of human resource development and management.

■ Fairly and accurately represent human resource development or human resource management credentials, qualifications, experience, and ability.

■ Contribute to the continuing growth of the society and its members.

Source: Reprinted from *Info-line, Ethics for Training and Development*, Issue 9515. Copyright 1995 by the American Society for Training & Development. Reprinted with permission. All rights reserved.

Although those examples might be extreme, subtle behaviors are more insidious and can cause as much damage. You may even be unaware of the behaviors you demonstrate. For instance, a trainer who pays less attention to new employees while giving more attention to veteran employees discourages the newcomers. The trainer may not even realize that he or she is doing that. However, learners will find it offensive and some may even regard it as favoritism. The same problem may exist if the trainer finds one participant interested and eager to participate and continually directs eye contact and questions to that person. If you become aware of such problems as a trainer, make every attempt to avoid them.

There are several actions you can take to surface your own undesirable behaviors as an instructor. One is to record your delivery on video. You (and others) can then watch the tape to look for subtle or overt behaviors that are unacceptable. If you find that videotaping is not practical because it reduces learner participation or otherwise interferes with learning, then ask a colleague to attend the program and give you feedback. You can also request feedback from past or present learners.

INAPPROPRIATE HUMOR

Humor can be used to gain learner attention, reinforce key concepts or points, and enliven the learning environment. But be careful in using it. Inappropriate humor can be damaging to your credibility as a trainer. Avoid telling off-color jokes and stories or jokes that possess a racial, ethnic, or sexual content. Realize that using humor is akin to walking a tightrope, and that you can fall off the tightrope even when you use humor that is offensive to only one person. Your overall credibility can still suffer.

There are several ways that you can avoid inappropriate humor. One way is to resist using humor at all. (That is sometimes recommended for speakers in professional or academic conferences.) However, we do not recommend that approach because humor can be highly effective if properly used. Another way is to request the opinion of colleagues or representatives of the intended audience regarding a joke you want to tell or a story you plan to share. Make an effort to view the humor from the learners' perspective and consider whether anyone might find it to be offensive. If you have any doubts, do not tell the story or joke.

There are also ways that are not so effective in avoiding inappropriate humor. One ineffective way is to qualify the joke by saying something like, "I hope no one will find this offensive, but did you hear the one about..." By making such a statement, you are not minimizing its offensiveness. On the contrary, you are drawing attention to just how objectionable it could be. It may also be ineffective to use the amount of laughter as a gauge. Many people may laugh at a joke, even though everyone may find it highly objectionable or offensive. Worse yet, some people may sit glumly as others laugh, thereby intensifying their deep and quiet anger. Misused humor may have legal implications as well. Offensive or degrading humor—particularly when directed at protected groups (such as women, minorities, or persons with disabilities)—may provide evidence of discrimination or harassment according to Equal Employment Opportunity guidelines.

Perhaps a better approach is to stick to humor that arises directly from the training situation itself. If you can demonstrate wit when confronted with a potentially humorous situation during delivery, you can build rapport with learners and create a relaxed, comfortable training environment. For instance, if loud music suddenly erupts from the room next door, you might make a dry remark such as "it sure sounds like they are doing good business in the disco next door." As another example, imagine a trainer who makes a spelling error when writing on a flipchart. When the error is pointed out, instead of making an excuse, the trainer may poke fun at herself and say, "Someone should invent a spell-checker for flipcharts!" Such comments can generate excitement and enthusiasm among learners while not offending anyone. (In fact, humor directed at yourself is usually offensive to nobody but you!) But when such spontaneous humor is misused, it can have a detrimental effect on learning. Imagine that in the same example the trainer tells the learner in a joking, but also terse and threatening, manner to make the spelling correction. That response may make learners feel uncomfortable, embarrassed, and intimidated, and it can cast a pall over the group that lasts for the duration of the training program.

BUILDING TRUST THROUGH INTEGRITY, DISCRETION, AND RESPECT

Integrity is a match between what a person says and does. It can be an elusive concept, but it is a manifestation of your actions and interactions. One way you can demonstrate integrity is by handling sensitive issues discreetly. For example, if you are providing learners with feedback about test results, do it privately to avoid embarrassing people who did not perform well. Discretion is appreciated by learners, and it builds trust and confidence in your personal integrity. Another facet of integrity is the degree of openness and honesty you demonstrate to learners. For example, when you dismiss some questions as confidential, learners may perceive that you have a hidden agenda or are only "following the party line." Show respect for all learners attending a training program. Demonstrate respect by listening to learners, being open to dissenting opinions, and treating everyone with respect and dignity. Doing this helps to create an atmosphere of mutual respect and trust, and that, in turn, bolsters your credibility and contributes to successful training experiences. Read the following description of a training professional who gained the reputation for having integrity.

> Ryann was a successful training professional in her organization. She had a great reputation for being honest, kind, and someone you could go to with a problem. When asked what it was about her that made people trust her so much, she responded with, "I do what I say, and say what I mean." Someone pointed out that her response was just a cliché. Ryann thought about it and explained that to her it was not just a cliché. It was more than that. She explained that when she said she was going to do something, she wrote it down and made sure she did it, no matter what. Further, unless she knew she could do it, she wouldn't say it. Ryann felt strongly that her actions and her words needed to match and this is how she could gain people's trust. It seemed to work very well for her.

PRESENTING TRAINING IN WHICH YOU DO NOT BELIEVE

Sometimes you may be asked to present information or advocate a position that you personally disagree with or that you seriously question. Delivering training that you question—or find objectionable—places you in a tough ethical spot. There is no simple solution to this problem. You may ask that someone else be assigned to do the training. When that is not workable, you may share your views in private with your immediate supervisor but make clear in the training course that you are serving as an official spokesperson for the organization, but that your personal opinions will not be discussed. If even that approach is suspect, then you may ask learners for their opinions or ask for guest speakers who do favor the company policy to address your learners.

DEMONSTRATING CONTENT EXPERTISE

To this point we have discussed acceptable personal conduct and social practices. But in this section we turn to content knowledge—which is sometimes called *subject matter expertise*. In this section we discuss how subject matter expertise plays a role in helping you establish and maintain credibility.

One trainer in our survey provided a critical incident that cited "lack of technical knowledge" as the most common problem he faced. The importance of content knowledge will vary depending on your audience and on the training topic. For example, a trainer leading a discussion with rocket scientists on the topic of "alternative fuels" should possess a high level of content knowledge. But a trainer leading a discussion about customer service may not need to possess content knowledge and could instead rely on facilitation skills to help learners pool their insights.

Content expertise can be demonstrated and communicated to the learners in many ways. Examples (of such ways) include professional and academic credentials, work experience, and subject matter mastery. Other ways include the ability to respond to content-specific questions and accept different opinions.

PROFESSIONAL AND ACADEMIC CREDENTIALS

One way you can communicate your content expertise is to describe your professional and academic credentials as they are related to the topic on which you are conducting training. For example, an accountant who earned the certified public accountant (CPA) designation possesses a well-known credential indicating specialized knowledge. Similar credentials exist in many occupations—ranging from the person who is a certified *master mechanic* to someone who has obtained a Ph.D. in nuclear physics. Such professional credentials demonstrate content expertise in specific areas.

In recent years the training field has also tried to establish professional certification. For example, the Chauncey Group International has developed knowledge and skill assessments leading to professional certification. These are called the Certified Technical Trainer (CTT) and the Certified Professional Development Trainer (CPDT) designations, and they are based on the fourteen IBSTPI instructor competencies that serve as the foundation for this book. Trainers attempting to become certified must pass a multiple-choice test consisting of over one hundred questions and then submit a performance video that shows the trainer demonstrating the competencies in a live training situation.

EXPERIENCE

While professional and academic credentials often indicate mastery of theoretical or conceptual knowledge, work experience indicates on-the-job performance. A trainer's experience in doing work related to a topic is perceived in U.S. culture as more valuable than academic credentials. (That is not true in all cultures around the world, however.) Examine the critical incident below that describes the difficulties experienced by one trainer in our survey who lacked appropriate experience:

The Cost of Inexperience

" I was instructing a group of high school students. There was one participant who did not like me and we did not get along well. I was a rookie trainer and the student was "testing" me because of this. I allowed this student to provoke me and we exchanged words/looks/attitudes in class. The tension was high and, needless to say, I lost control of my class. "

When you can say that you have had experience with the topic, you have more credibility than if you have had no experience. For example, in an executive development program attended by CEOs and other senior executives, the trainer who possesses executive experience will usually have more credibility with the participants than a trainer who does not. People with experience can tell "war stories" from their own lives that can dramatize the points they are making. That is one reason why subject matter experts (SMEs) are sometimes asked to deliver training. Such people have instant credibility based on their experience. Unfortunately, a person possessing subject matter expertise does not always possess *training delivery expertise*, the ability to conduct effective training and facilitate the learning process. For this reason, professional trainers are sometimes paired with SMEs to deliver training. That is an effort to balance subject matter expertise with training delivery expertise. Of course, it is also possible to ask SMEs to attend in-house or externally conducted train-the-trainer courses to help them build their training delivery competencies.

MASTERY OF CONTENT AND HANDLING QUESTIONS

The training topics offered by an organization may range from technical topics, such as basic metallurgy, to nontechnical subjects, such as teamwork. In many instances you may be asked to deliver training on subjects with which you have had little or no experience and in which you have little or no content expertise. That can, of course, lead to difficulty in establishing and maintaining your credibility with a group. One trainer in our survey faced such a situation, and reading about this example can dramatize the difficulties this situation creates for trainers:

Gaining Credibility with Learners

" *The worst experience I had relating to delivery of training involved a class of new employees, many of whom lacked motivation. To make the situation worse, I was required to train very detailed processes, some of which I only marginally understood myself. The challenge was to establish credibility and motivate the negative people in the class. I worked hard after hours to increase my knowledge accessing as many expert resources as possible. I was up-front with the group regarding my lack of expertise. I informed them that I was a generalist and would bring in experts when needed. Motivation for negative people was in the form of lots of individual attention. Most responded to this approach, but some did not.* "

Another critical incident shows what happens when trainers do not familiarize themselves adequately with the training material:

Preparation Is Paramount

" *The worst experience I ever had was going into a classroom unprepared. I hadn't reviewed the material as thoroughly as necessary and it was obvious.* "

If you are asked to present new information—or information with which you are unfamiliar—it is your responsibility to prepare for that. You must do your homework. There are several ways to do that. One way is to rely on a detailed instructor guide, assembled by instructional design experts and those possessing both training delivery competencies and content expertise. A second way is to work closely with SMEs to deepen your understanding of the content. You can also obtain and review reference manuals, technical documents, books, reports, or videos about the subject. A third way, if time permits, is to try to gain at least some limited experience. For example, if you are to deliver supervisory skills training but possess no supervisory experience, you could spend a day or two shadowing some supervisors. A fourth way is to invite SMEs as guest speakers. A fifth way is to invite SMEs to sit in on your training to field tough questions.

GAUGING YOUR CONTENT KNOWLEDGE

How do you measure your content expertise? There are various approaches. Some organizations may require you to become certified as an instructor. To do that, you may have to first attend the course as a participant, then co-teach the course, and finally deliver the training under the watchful eye of a master instructor. This authorization process is shown graphically in Exhibit 4–3.

Another way is to ask someone to watch and judge your ability to field questions about the content. That can be especially challenging when your participants possess more than rudimentary knowledge or when a training session contains both experienced and inexperienced participants. Be sure that, when you answer questions, your answers are accurate and thorough. Remember: your competence with the topic correlates to your confidence in delivering it. You may find that you have to deliver a training course several times before you exude confidence. But also keep in mind that overconfidence is not necessarily good, either.

ACCEPTING DIFFERENCES OF OPINION AND EXPERIENCE

You will always find some learners who will raise objections or will want to argue with you. (That is more often true in the United States than in other countries.) How you react to these situations is key to maintaining credibility. The worst way to react is to humiliate those who pose objections or difficult questions. It is almost as bad to become defensive or to dismiss objections or questions without making much effort to answer them. These behaviors not only damage your credibility but also discourage participation.

The desirable strategy to use when you find yourself under attack is to leverage the situation to strengthen the learning, provoke participant thinking, and make the learning situation more interesting. In fact, you may want to tell participants that they should feel free to express

Exhibit 4–3
Sample trainer authorization or certification process.

Demonstrate Content
Knowledge

Co-Deliver Program

Deliver Program Under
Supervision

Deliver Program Without
Supervision

themselves and voice differing opinions. Another strategy is to invite learners to agree or disagree with a statement you made or with a point made by another participant. You can do that by asking "Who agrees with that point?" or "Does anyone disagree?" By doing that, you show that you welcome differing views and opinions.

Just as learners may express disagreement with your comments, they might also come to training with varying levels of experience. As mentioned in Chapter Two, experience is a valuable resource. When you ask learners to share their experiences, you can enhance training by surfacing many practical problems and situations that underscore the value of the training. To conclude this section look at the following dialogue to see how a trainer manages to identify differing opinions in the classroom. Observe how he not only brings out concerns, but also attempts to involve learners in developing solutions to those concerns.

> **TRAINER:** *Let's see a show of hands of who agrees with this principle (several learners raise their hands). Okay, now let's see a show of hands of who does not agree with this principle (several learners raise their hands). Good. Let's explore this further. Of those that just raised their hands, why is it that you do not agree with this principle? What about it doesn't click with you? What experiences have you had that make you think it isn't effective?*
>
> **CATHERINE:** *I raised my hand because we have tried this principle before and it didn't work then, so why should it work now?*
>
> **TRAINER:** *That's a good concern that you raise. What went wrong the last time, and is there any way to prevent it from happening again?*

MODELING PROFESSIONAL AND INTERPERSONAL BEHAVIOR

How do you model professional and interpersonal behavior to establish and maintain your credibility? To answer that question, this section explores how to model professional and interpersonal behavior by showing respect, acting consistently, and avoiding such behaviors as illegal or unethical conduct.

SHOWING RESPECT

You should, of course, show respect for all learners. When you extend kindness and consideration to all learners, it is usually reciprocated. That creates a climate of mutual trust. Any training event may attract people possessing diverse characteristics. Your training course may include people from different races, sexes, and educational backgrounds, and with different physical appearances and physical capabilities. No matter who attends, however, you must demonstrate respect to everyone.

Of course, the opposite of showing respect is showing disrespect. Disrespect is conveyed through sarcasm, rudeness, neglect, favoritism, dishonesty, or unkindness. Disrespect directed at one learner has a ripple effect, creating negativity among group members, which seriously hampers learning. Put simply, disrespect can quickly and severely damage a trainer's credibility, sometimes irreparably so. Consider the following dialogue as an example of a subtle, and perhaps unintentional, form of disrespect.

TRAINER: *Can someone give me an example of a time that you used the paraphrasing communication technique on the job?*

TANIA: *I used it yesterday when I was working with my supervisor. She asked me to do several things by the end of the day. I wanted to make sure that I understood her so I paraphrased the assignments to her and got her confirmation.*

TRAINER: *What was the result?*

TANIA: *I successfully completed the assignments. I believe it also helped to strengthen our relationship.*

TRAINER: *That's a great example! It demonstrates what you did and how it helped you to be more effective. Thank you, Tania. Can someone else give me another example of how you used paraphrasing?*

CASSIE: *I often use paraphrasing with my subordinates to help me clearly understand their needs. They really seem to appreciate the two-way conversation and sometimes tell me that I'm a good listener.*

TRAINER: *Okay. Anyone else?*

SAM: *I use it to...*

While this may not seem like overt rudeness, Cassie probably feels overlooked. Additionally, the trainer probably does not even recognize what she did and will therefore not attempt to gain back Cassie's trust. That will only intensify the problem. Cassie will probably not participate or respond to other questions posed by the trainer. You need to be aware of, and avoid, creating even the perception of disrespecting any learner.

CONSISTENCY

You must demonstrate consistency not only during training delivery, but also in your words and actions outside of delivery. For example, assume that a trainer is involved in delivering a workshop on Quality Circles (QCs). During delivery the trainer talks about the value of the QC philosophy to the organization and urges employees to apply the tools they have learned to their job positions. Later, during an offline conversation with a participant, the trainer comments that she feels that Quality Circles have been tried before and it is really based on an obsolete philosophy that probably will not work. This trainer has not been consistent because she espouses the value of QCs in class but denounces it outside of class. This behavior sends mixed messages. People who notice such inconsistency are more likely to question the person's sincerity and credibility in training.

ILLEGAL BEHAVIOR

Credibility can be completely destroyed when a trainer knowingly engages in reprehensible activities, such as training people to exhibit illegal or discriminatory behaviors. For example, imagine a trainer involved in delivering a course on interviewing skills. This trainer is part of an organization that prides itself on being nonunion in a predominately unionized industry. The trainer deliberately teaches managers interviewing techniques that will help them identify job applicants who are pro-union so that these people will not be hired. Such behavior could be perceived as discriminatory and, if uncovered, potentially become a legal risk. However, not all illegal or unethical behaviors are as clear-cut. Breaches of confidentiality, copyright violations, abuse of power, and conflicts of interest could all raise ethical concerns. Each, however, could be very subtle and may not always be illegal. Further, you may be under pressure from managers (or others) to engage in questionable behavior. Obvious illegal activities are easy to identify and must be avoided. Just as you are advised to avoid humor that some learners may find offensive, you should clearly avoid illegal, immoral, or unethical behavior. When confronted with such dilemmas, you should consider consulting with peers, human resources professionals, or others who can look at the situation objectively and provide valuable advice.

FAVORITISM AND BIAS

Favoritism means giving preferential treatment to selected learners in a group. For example, if a small group of learners is chosen to be involved in a desirable aspect of training, such as lunch with a senior executive, while others are excluded, a perception of favoritism may arise. The learners left out may resent being overlooked and treated unfairly. Subtle favoritism can be just as insidious as overt acts. For example, providing more positive reinforcement to some people while ignoring others can be viewed as favoritism.

    Bias means making decisions or taking actions based on your own opinion or personal preference. While nobody can be completely objective, you should work to minimize personal bias that will have a negative impact on the learning process. Never pressure learners to accept a viewpoint they do not believe in. Bias leads to a loss of credibility.

DEMONSTRATING FLEXIBILITY

Your ability to be flexible affects your credibility. Be sure to use familiar terminology and make adjustments to your delivery based on learner needs and characteristics.

USING APPROPRIATE TERMINOLOGY

Jargon means terminology that is too technical. While jargon can be helpful to those in a specific industry, organization, or occupation because it makes for efficient communication, uninitiated people find it to be gibberish. The training field is riddled with jargon, especially acronyms. Consider acronyms such as ISD (instructional systems design), HPI (human performance improvement), OD (organization development), and ASTD (American Society for Training and Development). Also consider commonly used terms in the training profession such as flipchart, breakout room, behavior modeling, needs assessment, action learning, or competency. Using these terms and acronyms with people outside of the training profession, as well as some within it, can lead to confusion and frustration. However, to learners familiar with the training profession, such terminology would be useful.

    Some trainers find it difficult to avoid jargon during delivery. One trainer in our study provided the following critical incident that expresses the difficulties that arise due to terminology:

What Are You Saying?

" *I instruct people on computer software. Most of the problems I have are related to terminology differences. I may use one term and someone in the program has a different definition than the one I have in mind.* "

Avoiding jargon can be particularly challenging to subject matter experts involved in training delivery, because the jargon is deeply ingrained in their vocabulary. But several strategies can be effective. One strategy is to place yourself in the learner's position. Would you understand the term that was used? Another strategy is to explain all jargon so that learners become familiar with these special words. You could make the following statement to clarify a point that might represent jargon to some learners: "It is important for you to attempt to measure the ROI of training. ROI is an acronym for return on investment. Return on investment, or ROI, relates to the value or benefit that is received from an investment that is made. For example..." In this case, the acronym ROI is used and its meaning is clearly explained. Providing an example helps to clarify the meaning even further. If you intend to use a large number of unfamiliar terms, phrases, or jargon during delivery, another strategy you can use is to pass out a glossary listing new terms with their definitions for learners to use as a reference.

MAKING ADJUSTMENTS TO MEET LEARNERS' NEEDS

Demonstrating flexibility by showing a willingness to make changes can help you build your credibility because it shows learners that you are willing to make adjustments to meet their needs. One way you can do that is to change the speed or pace of delivery. If learners are completing individual reading assignments in twenty minutes when they are allowed thirty minutes, you can reduce the time required for similar assignments. A second way you can show flexibility is to spend more (or less) time on a subject based on learner needs. If learners are struggling with a difficult topic, you can dedicate more time to it. A third way you can show flexibility is by making adjustments based on learner needs, interests, and goals. For example, if learners prefer small group activities to large group discussions, you can make changes so that the delivery matches their preferences. Remaining sensitive to learner needs and interests shows flexibility. When you are perceived to be flexible, you gain credibility in the eyes of the learners. It conveys that your focus is on meeting their needs, not sticking to your agenda.

Veteran presenter Fran Solomon of Playfair Incorporated in Oakland, California, summarizes the importance of trainer flexibility and even suggests enrolling in an improvisation course as a way for trainers to enhance spontaneity. She offers this advice to new presenters: "Be willing to let go of your outline, speech, or expectations. Listen carefully to an audience's body language, noise level, and response. People should have a chance to move around every twenty minutes."[1]

MAINTAINING OR RESTORING CREDIBILITY

You begin to establish credibility with the first words and behaviors you exhibit during, and even before, delivery. Establishing credibility is not an event. Instead, it is a process that must be sustained throughout a training experience. In other words, credibility must be first established and then maintained during delivery. To build credibility before and during delivery, you should take specific actions—such as matching clothing with the learners, becoming well versed with the training material, and showing respect for learners. Greeting learners at the door or making engaging in informal discussions with learners helps you to connect with them before the program begins.

Unfortunately, there are times when your credibility may be damaged or even lost. When that happens, your effectiveness is diminished. In such cases, take immediate steps to restore credibility. What you should do depends on how you lost credibility. At times, a simple apology can be enough. At other times, you may have to take specific action, and several strategies you can take are discussed below.

MAKING ADJUSTMENTS TO ENHANCE OR REPAIR CREDIBILITY

Certain types of personal conduct can lead to damaged credibility. For example, if your clothing does not match the learners' clothing, then you might simply change clothes (or remove your tie and sports coat). But the most important thing to do is to recognize that a problem exists. Once you know that a problem exists (such as wearing a coat and tie), you can take steps to solve it and thereby begin to restore lost or damaged credibility.

RECOVERING FROM ERRORS

You may also have to rebuild your credibility when you make a mistake during delivery. The worst thing to do is ignore it—or cover it up. A better approach is to admit it, apologize if necessary, and correct the mistake. Unfortunately, you may be embarrassed or fearful that learners will look down on you because you made a mistake. In reality, when you openly and honestly admit a mistake, you will be viewed as more human by the learners. Learners appreciate this honesty. An exemplary trainer might even apologize, fix the mistake, and then crack a joke about himself or herself to lighten the atmosphere. Consider the following statement that a trainer could make to demonstrate his or her regret:

TRAINER: *Listen, Noah, I apologize for coming down on you a little hard during that last discussion. I know you are passionate about workplace safety. I was only trying to point out that there's only so much the company can do because of budget restrictions. Even still, I should not have cut you off like I did. Please accept my apology.*

DEVELOPING CONTENT KNOWLEDGE

You can build your credibility if you show that you know what you are talking about. That can be challenging, of course, if you are not an expert or are not familiar with the subject. But you can review the training material ahead of time, consult with subject matter experts, and try to get some firsthand experience to develop a deeper understanding of the content. However, you may still find yourself unable to answer a question. When that happens, simply admit that you do not know the answer, apologize, and promise to get the answer. By doing that, you will minimize the damage to your credibility. Of course, you should do what you promise and provide an answer to the question as soon as possible.

SUMMARY

This chapter focused on establishing and maintaining trainer credibility. Credibility is influenced, both positively and negatively, by what you say and what you do, including the following:

- Your personal conduct.

- Your good social practices.

- Your content knowledge.

This chapter also described how to minimize damage to your credibility and restore lost credibility.

STRATEGY LIST

Actionable Strategies to Improve Training Effectiveness:

Demonstrate Acceptable Personal Conduct

☐ Project an image of professionalism and serve as a role model. The learners' image of you is affected by your personal appearance as well as your personality.

Visual Appearance

☐ Match your clothing to that of the learners to avoid creating a barrier.

☐ Practice appropriate grooming (hair length and style, cleanliness, personal hygiene).

☐ Demonstrate good posture (relaxed and comfortable, do not slouch).

☐ Carry yourself with smooth movements and exude confidence.

☐ Avoid inappropriate or distracting movement and gestures (hair twisting, finger wagging, fidgeting).

Personality and Character

☐ Admit mistakes or lack of knowledge and apologize if necessary and appropriate.

☐ Avoid placing blame on others.

☐ Accept responsibility for correcting errors or getting the right answer for learners.

☐ Always followup with learners and keep any promises (real or implied) you make.

☐ Seek feedback about yourself from learners.

☐ Be aware of your personal conduct and correct any inappropriate words or deeds.

❏ Become familiar with and follow the ASTD Code of Conduct or other codes of ethics.

Demonstrate Acceptable Social Practices

❏ Demonstrate acceptable social practices to foster an environment of trust and mutual respect.

Acceptable Manners and Behavior

❏ Avoid unacceptable manners and behaviors (rudeness, arrogance, interrupting others).

❏ Provide all learners with equal amounts of attention and avoid favoritism.

❏ Use a video camera or seek feedback from colleagues to identify unacceptable mannerisms and behaviors.

❏ Avoid inappropriate humor (avoid potentially inappropriate jokes or consult colleagues before using).

Build Trust

❏ Handle sensitive issues discreetly.

❏ Demonstrate openness to learners.

❏ Show respect for all learners by listening, being open to dissenting opinions, and treating everyone with respect and dignity.

Demonstrate Content Expertise

❏ Demonstrate subject matter expertise to bolster credibility.

❏ Convey your content expertise by describing your professional and academic credentials and how they relate to the training topic.

❏ Work toward professional certification.

❏ Convey your content expertise by describing your work experience that relates to the training topic.

❏ Familiarize yourself with the training material and content.

❑ Prepare, prepare, prepare for training delivery!

❑ Review the instructor guide and participant guide in advance.

❑ Spend time with subject matter experts.

❑ Review reference material and other documents to learn about the subject.

❑ Gain some actual experience.

❑ Answer questions accurately and thoroughly.

❑ Accept difference of opinion and experience.

❑ Never humiliate or become defensive with those who pose objections or difficult questions.

Model Professional Interpersonal Behavior

❑ Show respect for all learners.

❑ Demonstrate consistency in your words and actions during training and outside of training.

❑ Avoid engaging in illegal, immoral, or unethical behaviors.

❑ Avoid bias and favoritism.

❑ Use appropriate terminology and avoid jargon.

❑ Demonstrate flexibility by showing a willingness to make changes to meet learners' needs.

CHAPTER 5

MANAGING THE LEARNING ENVIRONMENT

Take a moment to review the competency and associated performances that will be covered in this chapter. Consider your current level of proficiency in the competency as a whole as well as each performance and check the items where you feel you need to improve. As you read the chapter, concentrate on those areas most in need of development.

Competency:

❏ Manage the learning environment.

Associated Performances:

❏ Select initial presentation strategies.

❏ Involve learners in establishing an appropriate level of comfort.

❏ Adapt delivery to account for learner characteristics.

❏ Manage time available for the course.

❏ Provide opportunities for learner success.

❏ Manage group interactions and participation.

❏ Resolve learner behavior problems.

❏ Judge whether the learning environment facilitates successful performance.

Managing the learning environment is the fourth training delivery competency found in the IBSTPI Standards. It is also the second competency that is typically exhibited during training delivery. This competency is the focus of this chapter.

Whereas Chapter Three focused on the physical aspects of the learning environment, this chapter deals with the psychosocial conditions. *Psychosocial conditions* are intangible elements— such as group dynamics and group trust level. Other words sometimes used instead of *learning environment* include *learning climate* or *learning atmosphere*. A positive and secure climate facilitates learning. A negative or insecure climate impedes learning. As a trainer, you can affect the learning environment in positive or negative ways by what you say and do.

I Don't Want to Be Here!

"*As our company was going through a significant change a few years ago, going from 130 limited partnerships to one corporation, I was introducing many of our coworkers to legal compliance issues which they had never had to deal with before. One assistant manager in particular was vehemently opposed to the changes and spent the entire seminar alternately staring morosely out the window, upset at not being in his store where he could be "doing something worthwhile," or challenging every point of the policy on any grounds he could, philosophical, legal, or moral.*"

This chapter covers the following topics:

- How to set the tone of a training session and establish a positive learning environment.

- How to maintain interest and foster understanding by involving all participants.

- How to identify a need for adjustments during instruction and adapt your delivery to match learner characteristics.

- Strategies for managing time, since most training programs have finite time boundaries.

- Providing learners with opportunities for success.

- Management of group dynamics and participation, including

methods for resolving dysfunctional behavior problems among participants.

As you will discover, a large number of critical incident experiences were in the area of managing the learning environment. As you might guess, many of these are concentrated in the section on managing learner behavior problems. This large number of critical incidents is consistent with the finding in our study that this competency was found to rank third in terms of difficulty to demonstrate among the fourteen delivery competencies.

SELECTING INITIAL PRESENTATION STRATEGIES

One of the gurus of effective public speaking, Dale Carnegie, states that the key to all persuasive speaking is the ability to grab the attention and interest of the audience from the outset. This statement captures one of the primary purposes of initial presentation strategies, which is to capture learner attention and interest and set the initial tone of delivery.

ATTENTION GETTERS

Your initial presentation strategies can take many forms—depending on the situation, the participants, and your styles and preferences. But you can use six techniques to seize and hold audience attention at the opening of your session. This section focuses on those six techniques:

1. Providing examples.

2. Stimulating curiosity.

3. Using facts and statistics.

4. Posing questions.

5. Conveying benefits.

6. Incorporating props.

PROVIDING EXAMPLES

Providing examples—preferably something drawn from your own experience—is the first technique you can use to capture audience attention. Examples transform a boring topic into an interesting one and make abstract issues seem to be concrete. Further, examples have a way of galvanizing interest and stimulating curiosity.

Consider the following illustration of an attention-getter that relies on an example:

> **TRAINER:** *In this session we're going to be talking about the importance of safety. Before we get into specifics, I'd like to give you an example of what can happen when safety rules are not followed. About a year ago I was working out in the plant. It was the middle of the summer and it was like an oven out there. I decided to take my safety goggles off for a while. Well, I forgot to put them on, and the next thing I know my eyes were burning like fire! I stumbled my way to the emergency eye wash station and was then rushed to the hospital. Today, I cannot see out of my right eye.*

A short example like that emphasizes the topic of the training while also building the trainer's credibility as someone who knows how important the topic is.

When you consider an example or short story that you might incorporate into delivery, consider your own experiences or experiences with which you are familiar. Select an example that relates to the topic you are discussing or dramatizes a particular point you want to make. After you choose an appropriate experience you need to organize it. Keep the following in mind:

1. Introduce the example by stating how it relates to the topic under discussion.

2. Don't get lost in the details—make it brief and to the point.

3. If it is a personal experience, relate how you felt, what you did, or the result (positive or negative) of what happened.

4. When you have finished be sure to tie the example back to the topic under discussion.

5. Clarify any points that may have been confusing to your listeners.

STIMULATING CURIOSITY

Stimulating curiosity—usually by telling a story that arouses interest or builds suspense—is a second technique you can use to capture audience attention. The following story could be told by a trainer at the beginning of a training program on customer awareness and marketing:

> **TRAINER:**   *About ten years ago a company—and you have to name the organization—decided to introduce a new product into the market. This company was a very large and successful organization that had been in business for well over fifty years. A team of engineers, marketing specialists, and others was assembled to develop this product. After months of development and millions of dollars invested, the product was primed and ready for introduction. The big day arrived, the product was unveiled...and it fell flat. Sales were flat, team morale plummeted, the company's image was tarnished, and everyone wondered what went wrong. Can anyone guess the company I'm talking about?*

Most participants will, of course, think that the company is their own. That helps reinforce the importance of the training, making the topic realistic and valuable.

When attempting to stimulate curiosity among learners, one means by which to do this is to keep something hidden from the learners. In the example above, the trainer asked the learners to guess the company being described. Then, additional information was provided to learners to slowly give clues that would help them guess the correct company. This strategy helps to build learner interest and curiosity as they process the information and attempt to uncover the answer to the question, dilemma, or riddle you present to them.

USING FACTS AND STATISTICS

A third technique you can use to kick off a training session is to state an interesting fact or statistic. Facts and statistics capture attention—especially when people are unaware of them, find them shocking, or see the immediate relevance of them. Consider the following facts and statistics that could be used as session openers:

- The population of Asia is over 3 billion people.

- In 1995 U.S. companies invested more than $55 billion in employee training.

■ Just twenty-three trading days after the Dow Jones industrial average reached the 10,000 milestone, it surpassed the 11,000 mark.

Depending on the audience, the facts and statistics shown above can get people to sit up and take notice. Of course, the statistics should be meaningful to the listeners and should be somehow related to the training program. Facts are plentiful. To find them, you need only conduct an Internet search, visit the library, or read the newspaper.

POSING QUESTIONS

Posing questions—and asking for a show of hands—is a fourth technique you can use to open a training session. By doing this, you get people involved immediately and make them physically active. To make the learners even more active, you can ask them to stand instead of raise their hands.

As a simple example, you could ask your learners this question: "Who has been to a movie theater recently? Everyone who has been out to the movies within the last six months please stand up." This question not only gets the learners mentally involved but it gets them physically involved.

You can prepare questions in advance of training by reviewing your notes and instructor material and asking yourself, "What question can I pose at this point that would get the learners' attention or get the learners involved?" As you do this, questions will naturally emerge from the material. In the early stages of a program it is easy to ask learners questions about themselves and their experiences. For example you could ask, "How many people here are in the position of account manager?" or "How many of you have been with the company for less than one year?" Once you've developed your questions, we suggest that you practice asking them in advance, preferably with another person such as a colleague. This will help to ensure that your wording is correct and it is easy to understand what you are asking.

CONVEYING BENEFITS

Another attention-getter is to tell the participants about the benefits they can expect to receive from the training. That is typically done in subtle ways. But it can be effective to describe explicitly how your learners will benefit from the training. For example, you might say something like this: "When you finish this training program, you will be able to drive a forklift." Often the benefits can be derived directly from the learning objectives because the objectives describe what the learner will be able to know, do, or feel differently as a result of the course. To generate a listing of additional benefits beyond the course objectives, ask yourself questions like:

Why is this training important for learners?

What business need or workplace issue does this training address?

What benefits should learners expect from this part of training?

What impact will this training have on the job?

Why should the learners care about this aspect of training?

If learners apply this training, what benefits should result?

Answering these questions helps you to develop a list of the benefits. Once you have this list in hand, scan the program material to identify specific opportunities where these benefits can be inserted. Also, keep the list of benefits in mind so you can convey them spontaneously as you identify opportunities for doing so.

INCORPORATING PROPS

Using props is a sixth and final attention-getting technique to use as a session opener. A *prop* is something people can see, smell, hear, or touch. For example, you could hold up a measurement gauge that will be used later in training for learners to see. You could pass out the company's philosophy card for learners to see as well as touch. Or, you could distribute sample products made by the company to each learner. Each action represents a unique way of using a prop to get attention and stimulate interest during training. More specific strategies for using props during delivery are covered in Chapter Seven.

ICEBREAKERS

Icebreakers are activities used to "break the ice" at the opening of a training program. They are important for the simple reason that participants cannot work with you or with each other effectively in a training session if they remain strangers. Learner interaction is key to successful experience-sharing—that is really a key benefit of *group* instruction—and icebreakers are useful in building effective interaction and *esprit de corps* among participants. Icebreakers come in many shapes and sizes, ranging from short to lengthy and from silly to serious. This section summarizes some ways you can incorporate icebreakers effectively into your training sessions.

GUIDELINES FOR SELECTING ICEBREAKERS

When selecting an icebreaker, you should consider several issues—including group size, type of training activity, time available, and leadership. By considering these issues, you can determine what kind of icebreaker to use in different training situations. Ask yourself some questions to organize your thinking when you contemplate creating or incorporating an icebreaker into your training program. Many times, you may find that you have to create an icebreaker because you will not find one that suits the situation. (Published icebreakers are readily available. See the Annotated Resource Guide for sources.) Reflect on the questions appearing in Exhibit 5–1 when you select or create an icebreaker to open your training program.

How much time to spend on an icebreaker depends somewhat on the type of training, the purpose of the icebreaker, and the time available. The purpose of most icebreakers is to help learners get to know one another and thereby establish an effective learning climate. But do not go overboard: we do not recommend that you use a forty-five-minute icebreaker at the beginning of a two-hour brown-bag lunch training session. However, at the beginning of a two-week executive development program where participants will be working closely in small groups, a longer icebreaker may be more appropriate.

The type of training also affects the choice of icebreaker. For example, at the beginning of a four-hour technical training course on hydraulic fluids, simply ask participants to interview the person sitting next to them and then introduce that person to the group. (You might want to set a time limit on those introductions as well.) But in a team-building workshop, you might want to use a more elaborate icebreaker so that the learners begin to communicate on deeper levels. For example, you could request that learners not only introduce themselves, but also share something about themselves, such as a personal accomplishment or story. That sets the tone for the training as well as encourages effective interaction among learners.

What are some simple examples of icebreakers? One is to ask the participants to stand up and exchange business cards. Another is to ask people to stand and give their names, job titles, and key reasons for attending the course. A third is to hand out a sign-up sheet and announce that you will give a prize to the first person who gets the signatures of everyone in the room. As alternatives, you could work to establish an informal learning climate by using a humorous icebreaker. One example is to ask every person in the room to tell "one thing about yourself that you do not want anyone to know." Another example: "Tell

Exhibit 5-1
Guidelines for selecting icebreakers.

Key Questions to Ask	
What is the purpose of the icebreaker?	This is the most important question. The purpose of the icebreaker is always to "break the ice" among learners. However, it may also help to provide a preview of the training, build enthusiasm, or other sub-purposes.
What is the class size?	Class size will determine how involved learners can become in an icebreaker. Smaller class sizes are conducive to more in-depth icebreakers.
How much space is available? Can learners easily move around the room?	Some icebreakers may require a great deal of space and mobility. If learners' movement is impeded by tables, the shape of the room, or other objects, consider using an icebreaker that focuses on the individual or small groups rather than the full learning group.
Who will be leading the icebreaker? Learners? Instructor?	Some icebreakers require the learners to take the lead while others require the trainer to lead. The purpose of the icebreaker will largely determine the answer to this question.
How much time do you have to spend on the icebreaker?	Time restrictions play an important role in selecting an icebreaker. Large amounts of time will allow a more in-depth icebreaker that may not only introduce learners to one another but also provide insight into the training.
How will time be managed?	Sometimes icebreakers have a tendency to "get away" from trainers. Certain parts may take much longer than expected. For this reason, it is important for trainers to intervene to move things along and stay on schedule when necessary.

us the funniest thing that ever happened to you in your life." A third example: "Tell your small group two true statements and one falsehood about yourself so the others can guess which is the lie."

Avoid *icebreaker overkill*. If you overuse icebreakers, their impact is diminished. For that reason, you do not need to devote large time blocks to them—or use them to open every day of a five-day training course.

COMMUNICATING TRAINER AND LEARNER EXPECTATIONS

The opening of a training session is an ideal time for you to communicate your expectations and explain what you want from the learners. People will expend effort when they believe the results will be useful to them. For this reason, take time to clarify what benefits the learners will gain, how the training meets business needs and workplace issues, and how the training contributes to successful job performance.

Early in the training program, set the expectations about how the program will be conducted. For instance, emphasize that your intention is to create a relaxed learner-centered environment where participants should feel free to ask questions, voice concerns, and actively participate. You may also emphasize that, while you are responsible for doing the training, participants are responsible for their own learning. In fact, you could say that training may not be like the participants' previous educational experiences and that everyone can learn from one another. The following illustrates how a trainer can convey expectations to learners:

TRAINER: *Now what I'd like to do before we really get into the program is convey some things you can expect. I like to boil it down to three key guidelines: 1) stretch, 2) participate, and 3) have fun! Now you're probably thinking this is an exercise class! First, I challenge you to stretch yourself. Absorb and learn as much as you can. You'll be introduced to many new ideas and I encourage you to try them out. Some may be out of your 'comfort zone' but that's all right. You're here to learn and grow in a safe environment. Second, participate. I believe in creating an informal environment that enables you to learn. I don't like to lecture and I don't plan to do it. I believe we can all learn from one another so please, add your comments, share your experiences, and ask any questions that you have. Finally, have fun! This program has been designed to touch on many learning styles. It is also very hands-on. You'll be involved in stimulating group discussions, exciting projects, and even a few learning games. Our main goal here is learning and in order to maximize learning, I believe it should be fun and interesting. So, I encourage you to stretch yourself, participate, and have a little fun while you learn!*

LEARNER EXPECTATIONS

The opening of a training course is a time not only to communicate your expectations but also to hear from learners what they expect. Surfacing learner expectations at this point is important for several reasons. First, you can check whether learners have appropriate expectations, given the nature and content of the training course. Second, you can pinpoint individual needs, interests, and concerns. Third, you can find out how important it is to make modifications to the training to accommodate issues of concern to individual learners. An important point to remember is that significant differences in expectations must be clarified, or negotiated, early in the training process.

To illustrate the point, consider a situation we encountered. We were conducting an open-enrollment public seminar entitled "Training Needs Assessment." Early in the session, one participant emphasized that he wanted to learn about "Training Evaluation." The training objectives—which this participant admitted reading before attending the seminar—made no mention of training evaluation. He showed up anyway because the timing was convenient for his schedule, so he hoped that he could change the course objectives at the opening of the training. That was not possible, and other participants supported the trainers in sticking to the announced topic. He was rerouted to another seminar that would help him meet his needs better, even though the timing was not as desirable for him. While this situation did not allow the learner's expectation to be met, you will find that many times you are able to address individual goals, needs, and expectations expressed by learners.

COMMUNICATING ADMINISTRATIVE DETAILS

Administrative details are among the many topics that should be covered at the opening of a training session. Such details include explaining where restrooms are located, when lunches and breaks are scheduled, when the session will adjourn, and where supplies or materials are located. Unless these issues are handled at the outset, they can create distractions. Some trainers may choose to answer these questions on a handout to minimize the time required to cover them. While that can work, it will not be effective unless you also draw attention to the handout and emphasize its key points. Otherwise, some people will not read the information and will interrupt you anyway later to ask simple questions that were clearly answered on the handout.

SEQUENCING AND EFFECTS OF INITIAL PRESENTATION STRATEGY

You lay the groundwork for an effective training session by the supportive learning atmosphere you establish during the opening segment. Some experienced trainers waste no time: they conduct an icebreaker immediately. When that is finished, they cover the purpose of the training program, its objectives, its organization, administrative details, and then describe their expectations and solicit learner expectations. Other trainers prefer a somewhat different sequence: administrative details first, for instance. Sometimes it is better to begin with a brief icebreaker. But no matter what approach and sequence you select, understand that your decision affects the learning environment. Exhibit 5–2 illustrates the effects of the opening section. Use the exhibit to help you organize your thinking about what results you want from an opening.

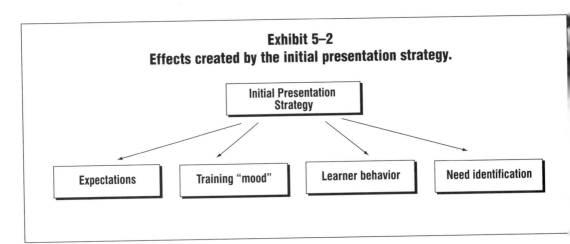

Exhibit 5–2
Effects created by the initial presentation strategy.

Initial Presentation Strategy

Expectations | Training "mood" | Learner behavior | Need identification

ESTABLISHING AN APPROPRIATE LEVEL OF LEARNER COMFORT

At the opening of a training session, some trainers will make a statement like "your participation is important to the success of this program." But that statement is problematic if the trainers do not create a climate that encourages learner participation and involvement. Evidence of learner involvement by their asking questions of you or other learners, learners responding to questions or prompts you provide, or learners actively participating in games, activities, and discussions.

Active learner involvement is important for many reasons. When learners participate, they share their experiences with you and other participants alike. In that way, everyone benefits from hearing different viewpoints and experiences. Further, when participants are collaboratively involved in the process, learning is enhanced because learners feel a sense of openness and ownership. Likewise, participation plays a useful role in giving you, as trainer, some information about how well learners understand what they have been learning. If learners remain passive and uncommunicative, you may have a difficult time determining how well they understand the content. In contrast, when learners are asking questions, answering questions, and even arguing with you or others, they are involved in the learning and provide useful information about how closely they have been paying attention and how well they are learning.

In Chapter Eleven we will discuss other instructional strategies that you can use to involve learners. Those strategies include using small group discussions, interactive games, simulations, questions, and team-based problem solving. Used collectively or individually, they can encourage learner involvement and participation.

Your role is to create, through your words and actions, a climate where learners feel comfortable being actively involved in the training. However, certain individuals, regardless of the participatory environment you create, will not become actively involved. Their reasons may vary. You may, for instance, encounter participants who are shy, who are facing deep personal problems, who resist participating because they do not want to be in the training session, and who (in international settings) have trouble with the language. Do not become obsessed with getting involvement from all learners. However, make every effort to involve people by showing an open, approachable attitude and by reinforcing people positively when they do participate.

LOOKING FOR OPPORTUNITIES

Throughout a training session, you should find countless opportunities to boost the learners' comfort with the learning climate. When learners make mistakes by answering questions incorrectly, display errors when demonstrating a procedure, or make other mistakes, your method of dealing with that situation sends a powerful signal that sets the tone. If you ridicule one person, on the one hand, you will have trouble getting anyone to talk again. On the other hand, if you are good-natured about it and make a comment such as "I was looking for another answer," then you encourage people to participate while not putting them down.

A simple example might dramatize this point. One of the authors had occasion to teach twenty graduate classes in the People's Republic of China. The MBA students there expressed amazement at his approach. They said, "You never tell us we are wrong, like our professors take such great pleasure in doing, but you always encourage us to think instead." You might ask, "How did you do that?" The answer was simple. Whenever someone answered a question incorrectly, the author would say, "That's a good effort at answering, but there are better answers." When someone answered correctly, the author would give him or her a candy bar. As the students said, "It is not the candy but the approval the candy represents that makes it so worthwhile." This example illustrates an important point: always encourage people to participate and, to the extent you can, give them reinforcement for it. If you do, you will encourage them to participate and to be motivated to learn. Reinforcement need not always be tangible; verbal praise and acknowledgment can go a long way.

BALANCING LEARNER COMFORT AND CHALLENGE

Do not draw the conclusion from the previous sections that you should substitute learner comfort for challenge. Change, growth, and development are, after all, the purposes of training. However, minimize the personal risk and consequences resulting from failure or error. Always focus on creating and maintaining an environment where learners feel secure enough to get involved and take risks. Consider the following dialogue during a training class on coaching skills.

> **TRAINER:** *Can someone tell me what the first step is in the coaching process?*
>
> **MORRIE:** *The first step would be to identify possible solutions.*
>
> **TRAINER:** *You're very close because you definitely need to identify possible solutions early on. However, that is not the very first thing you do. Any other thoughts on what the first step is (as the trainer turns to the whole group)?*

Note that the trainer's response to Morrie was positive because the trainer moved the focus from the person to the positive aspects of the response. The learner in this situation would most likely feel encouraged to respond again in the future or even to the trainer's follow-up question. Unacceptable responses, on the other hand, would include such statements as, "If you were listening, you would know that the correct answer is..." or "Someone didn't do their homework, did they?!" While exaggerated, statements like these will damage learner self-esteem and send a message that the trainer is playing a game where only one response is correct.

MATCH COMFORT LEVEL TO TRAINING TASK

As a final point, let us stress that learners' comfort in training should be matched to the challenge the learner will face when applying what he or she has learned. To illustrate this point, assume that airline pilots are receiving training on how to make emergency landings. The real-life performance of such a task is highly stressful and demanding. The training, therefore, should mirror this reality as closely as possible. In that situation, if you established a climate that was too comfortable for the learners, you would not help them master the stress that would be a key issue in performing under the circumstance of an actual emergency landing.

ADAPTING DELIVERY TO MATCH LEARNER CHARACTERISTICS

In Chapter Two we discussed the importance of matching course material to learner characteristics. We also discussed how to make spur-of-the-moment adjustments to improve that match. In this section, we will describe areas where you may need to adapt your delivery methods to bring them into alignment with learner characteristics.

To begin thinking about this topic, reflect on the following critical incident, where the trainer adjusted the material and the delivery to reduce the anxiety level she detected:

Dealing with Math Anxiety

" *The most typical problem I encounter is a quiet anxiety about mathematical problems. Many individuals are deficient in very basic math skills and some are even traumatized to a degree. My own approach involves sizing some basic industrial components used with compressed air, namely air cylinders and valves. The math involves simple multiplication, division, addition and subtraction, substitution of a number for a variable, and the use of a calculator. The approach that I use that works best with these people is to break the problems down into a numbered, step-by-step format. Practicing problems in class with empathy and understanding are the key elements to encouraging a discouraged adult. I always remind people that if you want to learn, no one can stop you...if you are determined. Partial credit is always given (reinforces and encourages), and complete answers are provided so the solution can be studied as well as the problem. Tracking the results is a short-term exercise for me, but I have received feedback that my step-by-step approach works well. On occasion, I have been able to encourage individuals to enroll in classes to further their education. This, I feel, is the real long-term reward to my position.* "

Note that this trainer uses encouragement coupled with step-by-step problem-solving to make the training progress easier for learners.

MAKING CHANGES TO EXAMPLES

You may find it necessary to make changes to examples to match the training content to the learners. As mentioned earlier in this chapter, examples can make otherwise dry content more vivid and memorable. Examples are often used in training to reinforce key points. At times when you provide an example, learners may still not comprehend the point you are trying to make. In such cases, you may have to think of using more, different, or easier examples to help learners understand your point. Of course, you can also ask the learners for examples from their own experience. If one example is particularly useful, document it and report it to instructional designers so that it may be used in the future or included in a course instructor guide. We recommend that you have a collection of examples at your disposal so that if one does not work, you can introduce another.

MAKING CHANGES TO REFLECT CONTENT CHANGES

You may also find that you must make changes to the training when the work itself changes. Assume, for instance, that a training program focuses on the intricacies of operating a 100-ton stamping press. During the program, a participant points out that a new button was recently installed on the machine and that this new button has changed the way the machine works. In this situation, you should document this change and report it to instructional designers so that future courses will include a discussion of the new button. If this actually happens, thank the participant who volunteered this information and build upon that by asking the group if they are aware of any other changes. When you show a willingness to receive feedback from learners, you contribute to an open environment that encourages involvement and ensures that the content reflects work-related changes.

MAKING CHANGES TO TRAINING METHODS

Sometimes you may need to alter an instructional method or exercise to meet the needs of the learners. For instance, assume that a case study was the method planned to be used at a particular point in a training segment. When that point was reached, the learners were engaged in a discussion that everyone considered valuable. In this case you might drop the case study and continue with the discussion.

RATIONALE TO SUPPORT ADJUSTMENTS

Whenever you make or consider alterations during delivery, always do so with sufficient rationale. Your delivery should be adapted to achieve a better match with the learners' characteristics. Adjustments should support objectives and facilitate learning.

MANAGING TIME

The ability to manage time is an important skill for you to possess. Most training programs have limited time available and must be well managed so that all learning objectives are met. If designed properly, training should follow a schedule that is usually provided in the instructor or participant guide. This schedule lists activities and provides estimates of how long they should take. Some schedules are very detailed and show estimated times for every part of the course, while others simply show primary course sections and estimated times. Most time frames are somewhat flexible. A general rule of thumb is to stay within ten minutes of the planned schedule. If you stray too far from the scheduled agenda, you cannot achieve the course objectives and may risk giving learners the impression that they are in a runaway training session. Most schedules, however, are intended to be guidelines only. They are not meant to be so restrictive that they remove your ability to fit the time to match learners' needs.

STARTING TIMES

Do your best to adhere to the scheduled start time. Starting a training session late is one of the most costly mistakes you can make. While some trainers who start late believe they are being courteous to tardy participants, they are actually rewarding lateness and penalizing those who arrived on time. Worse yet, starting a class late can give the impression that you are not prepared.

Late Arrivals

" *People arriving late is a common problem. I advertise, to the extreme, the starting and ending times. I begin as scheduled… those who come in late, stay late, or are the first volunteers for any exercise.* "

Latecomers often disrupt a session by asking questions that were answered while they were absent or by making it difficult to establish and maintain effective interpersonal relationships, which can be so important in group training. If the problem occurs repeatedly, find out why it happens. There may be reasons that interfere with the start of training, such as working parents who need to drop their children at school or managers whose daily staff meetings are scheduled at times that interfere with the start of training.

BREAKS

While flexibility is important, some events should be controlled carefully. Taking breaks is one of those. While the frequency and length of breaks can differ, the point is to stick to the time allotted. Inform the learners when breaks will take place. Avoid extending breaks longer than the announced time, since that will give the impression that you do not value time. Breaks are important because they offer learners the opportunity to regenerate and renew their focus. They also enable offline discussions among learners and with the trainer. As a general rule of thumb, try to give breaks about once every ninety minutes.

RETURNING FROM BREAKS

Most trainers experience difficulty getting people back from breaks. This problem is most pronounced when participants are high-level managers, whose cell phones ring constantly and whose decisions are needed before their employees can take action. The problem can also be acute when the organization is undergoing a major change—such as a downsizing, restructuring, or a merger—when participants may worry about their job security or have pressing issues on their minds while they are attending a training course.

How can you get participants back from break? That is a topic that has often been discussed in books and articles about training. There are many techniques, and some work better with some participants than others. For instance, you might say, "Let's take a seven-minute break...I say seven because I know you'll take ten...so be back in no longer than ten minutes!" Using unusual durations and changing those durations for each break can be more memorable to learners. However, it might confuse some people. Another strategy you could use is to provide incentives, such as candy or a small prize, to those returning on time or provide good-humored "punishment" to those who are late. For example, you could present an obnoxiously "loud" tie to the last person who returns late from break and explain that it must be worn until it can be passed off to the last person returning from the next break. Requiring late learners to sing or whistle a short tune is another strategy you could use. We do not recommend any one technique over another. It depends on the group, the need to have learners arrive on time, your style, and your willingness to risk embarrassing learners.

We have discovered that one particularly effective way to encourage learners to return on time is to emphasize the importance of the training and the established schedule. Another way is to say, "If we go over on breaks, we will have to make up the time by starting earlier, taking it out of the lunch hour, keeping you later, or giving you homework that must be completed with your boss." (While in reality it may be difficult to make good on the latter comment, the statement makes enough of an impression that it has an effect.) These strategies communicate the importance of returning from breaks on time so that training objectives will be reached. It helps to shift some of the responsibility for time management to the group. In contrast, if you do not communicate this, or if you do not adhere to it, learners will probably not take time management seriously.

RESUMING DELIVERY FOLLOWING A BREAK

One effective technique to manage break time is to provide a time limit and stick to it. You should begin immediately at the end of a break, even when people have not returned. By doing that, you send the message that you mean what you say. It also shows respect to those who return from the break on time and emphasizes that training will begin on time, with or without everyone present, which places responsibility on the learners. We should note, however, that if you use this technique, then you become the role model for returning promptly from break!

CULTURE AND PERCEPTION OF TIME

A caveat that must be mentioned in any discussion on managing time is the impact of culture. Different cultures have varying perspectives on the concept of time. For example, Asian cultures tend to place a high emphasis on building relationships before discussing business, sometimes a time-consuming endeavor. Some Western cultures, on the other hand, view idle chitchat as a time waster and prefer to "get down to business." In some societies, early or prompt arrival to training is considered rude and the value is on late arrival. Such cultural differences can create frustration if you have a rigid schedule with tight time frames. For this reason, the cultural norms should be clarified in advance and accommodated when possible.

Organizational culture must be considered as well as national culture. To emphasize that point—and the importance of getting norms clear in advance—consider the following critical incident.

Where Did They Go?

"*The worst experience I had related to the delivery of training was a four-hour session I was giving to a group of maintenance personnel in a large manufacturing facility. The initial session started well with a participative class. After about an hour and fifteen minutes of instruction I asked everyone to take a ten-minute break. Twenty-five minutes later the trainees returned, at which time I politely asked if we could hold our breaks to just ten minutes, this would help us get through the material on time. A minor rebellion ensued. One individual announced he wouldn't be told how long the breaks would last, crossed his arms, and clammed up. The others followed suit. I spent the next hour or so answering my own questions to a tight-lipped group. Then it was time for another break. I waited patiently for everyone to return and then I asked, "OK guys, what did I do wrong?" It was explained to me that the union guaranteed these men so much break time in a four-hour period and that I couldn't limit their time to ten minutes. I also learned with a little questioning that most of these men had worked ten- or twelve-hour shifts already and were required to attend this additional four-hour session. Two of the men were brought in on their day off. Tough crowd, but with good reason. I apologized, told the men honestly how I misunderstood their requirements, and continued with a much more cooperative and successful class. I am always more careful to qualify the trainees and their concerns before I begin training sessions.*"*

THE SOCIAL VALUE OF BREAKS

A final word about breaks. One reason breaks get out of hand is that they provide an opportunity for socializing. Breaks give learners a chance to discuss the training off-line, ask you individual questions, get reacquainted with colleagues, and establish new relationships. While it is important for you to control time, you should also realize the value of breaks and even encourage socializing during breaks. However, be sure to strike a balance between managing time effectively and providing opportunities for relationship building among learners.

THE PACING OF DELIVERY

Instructor guides typically provide time estimates for each instructional segment. But remember: it is important to alter activities at least every fifteen or twenty minutes to sustain learner interest. The *pacing of delivery*—which refers to the speed at which information is presented and the activities in which participants engage—depends on learner needs as much as on established time frames. Resist cutting activities short or skipping sections simply to stay on schedule. Effective pacing depends more on the learners and the course objectives, and less on time estimates published in instructor guides.

ADJUSTING THE PACE

Use several ways to adjust pacing to meet time constraints and learners' needs. First, alter the depth of coverage, thereby adding or reducing the time necessary. Certain sections can be skimmed to reduce the time while still allowing adequate coverage. If you skim sections, or skip them completely, be aware of what impact this may have on learners— and their ability to deal with later sections of the same course. Do not skim or skip course sections if that will mean learners lose track of how the topics are related or if they will be unable to achieve the required course objectives.

TIME MANAGEMENT STRATEGIES

Always remain aware of the current time and how it relates to the schedule. It is easy for you to lose track of time if you are immersed in delivering the training. A simple way to solve this problem is to position a clock or watch in a visible place near you, such as on the overhead projector or on the back wall. When a clock or watch is easy to see, you are reminded of the need to stay on schedule and are more likely to do so. One caveat: Avoid checking the time obviously and frequently. If you do that, the participants might think you are more interested in the time than in them. Further, it may focus their attention on breaks, lunch, or other schedule-related issues, distracting them from the training. For this reason, check time inconspicuously so as to avoid making it the centerpiece of attention. Removing your wristwatch and placing it in a nearby location can help you avoid the temptation to look at it frequently.

STATING THE AGENDA

If you state the agenda at the opening of training, a technique described earlier, it communicates the time frames and activities to be completed. By providing this "road map" early on and then periodically revisiting it, you help learners see where they were, where they are, and where they will be going. It also helps to show learners when adjustments to schedule may be needed.

CONTINGENCY PLANNING

Contingency planning is the process of establishing and, as necessary, implementing backup plans when adjustments are required. One example of contingency planning is reviewing training content before delivery to predict where activities may need to be expanded, reduced, added, or eliminated based on time constraints. Once you know where training could get off schedule, you can determine what backup strategy you should use if your prediction comes true. For example, you may project that a discussion about a sensitive subject will spark a heated debate. To deal with that possibility, you might reduce the time spent on other, less controversial, activities so that the discussion can be extended if necessary.

TIME BUFFERS

A *time buffer* is scheduled time, built into an agenda, to permit a range for the treatment of a topic. Buffers are sometimes built in during the instructional design phase. For instance, sixty minutes might be allowed for an activity estimated to actually require fifty minutes. The extra ten minutes is a buffer you can use, if needed, without adversely affecting course timing. This strategy helps you manage time by building in more flexibility.

PROVIDING OPPORTUNITIES FOR LEARNER SUCCESS

Throughout a training program you should create opportunities for learners to be successful. Learner success is important for several reasons. First, it permits participants to gauge their own progress and development. Additionally, it enhances learner motivation to exert more effort toward task accomplishment or it rewards them for successful task completion. Further, learners must feel a sense of accomplishment, completion, and closure before they move on to another topic. When learners are successful they become more self-confident and are more likely to apply what they learned back on their jobs. In contrast, if learners are not provided with opportunities for success, they may lack self-confidence, which will decrease the likelihood that they will apply those skills in the future.

ENCOURAGE GROWTH

You should encourage learners to stretch and grow by presenting increasingly challenging problems and providing learners with sufficient opportunities for success. This relates strongly to the environment that you create. In a safe environment learners are typically more willing to take risks that lead to success because they do not fear negative consequences. As was mentioned in the section on involving learners in establishing an appropriate level of comfort, the personal risk to learners should be minimized while growth and development are maximized.

METHODS TO EVALUATE LEARNER SUCCESS

There are many ways you can provide opportunities for learner success. You can build assessment and evaluation methods into training. You can use tests and quizzes that assess learning to create opportunities for participants to demonstrate their knowledge and skills to themselves and to you. You can also use practice exercises with feedback to help learners confirm their own skills and abilities. Tests, quizzes, and skill practices are somewhat formal and sometimes anxiety-producing methods of providing opportunities for learner success. A more informal but highly effective way is through what you say and how you act with the learners. You can acknowledge and praise participants who answer questions correctly, who show that they are making an effort, or who complete a learning task. Each is an opportunity for learners to be successful. When they are successful, you can recognize and reward this success through simple oral acknowledgement. Discretion and caution, however, should be used to avoid embarrassing people with too much—or with insincere—feedback.

MANAGING GROUP INTERACTIONS AND PARTICIPATION

Group activities include small group discussions and small group problem-solving exercises. You will probably find yourself using many small group activities, and you must be able to manage group interactions and individual participation successfully to be competent as a trainer. One common mistake is to start the learners in a group activity and then abandon them while you look over your notes or take your own short break. However, when learners work in groups your job is not over. Sometimes your role may grow more difficult—especially if you are dealing with multiple groups, personality conflicts, or complex assignments with detailed directions. When responsibility and control are shifted to the learners during a group activity, you must carefully monitor the groups to ensure that people understand the directions, stay on task, avoid problems, and meet expectations. In this section we discuss stages of group development, the importance of remaining aware of group dynamics, and the strategies for managing interaction and participation successfully.

STAGES OF GROUP DEVELOPMENT

Teams and groups typically progress through predictable stages that include forming, storming, norming, performing, and adjourning.[1] During the *forming* stage learners experience confusion about what to do, how to interact, and why the task before them is important. During *storming*, as the name implies, learners face conflict as they clarify issues, overcome indecisiveness, deal with power struggles, and cope with impatience. *Norming* is typified by clear tasks and purposes, spoken and unspoken rules about interactions, and relief. In the *performing* stage the learners achieve maximum productivity and performance. Finally, in the *adjourning* stage the group prepares to disband.

HELPING GROUPS MOVE THROUGH THE STAGES

Your awareness of the stages of team development can help you and the learners working in groups identify where they are positioned in the development cycle and can suggest strategies for you to use to help a group move from the early stages to the ideal (performing) stage. For example, during the forming stage, be directive as you help the group understand its task and how to interact effectively. During the storming stage, help the group pinpoint dysfunctional behaviors and develop strategies to overcome them. In the norming stage, shake the predictable complacency of a group by raising questions and challenging learners to stretch and grow. In the performing stage, offer praise, encouragement, and positive reinforcement to preserve group effectiveness. Finally, during the adjourning stage, lead learners though a debriefing of key learning points and help them plan how they will apply their new knowledge and skills in their jobs.

GROUP DYNAMICS AND GROUP PROCESSES

Group dynamics, as defined in the IBSTPI Standards, means "actions and interactions—positive and negative—that occur when individuals become part of groups." Group dynamics involve behaviors, actions, and interactions that take place simultaneously. Group dynamics include both positive and negative behaviors. *Positive behaviors* help a group become more effective. When each individual's viewpoints and unique contributions are valued and sought out, this is positive behavior. *Negative behaviors* can cause a group to become less effective. One or two people dominating a group is an example of negative behavior. You should identify and isolate positive and negative behaviors so that you can help group members interact effectively—that is, use effective group processes.

TRUST IN GROUPS

Trust is the belief or faith one person has in another person's motives and actions. It involves both how people feel about others and what people think about others. When group members share a foundation of trust, which stems from their interactions, the results include cooperation, mutual respect, and openness, which lead to group success. For this reason it is important for you to encourage functional (positive) interactions and discourage dysfunctional (negative) interactions. Conveying clear expectations, establishing interaction ground rules, and facilitating group processes are among the ways you can help to foster trust in groups. These methods will be discussed below.

FUNCTIONAL GROUP BEHAVIORS

Functional behaviors include showing respect for others, encouraging others, ensuring that everyone is given a chance to participate, expressing enthusiasm, and supporting divergent viewpoints and opinions. The effects of such functional behaviors are obvious. Trust and group cohesiveness lead to enhanced learning. It is important for you to ensure that group dynamics remain functional so group effectiveness is maintained. You can do that by modeling desired behaviors. You can also explicitly identify and explain functional behaviors and their importance, thereby creating the expectation that such behaviors will be demonstrated. For example, you could inform the group that each member brings a unique perspective to the table and therefore should be encouraged to participate.

DYSFUNCTIONAL GROUP BEHAVIORS

Dysfunctional behaviors weaken group effectiveness and are the antithesis of functional behaviors. Examples of dysfunctional behaviors include dominating discussions, showing disrespect, intimidating other people, dismissing certain viewpoints or opinions, and making negative comments. Defensiveness is the product of dysfunctional behaviors, and it impedes the learning process. Additionally, dysfunctional behaviors will reduce learner involvement and participation because they produce low levels of trust and group cohesiveness.

Dysfunctional group behaviors are also exemplified by groupthink and social loafing.[2] *Groupthink* occurs when no individual member is willing to express alternative opinions or viewpoints because he or she does not want to be at odds with the group. Groupthink results in poor, uninformed decisions—and occasionally even catastrophic errors. One of the theories for the space shuttle *Challenger* disaster was that groupthink replaced objective decision making and stifled dissenting views. *Social loafing*, as the name aptly implies, describes the phenomenon when individuals assume less responsibility in a group situation because they do not see that they are held accountable or because they believe other people will do the work.[3]

STRATEGIES FOR EFFECTIVE GROUP WORK

You can use many strategies to manage learner participation and interaction during group-based training. These include introducing group activities effectively, using ground rules, and becoming a facilitator.

INTRODUCING THE GROUP ACTIVITY

When introducing a group activity, be sure to provide a thorough description of the directions. Avoid the confusion that stems from unclear goals and expectations. Take ample time to introduce the activity and its purpose, state your expectations, communicate any time constraints, and describe what final product the learners should supply upon completion of the activity. By doing this, you will help ensure that the activity runs smoothly.

Avoid making remarks like "If anyone has questions, don't hesitate to ask." Instead, walk around to each group after they have assembled to ensure that everyone knows what to do. Despite giving clear directions in both verbal and written form, you will often find that learners do not know what to do when they begin or during the activity. For that reason, your presence on-the-spot will help to clarify directions and make sure people are on target.

USING GROUND RULES

Ground rules are guidelines for interaction. Ground rules often cover interpersonal behaviors to encourage functional behaviors and discourage dysfunctional behaviors. Be aware, however, that some learners may be insulted if you suggest that ground rules are even needed because they believe such ground rules are "common sense" and "part of the taken-for-granted rules of the corporate culture." One way to avoid the chance that you may offend someone is to ask the learners if they feel a need to adopt ground rules. If people believe that problems are likely to arise, they will welcome your offer to adopt such guidelines. Sample ground rules, suitable for use in a group situation, are presented in Exhibit 5–3. Start with this list, if you wish, and post it on a flipchart or wall. Refer to it when you believe a rule has been violated. Also, you can ask the group for additional rules and add them to the list as appropriate.

Exhibit 5–3
Sample ground rules for groups.

1. We will encourage everyone in the group to participate.

2. One person will not be allowed to dominate the discussion.

3. We will be open-minded to new ideas and opinions.

4. We will manage our time and complete our tasks on time.

5. When someone is speaking, the others will actively listen.

6. Everyone is free to express their views and opinions.

7. If someone uses jargon, explain what it means.

8. No interrupting others when they are speaking.

9. We will strive to reach consensus in our decisions.

BECOMING A FACILITATOR

You can become a facilitator in a bid to manage group interaction and participation. While the term *facilitator* is sometimes used synonymously with instructor or trainer, we believe that a clear distinction exists. *Facilitation* is a process in which you help a group define its goals and objectives, create an open climate, facilitate problem solving, and evaluate results. Instructors or trainers, on the other hand, are much more directive. They view their role as one of disseminating information. By actively assuming the role of a learning facilitator and exhibiting facilitative behaviors, you can better manage interaction and participation and help groups become more effective. Trainers often find themselves switching between the roles of trainer and facilitator during training delivery, especially when group activities or projects are incorporated.

RESOLVING LEARNER BEHAVIOR PROBLEMS

The following critical incidents provided by two different trainers in our survey will introduce this section on learner behavior problems. Each dramatizes special problems that you may face with learners. How would you handle them?

You Call That Customer Service?

" *A supervisor in one of my courses, in front of her subordinates, stated that she has no problem telling the customer to 'kiss my XXX!'* "

The Gossipers

" *The worst experience was when I first started training. I had several managers in my first time management class. They did not buy into the training and started to gossip about someone in the company. I have since developed my skills in dealing with this type of audience.* "

RECOGNIZING TYPICAL BEHAVIOR PROBLEMS

Many humorous, but descriptive, labels can be attached to learners who exhibit dysfunctional behaviors. Examples of such labels include prisoners, class clowns, daydreamers, hermits, vacationers, and social butterflies or talkers. The behaviors associated with each label are probably apparent.

The first step toward solving learner behavior problems is recognizing them. Some behavior problems are easy to spot because they involve visible actions or words. For example, two learners carrying on a side conversation is an easy problem to notice because the behavior will probably be distracting to you. Other behavior problems may be more subtle, such as the person who appears to be listening but is really deep into a daydream. This section discusses typical learner behavior problems and solutions to them.

Dealing with difficult learners is inevitable. Every trainer, sooner or later, will encounter at least one problematic participant who can catch him or her off guard or damage the learning environment. Dealing with behavior problems was a frequently mentioned problem in our survey of trainers. Such problems include people who talk during class, challenge your expertise or authority, or show up late. Be aware of what problems may come up and be ready to solve them.

PREVENTION

Prevention is perhaps the best solution to behavior problems. By taking several preventative measures before training or at the start of a session you can avoid many common behavior problems. One approach is to set the expectations with learners and managers before training begins by describing the course content, expectations about the learners' performance, and the rules of conduct appropriate during class. When you make the expectations explicit, you transfer responsibility from yourself to the shoulders of the learners and their supervisors. As a result, participants should have a better understanding of why they are in training, what they are supposed to learn, and how they should act. Providing managers with this information in advance will also give them the opportunity to assign learners appropriately to training and hold them accountable while they are there.

DECIDING IF AND WHEN TO INTERVENE

Unfortunately, all the preparation in the world will not avoid every behavior problem. Some problems will occur regardless of the preventative measures you take. When this occurs, make a quick diagnosis of the problem, determine the impact and the consequences of the behavior, and implement the appropriate intervention to solve the performance problem. Select the interventions based on the severity of the behavior problem. It is also important to determine whether you even need to intervene. To provide some guidance on this, take measures to eliminate behavior problems when they become distracting to you or others.

STRATEGIES FOR HANDLING TALKERS

Talking in class was one of the most frequently cited learner behavior problems in our survey of training practitioners, as the following critical incident demonstrates.

Feeling Like a Baby Sitter

 " My worst experience was complete disregard for me during a sexual harassment class I was conducting. No one was listening and people were talking. Their supervisor was even in the room. I confiscated notes that were being passed around, got their attention by being louder than normal, lectured them (like kids) why the subject was important and went on with the class. I got a formal apology from the students and their managers about their behavior in class. But I still feel they don't understand the material. "

Participants carrying on discussions during class can be productive. Students will often ask each other for more information or clarification on issues rather than disrupt the whole class by asking you. This is especially true for learners who do not like to call attention to themselves. In the incident above, however, the class was out of control, with detrimental consequences; if the problem had been handled more effectively when it was first noticed, it might not have gotten out of control. When dealing with behavior problems, address them immediately. Here are some tips on how to handle talkers.

- Remain calm and composed. While it can be frustrating and tiresome, take a deep breath and remain level headed.

- Start asking questions. Most learners feel the need to pay closer attention when they know there is the possibility that they may be asked a question.

- Stand close to talkative people. This reminds them that you are present, that you are probably aware of what they are doing, and that you may do something, such as call on them.

- Acknowledge the talkers' presence by referring to an earlier statement or comment made by them. By putting the spotlight on them, you grab attention and will probably stop their discussion.

- Shift into an activity that requires some other training method, such as group work or an individual activity, which will force participants to move and thereby separate the talkers.

- If the behavior persists, give the class a break, take the chatty participants offline, and ask them to refrain from talking during class because they are becoming a distraction to the others.

Reinforce that participation is encouraged but that it would be more helpful to participate with the whole group.

- If all else fails, ask participants to leave the class. Do that in private and not in front of others. While this creates an uncomfortable situation, the welfare of the entire class is at stake and must be protected. If a participant refuses to leave—and some aggressive individuals will sometimes do just that—then call their supervisor directly and explain what is happening right then. If the supervisor will not take action, ask building security to remove the disruptive person and then inform the human resources department and the supervisor's immediate superior in writing of what happened.

Following are three more critical incidents that relate situations where talkers created distractions. The first involves a person who asked so many questions that it became a problem. The second shows the difficulty of competing with learners who are talking. The third relates to learners getting sidetracked. Note the techniques used by the trainers in each case.

Endless Questions

" A rep in the front of the class had many, many, many questions. She was monopolizing my time. It was hindering the rest of the class. In the afternoon I spent less time in the front of the class where she could easily ask me questions. When I was not in front of her, the questions diminished greatly. Keep in mind, these were not ordinary questions. I had to speak with her aside from the group and ask her not to ask questions that did not pertain to the subject we were on. "

Competing with the Talkers

" Large classes are the most difficult. People tend to talk to each other and share experiences. If this continues, I usually will walk in the direction of the distracting people and continue to teach with my voice raised just slightly. If this does not work, I will stop my presentation and explain that I cannot compete with them and kindly ask them to refrain from this until the class breaks. If this continues, I will speak to them in private on a break and ask them to refrain. "

Off the Beaten Path

" *The common problem I have is keeping participants on track. Participants are in a call center environment and any training opportunity gives them time off of the phones. Most phone representatives see this as an open opportunity to chat, talk to their friends, and catch up on topics that are not relevant to the topic being facilitated in the classroom. I usually allow them a few minutes' cushion time prior to class for their chitchat. During class, I post a "parking lot" flipchart on the wall and will "park" any issues or topics that come up that are not relevant to the class. I always make a point to acknowledge their comments and give them value. However, I don't want unnecessary talking or topics to dominate over the training at hand.* "

The topic of the "parking lot," mentioned by the trainer in the third critical incident above, will be discussed in more detail in the following sections.

STRATEGIES FOR HANDLING CHALLENGERS

Challengers are learners who question the value of the material, the trainer, or the learning environment.

The Heckling Supervisors

" *I was delivering supervisor training to over twenty incumbent supervisors. Two of them thought they didn't need the training and commenced heckling and making snide comments causing disruption. The training was mandatory and I told them to leave the class and notified their managers and they called to apologize. I allowed them into the next class and they knew I wouldn't tolerate that behavior.* "

Challengers pose questions such as, "Why are we here?", "Why isn't my boss here if this is so important?", "What does this have to do with my job?", or "How would we do it in the 'real' world?" In short, challengers want to question what you are presenting or what expertise you possess to be doing the training. These questions number among the most difficult you will encounter as a trainer. Although these questions are challenging, they may also be valid. Learners should know why they are there, how the training will help them in their job, and how the skills will transfer to the "real" world (their jobs).

If you set the right tone at the outset of the training experience, you should effectively diminish the chance that challengers can be successful in what they are doing. Be sure to explain your expectations, establish group behavior norms, and then point out behavior that departs from the expectations or the norms. However, if these problems come up during delivery, you should remain calm and patiently answer the questions. Above all, avoid being defensive.

STRATEGIES FOR HANDLING DERAILERS

A *derailer* is similar to a challenger. A derailer wants to change the focus of the training. As the next two critical incidents portray, derailers go off on tangents to discuss obscure issues or raise questions that are not really pertinent to the topic.

Off on a Tangent

" I was conducting a training class at a remote location. It was at the union side of the company, our division is nonunion. These employees were constantly trying to bring the subject back to us being nonunion. I handled it by stating, "I would prefer not to discuss these issues. I accept your viewpoint, however, I have no control over these issues and I really want to help you." Since I am so young, and most of the employees could be my mother, they stopped and let me train. "

Getting Them Off the Soapbox

" I was in a very ethnic city doing eight-hour sales training for one week. I had never met the employees before. They were in the middle of a union dispute and tried to use my classroom as a soapbox. After the second day, I had to tell them very bluntly that I was there for a specific reason and would not put up with what they were doing. It worked. "

The trainers in these critical incidents were successful in dealing with these derailers. The "parking lot" method, which was mentioned earlier, is another way that this could be handled. This technique allows you to place issues that are outside the scope of training or that cannot be dealt with during the time allotted on a list for later discussion. The caution with this approach, however, is that it leaves the door open for future discussion. In reality, it is often necessary to dismiss the subject entirely, especially when the intent was nothing more than to derail the training. What follows is another critical incident related to the problem of derailers. Note the approach that was used by the trainer in this situation. While we do not necessarily endorse this action, it appeared to be effective for this person:

Those Foolish Questions

"*I was conducting a course on employee benefits and performance evaluation to a mixed group of union and salaried employees. Two union employees (out of a total class of thirty-five people) attempted to disrupt the presentation by asking foolish questions. At a point when I could not control these two individuals and when I became exasperated, I told them to pick up the want ad section of the* Chicago Tribune *and look for another job. They looked at each other, picked up the newspaper, and left.*"

While this example is extreme, realize that other participants are also watching how you handle these situations. In some cases, they will actually cheer when a derailer with a special ax to grind is treated in this way.

STRATEGIES FOR HANDLING LATECOMERS

Latecomers are people who consistently show up late for training, take long breaks, and depart early. Attendance expectations should be conveyed during the opening remarks; you should make it clear that if participants are unable to meet the expectations, they should not attend the training at all because they risk missing valuable information or distracting other people. If that strategy does not work and the behavior continues, talk to the individual privately about attendance. If a tardy participant is taken aside, you may discover that there is a legitimate reason for lateness—such as a medical problem or even an unreasonable boss. At this point, you need to make a decision. Either make special accommodations for this session, or ask the learner to reschedule training when the time is better.

STRATEGIES FOR HANDLING EAGER BEAVERS

The *eager beaver*, or *show-off*, is a participant who thinks he or she knows all the answers and wants to demonstrate his or her knowledge to others. (Some trainers call them showboaters.)

Leading the Know-It-All

" *Because I design and develop training to meet regulatory requirements of OSHA, EPA, Department of Energy and Department of Transportation, the biggest challenge I face is from people who are the "know-it-alls." When delivering the training, I weigh the benefits of what they have to offer against the potential bad effect of them giving inaccurate information to the rest of the group. Asking those individuals questions that will lead the rest of the class to the correct (accurate) information works best for me. When they have to respond to questions from the instruction, they are less likely to challenge statements from other participants (for fear of looking foolish).* "

While it can be exciting to have knowledgeable, enthusiastic learners who are willing to share their knowledge, that turns into a problem when it prevents others from participating. If this occurs, acknowledge—and even thank—the eager learner for his or her willingness to share knowledge. But then state that it would be good to hear from others. Make direct eye contact with those who appear overly enthusiastic about answering questions or making comments.

The eager beaver is also someone who dominates the group by asking too many questions. That can be exciting at first, because it helps you keep the interaction lively and upbeat. However, too many questions can get things off track. The key lies in determining if the new track is going to help or hinder learning. If it will help learning then it may be worth pursuing. Otherwise, you should attempt to get the class back on track as soon as possible. Many trainers find the "parking lot" technique effective in dealing with this problem. If a question is asked that is not relevant or runs the risk of getting the class off track, place it on a flipchart or chalk-board to be discussed at a later time. Participants will usually get the "hint" to stick to the issues at hand. Then, if time permits, guide the dis-cussion back to the questions appearing on the "parking lot."

STRATEGIES FOR HANDLING THE UNINVOLVED

The *uninvolved*, sometimes called *hermits*, are those who do not attempt to participate. They do not answer questions, or make com-ments, or share experiences. While it may be easy to label people exhibiting these behaviors as uninvolved, remember that not every-one learns the same way. Some people prefer to learn while remain-ing silent and anonymous. Forcing them into a more interactive role during training may actually hinder their learning. Instead, try to stimulate the hermits by using varied training methods such as group work, presentations, individual activities, or role plays. Encouraging them to participate may also make them feel comfortable enough to do so.

STRATEGIES FOR HANDLING WHINERS

The *whiner* complains about anything and everything. These individu-als often view training programs as opportunities to vent about the lat-est issue or complaint. Whiners can effectively derail a course because they shift the focus away from the topic and get on a soapbox. The fol-lowing critical incident dramatizes this problem.

The Whiners Take Control

" One of my worst experiences was with a group of fifty associates, all hourly and not really interested in topic being presented. It evolved into a gripe-session. Myself and two supervisors were leading the training. It was our third two-hour presentation of the day, starting at 6 P.M. The associates were used to starting work at this hour, but we were exhausted. They took over and it was unproductive. "

Be sure that you can tell the difference between valid concerns and irrelevant complaints. If you determine that the issue needs to be addressed, provide a response. That is a judgment call. But you face the danger of letting the genie out of the bottle. If you can talk about the complaint in an acceptable time frame, address the issue. However, if you have neither the time nor ability to respond, defer the issue to another forum or to a one-on-one conversation with the disgruntled learner during a break or at a future date. The parking lot technique, discussed earlier, may be another way you can put the issue on hold for later discussion or to be addressed by someone who is better able to respond, such as the person's manager, human resources, or someone else in the organization.

STRATEGIES FOR HANDLING OTHER PROBLEM BEHAVIORS

The paragraphs above attempted to highlight some of the more commonly encountered learner behavior problems that you might face. While there is obviously some overlap between the problem behaviors, it can be useful to label the problem so that it can be readily detected. You should keep in mind, however, that behavior problems should be verified as such. Sometimes, an eager participant may be inaccurately labeled as a derailer, and any corrective action you take could diminish his or her enthusiasm. For this reason, verify your perceptions first and avoid jumping to conclusions. Further, handle all behavior problems with care and sensitivity.

The following critical incidents highlight additional problems you may face and suggest ways of solving them. It is difficult to prepare for every possible problem in advance. But it is important for you to prepare as much as possible and, more importantly, act in a flexible and adaptable way.

Immediate Corrective Action

" *I was uncomfortable dealing with a hot-tempered rep who did not receive being corrected well. I had to immediately correct and address his inappropriate behavior in front of the group. He made the other reps uncomfortable.* "

BOB PIKE

We interviewed training guru Bob Pike and asked him, "What are the most common difficulties you face in instructing groups and how do you resolve these?" He responded, "I find that there are really four categories of people that are in most training situations. The 'learners' who are there because they want to learn. The 'networkers' who view the educational event as an opportunity to connect with other people. To them the content is incidental. You also have 'vacationers' who think that any place is better than being back at the job. Finally, you have the 'prisoners' who were either sent there and didn't want to go, or who think they already know it all. The prisoners are the real problems in training situations, especially when there is more than one. If there is more than one in a class, they will often find each other, and sit together in the back of the room.

"What I do is try to prevent problems with prisoners from ever happening. What I do, 98 percent of the time, is use small groups of five to seven people. I generally have the room set up with tables around which the groups sit. This makes the prisoners part of a group right off the bat. In this way they are accountable to the group and not just to the trainer.

"The next thing I do is rotate groups on a fairly frequent basis. This provides opportunities for networking and relationship building. One thing I do early in the program is ask people 'how many of you are sitting with people you know?' Most people typically raise their hands. Rotating through different groups mixes things up and provides opportunities to meet new people. The other thing I do is rotate the groups from back to front. This is another way to get the prisoners, who may have taken a seat in the back, into the training.

"I also incorporate a number of group activities into the training. Anyone can ignore the instructor, but it is difficult for most people to fight the group. Related to this, the other thing I do is change group leaders for each activity. We have identified fifty-seven ways to choose a group leader. One thing we do is have them turn to a certain page in our book and use one of the methods that is shown on that page to choose the leader. This helps to keep interest piqued. Another way to do it is to have the last leader choose the next leader. We have found that groups of five to seven work well because it is difficult for one dominant person to overcome four others. When there are more than seven people in a group the shy or quiet people have a tendency to get lost in the crowd.

"Another strategy I use is to have an activity on the table for participants to work on before the class gets started. This is a good barometer to see how participative people will be in class. Some people will jump in and start the activity right away, while others won't. This gives you an advanced indication of who is participative."

SUMMARY

This chapter focused on managing the learning environment. As the chapter has shown, trainers have an important responsibility to establish and maintain a climate that supports and encourages learning. This chapter covered the following topics:

- Setting the tone of a training session and establishing a positive environment.

- Communicating both your and the learners' expectations.

- Adapting delivery during instruction to match learner characteristics.

- Time management.

- Helping learners find opportunities to be successful.

- Managing problem behaviors demonstrated by participants.

STRATEGY LIST

Actionable Strategies to Improve Training Effectiveness:

Set the tone for training by Grabbing Learners' Attention

❐ Provide learners with examples from your own experience.

❐ Tell short, interesting stories to enhance training. If possible, pilot the stories to a co-worker before going "live" to ensure you are sending the correct message and to make it smooth.

❐ Introduce relevant facts and statistics that will generate interest and enable you to drive a point home.

❐ Ask the learners questions to get them involved and to stimulate their thinking. Plan these questions, as well as several follow-up questions, in advance.

❐ Convey the benefits learners can expect as a result of the training. Adult learners are more willing to learn and participate when they know what's in it for them.

❐ Use props when possible to pique interest and involve more senses (sight, touch).

❒ Use icebreakers to energize learners, lighten the mood, or to help learners get acquainted. Caution: Avoid *icebreaker overkill* by conducting too many icebreakers.

Communication

❒ Convey your expectations regarding the format and style of the class as well as learner conduct.

❒ Ask learners at the beginning of the class what their expectations are. Incorporate those expectations into the program whenever possible and address those that will not be met during training.

❒ Address administrative details at the beginning of class (restrooms, breaks, location of supplies).

Create a Comfortable Learning Environment

❒ Acknowledge all those who attempt to answer question–seven if they are wrong. Use statements like, "That's a good point, but can you further explain...."

❒ Never ask learners to do things with which they are uncomfortable or that will make them look foolish in front of the rest of the group.

❒ Match the comfort level of the training to what they will actually be doing on the job, enabling them to experience a more "real world" training environment.

❒ Provide opportunities and encouragement for learners to stretch their skills and grow.

❒ Demonstrate emotions such as concern, understanding, or empathy when appropriate.

❒ Demonstrate willingness to change the program to suit your audience needs. Caution: Avoid comprising the integrity of the original design so that objectives are not attained.

❒ Add humor to lighten the mood—but only if you have had the opportunity to test out the humor with several co-workers for a "taste" test.

Managing Time

☐ Manage your time so that you can stick to your agenda.

☐ Start on time.

☐ Welcome latecomers into the classroom without allowing them to disturb the rest of the class. Help them catch up over a break.

☐ Schedule breaks about every ninety minutes and stick to the designated duration times. Start class on time, even if some people are missing, to send the message that they should arrive on time.

☐ Adjust the pacing of your delivery to accommodate learning. Be prepared to add or eliminate material based on the needs of the group.

☐ Keep a watch or clock in an inconspicuous place nearby so that you can monitor the time. Caution: avoid constantly looking at your watch.

☐ Add time buffers into the training material to allow maximum flexibility.

Assessing Learners

☐ Create opportunities for learner success to build confidence and future skill application.

☐ Evaluate learner success formally and informally throughout training. Listen, ask questions, and observe to identify whether or not learners understand.

☐ Monitor groups to assess the involvement of each individual in the group.

Working in Learning Groups

☐ Monitor the stages of group development and help learners move through them (forming, storming, norming, performing, adjourning).

☐ Conduct a debrief with groups to reinforce learning and to encourage application of the learning to their jobs.

❏ Plan activities and encourage functional interaction among groups so that they can build trust with one another.

❏ Walk around the room and sit in with each group to monitor performance. Help them overcome dysfunctional behaviors by pointing them out and facilitating their resolution.

❏ Provide ground rules before learners start working together.

Dealing with Difficult Learners

❏ Remember that prevention is the best cure, so explicitly state your expectations for learner conduct at the beginning of the program.

❏ Intervene when behavior problems occur. Match the severity of your intervention with the severity of the behavior.

Talkers

❏ Stand close to them.

❏ Ask them questions.

❏ Acknowledge their chatter by asking them if they have any questions.

❏ Shift to an activity that separates the talkers.

❏ Approach them during break if the behavior continues and ask them to refrain from talking during class because it is distracting to the other learners.

Too Many Questions

❏ End a question and answer session by stating, "Let's take one more question and move on."

❏ Use the Parking Lot technique (ongoing list of questions to be answered at a later time).

Challengers

❏ Set expectations up front regarding learner conduct to prevent potential problems.

☐ Clarify and respond to learner challenges regarding why they are there and what they will learn.

☐ Approach challengers during a break if their behavior continues. Ask them not to disrupt the class and explain that their comments are distracting to the other learners.

☐ Do not allow yourself to become frazzled by hecklers. If you need to, call for a short break to regroup.

☐ If necessary, ask the challenger to leave.

Know-It-Alls

☐ Acknowledge their expertise and ask them to explain concepts or ideas to the group. If appropriate, continue using this person as a resource. Caution: make sure the information being conveyed is accurate.

☐ Don't allow the know-it-alls to prevent other learners from participating. Encourage a balance of participation.

Uninvolved

☐ Make sure you have created an environment where everyone feels comfortable participating.

☐ Do not feel as though everyone has to verbally participate to learn. Some people learn by listening to the experiences and comments of others.

CHAPTER 6

DEMONSTRATING EFFECTIVE COMMUNICATION SKILLS

SKILLS ASSESSMENT

Take a moment to review the competency and associated performances that will be covered in this chapter. Consider your current level of proficiency in the competency as a whole as well as each performance and check the items where you feel you need to improve. As you read the chapter, concentrate on those areas most in need of development.

Competency:

❏ Demonstrate effective communication skills.

Associated Performances:

❏ Use appropriate verbal and nonverbal language.

❏ Adapt verbal and nonverbal messages to learners' needs.

❏ Use frames of reference familiar to learners.

❏ Determine if learners understand messages.

❏ Judge the effectiveness of the communication.

Communication skills should be extremely important to you as a trainer because much of your time is spent transmitting, receiving, and processing verbal and nonverbal messages. In our survey, training practitioners rated *demonstrating effective communication skills* as the second most important of the fourteen training delivery competencies. This chapter concentrates on the trainer as the primary means of transmitting information and on the communication skills required to do that effectively.

It has been said that it is impossible for people to avoid communicating, since silence itself is a form of communication. This chapter covers the following topics:

- The basic communication model.

- Verbal and nonverbal language.

- Adapting both verbal and nonverbal language to meet learners' needs.

- Using familiar frames of reference to enhance learning transfer.

- Practical ways to determine whether learners understand a message.

In short, this chapter emphasizes how important it is in your role as a trainer to manage communication so that you can maximize learning and help learners achieve the instructional objectives of a training program.

This chapter is the first of four devoted to vaious elements of communication. Chapter Seven deals with *presentation skills* that you can use to engage learners and stimulate interest and enthusiasm. Chapter Eight covers the use of *questioning skills and techniques.* And Chapter Nine discusses *responding appropriately to learners' needs for clarification and feedback.*

BASICS OF COMMUNICATION

Communication can be understood to mean a dynamic, two-way process whereby information is transmitted and received. In training delivery, dynamic communication is especially important. *Unidirectional communication*—in which the trainer speaks and students only listen—is not only boring but is also ineffective for encouraging learning.

A BASIC COMMUNICATION MODEL

A *communication model* is a simple way of depicting the communication process. A basic communication model is shown in Exhibit 6–1. In this model, the *sender* prepares a message, and the *receiver* gets the message. The *message* is what is sent; the *medium* is how it is sent; *noise* is anything interfering with the communication process; and *feedback* is any message sent back from the receiver to the sender that indicates whether the

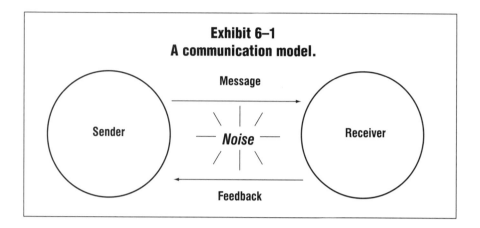

Exhibit 6–1
A communication model.

Sender — Message → Receiver
Noise
← Feedback

message was received and understood. *Understanding* exists when a match occurs between the message sent and the message received.

When the model is applied to the typical, instructor-led training process, the trainer is the sender, and the learners are the receivers, and the message is the training content. Understanding exists when the learner successfully receives the information sent by the trainer. Questioning is a means by which trainers can test how much and how well learners received and understood their message. If learners did not receive the message successfully, they may need clarification or feedback.

Noise is any disturbance or distraction that interferes with, or distorts, the transmitted message. Noise can negatively affect the coding of the message by the sender, the transmission of the message, and the decoding of the message by the receiver. Noise may involve actual, audible noise produced by some source in the training environment—such as a loud ventilation system. If severe enough, noise drowns out the message.

The Noise! The Noise!

" I was delivering a leadership training program in a hotel conference room. Halfway through the program I heard loud noises coming from the room next door. It turned out to be a saw cutting into wood and hammers pounding nails. There was a crew of construction workers renovating the room. "

The pounding and sawing in this critical incident posed a distraction for the learners and interfered with the learning process. Noise may also be internal to the sender or receiver. For instance, a daydreaming learner is experiencing internal noise, since the daydreaming interferes with message reception.

CRITICISM OF THE BASIC COMMUNICATION MODEL

The communication model shown in Exhibit 6–1 is useful for describing key aspects of the communication process. But it is not without its critics. The main problem with this model is that it gives an overly simplified view of the communication process. It implies that communication is a one-way process and that it occurs in a linear (step-by-step) fashion. In reality, however, communication is more complicated: Both sender and receiver are simultaneously sending and receiving information. In this sense, then, communication is more akin to a dance. The dance metaphor is an apt one, since it highlights the dynamic, fluid nature of the communication process.

Another problem with the basic model is that communication appears to be isolated from a *context* (setting) that influences and shapes it. But context plays a large role in the communication process. For example, the history and corporate culture of an organization might significantly influence the dialogue between a manager and her direct report or between a company trainer and his learners. If one norm of the corporate culture is the (unspoken) expectation that people should work seventy hours per week, that could play a role in the communication process when a manager assigns a project. Context is also an issue when communication occurs across national cultures or across genders.

COMMUNICATION IS A SHARED PROCESS

By reflecting on the criticisms of the model presented above, we can gain a deeper understanding of the communication process. Communication is not a one-way street but is a shared process involving two or more people who interact dynamically. This highlights our belief that effective training should be led by an instructor, but also *participant-centered*. When both the trainer and the learners are effectively involved in dynamic communication, learning and understanding is more likely. Communication, to be effective, must also be grounded in a common context so that the communicators develop a shared understanding. This underscores the importance of ensuring that training reflects the realities of the work situation as closely as possible.

When two people engage in a conversation, they should also follow some commonly accepted guidelines. When one person speaks, for example, others should refrain from interrupting and should demonstrate active listening through body language, such as eye contact or nodding. Imagine what would happen if two people do not share the same understanding of how communication takes place. What if the speaker never made eye contact or if the listener constantly interrupted? Communication would be disrupted. Lack of common ground sometimes stems from differences in gender or culture. For example, when a trainer asks learners if they have any questions or comments in Japan or some other Asian countries, it is common for learners to look to the older participants to contribute first comments. This cultural norm displays respect for the wisdom of the more senior members of the group. Creating a common ground for communication can facilitate efficient and effective interactions.

COMMUNICATION INVOLVES VERBAL AND NONVERBAL LANGUAGE

Communication involves both *verbal* (spoken or written) and *nonverbal* (body) language. Interpersonal interaction occurs on multiple, simultaneous communication channels. For example, as you speak to transmit a message, your concurrent facial expressions or gestures represent additional channels. When you ask, "What expectations do you have?" you might simultaneously raise your eyebrows and make eye contact with several learners. This combination of verbal and nonverbal messages represents multiple channels. It should be noted that when multiple channels are used, they should send complementary messages. If you ask, "What expectations do you have?" while looking at the floor, you are sending a mixed signal that reduces the likelihood of a response. The important point is that communication occurs on many channels at once.

USING APPROPRIATE VERBAL AND NONVERBAL LANGUAGE

Say the word *communication* to most people, and they will think first of spoken language. But spoken language is only the tip of the communication iceberg. Nonverbal communication plays a key role in promoting understanding. This section begins with a brief discussion of verbal language and then covers nonverbal language, including gestures, eye contact, and movement, and how they can enhance training.

VERBAL LANGUAGE

Verbal language includes spoken sentences and words used during training. It also includes printed and other written material. It is important for you to use appropriate grammar and syntax, and to gear the word choice and vocabulary to the learners. For example, avoid using highly theoretical or conceptual vocabulary with plant maintenance employees, who are probably accustomed to more down-to-earth, practical terminology. Other aspects of spoken language—such as volume, rate, and inflection—will be discussed in Chapter Seven.

HOW WORDS ARE SPOKEN

How you speak conveys as much meaning as *what you say*. That is as true for the learners as for you. How you speak includes your vocal pitch, tone, rhythm, pauses, laughter, groaning, yawning, and other modifiers that are not considered language but that do convey meaning. For instance, if several learners begin yawning and stretching toward the end of the day, their behavior may convey fatigue or boredom. While nothing has been spoken, it is important for you to be aware of such cues and take necessary action, such as asking everyone to stand up and stretch or calling a short break. Variations in vocal pitch can reflect a range of feelings, including boredom, anger, sadness, happiness, surprise, or disgust. By remaining aware of variations in the vocal pitch used by learners, you see beyond spoken words and detect important clues related to underlying meanings. When such signals occur, check for accuracy. An easy way to do that is to say something like, "I sense that some of you are getting tired. Am I reading this correctly? Do you need a break?" If learners need a break, they will be thankful for the opportunity to provide the feedback.

SILENCE AND PAUSES

You can use your verbal skills to emphasize important points during training delivery. But silence and pauses can also serve useful purposes. By deliberately pausing after you make an important point, you help learners sense its importance and provide them with time to reflect on it and absorb it. Adding a brief or extended period of silence before introducing a point is another technique you can use to focus learners' attention. Sometimes when learners become aware of the silence, they take note of it. It arouses their curiosity and captures their attention. You can also use silence following a question. A pause after a question communicates to learners that they are expected to respond. Sometimes an extended pause following a question can create discomfort, prompting silent learners to respond when they might otherwise have remained silent. Become comfortable with silence and pauses and incorporate them into your delivery. This is sometimes easier said than done because many people, even in casual conversation, are not comfortable with moments of silence. For this reason, practice injecting silence and pauses into your delivery so that you will become accustomed to the "sound of silence."

NONVERBAL LANGUAGE

Nonverbal communication includes visibly observable behaviors between people that convey meaning without the use of written or spoken words. Nonverbal communication is sometimes more important than the words that are spoken, for several reasons. First, more time is typically spent in nonverbal than verbal communication. Second, nonverbal cues tend to be more reliable than spoken words. Third, some elements of nonverbal language, such as facial expressions, point to underlying emotions.

This section discusses eye contact, facial expressions, gestures, body movement, touch, and distance. Each behavior has great significance for you because it can be used to support, replace, or extend verbal messages during delivery. Unfortunately, the possibility exists that nonverbal messages can interfere with verbal messages when a mismatch between them exists. It is therefore important to ensure *congruence*—that is, a match—between them.

EYE CONTACT

Eye contact is an important form of nonverbal communication in training delivery. Eye contact is established when one person looks directly into the eyes of another person. It is crucial for you to attempt to make eye contact with all learners on a regular basis throughout delivery. On the other hand, avoid too much eye contact—such as staring at one person—because it creates uneasiness and poses a distraction for learners. Eye contact is important because it can capture attention, convey meaning, express emotion, provide guidance, and maintain trainer control. Eye contact can also convey information, such as understanding, appreciation, and attentiveness. Further, differences of status can be communicated through eye contact; people tend to make direct eye contact less often and for shorter duration with those they perceive to be of higher status.

When you guide interactions, your eye contact can initiate communication. When you ask a group of learners a question, scan the room for someone who is making eye contact to determine who, if anyone, is willing to respond. When a person avoids eye contact following a question, it usually signals that the person is unsure of the answer or is unwilling to risk responding. So when learners return eye contact, you can generally assume a willingness to participate. When many learners avoid eye contact, you may need to clarify your point or your question. And when most learners avoid eye contact, it can signal an environment that is not conducive to learner participation and involvement. If, for example, the learners fear they may be put on the spot if they respond, then they might refrain from participating. In such cases, work to build trust and establish an open learning environment where learners feel more comfortable and relaxed.

Eye contact can also help to maintain communication by giving you an indication that people are paying attention to what you are saying. When learners don't make eye contact with you, it may indicate that they disagree with what you are saying or are bored by it.

You can also use eye contact to exercise control or facilitate persuasiveness during delivery. By initiating and holding eye contact you capture learner attention and convey urgency, importance, or authority if necessary. Further, as we mentioned in Chapter Five, direct eye contact is a technique that you can use to resolve learner behavior problems.

During delivery, remain alert to your eye contact with the learners and what it means. Make adjustments to your delivery if you detect problems based on your observations. Maintaining good eye contact is an important delivery skill, and it can be learned. Novice public speakers and trainers often have much trouble mastering it. They may look at the wall, ceiling, the notes in front of them, or out the window—but they do not scan the participants in their training session.

One of the authors, when trying to teach eye contact to a group of novice trainers, used the technique of holding a twenty-dollar bill up in the air. He told them that they could have the money if they could see it—and the author moved around in the audience to encourage them to scan the audience. Surprisingly, the novices had difficulty mastering good eye contact even with that unusual—and what you would expect to be effective—approach. So the author resorted to standing directly behind each novice trainer and telling him or her where to look and when to do it. That one-on-one coaching technique worked to improve their eye contact much faster and soon it became natural.

FACIAL EXPRESSIONS

People express themselves through facial expressions as well as by their spoken language and their eye contact. *Facial expressions* convey such emotions as surprise, distress, anger, joy, sadness, and displeasure. Smiles, frowns, raised eyebrows, squinting eyes, wide open eyes, and crinkled forehead all represent visible facial expressions that are linked to emotions. Incidentally, these emotions have been found to be consistent across cultures. Armed with a solid understanding of facial expressions and their associated emotions, you will be better able to assess the feelings of learners and respond accordingly. For example, during an intense discussion about a particularly sensitive topic, you may detect anger brewing among participants simply by observing facial expressions, such as frowns, pursed lips, or red faces. In such a case, intervene as necessary.

GESTURES AND BODY MOVEMENT

Messages can be communicated through your body movements and gestures. Gestures support or replace spoken language and may help you emphasize a point and help a learner understand it. Gestures linked to verbal language are called *illustrators*.[1] Describing a prop by pointing to it is an example of using an illustrator. Gestures not directly linked to verbal language, on the other hand, are called *emblems*.[2] A wave of a hand to express a greeting, which can be used independent of verbal language, is an example of an emblem. During training sessions you will have many opportunities to replace or complement your verbal messages by incorporating illustrators and emblems into delivery.

Unlike facial expressions, gestures can have different meanings across cultures. For example, a military salute may not have the same significance as the same gesture in another country. You can use illustrators and emblems during delivery to dramatically enhance the impact of your presentation.

TOUCH

Touch, another form of communication, can have a powerful effect on behavior. In various situations, some people react more favorably, or feel less anxiety and less fear, when touched. For example, trainers can alleviate learner anxiety by placing a hand on the shoulder of the learner. Some trainers make a practice of greeting learners with a handshake during introductions or as they enter the room. Physical contact like that can sometimes help to relax learners and prepare them emotionally for training. Plan and deliberately incorporate them into training at appropriate places.

However, touch can also be a sensitive issue for those involved in training delivery. Some learners may be offended by physical contact, especially by contact that could be construed as intimidating, threatening, or even harassing. Some trainers avoid all physical contact with learners so that they do not risk sending a mixed or inappropriate message. You may want to follow that example, or ask learners for permission before you touch them. For example, a computer software trainer might find it to be helpful to place his hand on the learner's hand, which is on the mouse, to show how to point and click to activate different functions of the software package. In that situation you should ask learners if they mind this approach before actually touching them.

One of the authors has found this technique to be highly effective when working with people who enter software training with an aversion to computers or who have never used a mouse. In one situation a learner's first reaction when instructed to use the mouse to point to a particular icon was to pick up the mouse and point it at the monitor as if the mouse were a remote control. The concept of maneuvering a mouse was totally foreign and awkward to this learner, but the use of touch to demonstrate pointing and clicking was tremendously helpful and facilitated learning.

DISTANCE

The physical distance between trainer and learners is a nonverbal means by which to communicate. Various categorization systems have been established for understanding interpersonal distances and the messages they convey. These zones have been labeled the intimate, personal, social, and public zones.[3] Unlike many professions, trainers may find themselves in all of these zones during training delivery. The *intimate zone* is about eighteen inches. If you get that close to another person, you are showing a high degree of intimacy, which can be uncomfortable to some people. The computer trainer mentioned in the previous section was undoubtably in the intimate zone because physical contact with the learner was made. The *personal* distance ranges from eighteen inches to about four feet. From four to twelve feet is considered the *social zone*, and from twelve to twenty-five feet or more is regarded as the *public zone*.

One characteristic of the various zones that relates to training is the degree of formality. In formal presentations, the distance between the trainer and the learners is usually great. But if you want to establish a more socially close learning environment, you should get closer. One way to do that is to eliminate barriers such as podiums or a stage that separates you from the learners. You can also roam around the room so that you are closer to where the participants are sitting. Moving among the learners is an excellent way to connect with them because you physically as well as psychologically become part of the group itself.

DISTANCE AMONG LEARNERS

You can gain valuable insight merely by examining the physical distance separating the learners themselves. Learners who are comfortable with each another, such as peers, will sit closer together than those who are not acquainted or are not comfortable together. The degree of familiarity among the participants can affect learning because it influences the existing learning environment. This is one of the reasons that icebreakers, which were discussed in Chapter Five, are used to help learners become acquainted. However, other factors, such as status, can influence the distance between people. For example, you would expect to find a greater distance between an executive and a first-line supervisor than between two executives who are peers.

ADAPTING VERBAL AND NONVERBAL MESSAGES TO LEARNER NEEDS

The previous section covered many important aspects of verbal and nonverbal communication. This section discusses the importance of adapting such messages during delivery to meet the needs of learners, regardless of training content.

By understanding learning styles, you discover when it is necessary to adapt verbal and nonverbal communication to accommodate learning preferences. If you determine that a visual learning style is the predominant style of the group, for instance, then adapt your communication style to that preferred mode. Incorporate more gestures, movements, or visual aids to capture learner attention and to reinforce key points in a visually stimulating manner. Since you will probably encounter a variety of styles present in any given group, your communication should appeal to a range of preferences. Alter your delivery methods to cater to the various learning styles that are present.

REPEATING MESSAGES TO ACHIEVE UNDERSTANDING

Another way you can adapt your communication style to the learners is to repeat messages. Repeating does not mean simply reproducing the same message like a tape recorder. Instead, it means revising, rephrasing, or completely restating the message in ways that encourage understanding. If learners provide verbal and nonverbal cues indicating confusion, you may need to repeat a message. Sometimes learners will indicate, through comments or questions, that they do not understand. More often, however, you must assess their nonverbal cues to pick up on their confusion. Look for such cues as lack of eye contact, a general unwillingness to answer questions, puzzled facial expressions, or increased whispering. In these cases, do not focus your attention on one person but focus it on the entire group. Ask the group if clarification is needed—or if their need for clarification is obvious, then you can restate the message. Simple statements, such as "I sense that this point needs some clarification," can provide a signal that you will be repeating a message. Avoid making negative statements such as "I guess you are all confused," since that will diminish your credibility as a trainer who gives clear directions.

Sometimes repeating messages can be useful even when the learners do understand. By first communicating a message and then rephrasing it in a slightly different way, you make the message clearer because you are reinforcing and clarifying the first transmission. To do this, make statements such as "in other words" or "another way of describing this," followed by a revised, rephrased, or restated version of the original message. This technique is especially useful when you are introducing terminology or language that may be new, confusing, or unfamiliar. In these cases, statements such as, "the (*new term*) can be defined as..." are helpful to learners because they provide clarity and aid understanding. That statement may then be followed by yet another clarifying statement such as, "A useful way of thinking about (*new term*) is to view it as..."

FAMILIAR FRAMES OF REFERENCE

Each of us views the world with a unique frame of reference, which represents ways in which we perceive reality. Try to use frames of reference familiar to your learners. Learners can better understand the training content when they can identify with your perspective. For this reason, do the homework necessary to find examples from the learners' workplace(s) or other real-world applications.

Assume, for the sake of example, that you are delivering a coaching skills workshop to supervisors. To do that most effectively, draw on actual situations (or critical incidents) confronting supervisors as they try to coach people, rather than just describing effective coaching principles in the abstract. When learners are not given examples that are grounded in their daily work reality, they will find the training boring or confusing. A sure sign this has happened is when a participant says something like, "This theory is quite interesting, but when will we hear how to apply this?"

Using familiar frames of reference helps learners see how the training applies to their work. That means they are more likely to take the learning back to their jobs and apply it, and the learning from the training environment to the work environment is more likely to be successfully transfered.

TAP INTO LEARNERS' EXPERIENCES

One of the most effective ways to use familiar frames of reference is to draw upon the knowledge and experiences of the learners themselves. Adult learners sometimes have years and years of experience, and when asked to apply that expertise or relate it to the course material, they often can provide excellent real-world examples. One of the authors remembers instructing a group of factory workers in the topic of self-directed work teams. Learners remained skeptical even though he provided examples from world-class organizations where the move to teams had been successful. He elected to shift gears and asked the learners if they had experience with successful work teams. A burly press operator spoke up and gave one of the most eloquent and compelling descriptions of the power of self-directed teams with a detailed rationale as to how it could benefit the organization. This operator, through his years of experience and personal credibility, was highly respected by his peers, and the result was startling to the trainer, who had tried in vain to provide a convincing case.

Master presenter Lance Dublin, of EPS Solutions in San Francisco, sums it up this way: "Never give away any answers. Most likely, someone in the audience will know as much or more about the topic than you do. And most people will know something. Use that. The more an audience is involved in the presentation, the easier and more fun it is for the presenter, and the more effective it is for the audience."[4]

DETERMINING WHETHER LEARNERS UNDERSTAND MESSAGES

Effective trainers focus on the learners. They do not regard their role as mere presenters of information. Instead, they see themselves as learning facilitators. They strive to be the "guide on the side," not the "sage on the stage." They ensure that learners understand what they have been trained to know or do. An important part of the trainer's role, then, is to determine whether learners understand the training content.

GAINING UNDERSTANDING

As we stated in an earlier section, one way to encourage learner understanding is to repeat what you say. Use verbal cues—such as the learners' responses to your questions—to check their understanding, and watch for telling nonverbal cues, such as unwillingness to make eye contact, prolonged silence following questions, or confused looks.

Once you have repeated your message, you need to check for learner understanding again. One way to do that is to ask, "Do you understand now?" Perhaps a better way is to ask some simple questions to check learner understanding. If the learners understand, several should acknowledge that. If they do not, you will need to probe deeper to find the source(s) of confusion.

JUDGING COMMUNICATION EFFECTIVENESS

How can you judge the effectiveness of your own communication skill? In this section we focus attention on three key issues of importance in judging your communication skill:

1. Evaluating your nonverbal behaviors.

2. Evaluating your frame of reference.

3. Asking your learners for feedback.

For the most part, however, you will find it exceedingly difficult to be an objective judge of your own communication effectiveness. To gather more objective feedback, ask colleagues or other people to observe and evaluate your training delivery skills and provide you with feedback about your strengths, weaknesses, and development needs. You may also find it helpful to videotape your training delivery and then review it. When you see yourself in action, you will easily notice ways you can improve.

EVALUATING NONVERBAL BEHAVIORS

Nonverbal behaviors (body language) should, of course, match and enhance what you say. To be effective, you should strike a balance between what you say and what body language you use. For example, if you want to make a serious point, your gestures should match it—and should not be exaggerated. If you are trying to demonstrate your enthusiasm about a topic, don't remain stonefaced. Such mismatches between body language and spoken language will (at best) confuse learners and (at worst) raise questions about your sincerity.

EVALUATING FRAMES OF REFERENCE

Evaluate the frames of reference you use. Be sure to use examples, activities, and job applications that are familiar to your participants. One way you can judge your success is to ask learners periodically if the examples seem realistic. If not, then solicit more realistic examples from your participants if possible. Learners will also let you know if examples do not seem relevant. They will ask for additional examples or ask you how a particular concept or idea is applicable to their work situations. Such questions from learners should signal you that new or better examples are needed to solidify understanding and demonstrate application. Again, soliciting examples from the group can be an effective strategy.

ASKING LEARNERS ABOUT THE IMPACT OF YOUR COMMUNICATION

Finally, ask learners how effective they find your communication skills to be. You may do that through end-of-course evaluation sheets, of course, but it's better not to wait until the end to find out. Take the temperature of the group on your performance by asking them periodically—right after break and right after lunch is a particularly opportune time—or by administering short written evaluation sheets at the end of each day of training. Evaluating trainer performance will be covered in greater depth in a later chapter.

SUMMARY

This chapter introduced the basics of communication. Effective communication skills are important to successful training delivery. In fact, this competency was rated as the second most important delivery competency in our survey. That should come as no surprise, since many trainers view themselves to be communicators.

This chapter covered the following topics:

- Description of communication and the basic model of the communication process.

- The uses of verbal language and nonverbal language.

- The challenge of adapting your communication style and delivery to meet learner needs.

- The use of familiar frames of reference to enhance learning transfer.

- Practical ways to determine whether learners understand a message.

STRATEGY LIST

Actionable Strategies to Improve Training Effectiveness:

Verbal Communication

☐ Recognize that communication is a two-way process and involves verbal and nonverbal elements.

❏ Create common ground when communicating.

❏ Remain aware of variations in vocal pitch that can help you to understand underlying concerns or issues learners may have.

❏ Pause after asking a question in order to give learners time to respond.

❏ Add a brief period of silence before introducing a point to focus learners' attention.

❏ Use words and examples with which learners are familiar.

❏ Repeat information that is particularly important.

Nonverbal Communication

❏ Use active listening skills such as paraphrasing, leaning forward, and making eye contact.

❏ Ensure that your verbal communication (your words) matches your nonverbal communication (your facial expressions, gestures, body movements).

❏ Use eye contact to demonstrate your attention to learners. Caution: Avoid extended eye contact and staring.

❏ Use eye contact from learners to assess their understanding, interest, or willingness to be involved.

❏ Ask learners and/or colleagues for feedback regarding your verbal and nonverbal messages.

❏ Use gestures to support or replace your words. Caution: Certain gestures may have different meanings in different cultures.

❏ Use distance to support your messages (close proximity is generally less formal and more intimate).

❏ Scan the room to identify nonverbal cues regarding learner emotions and problems such as confused looks, staring out the window, or blank stares. Caution: verify these cues to ensure accuracy.

CHAPTER 7

DEMONSTRATING EFFECTIVE PRESENTATION SKILLS

SKILLS ASSESSMENT

Take a moment to review the competency and associated performances that will be covered in this chapter. Consider your current level of proficiency in the competency as a whole as well as each performance and check the items where you feel you need to improve. As you read the chapter, concentrate on those areas most in need of development.

Competency:

❏ Demonstrate effective presentation skills.

Associated Performances:

❏ Use the voice effectively.

❏ Use eye contact effectively.

❏ Use gestures, silence, movement, posture, space, and props effectively.

❏ Organize content effectively.

❏ Use anecdotes, stories, analogies, and humor effectively.

❏ Judge the effectiveness of a presentation.

While Chapter Six introduced communication skills, this chapter focuses on presentation skills—sometimes called *platform skills*. Presentation skills add excitement, variety, and drama to training delivery. This chapter covers the following topics:

- The importance of effective presentation skills.

- The use of voice, eye contact, nonverbal behaviors, and props during delivery to stimulate interest and facilitate learning.

- Organizing content to enable smooth and seamless transitions.

- Using anecdotes, stories, analogies, and humor effectively.

THE IMPORTANCE OF EFFECTIVE PRESENTATION SKILLS

Effective presentation skills help you speak in a more entertaining way. In fact, you can benefit from using the presentation techniques perfected by actors, magicians, and other professional entertainers. These skills, when used appropriately, can motivate learners and add excitement to training. They can make training sessions more dynamic and powerful, thereby increasing the chance that learners will remember—and apply on the job—what they learned in training.

What happens when your presentation skills are ineffective? To find out the answer to that question, reflect on the following critical incident, which dramatically demonstrates the impact of poor presentation skills:

Trainers Are Still Learners

" The worst experience I had was as a participant. The presenter had a dry, boring presence, total data dump of information, no involvement of the participants, no handouts, and a hot room after lunch. The participants were executives and trainers. It taught me a lot of valuable lessons about what not to do as a trainer. "

The trainer described in this situation had not developed effective presentation skills. Fortunately, the writer of this incident received some benefit from the experience by learning what presentation behaviors to avoid.

USING VOICE EFFECTIVELY

Using voice effectively refers to how enthusiastically you speak (emotional range), how loudly you speak (volume), how quickly you speak (rate), and how you pronounce what you say (inflection). Using your voice effectively is critically important to the effectiveness of how well you deliver training in group settings. This section covers these and other important aspects of voice and provides some tips for using your voice effectively to enhance your presentation and thereby foster participant learning. Using your voice also includes the studied use of silence and pauses.

CONVEYING ENTHUSIASM

You have undoubtedly heard the saying that "enthusiasm is contagious." That adage clearly applies to your training delivery. If you speak in a monotone and appear unenthusiastic about the material you are delivering, the effect on learners is detrimental. Learners may visibly begin to drift off, or they will struggle to keep their eyes open.

In contrast, when you show excitement and interest in your material, you bring an otherwise dry topic to life. You can show enthusiasm in many ways. For instance, you can use varied tones when you speak, make sweeping gestures, move about the room, make frequent eye contact, smile, and show genuine interest in your material and your learners. When you are enthusiastic, you capture the interest and attention of learners. Participants, when engaged, lean forward, reciprocate eye contact, and provide other verbal and nonverbal signals to show they are involved. When people are fully stimulated, they are likely to learn more because they are focused on you and your message.

VOLUME, RATE, TEMPO, AND INFLECTION

One of your goals is to ensure that all participants in your training session can hear you. Your voice should thus be neither too loud nor too soft. When your voice is too soft, learners miss key points—or eventually give up—because listening is just too difficult. Likewise, when your voice is too loud, it can intimidate learners and cause discomfort. Of course, your challenge in speaking at just the right volume is compounded when the size of the group is large or the physical distance between you and your participants increases. Throughout your delivery you can change how loudly you speak to achieve specific purposes. For example, lowering the volume of voice can capture participants' interest and cause them to concentrate on what you are saying. Likewise, you can raise your voice to emphasize important points or seize sudden attention.

RATE OF SPEECH AND TEMPO

Rate refers to the speed at which you speak. When the rate of your speech is too rapid, several problems can arise. If you speak too fast, learners find that distracting and difficult to follow. Important points are missed because learners, while attempting to comprehend earlier parts of the message, miss subsequent parts. Just as rapid speech can be problematic, you will also have problems if you speak too slowly. Learners find a slow rate of speech tedious to follow and tune the speaker out—or become distracted by something else.

Tempo involves the rhythm of speech. Tempo should be even and, as with rate of speech, not be distracting due to uneven or erratic rhythm. Try to find a tempo that is appropriate to the learners. Self-awareness of rate and tempo may be difficult, so you might want to ask a colleague or the learners themselves how you are doing, and make adjustments as indicated.

MINIMIZING DISTRACTING VOCALIZATIONS AND VERBAL EXPRESSIONS

Vocalizations are utterances that are distracting if they are used too frequently. Common distracting vocalizations include the use of "ah" when speaking. (Note that such distracting vocalizations vary by language, and "ah" is one "filler" used in English.) This utterance often appears as a filler and is used between sentences or when people gather their thoughts. It can become habitual and even unconscious.

You can identify distracting vocalizations by asking another person to listen for them and even count how frequently they appear. In addition to tracking their frequency, you may find it helpful to ask other people to pinpoint when they are used, such as when you change thoughts or transition to another topic. This knowledge can help you avoid them because you are aware of the times they happen. Another strategy is to videotape a training session and review it, concentrating on which vocalizations occur, how often, and when. Use the checklist appearing in Exhibit 7–1 to monitor vocalizations and distracting expressions.

SUBSTITUTING SILENCE

Once you become aware of any distracting speech mannerisms that you are guilty of using, you should work to correct them. One way is to learn how to be comfortable with silence. In situations when you might normally say "ah"—such as when transitioning between sentences—you can use silence to fill that transition. That can be uncomfortable for you at first because you may have used vocalizations to minimize the frequency and length of pauses. When silence is substituted for the distracting utterances, it can become somewhat unpleasant until you realize that the

Exhibit 7–1
Vocalization checklist.

Directions: Use this checklist to track the frequency and type of various distracting vocalizations and verbal expressions exhibited by the trainer during delivery.

Name: _____   Observer: _____

Start: _____ Finish: _____   Date: _____

Vocalizations or expressions	Frequency	Comments
"Ahh"		
"Like"		
"Okay"		
"As it were"		
"If you will"		
"Basically"		
"Well"		
Others:		

pauses are typically brief, that silence and pauses are normal, and that they are a distinct improvement over using distracting fillers.

OTHER DISTRACTING EXPRESSIONS

"Ah" is a nonlanguage vocalization, because the sound itself has no meaning. But language vocalizations can become distracting during presentations, too. Verbal expressions include such phrases and words as "you know," "like," or "okay." They can grow annoying when used too frequently. Such expressions are often an unconscious part of the trainer's vocabulary and, as in the case of vocalizations, must be brought to the attention of the person using them. Often, both vocalizations and verbal expressions are part of everyday speech patterns. Awareness of the expression is the first step toward eliminating it.

Ask someone to point out each time the undesirable expression is used during your daily (nontraining) conversation. Each time you use the phrase, the other person should be instructed to interrupt you and point it out. Doing that can help you begin to be aware of—and eventually minimize—its use. At first this approach may seem ridiculous, but the more timely the feedback, the more likely you are to reduce the negative behavior. Obviously, such practices should only be done at appropriate times and with discretion. The following vignette illustrates the efforts of a trainer, Mallory, to eliminate distracting vocalizations from her delivery.

> Mallory worked for a small technology firm as a management development specialist. After her training sessions, she passed out an evaluation sheet asking for feedback on her performance. She noted that several learners remarked on her use of distracting vocalizations including "ah," "look," and "at any rate." Unaware of this, she was determined to eliminate this behavior. Mallory enlisted the help of two of her more trusted colleagues, asking them to listen to her communication and point out these vocalizations as they occurred. She was astonished at the frequency with which they interrupted her. Her heightened awareness helped her to gradually eliminate this behavior. Over time, Mallory caught herself before she uttered these words and was eventually able to extinguish them from her vocabulary by simply remaining silent or by substituting appropriate dialogue.

USING MICROPHONES

Microphones are appropriate to use when there is a greater than normal physical distance separating you from your participants, such as in large rooms or in large groups. Today's microphones can be quite sophisticated. Most common are wireless clip-on microphones, wireless hand microphones, wired hand microphones, podium microphones, pole microphones, and boom microphones. A clip-on goes on your tie or lapel; wireless hand mikes fit in your hand; wired hand microphones fit in your hand but have a trailing cord; podium microphones sit on a podium; pole microphones are positioned on a stand; and boom microphones are suspended above the speaker.

Each microphone has distinct advantages and disadvantages. Wireless clip-on microphones permit freedom of movement. There are no unsightly wires that can lead to the graceless vision of a presenter tripping over cords. Unfortunately, wireless clip-ons may be turned on and forgotten by the unwary—with the result that people could hear what you say to a colleague when you leave the room briefly.

Wireless handheld microphones are well known because they are frequently used by talk show hosts and newscasters doing person-on-the-street interviews. Such microphones are more limiting than lapel microphones because they must be held properly to capture your voice. That, of course, affects your ability to use expressive gestures, hold objects such as props, or even drink water from a pitcher. Handheld microphones with cords limit your movement and may invite distractions as you pay attention to the cord instead of participants.

Mounted microphones, like those found on podiums or on microphone stands, are fixed in one place. That makes it easy to manage them, since they are not as easily lost (or stolen) as wireless lapel microphones. But they limit your movement and, when you do move, limit the participants' ability to hear you.

Boom microphones are rarely used in group training. But they are commonly used in television productions so that viewers do not have to be distracted by watching microphones traded around. You may have occasion to use boom microphones when your training session is videotaped or when you are using distance learning methodologies such as videoconferencing, so you should be aware that they are useful only when you are positioned directly under them. That may mean that you have to look up occasionally to find out where the microphone is, and you will need a boom operator to make sure that you are standing sitting in the right place.

TESTING MICROPHONES

Always test a microphone and the speaker system before using them. Make sure that, like audiovisual support, you have audio support in case microphones or speaker systems do not work. Note the positioning of speakers so that you will see where the audience is supposed to sit. If you plan to shift seating arrangements, plan ahead about what that might mean for people trying to hear you.

MAINTAINING LEARNER INVOLVEMENT

Maintaining learner involvement is a key issue when using microphones. Generally, you are the primary user of the microphone. When learners speak without a microphone, not everyone will be able to hear what they said. In these cases you should repeat or paraphrase the question or comment being made. For example, if you are wearing a clip-on microphone during a conference presentation and someone asks a question, you should say something like, "That was a good question. For those who did not hear, the question was…" followed by a repeated or paraphrased version of the original question. Doing that ensures that everyone knows what was said.

Of course, you could also have several microphones positioned around the room for use by the participants. That technique is used in conferences, televised talk shows, or town meetings. When people from the audience have a question or comment, they are handed a cordless hand-held microphone or move to a nearby microphone. With this method everyone can hear the question directly from the learner at an audible volume.

BECOMING COMFORTABLE WITH MICROPHONES

You may find it uncomfortable and awkward the first time you use a microphone. Further, when you experience screeching feedback or improper volume, you (and your learners) can become rattled. The impact of that on your presentation—and on participant learning—can be devastating. However, with practice and with the assistance of a competent audio technician, you can learn to use microphones effectively. The benefits outweigh the disadvantages, because microphones will help your learners hear you and each other.

USING EYE CONTACT EFFECTIVELY

This section focuses on using eye contact to enhance presentation effectiveness. During presentations you should attempt to make direct eye contact with each learner in the audience. Eye contact engages learners in your presentation and gives one-on-one attention to learners in a group setting. Making eye contact, in effect, draws each learner into the process.

Avoid making eye contact with only some learners and not others to avoid being perceived as showing favoritism or exclusion. Obviously, eye contact with all learners becomes difficult, if not impossible, with large audiences. During conference presentations, for example, there could easily be an audience of several hundred or even several thousand listeners.

Try to make eye contact on a regular basis throughout the presentation. Be aware of the duration of the eye contact you make to ensure that it is neither too short nor too long. Brief eye contact can give the impression that you consider some learners less important than others. Extended eye contact turns into staring and can be awkward for learners.

PURPOSES AND MEANINGS OF EYE CONTACT

Eye contact serves many purposes. You can use it to check for learner understanding and willingness to participate. Learners refusing to make eye contact may be signaling that they do not understand the material. In such cases, you may need to revisit a point or clarify an issue. Learners may also avoid eye contact when they are uncomfortable or feel that responding may lead to embarrassment. In contrast, fully involved learners will try to make eye contact with the trainer to signal a willingness to make a comment, volunteer for an activity, ask a question, or respond to a question. Always scan the room, looking for signs of participants who want to speak.

How do you know if you are using eye contact effectively? One way is to ask learners directly by including a question about eye contact on participant evaluation forms or conducting written surveys. The survey appearing in Exhibit 7–2, for instance, can be used to solicit feedback from learners regarding your eye contact.

USING NONVERBALS EFFECTIVELY

Nonverbal behaviors can complement or enhance your presentation delivery. This section describes how you can make effective use of gestures, movement, silence, posture, and distance in your presentations.

GESTURES AND MOVEMENT

Gestures support or can even take the place of spoken language. When using gestures, you should always be sure they are appropriate.

Exhibit 7–2
Survey of eye contact usage.

Directions: As a trainer, I am always attempting to improve my delivery skills. One area that I am working on is eye contact. Please answer the following questions as feedback for my development efforts. Thank you!

1. How frequently did the trainer make eye contact with you?

1	2	3	4	5
Never made eye contact with me	Seldom made eye contact with me	Made adequate eye contact with me	Made too much eye contact with me	Stared at me

Complete the following sentence:

2. When the trainer made eye contact with me, I felt…

3. What other comments do you have about the trainer's performance?

Appropriate gestures add meaning and enhance your message. Inappropriate gestures can become distracting by taking attention away from the message and placing it on the gesture.

To illustrate, imagine a training situation where the trainer frequently runs his fingers through his hair. While this seems like an innocent gesture, if it is noticed by the learners and becomes a distraction to them, then it may prevent them from paying attention to the message. In the same way, not using any gestures can be equally problematic. Imagine a trainer who rigidly stands in the same place and never moves her arms. That would look unnatural and would create a distraction.

Why might someone use distracting gestures and movement? The most common reason is *stage fright*. Novice trainers, like stage actors making their first appearances, may be fearful of public speaking. Their main goal is to deliver the message. That can lead to distracting mannerisms and posture. Novice trainers are well advised to stand with their arms at their sides or behind their backs, avoid leaning on objects such as desks or podiums, and stand with their legs firmly on the floor.

Doug Malouf, an expert trainer with DTS International in Sydney, Australia, offers the following advice to new trainers who want to combat stage fright: "Practice, rehearse, and drill. In one study, people were asked to rank their fears in order. Sixty-eight percent said death was number one; 32 percent said public speaking was number one. That means that one-third would rather die than speak. Many trainers feel the same way. The only way to overcome such fear is to practice and rehearse. You never lose the fear, you learn to control it."[1]

MATCH GESTURES TO THE MESSAGE

One key to your success as a presenter is to match the gestures to your message. Look at Exhibit 7–3, which describes some common gestures and their possible meanings. Use that exhibit to select gestures for your presentations. You may also use it to improve how well you interpret the gestures of your participants.

SILENCE

You can enhance your presentation by using silence strategically. Use silence before or after making important points, following a question, or at other times during delivery. Silence can arouse learner interest and curiosity. When learners become aware that you are silent, they wonder why. When learners focus their attention on you, you can

Exhibit 7–3
Common gestures and their possible meanings.

Gestures	Possible Meanings
Nodding head	Demonstrates agreement or acknowledgment of positive behavior.
Pointing at an object	Draws attention to the object.
Raising hands	Emphasizes importance or depth of feeling about the topic or issue.
Facial expressions	Demonstrates a variety of emotions and feelings such as confusion, anger, concern, or happiness.
Touch	Shows concern, friendship, or acceptance.
Pointing at a learner	Singles out a learner for selection or reference.
Leaning forward	Conveys active listening.
Distracting gestures, such as running fingers through hair	Demonstrates anxiety, frustration, nervousness, or tension.

In the space below, list some of the common gestures that you use. What messages are you sending through these gestures?

deliver the key learning point with full impact because you have their undivided attention.

To illustrate just how powerful silence can be, assume that you make the statement "this is a very important point" and then pause. This deliberate moment of silence stimulates interest and allows the learners to focus their attention on you and your message.

WHEN TO USE SILENCE AND PAUSES

Pausing briefly after a key learning point is another way you can use silence to enhance your presentation. Immediately following an important learning point you can become silent to permit the gravity of the point to sink in. Silence also provides the learners with adequate time to reflect on, and process, the message. As with many delivery skills, one effective way to improve your ability to use it is through continuing practice and feedback.

Another technique you can use is to incorporate planned pauses as you use media. For example, when you use overhead transparencies, you can cover part of the slide with a bulleted list and reveal each bullet as you discuss it. As you progress from bullet to bullet, you move the paper. The motion required for you to go to the overhead and move the paper to reveal each point permits a moment of silence that builds interest and attention. It also allows an effective transition between points.

You can also use silence for impact when you are delivering a message with a strong emotional component. Suppose you tell a sad—or inspirational—story to reinforce a concept, change an attitude, or excite the learners to take action. To increase the story's impact, you can pause at appropriate times throughout delivery and at the end. Such periods of silence are most effective in conveying your emotion and evoking feelings among your listeners.

Silence can also be used after you ask a question. Such pauses send a message to learners that you expect a response. In addition, silence after a question allows time for learners to consider the question and, if possible, formulate an appropriate response. Watch out for the mistake of not allowing people enough time to think of an answer to your questions. Worse yet is to permit insufficient lead-time to answer a question and then provide the answer to the learners. You should practice how you pause after asking questions. During the silence you should scan the room to identify individuals willing to participate. By doing this, sometimes for extended time periods, you may elicit a response from among the most reluctant participants.

When silence follows a question, learners realize that someone must answer. The tension created by silence usually prompts someone to volunteer. If you do this several times, you will condition the learners to answer questions.

DISTANCE

The physical distance separating you and the learners sends a powerful nonverbal message. The closer you are to the learners, the more intimate and informal the learning climate becomes. Conversely, the farther away you are from the learners—and the more objects like podiums, tables, and audiovisual equipment are in the way—the more formal the learning climate becomes. Distance can thus affect the willingness of learners to participate. Generally, people talk less often when they are in formal settings and talk more when they are in informal settings. To create a more personal, intimate environment, you should set up the classroom so that you are positioned in close physical proximity to the participants. This will set a tone that encourages learners to interact in a more casual, relaxed manner.

You can change your proximity at different points in your delivery to match the message you plan to send. If you want to preserve formality at the opening of a training session to dramatize the impact, stand behind a podium to show authority and stress your position as trainer. On the other hand, if you wish to encourage discussion, move away from the podium and toward the learners. The closer you can get to them, the better.

Perhaps a simple example will emphasize how the instructor's proximity to the learners can set the tone. One of the authors was presenting to a group of senior college professors. The first session was conducted formally: The participants sat in neat rows, like students in a traditional college classroom, and the instructor stood behind a podium and delivered a PowerPoint presentation. But in the second session—which happened to focus on "how college professors can facilitate discussions"—the instructor modeled the role of facilitator by moving from behind the podium and sitting facing the front row of participants. The physical separation was reduced, and the participant interaction was dramatically improved.

USING PROPS EFFECTIVELY

A *prop* is any physical object used for demonstration during training. Almost any object can serve as a prop, a term which is drawn from theater. For example, in an introductory computer course, a 3.5-inch floppy diskette might serve as a prop. You could display the disk when you begin discussing data storage methods. By doing that, you show learners a representative example. Some learners find it easier to understand when they have physical objects or other examples to see, touch, and examine.

Another example of a prop might be the finished product from a particular manufacturing process. A properly written memo could serve as a prop in a course on effective business writing or a sample of a defective product could be introduced during quality-related training. Regardless of the actual prop that is used, the key is to recognize how and why it is used. Props should not be used without a specific purpose or intent. Props should be used for demonstration purposes to help support or reinforce learning and achieve the course objectives. Props should be used to gain interest, focus attention, provide a big picture, or provide learners with a hands-on opportunity. It is not recommended that props be introduced simply because they are interesting or nice to use.

WHEN TO USE PROPS

Props are excellent attention-getters to use when introducing a topic during training delivery. When you display a prop, it commands attention. People gaze at it, naturally curious what it is.

Some trainers will cleverly joke about "show-and-tell" time, reminiscent of kindergartners bringing something interesting to class.

Props need not be limited to use during opening segments, but they can be used throughout training. They can be an excellent way to provide learners with a big picture view of the training. In some cases the prop could actually be the central focus of the entire training program. For example, in a technical training course on using a voltmeter, the program itself may be centered around that device.

STRATEGIES FOR USING PROPS EFFECTIVELY

Using props effectively can be challenging depending on the nature of the prop, the purpose for which it will be used, the learners, and the training situation. When using a prop, its purpose is the first, and arguably the most important, issue you should consider. In considering the purpose of the prop, examine the course objectives. What prop would help to support the objective? When should the prop be introduced? How should the prop be introduced? What is the most effective use of the prop? What problems or barriers could present themselves that might diminish the effectiveness of the prop? Answering these questions can help you to make best use of the prop to help achieve an objective.

Once you have thoroughly assessed the purpose of the prop, reflect next on how you plan to use it during the presentation. Consider how you will display the prop. Will you hold it up and then pass it around? Is the prop so large or heavy that you must position it somewhere in or near the classroom? How difficult will it be for learners to see the prop?

If you think that learners will have difficulty seeing the prop, you have several options. One is to pass the prop around. Another is to ask learners to gather around it, if the prop is large. A third option is to have enough props (for example, computer terminals) for learners to cluster around in small groups. To illustrate, two of these methods were used by one of the authors some years ago during a general plant safety training course. During the program he handed out a pair of safety glasses to each participant when eye protection was covered. Each participant was encouraged to observe key features, such as the wrap-around shields, and actually to try wearing the glasses. Later in the same program the learners were asked to gather around a mock electrical utility box to observe as the trainer demonstrated the lockout-tagout procedure. Volunteers were then given the opportunity to perform the same tasks the trainer had demonstrated. Using these props helped the trainer to foster learning because it allowed participants to see and feel the material in a way that descriptions alone would not have allowed. Thus, their understanding was deepened.

What do you do with props when you are finished using them? You may want to leave the prop in a visible location so learners can view it as you continue your presentation. Doing this can be helpful when the prop is referred to later in the training session. One disadvantage of this approach is that it can become a distraction to learners. If they continue to focus on the prop, they could miss key points you are presenting. On the other hand, you can choose to place the prop in a location so it cannot be seen, such as under a skirted table. Again, this strategy has potential advantages and disadvantages. If the prop was taken away, the focus of the learners can be returned to the training content. On the other hand, if the prop was removed from sight just as the curiosity of learners was peaking, then they may continue to focus on the prop even if it is out of sight, thus creating another divergence of focus. Consider this issue carefully before deciding what to do with a prop.

Be sure to try out a prop before using it in training. Allow other people to look at the prop to see if it functions as intended. Consider whether it is in working order. Does it need anything for operation such a batteries or a light bulb? Will the prop be understood by all learners, or is it more appropriate for a small group?

ORGANIZING CONTENT EFFECTIVELY

Take a minute to think about a training session you have seen that was not well organized. What did you notice that made you think the training was disorganized? This section describes some ways that training can be presented in an organized way—and what happens when it is not.

The Case of the Missing Slides

" *The worst experience I have had related to the delivery of training is with the previous trainer for a class who had left the slides all out of order and some of the notes were missing. I did not have time to prepare because of other commitments and because I knew the material well. A new trainer was observing me during the class so I wanted it to be done well. I wound up just getting through the material off the top of my head, making it more interactive, and then straightening out the slides over the break. It actually went quite well because it forced me to ad-lib on material I knew and has probably made me a more effective presenter who can deviate from the script notes.* "

This trainer was fortunate in that he coped with overheads that were not assembled in order. But that could have turned into a disaster if he had not been familiar with the training content.

What should you do when confronted with a situation in which you must ad-lib? Here are some practical tips:

■ Take a deep breath, pause, gather your thoughts, and continue.

■ Ask the learners to take a short break of less than five minutes while you organize your notes, overheads, or other material.

■ Provide the learners with an activity, exercise, or other useful task that permits you breathing room to organize your material.

■ Ask the learners open-ended questions to get involvement without lecturing.

LINKING CONTENT TO OBJECTIVES

The most obvious evidence of disorganized training is when there is a mismatch between the stated purpose and objectives of the course and its actual content or activities. Learners will be quick to notice that. They will then make statements like, "Why are we in this training?" or "What did we just learn, and why was that important?" To avoid this problem, be sure to spell out early in the program why the training is being conducted and how it will meet business needs or workplace issues. Then reemphasize that point throughout the course. When learners see the practical value of the training, they will pay attention and will be more motivated to learn.

USING RELEVANT EXAMPLES AND INFORMATION

Use examples and content that are tied to the organization and to the learners' experience. When examples seem out of place, learners can become confused and wonder why they are included and how they fit into the course. For this reason, continually strive to relate content, examples, and other instructional matter, such as activities, to the over-all premise of the course. After you provide an example, for instance, make a linking statement to demonstrate to learners why the example is important and how it fits the course, the corporate culture, and the industry of which the organization is part.

Try to use examples and facts that are realistic and relevant to the participants in your training course. The learners should see how the content is applicable to their personal or professional lives. Explain and demonstrate the relevance or benefits of the training to the learners. In a training course on tools for quality improvement, for example, you could reinforce the relevance of a specific tool by demonstrating an on-the-job application to which learners can relate. Even though the relevance of content may be self-evident to learners, always state the relevance to make it as explicit as possible.

STRATEGIES TO GUIDE LEARNERS

Adult learners, unlike children, should be self-directed and willing to exert some effort to learn when they see reasons to do so. But adult learners often still prefer some structure to their learning and want to know what immediate practical value their learning will have. You can structure training more effectively by using overviews to introduce topics, summaries to synthesize and conclude a topic, and seamless transitions between topics.

OVERVIEWS

An *overview* presents a big-picture summary of what is to come. An overview is often provided at the opening of a training program or of a part of a training program. (A part of a training program might include a single day in a multi-day course or an afternoon in a one-day course.)

To get an idea of what an overview is all about, think about the old statement that military training should be structured so that you "tell them what you are going to tell them, tell them, and then tell them what you told them." An overview serves the purpose to give them advance warning of what is to come. It "tells them what you are going to tell them" and thus presents a flash-forward of the training contents.

An *advanced organizer* is a special overview technique. As the phrase implies, it aids learners by preparing them in advance for what will be presented during training. Advanced organizers can take many forms. If you show an agenda, an outline of the training content, or a flowchart depicting the organization of the course, you are providing advanced organizers. They prepare learners for the training. They also help learners gain a broader perspective of the training by informing them of where they are and where they will go. In that sense, it is like a building map or city street map, where "X" indicates "you are here."

Overviews help provide learners with a context for each segment, answering the question "why are we covering this, and where is this leading?" Overviews may be simple statements that you can make, such as "In this segment we will be discussing (*topic to be discussed*). This is important because (*reasons the topic is important*). This section relates to the objective (*relevant objective*)."

SUMMARIES

Summaries or conclusions are usually provided at the end of a training segment. They help learners synthesize what was covered and distill the training into the key learning points. Summaries help "bring it all together," connecting all points. You might think of a summary as akin to an activity debrief in which learners discuss what they learned and draw conclusions about it. Summaries are also helpful in reinforcing how the training was useful and how it can be applied on-the-job.

TRANSITIONS

Transitions are the connections between training segments. They link otherwise independent sequences. Transitions often take the form of statements that bridge the gap from the conclusion of one section to the introduction of the next section. Exhibit 7–4 depicts schematically how transitions help link together training segments.

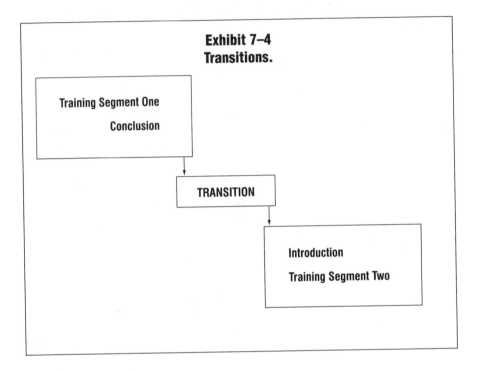

**Exhibit 7–4
Transitions.**

Training Segment One
Conclusion

TRANSITION

Introduction
Training Segment Two

Transitions should provide a bridge from one topic into the next. When transitions are seamless, the flow of training is smooth. But poor transitions indicate a disorganized trainer. What are some examples of poor transitions? They include extended pauses and the shuffling of papers or overheads in an effort to move on. Learners grow confused because they may not see how the next section relates to the last one. They are thrust into a new topic without preparation. Some learners may also express impatience because they feel time is being wasted. Here follows an example of an effective transition from one training topic to the next.

TRAINER: *I'd like to close our discussion on the importance of building trust in work teams. Keep in mind the three reasons we men-*

tioned: one, higher morale and job satisfaction; two, more productivity and better performance; and three, more open communication.

Now we're going to shift gears and talk about specific ways you can build trust in your teams. We're going to begin with a quick exercise to identify a list of trust-building activities....

Notice how the trainer brought the first section to conclusion by providing a summary of the key points. Next, the trainer explicitly informed the learners that a new topic was being introduced through the statement "now we're going to shift gears." Then the trainer provided an introduction to the next section by explaining to learners what would happen next.

MANAGING TIME AND AVOIDING DIGRESSIONS

As a trainer, you must ensure that time is managed effectively. If you have distributed an agenda with time estimates, try to stick to them. Rehearse the course in advance to get realistic time estimates. Your goal is to ensure that each training segment is covered in sufficient detail to achieve the learning objectives.

Now, it is quite true that learner groups differ dramatically. Each group is unique. Some groups simply require more time than others to master the same material. One group may have more experienced learners who require less background or less explanation, or another group may have more motivated learners. Whatever the reason, you should realize that no two groups will progress through material at the same pace. Your job as trainer, however, is to ensure that all groups emerge with equivalent competence, having mastered the learning objectives for the training.

Digressions are diversions from the intended topic that may (or may not) work against achieving the learning objectives. A digression is when a learner accidentally or deliberately diverts the presentation into an unrelated area by asking a question or telling a story. This can be called *taking the group off on a tangent* (also known by other names, such as "going on a wild goose chase" or "going on safari").

Digressions are natural. They occur because learners may associate one topic in the training with other topics they have curiosity about. Alternatively, the training course may hit on a topic about which participants have axes to grind, and they use the training program as a bully pulpit to state their positions, try to build support, or to vent their feelings.

When digressions are short and do not derail the logical relationship among topics in the training course, they can be beneficial because they may introduce new, insightful, and highly relevant perspectives. However, when diversions become lengthy, they jeopardize the chance that the training objectives will be met. Worse yet, some learners in a group may not want to pursue the unrelated topic, and they will feel that the time is wasted and will usually say so—either during the course or on end-of-course participant evaluations.

CORRECTING DIGRESSIONS

Take corrective action when you sense that a digression is becoming too lengthy or is beginning to wear out its welcome with most learners in a group. If you have made the digression by telling a story, for example, cut it short and move right back to the topic. If a participant made the digression, then interrupt him or her and say something like "this is quite interesting, but it does not seem related to the topic. Let's move on so that we can achieve our course objectives in the time we have." As another option, ask the participant if it would be okay to return to that topic when more time was available for it. Often people do not realize that their well-intentioned comments, questions, stories, or observations have turned into digressions. However, typically, when learners recognize that they have strayed from the intended topic, they are more willing to return to it.

Redirecting digressions back to the planned topic for discussion helps the learners stay focused. It also gives the impression that you are well organized with specific goals and tasks that need to be achieved. On the other hand, when you allow digressions to run unchecked, you give the appearance of being disorganized.

LOGICAL FLOW OF THE PRESENTATION

The overall flow of the presentation should be derived from the instructional design of the training. However, the actual word usage, sentence choice, and organization often comes from the trainer. In other words, designers create the overall structure that guides training, but you must implement that design through the delivery process. Words and sentences used during delivery should be carefully chosen and arranged logically to achieve smooth and even flow. When the flow of delivery is not logical to learners, it can lead to frustration because they become confused and unable to make sense of the content or connections being made between content points.

CONCLUDING STATEMENTS

Concluding statements are an important, but often neglected, part of a training course. They are important because they provide closure. Concluding statements may appear at the end of a large segment of content or immediately preceding transitions. (The topic of summaries, which help to provide learners with guidance, was discussed earlier in this chapter.)

Concluding statements, like summaries, bring closure to a delivery segment. When concluding statements are absent from delivery, learners are left hanging. A useful strategy is to plan concluding statements or points before you deliver the course or section.

Here are some practical tips for concluding statements:

- Check for understanding. Say something like, "We have now reached the end of this section (or course). We have covered topics a, b, and c. What further questions do you have about this material before we move on to the related topic of d (or before we adjourn)?"

- Try to stimulate creativity. Say something like, "We have now reached the end of this section (or course). But, I wonder, are there more creative ways to view this topic? What are your thoughts on specific ways we could do that?"

USING ANECDOTES, STORIES, ANALOGIES, AND HUMOR EFFECTIVELY

Anecdotes, stories, analogies, and humor can enliven your training, making it memorable and interesting. When used appropriately, they can reinforce key points and drive home important information. They are especially useful for showing the practical applications of otherwise abstract ideas. This section describes each technique and provides strategies for incorporating them effectively into your presentation. Use the job aid appearing in Exhibit 7–5 to help you plan to use stories, anecdotes, and humor.

STORIES AND ANECDOTES

Storytelling is an ancient art that has been used to pass information from one person to the next for millennia. A *story* is a real or fictitious tale told to convey meaning. An *anecdote* is similar to a story but is generally shorter and more direct. Stories and anecdotes used in training

Exhibit 7–5
Job aid for using anecdotes, stories, and humor effectively.

Approximate length of anecdote, story, or humor: _____

What is the purpose or the key message of the story?

What is your opening statement? How will you gain the attention of the audience?

How will you bridge into your key message?

How will you close your story? How will you drive the main point(s) home?

What are your transitional phrases? When will you use them?

What emotion(s) do you plan to convey? How?

What props will you use? How and when?

What gestures will you use for impact? When?

should have a specific direction or purpose. They should not be told for their mere entertainment value.

Stories and anecdotes about people and situations are helpful in organizations because they can communicate important information about the corporate culture, the taken-for-granted assumptions about the "right" and "wrong" ways to "do things around here." For instance, a story about a company president who arrives at the office at 5:30 A.M. on a snowy winter morning to shovel the sidewalk could be told to convey a number of corporate values, such as the importance of work ethic, the value of having concern for employees, and the organization's tradition of leadership sacrifice. Some stories are told so often that they become exaggerated, transforming people into myths and legends and making events more dramatic than they were in reality.

When stories or anecdotes are told without an express intent they can leave learners confused as to how they relate to the content of the program. For this reason, if you choose to use stories or anecdotes, first consider the purpose that will be served. Next, select a story or anecdote that will achieve this purpose. If you are developing the story, then first consider the one or few key points to be conveyed based on the predetermined purpose, and then design the story around those key bullets. Lay this initial groundwork before incorporating the story or anecdote into the presentation. The next section discusses important delivery considerations.

PRACTICE TELLING STORIES IN ADVANCE

Some people are natural, gifted storytellers. Others find telling stories or anecdotes difficult and therefore use them minimally. Whether or not you are one of the gifted, it helps to practice telling your story before you deliver it to a group in a training session. *How* you deliver the story is key. Practice helps you make the story concise. It also helps you learn how to make smooth transitions, keep elements of the story in the right sequence, and incorporate appropriate nonverbal behaviors—such as gestures and facial expressions—into the delivery. Practice makes the delivery smooth and gives it maximum impact.

USE YOUR EXPERIENCES

Direct experiences are usually easy to relate because they represent a recollection of your memory of those occurrences. Dale Carnegie, one of the gurus of public speaking, states that one of the cardinal rules of public speaking is to talk about a topic you have earned the right to discuss, and he cites experience as one method for earning that right. Experience can often be recounted in great detail. Some memorable stories incorporated during training are tales of real, or sometimes exaggerated, events experienced or observed by the trainer. These events may be positive, negative, challenging, humorous, or interesting, and they are designed to convey a specific message to the listeners that tie back to the content and to the objectives.

But let us be clear. If you do not plan a story or anecdote but rather tell an impromptu story, you risk creating a diversion. Make sure that the point of the story is clear and is related to your topic, or it becomes a *war story* or (if illustrating a nightmare scenario about something gone badly awry) a *horror story*. Stories told effectively and on point may also illustrate your own adherence to the principle illustrated in the story while building your credibility as someone who lives by the principles he or she teaches to others.

USING LEARNERS' STORIES

In a training session, you are not necessarily the only one who has had firsthand experience with the topic. The learners may also have had that experience. Consequently, you can tap into that experience by asking the learners to share their experiences by telling stories or anecdotes to your group. These stories are examples, told in the words of the learners without rehearsal, and they can be powerfully instructive. Further, you can adopt stories and anecdotes provided by learners and incorporate them into future training sessions. If you do that, however, you should either obtain permission or approval from the person to use the story or else carefully disguise identities.

Such stories, when told originally by a well-respected or highly regarded individual, often have instant credibility with a group of learners. Telling a group of learners, "Several weeks ago our CEO sat in this seat and told the group a story, and I'd like to share with you the experience that she related to us," would be likely to gain their attention and command interest.

How can you solicit stories or anecdotes from learners? The simplest approach is to ask them to share experiences they have had. This off-the-top-of-their-head approach can yield spontaneous expressions of thoughts and feelings. The stories can be highly entertaining and instructive. But be careful: Use this approach only if you are certain that there are veteran workers in your audience. Soliciting stories from novices will lead to uncomfortable silences, since they have had no experiences and thus have no stories.

Even when the learners are experienced and have powerful stories to share, you must take care that the storyteller stays on track and does not talk in circles. Another danger you must watch for is that some storytellers will use this opportunity to drone on forever or get on a soapbox. In these cases, others may begin to roll their eyes, drift off, or in other ways lose interest and become distracted. When this happens, you'll need to intervene and either cut the story short or help the speaker focus and deliver the key message.

A true story is in order here. One of the authors was teaching a course on career planning to executive MBAs in China. At one point, he asked participants to tell short stories from their experiences that illustrated what their career goals were and why they considered those goals important. One student took the opportunity to spend over ten minutes telling an inspirational story from the life of Buddha and using that to justify his avowed career goal of "converting the world to Buddhism." The author still remembers the rolling eyes, the silent laughter, the whispered comments, and the agonized looks he got from other students during the tortured time that the student droned in a monotone to tell his story. The point is that the author learned from the experience that it is important to give people advance cues about how long their stories should be and what will happen if they devote too much time. Now he introduces that section by saying "before we begin, let me remind you to keep your story short—under two minutes—or else we will cut you off and move on to the next person so that everyone has an opportunity to speak."

GATHERING CRITICAL INCIDENT EXPERIENCES

Another method you can use to solicit stories from learners is to ask them to use the *critical incident technique* to structure storytelling, either by writing about or telling of a *difficult situation* they have encountered in their work lives. This method gives learners an organized structure to follow in telling their story. You can solicit critical incidents and then read the stories to others or use them as guides when conveying the information. The written critical incident technique can be useful for giving structure to the story and focusing the topic in specific directions. In the critical incident method, learners are asked to recall an experience they have had in a specific area of focus and describe it in detail. Incidentally, we used the critical incident method in the research study we conducted for this book. We asked practitioners to respond to the following:

Please describe the *worst experience* you have had related to the delivery of training. Provide as much detail as possible including what happened, who was involved (positions only), what you did, and the results.

Please describe the *most typical problem* you face on a regular basis related to the delivery of training. Provide as much detail as possible including the situation, how you handle it, and the results.

We then used the responses we obtained from trainers as the critical incidents that appear in this book. They relate real-life experiences, which in many cases are very enlightening because they provide common and worst-case scenarios of what trainers encounter when delivering training. Virtually any subject could be used to solicit critical incidents. For example, critical incidents could be gathered about such topics as customer service, new technology, or dealing with a manager or supervisor. Critical incidents need not focus only on negative experiences or problems but can be used to gather positive information as well. For example, learners could be asked to describe in detail the best treatment they have received as customers. Regardless of the content, responses that learners provide to critical incidents can be used in training in various ways. You can have the learners read stories aloud, share them with others in a small group, or use them during future training sessions.

ANALOGIES

An *analogy* is a comparison between two things that are otherwise dissimilar. For example, a supervisor who is described as a "battle-ax" is easily recognizable as someone who uses an autocratic, traditional management style. Analogies are useful in training because they simplify complex concepts or ideas. For example, in a basic computer hardware course, a trainer uses the brain as an analogy for the microprocessor chip of a computer. Continuing the analogy, the brain can receive information, such as numbers; perform calculations on the numbers, such as adding them together; and produce a result, such as the sum of the numbers. The workings of the brain in this example could be compared to many microprocessor functions. Obviously analogies will tend to break down if extended too far, but they can be useful in illustrating a complex idea or an abstract concept through a notion with which most learners are familiar.

When you use analogies, make sure that they are clear. Tell learners that you are using an analogy and then isolate key elements of two unlike items for comparison. You should also consider aspects of the analogy that do not hold true or ways in which the analogy could produce conflicting information or confusion. In the example of the brain and microprocessor, a learner might ask if the microprocessor has the ability to reason since the brain has that capacity. The trainer in this case should be prepared to deal with such questions or others that might arise about the analogy. The job aid shown in Exhibit 7–6 can be used to assist you with effectively incorporating analogies into delivery.

HUMOR

Humor includes jokes, tricks, stunts, funny stories, or other actions that are used for entertainment as well as for learning. Humor helps to create a relaxed, informal, and energized learning climate, such as the trainer who enters the room riding a unicycle or wearing Groucho Marx–type glasses. In addition, humor and tricks can be effective ways to illustrate key information. For example, a trainer may juggle more and more balls in the air until they eventually fall to the ground as a way to make the point that the job of the supervisor is often like a juggling act.

As with storytelling, using humor is an art. Two types of humor that can be used are *planned humor* and *spontaneous humor. Planned humor* involves predetermining a time during training when humor, such as a joke or funny incident, will be used. This type of humor can be practiced and refined in advance to ensure evoking the intended response from learners. *Spontaneous humor,* as the name suggests, is unplanned and arises during delivery. This type of humor is often the result of something that happens during delivery, such as a participant comment, or a faux pas that a quick-witted trainer converts into humor. Such humor is often without specific purpose or intent but can be used to foster a relaxed or energized learning climate.

INAPPROPRIATE HUMOR

Avoid inappropriate humor that is uncomplimentary to specific people or groups, and avoid so-called practical jokes that may hurt someone. If you must use humor that puts people down, direct it at yourself. Otherwise, stick to humor that makes the point without taking the risk of offending anyone. When in doubt, ask other people before you use the joke or humorous story.

STRATEGIES FOR INCORPORATING HUMOR

There are several strategies you can use when incorporating humor into the training situation. These guidelines apply primarily to

Exhibit 7–6
Job aid for using analogies effectively.

What is the purpose or the key message you want to convey through the analogy?

Does the analogy make your message or concept clearer? How do you know? Have you tested it on anyone?

What concepts are you comparing?

What are the similarities of the concepts? How will you convey this information?

What are the dissimilarities of the concepts? (Where might the analogy break down?) How will you convey this information?

How will you drive your main point(s) home?

Will you use an object or prop to demonstrate the analogy? Will the prop make your analogy clearer?

planned humor. As in using stories or anecdotes, use humor with a specific purpose in mind. What is the overall objective or purpose of the joke? Is it to gain attention? Is it to convey an important content point in a humorous way? Is it simply to entertain learners? You should be aware that using humor for entertainment purposes only can be dangerous. When this happens, learners may leave the session feeling positive about the experience, but when they reflect on the actual content and application of that learning, they may discover that it was lacking. For this reason, use humor in training to serve a specific purpose, such as reinforcing a content point or energizing the group. As with stories and anecdotes, practice telling the joke. Do that to ensure maximum impact.

TIMING OF HUMOR

Often the success of humor in training hinges upon its timing. This is especially relevant with spontaneous humor, which arises from the situation. If you are able to incorporate humor as it presents itself, it can be highly effective because it is genuine and relevant. Situations that might be the catalyst for spontaneous humor include unplanned mishaps, such as mistakes in the materials or inappropriate environmental noises. In essence, you are playing off something that was not supposed to happen, diminishing its potentially harmful impact while relaxing and energizing the learners.

With planned humor, timing is critical as well. A joke or funny story that is told out of place may fall flat because it was delivered too early or too late. When planned humor is not timed well, learners may not make the connection between the content and the humor, if the purpose was to reinforce content. This may lead to confusion.

The way in which you introduce humor is important as well. Sometimes when you begin to tell a funny story some learners may not be tuned in and therefore miss enough of the story to minimize its overall impact. Take time to set up the use of humor to ensure that you have everyone's attention. One strategy is to pause or remain silent prior to delivery. As mentioned earlier, such silence can capture interest and focus learners' attention. During delivery, incorporate appropriate and matching nonverbal behaviors to fully maximize delivery, such as eye contact with the learners during delivery, gestures and movement to dramatize the humor, and facial expressions to complement your verbal language. During delivery, also attempt to gauge learner reaction and adjust appropriately. For example, if some learners appear to be drifting, increase your level of enthusiasm or change your voice.

ENDING HUMOR

The final aspect of using humor is knowing how to end it. If the punchline to a joke falls flat or is lost, or if the funny story ends abruptly, the overall impact is reduced. Therefore, pay close attention to the ending, which often contains the key learning point. Humor may be unsuccessful for a variety of reasons. When a joke or other humor does not achieve its intended purpose, you must attempt to recover. Sometimes ineffective planned humor gives you an opportunity to incorporate spontaneous humor. For example, if you bumble through telling a joke and it fails, saying, "I should have let someone else tell that one!" may help in recovery. A statement like this can add humor to an otherwise embarrassing situation, and it also demonstrates to the learners that you can laugh at yourself. This is similar to admitting mistakes. If the intent of the failed humor was to make a content point, then you may need to address that issue by saying, "The point I was trying to make through that miserable joke was…" This ensures that, although the method of making the point was not successful, the point received enough attention and reinforcement.

The use of stories, anecdotes, analogies, and humor is an art as well as a science. It is a science because of its potential to enhance learning, and it therefore should be designed and incorporated with precisely defined objectives in mind. It is also an art because creativity is essential and the difference between success and failure in using humor is often dependent on subtle nuances that are difficult to reproduce.

DO NOT INSULT, OFFEND, OR CONFUSE LEARNERS

Regardless of the technique being incorporated into delivery there are some key elements that must be considered. Make sure that no learners are insulted or offended by the story, anecdote, analogy, or humor. Some learners may take offense because a joke offends their culture, race, gender, religion, or other characteristic. Knowingly using potentially offensive humor can hamper learning and raise serious ethical questions. Further, if such humor is unwittingly used, the damage it causes may be irreparable. Therefore, think carefully before using such techniques.

In addition to avoiding potentially offensive stories, anecdotes, or humor, make sure that jokes or other stories are free of jargon or technical terminology that could confuse learners. Or, if you must use such terminology, be sure to clarify its meaning.

SUMMARY

Many issues contribute to your ability to demonstrate effective presentation skills, as this chapter has shown. When judging the relative success of a presentation, always think first of how well it supports the achievement of learning objectives. This chapter has described and emphasized the importance of the following:

- Adhering to allotted time.

- Using your voice effectively.

- Using nonverbal behavior to support training information.

- Organizing the logical flow of a presentation.

- Using stories, anecdotes, analogies, and humor effectively.

STRATEGY LIST

Actionable Strategies to Improve Training Effectiveness:

USE YOUR VOICE EFFECTIVELY

- ❏ Vary your vocal tones to convey enthusiasm, sincerity, seriousness, and other emotions.

- ❏ Use volume, rate, tempo, and inflection to ensure that everyone can hear, to stimulate interest, and to enhance your message.

- ❏ Identify distracting speech mannerisms ("ahh," "like," "you know") and attempt to correct them. Ask a co-worker to watch you during training and point them out to you. Learn to substitute these mannerisms with silence.

- ❏ Use microphones when you are training a large audience. Caution: Turn microphones "off" when not in use.

USE APPROPRIATE NONVERBALS

Eye Contact

- ❏ Use eye contact to demonstrate one-on-one attention to learners and to draw learners into the training process.

- ❏ Avoid making eye contact with some learners and not others.

❏ Scan the room on a regular basis to periodically make eye contact with every learner. Caution: Do not pause too long or stare at learners.

❏ Recognize a lack of eye contact from learners may mean they do not want to participate, they are bored, or they are distracted. This may signal a need to take a break.

❏ Ask learners or colleagues for feedback on how well you make eye contact.

Gestures

❏ Use gestures to support or replace your message.

❏ Test gestures with colleagues and learners for their appropriateness and impact.

❏ Ask for feedback regarding distracting gestures you may exhibit.

❏ Practice, rehearse, and drill to get your gestures right.

❏ Be certain that your gestures match your message. Ask for feedback from your co-workers and learners.

Silence

❏ Use silence before or after important points, following a question, or at other appropriate times during delivery to arouse interest and stimulate curiosity.

❏ Use silence before a statement to convey its importance.

❏ Use silence to encourage learner reflection on your message.

❏ Use silence to evoke emotion among your listeners.

❏ Use silence after questions to encourage learner response and participation.

Distance

❏ Move closer to learners to create a more intimate and informal learning climate. Caution: Be careful not to invade someone's air space by getting too close.

❏ Move away from learners to create a more formal learning climate.

❏ Change your proximity to learners throughout training to match the message you plan to send and to add variety.

Using Props Effectively

❏ Use props to support or reinforce learning and achieve the course objectives.

❏ Use props to gain interest, provide a big picture, focus attention, or to provide learners with a hands-on opportunity.

❏ Be aware that using props can take learner attention away from what you are saying and become distracting.

❏ Determine how and when to use props before training occurs. Ask for feedback from co-workers regarding your timing and use of props.

❏ Determine in advance how the prop will be displayed or passed around to learners.

❏ Use props that are relevant to the training and familiar to learners.

❏ When you are finished using the prop, remove it from view so that it does not become distracting.

❏ Avoid using props that could be potentially dangerous.

STRATEGIES TO GUIDE AND FACILITATE LEARNING

❏ Link the training content and activities to the course objectives.

❏ Use examples and content that are tied to the organization and to the learners' experience and work environment.

❏ Provide learners with an overview or big picture of the training at the beginning of the course. This can be in the form of a flow-chart, outline/agenda, or a graphic.

❏ Provide learners with summaries at the end of training segments to help them synthesize important learning points.

☐ Use transitions between training segments to demonstrate the link or connections between them. Transitions provide a bridge from one topic to the next.

☐ Manage time so that each segment is covered in sufficient detail to achieve learning objectives.

☐ Use digressions in the conversation to make or enhance your message without derailing your learning objectives.

☐ Use concluding statements at the end of segments to provide closure to a topic.

ENLIVEN YOUR TRAINING

Stories/Anecdotes

☐ Use stories and anecdotes to communicate important information and reinforce concepts and ideas.

☐ Link stories and anecdotes to the objectives. Identify this in advance and test your strategies with several coworkers.

☐ Practice telling stories in advance to ensure smooth and natural flow.

☐ Base stories on your actual experiences.

☐ Ask learners to volunteer sharing their relevant experiences and stories with the groups.

Analogies

☐ Use analogies to simplify complex concepts or issues.

☐ Make sure that your analogies are clear, familiar to learners, and easy to connect to the analogy and the concept you are attempting to convey.

Humor

☐ Use humor to lighten the mood, emphasize a point, illustrate key information, or enliven your audience.

☐ Ask for feedback from several co-workers regarding humor you plan to use. Ask them if the humor is appropriate, funny, and supportive of the message.

❏ Be aware of your own ability and limitations to be humorous and do not attempt to exceed them.

❏ Avoid inappropriate humor that is uncomplimentary to specific people or groups. Caution: Do not allow anyone to be the target of humor. Stick to humor that makes the point without offending someone.

❏ Use a period of silence before using humor to capture learners' attention. This will prevent them from missing key information.

CHAPTER 8

DEMONSTRATING EFFECTIVE QUESTIONING SKILLS AND TECHNIQUES

SKILLS ASSESSMENT

Take a moment to review the competency and associated performances that will be covered in this chapter. Consider your current level of proficiency in the competency as a whole as well as each performance and check the items where you feel you need to improve. As you read the chapter, concentrate on those areas most in need of development.

Competency:

❐ Demonstrate effective questioning skills and techniques.

Associated Performances:

❐ Use appropriate question types and levels.

❐ Direct questions appropriately.

❐ Use active listening techniques.

❐ Repeat, rephrase, or restructure questions.

❐ Provide opportunity and adequate time for learners to state questions, comments, and concerns and respond to questions.

❐ Judge the adequacy of instructional questions.

Asking questions, as we mentioned in Chapters Six and Seven, is key to your success in your role as an instructor in training. Because asking questions is so important, this chapter focuses on that competency. The chapter asks and answers the following questions:

- What purposes are served by questions, and why are they so important?

- What are the types of questions?

- What levels of questions exist?

- How should questions be directed appropriately?

- How is active listening related to questioning?

- How can questions be successfully repeated, rephrased, and restructured?

- How should you provide learners with time to respond?

WHY ARE QUESTIONS SO IMPORTANT?

The art of asking questions has enjoyed a venerable history in Western civilization.

Socrates, one of the most famous teachers of all time, never lectured his students at all.

As Plato showed in his *Dialogues*, Socrates did nothing more than keep asking questions—questions that were directed to his students with such skill and panache that they are the envy of trial lawyers even today.

Questions serve various purposes in training, and they are important for each purpose that they serve. One purpose is to encourage active participation and involvement among learners. A quick way to turn a boring lecture into an exciting discussion is to stop *telling* and start *asking*. Questions are open invitations to learners to respond. When learners respond, they accept the responsibility to take part in their own learning process. In acknowledging the powerful role that questions can play in encouraging interaction, presentation expert Dianna Booher, of Booher Consultants Inc. in Dallas/Fort Worth, observes, "A reflective question followed by a long pause can be a more effective way for participants to examine new ideas than to play three games without their brains in gear."[1]

A second purpose of questions is to capture learner interest and hold attention. Questions focus learners on what you want them to look at and think about. They can also encourage creative thought, transforming learners into instructors in their own right. Another master presenter, Lance Dublin, of EPS Solutions in San Francisco, urges trainers to "be a provocateur, not a presenter." He encourages presenters to try delivering most of your content through a series of questions rather than statements. For each slide, develop a provocative question that will unveil or lead people to answers or points you want to make."[2]

A third purpose of questions is to gauge learners' understanding. The response to a question shows how much a learner has comprehended, it thereby giving you feedback about the program. Armed with this feedback, you can take corrective action when necessary to ensure that learners understand important information.

A fourth purpose of questions is to elicit learners' decisions and preferences. A key premise in adult learning theory is that adult learners should take an active role in their learning process. In one sense, that means learners should be given a say in decisions affecting them and the learning process. Questions can facilitate the learners' decision-making and can afford them opportunities to state their preferences.

Asking questions effectively is a more difficult competency to master than it might appear to be. In fact, some authorities regard it as one of the most difficult to do well. In our survey study of training practitioners, they rated this competency as the fourth most difficult to demonstrate. One reason this competency is more difficult than others is that trainers are presented with the challenge of striking a balance between asking questions that challenge learners and asking questions that build learner confidence. For example, a trainer may ask several probing questions to push the learner to thinking about connections and relationships between different principles. However, if the trainer pushes too hard, it may make learners feel incompetent, diminishing their confidence. Remember that each learner is different and will respond according to his or her own level of comprehension. It is your responsibility to identify this level. One strategy for accomplishing this is to float several test questions and listen to the responses you receive to determine the learners' current level of comprehension.

WHAT ARE THE TYPES OF QUESTIONS?

There are numerous types of questions at your disposal as an instructor in a training session. This section defines and illustrates these question types, which are also summarized in Exhibit 8–1.

CLOSED AND OPEN QUESTIONS

A *closed question*, sometimes called a closed-ended question, is designed to elicit a "yes" or "no" response. A simple example is "Do you have any questions?" That is a closed question because the participant

Exhibit 8–1 Types of questions: characteristics and uses.		
Types	**Characteristics**	**Uses**
Open	Open questions require respondents to elaborate with a narrative response.	Open questions enable trainers to gauge the level of understanding among the learners. They also encourage involvement and participation.
Closed	Closed questions are typically answered with a "yes" or "no" response.	Closed questions can be used to drive a point home, gauge opinions among learners, introduce topics, or change topics.
Overhead	Overhead questions are questions asked to the entire group. They are often rhetorical.	Overhead questions can focus the learning to a particular topic and encourage participation. They can also be used to avoid embarrassing a learner who gives an incorrect response.
Direct	Direct questions are directed toward an individual learner.	Direct questions can be used by the trainer to gauge the understanding of an individual learner. They can also be used to gain learner attention or involve a nonparticipative learner. One danger with direct questions is that they may cause embarrassment by putting a learner on the spot.
Reversed	Reversed questions are statements rather than questions. These statements paraphrase questions asked by learners to ensure that the question is presented very clearly.	Reversed questions clarify learner questions so that they hear and understand the question. Additionally, they help to ensure that the trainer is answering the correct question.
Redirected	A redirected question is a technique used by trainers to redirect a question to the group instead of answering it.	Redirected questions can encourage involvement and reflection as well as create ownership of problems by shifting the responsibility of knowledge transfer from the trainer to the learners. Also useful when the trainer is unsure of the answer.

must answer with either a "yes" or a "no." Closed questions often start with words like *do, are,* or *is.* Other examples of this type of question are "Is everyone ready to move on to the next module?" and "Are you comfortable with the skill practice?"

An *open question*, sometimes called an open-ended question, is designed to evoke a response other than a simple yes or no. Open questions encourage people to elaborate. A simple example: "What questions do you have?" That is an open question that cannot be answered with a "yes" or "no." Instead, the participant must provide an essay response. Open questions typically begin with certain words including *what, why, how, when,* or *where.* Examples of open questions are "Why do you believe some people resist the idea of merging with another bank?" and "How would you go about responding to a customer who berates you?"

RECOGNIZING WHEN TO USE OPEN AND CLOSED QUESTIONS

Both closed and open questions are appropriate to use during training. One type is not better or worse than the other, and both serve useful purposes. What is important is to know when to use each type and how to apply the skills to use each type of questions appropriately.

Use closed questions to gauge participant reactions or opinions. For example, you could ask, "Is teamwork important?" The yes or no responses to this closed question, with a request for a show of hands, can help you to take an on-the-spot poll to measure learner opinions about the importance of teamwork. Later, if appropriate, you can follow that up with an open question to explore the issue in greater depth. It is also typical to use closed questions near the end of a training segment or when you want to limit questions to only those topics about which learners feel strongly. A question such as "Are there any questions or commnets before we end for the day?" can minimize the chances for a long-winded response because it informs learners that the class will end if there are no questions. This should prompt learners to ask only questions that are critical or that they feel strongly about.

Open questions are a premier method for expanding the discussion of a topic. As such, open questions are useful for encouraging participation and involvement among the learners. For example, if you ask the group of learners "How do you feel about teamwork?" learners will be more likely to provide a lengthier reply. Open questions gain learners' attention, especially at the opening of a training segment. When you pose an open question to the group it represents something that learners must attend to, think about, and focus on. In effect, it stimulates cognitive processing. In contrast, opening a segment with a statement or a series of statements does not necessarily demand focus and allows learners to be more passive. Imagine sitting in the beginning of a training class. The trainer begins by introducing herself and telling you why the topic of the course is important to you. Now imagine the same course but instead of the trainer telling you why the course is important to you, she asks you to tell her why it is important to you. If the training program is on measuring employee performance, for example, the trainer could ask, "Why is it important to measure employee performance?" In doing this, she has changed the course from passive learning to a more engaging and interesting environment by simply asking an open question.

Inexperienced trainers have a tendency to use too many closed questions, and you may find that to be a problem for you at first. For example, when you want to find out if learners have questions you might ask, "Does anyone have any questions?" Often this closed question does not yield any responses, leading you to conclude that there are no questions. In reality, however, learners may have questions, but don't feel encouraged to ask them, given your approach. Maybe you use closed questions because you assume that the mere act of posing questions is what is important. But that is not the case. Open questions are far more effective than closed questions in building participation. In the example above, you could rephrase the query to "What questions do you have?" (followed by silence), and you would find that much more effective in prompting learner participation. Using that type of open question can also be less threatening, because it sends a message that you as the trainer are expecting questions, thus putting the learner more at ease and able to admit to having questions. The closed question implies only that there could be questions, leaving the learner to believe that he or she might be the only person with questions.

To improve your questioning skill, begin by assessing what question types you ask most frequently. If you discover that most questions you pose are closed and you would like to increase the number of open questions you ask, practice by consciously transforming closed to open questions by restating them and beginning them with words such as *what*, *why*, or *how*. Exhibit 8–2 supplies examples of closed questions that have been converted into open questions.

Additionally, once a closed question has been asked, it can be converted into an open question by using follow-up inquiries such as *Why?*, *To what degree?*, *How?*, or *How would you explain that?* Doing

Exhibit 8–2
Converting closed questions into open questions.

Closed Questions	Open Questions
Do you agree with these principles?	Tell me why you agree or disagree with these principles?
Do you have any questions?	What questions do you have at this point?
Is this clear?	What about this is not clear?
Does everyone understand?	Can someone explain this to me in their own words?

this enables you to probe deeper into the learners' knowledge to determine their level of understanding of the issues at hand. Consider the following dialogue where a trainer starts with a closed question and then leads into an open question. This method of questioning also allows a trainer to identify those who know the answer without putting them on the spot. As you read further, note the similarities between a closed question and an open question:

TRAINER: *Can this principle be applied to your everyday work?*

JOSH: *Yes.*

TRAINER: *Josh, tell me more. How can it be applied and how does that differ from the way you are currently doing it?*

JOSH: *Well, it can be applied by…*

OVERHEAD AND DIRECT QUESTIONS

In addition to closed and open questions, there are overhead and direct questions. An *overhead question* is asked of an entire learner group. For example, "Who has seen the movie *The Shining*?" is an overhead question because it is posed to the entire group and not just one individual.

A *direct question*, as its name implies, is directed at an individual learner. For example, "John, do you know what type of valve connection this is?" is a direct question asked of John. That is not just a direct question. It is also a closed question because it prompts a "yes" or "no" reply from John. Overhead and direct questions serve different purposes and can be either open or closed.

OVERHEAD QUESTIONS

Overhead questions tend to increase the likelihood of producing a correct response from the learners. An overhead question often represents an invitation to the entire group of learners to respond if they are comfortable and if they believe they have a correct or appropriate answer. Those who respond to an overhead question are usually confident that they have a correct answer. Otherwise, individuals would be unlikely to answer. The actual answer may not be correct, but the probability of accuracy tends to increase when people volunteer to respond to overhead questions.

When you ask an overhead question and no one answers, reframe the question, repeat it, provide clues as to the answer, or assume that no one actually knows the answer and therefore decide to provide the correct answer with a supporting explanation. When too many learners try to respond, you can select the learner who answers first. When you do that, however, you risk making other learners feel excluded. To deal with that perception, say something like, "Let's start with Victor." That indicates to the others that they will have a chance to provide their response after Victor provides his. Another tactic is to acknowledge the first learner who attempts to respond and select that person to provide the answer.

Remember not to overuse overhead questions, because learners may get bored with this technique and stop answering them. This is especially true if the overhead questions are remedial. For example, imagine a training situation where the trainer always starts by saying, "Are we happy to be here?" or "Are we ready to get started?" The first time or two, learners might respond. But soon responding will seem silly and learners may begin to stare back at the trainer or respond sarcastically.

THE DANGERS AND BENEFITS OF DIRECT QUESTIONS

Unlike overhead questions, direct questions single out individuals. They can be risky for that reason. A direct question can startle individuals and cause them to answer incorrectly or draw a blank. It also puts a person under the spotlight and may therefore cause discomfort. In this way, direct questions may remind some learners of negative experiences they had while in school. Direct questions can create a threatening, psychologically uncomfortable learning climate as well. On the positive side, however, direct questions can condition learners to speak up.

Learners are more likely to concentrate and pay close attention when they know they might be singled out and questioned without warning. Chapter Five discussed the technique of questioning as a way to deal with learner behavior problems. Direct questions can be excellent tools by which to accomplish this goal. Direct questions can also be used effectively to assess the comprehension of an otherwise quiet individual. Finally, direct questions can also be a way to involve a non-participative member of the group. For example, you could attempt to draw out a silent learner by saying "Jill, do you have anything to add?" or "Chris, you look like you wanted to say something."

STRATEGIES FOR USING DIRECT QUESTIONS EFFECTIVELY

Use direct questions sensitively to ensure positive outcomes. To do that effectively, forewarn learners that you will use this technique. That gives them a clue to pay close attention so that they are not caught completely off guard. In addition, when you use direct questions, deliver them in a positive way. Do not set out to embarrass people; rather, use direct questions to encourage learners to pay closer attention and participate. You might even want to qualify your direct question by briefly stating why you are asking them. Look at the following examples. Observe how much less threatening the question can be when softened with a qualifying statement. This technique turns the "test-like" questions into nonthreatening conversations.

TRAINER: *Don, since you work in purchasing, can you tell us your perception of how the recent deregulation has affected our vendor relationships?*

TRAINER: *Valerie, in light of our conversation at lunch, what do you think will be our next step in the assimilation process?*

TRAINER: *Paul, with your background in aeronautics, how will this new procedure affect the aerospace industry?*

The way in which you handle the first few direct questions sets the tone. If participants are not made to look or feel foolish, they are more willing to answer questions. You can also tell them that they can "take a rain check" or "pass" on a question, thereby avoiding the chance that they might be embarrassed by giving them an "out." That will keep the learning climate positive and upbeat. Another strategy you can use to enliven the question-asking process is to throw a beanbag or sponge ball to a person, indicating that they should respond to your question. For the next question that person gets to toss the ball to the person of their choosing. A rule you can add is that the ball must always be passed to someone who has not yet answered. This ensures that everyone is eventually involved.

REVERSED QUESTIONS

A *reversed question*, sometimes called a *reflective question*, is typically used when a learner makes a comment or asks a question. It is essentially a restatement, by the trainer, of the learner's original question. Sometimes when a learner asks something it may be confusing to other learners—and even, perhaps, to the trainer. The primary purpose of a reversed question is to clarify what the learner has asked. If the question is lengthy or contains mutiple questions (sometimes called a *double-barreled question*), it may become difficult to understand. A reverse question is introduced in such instances to focus attention on what has been asked and to make it clear and succinct. You may also want to break problems down into several smaller, more focused parts so that you are sure to capture all of the intent or concern behind the questions being asked.

Reversed questions are helpful to learners because they tend to clarify questions. However, they are not without danger. One problem is that when restated, the meaning of the original question can be lost or altered by the trainer in an honest attempt to make it clearer. That can provoke anger, resentment, or frustration from some participants. The best strategy is probably to present a reverse question and then ask the questioner if the reversed question has adequately captured the meaning of the original. When you use a microphone, you should repeat questions. In that way, you ensure that everyone can hear it. A reversed question is appropriate in such cases because a summary of the original question is sufficient to convey its content to others and because it would probably be difficult, if not impossible, to repeat it verbatim.

REDIRECTED QUESTIONS

A *redirected question* is a technique that you can use when a learner asks a question or makes a comment. Instead of answering the question, as many trainers might be tempted to do, you simply redirect it to others. Questions can be redirected to several targets, of course: to the person who initiated the question, to another learner, or to the learning group as a whole. Below is an example of a trainer redirecting a question to the person who asked the question.

> **MYRNA:** *I have a question for you: how does what you're saying relate to the philosophy of empowerment?*
>
> **TRAINER:** *That's a good question, Myrna. How do you think it relates to empowerment?*

Here is an example of a question that the trainer redirects to the entire learning group:

> **BOB:** *Do you really believe our CEO is going to adopt this idea of "open book" management?*
>
> **TRAINER:** *Bob, thanks for the question. Instead of giving my opinion, let me ask the group. Does the group think our CEO is on board?*

There are several purposes for redirected questions. One is to encourage learners to take ownership of the problem and formulate answers rather than rely on the trainer to provide all the answers or the one "correct" answer. Spoon-feeding learners will not teach them to think on their own or internalize the answer to a question.

Another purpose of a redirected question is to avoid informing learners that they have given an incorrect response. When a learner gives an inaccurate response—or makes a questionable comment—you can ask, "What do others think about that response?" Doing that does not place the learner in an embarrassing spotlight and provides others a chance to respond correctly. You can also use a redirected question when you do not know the correct answer to a question yourself. You can simply state, "I'm not really sure about the answer to that, so what do others think?" That should not be done too frequently because it risks damaging your credibility. As an alternative, you can simply say "That's a good question, what do others think?" That redirects the questions without bringing your own credibility into doubt. It also permits you extra time to reflect on the question.

Redirected questions can also be guided in several directions. You can refocus a question back to the questioner by asking, "What do *you* think the answer is?" Doing that can help a learner work through an issue to obtain clarity and comprehension. Such involvement can result in deeper understanding because the person was not provided with a quick answer but was invited to think it through to arrive at his or her own solution.

Be sure to keep track of the questions you ask to see if you are maintaining a balance. Use the checklist shown in Exhibit 8–3 to track the patterns of your questions and determine what question types you favor and which types you should use most frequently. The checklist can be used by a colleague sitting in to observe your presentation style or can be used to do a question count by type from a videotape of your presentation.

WHAT ARE THE LEVELS OF QUESTIONS?

The previous section addressed the many types of questions that you can use during delivery. This section covers the different levels that questions can assume. The *level* of a question refers to the depth to which the question probes the learners' knowledge of the subject matter. Deep questions require more knowledge to be answered correctly, while shallow questions can be answered with less knowledge or understanding of the topic. Consider, for instance, the following questions:

1. What is organization development?

2. How is the Action Research Model, which is the underpinning for most organization development interventions, different from the Instructional Systems Design model that is the underpinning for most rigorously designed training efforts?

Both questions gauge the learners' understanding of organization development, but the second question requires deeper knowledge to answer than the first. To answer it, learners not only need to know what organization development is but also what it is not and how it compares to training. Use different levels of questions to assess the depth of learner understanding and their readiness or confidence to provide answers.

When you ask questions, normally start by asking shallow questions and gradually move into deeper ones as the learners' knowledge increases. Take care not to leap into deep questions that are far beyond the learners' ability to answer, since that will reduce their confidence in

Exhibit 8–3
Question type checklist.

Directions: Categorize the questions asked during training by type. Count the number of each question as well.

Types	Questions asked during training	Total number of questions asked for each type
Open		
Closed		
Overhead		
Direct		
Reversed		
Redirected		

their own ability. Try instead to build their confidence by matching questions appropriately to their level of understanding.

HOW SHOULD QUESTIONS BE DIRECTED?

The direction of a question has to do with the way it is framed and delivered. Directing questions appropriately ensures that you achieve intended purposes. When questions are directed effectively, the learners' confidence level is enhanced. This section provides more information about issues you should consider and strategies you should use to direct questions effectively.

PROMOTING PARTICIPATION THROUGH QUESTIONING

As mentioned earlier, one primary purpose of questions is to encourage learner involvement. Questions should be delivered in ways that do not threaten learners and decrease participation. Overhead and direct questions are the most important here. If the chance exists that direct questions may cause anxiety among learners, substitute an overhead question. An overhead question encourages any learner to respond. If many overhead questions are used throughout delivery, all learners are presented with repeated opportunities to participate. This strategy does not guarantee the involvement of everyone, but increases the likelihood of that. Further, if certain learners consistently choose not to respond to overhead questions, use a "softly" delivered direct question to nudge a reluctant or shy participant.

HANDLING RESPONSES TO QUESTIONS

How you handle responses to questions is important in encouraging learner involvement. Learners will not respond if they feel you will punish them with embarrassment, condescension, or sarcasm when they do not provide correct answers. On the other hand, if all responses are welcomed with no penalty or negative reaction, then the learners' comfort levels increase and they are more likely to participate.

Several ways exist to handle incorrect answers. One is, of course, to redirect the question to other learners. A second is to praise any portion of the question that was answered correctly. A third is to praise or recognize the first person to try to answer—even when the answer is not correct. You can recognize learners in many ways, such as giving them a round of applause, verbally praising them, giving them a prize, or giving them a reward (like candy). Doing this helps people feel that attempts at participation are as important as the response itself. While the response is not necessarily rewarded, the effort is.

MATCHING THE LEVEL OF UNDERSTANDING

Frame your questions to match the learners' level of understanding. As you progress through training, the questions should become more challenging. But asking questions that are too difficult will only reduce or stop participation. Once again, the difficulty with this is that all learners have varying levels of understanding. You must be able to gauge each learner's level when asking questions so that you do not overwhelm some of them and bore others. You can attain this fine balance by constantly observing learners' behavior.

USING AN APPROPRIATE NUMBER OF QUESTIONS

You need to remain aware of how many questions, as well as what type of questions, you are using. If you provide too many questions at once, learners will not know how to start answering. They may feel overwhelmed or confused.

Some experts claim that you should pose about one question every five minutes. That rule of thumb, however, may be inappropriate for some training, such as technical training. Still, the more effective questions you ask, the better.

SELECTING RESPONDENTS

Selecting respondents is a topic related to questioning that is rarely discussed. Sometimes a few learners will monopolize all answers. Their hands shoot up every time a question is asked, but nobody else seems to be willing to answer. In such cases, selecting who will respond becomes easier due to the small number of choices. When only a few learners respond to all questions, it becomes important for you to involve those not responding so that the voices of a few do not dominate the entire program. Making an effort to involve others, through direct questions or other methods, can help to distribute the responses evenly among all learners.

At the opposite end of the spectrum, sometimes a large number of learners want to respond to questions. When this happens you have the dilemma of choosing whom to select. One option is to let one learner respond but then afford others the opportunity to build on to what the first person said. Another viable strategy is to vary deliberately on whom you call. If you attempt to let each learner respond to questions, different perspectives will be heard, which will enrich the learning experience. A third strategy is to vary your way of selecting people to answer questions. You may, for instance, explain that you will only call on someone seated in a specific row of seats. Read the following training dilemma and how a savvy trainer was able to overcome it.

> Lea was new to her organization and was immediately identified as a good communicator. Consequently, she was asked to conduct several communication workshops. She was excited at the prospect of this new venture and the workshops started out well. She was well prepared to get people involved by having a list of questions ready to keep the conversation moving and was amazed at how well people responded. However, after some time, she realized that only three of the twenty people in the class were answering questions. In fact, it got to the point that the other learners expected the three eager students to answer the questions, so they made no attempt to respond. Lea knew she was losing the class so she immediately put them into five smaller groups containing four people. Then, she asked the questions, instructed them to answer the questions as a group, and then had them elect a spokesperson to answer the questions to the larger group. After every group had their chance to speak, she asked them to change spokespersons. The result was more participation from everyone.

HOW IS ACTIVE LISTENING RELATED TO QUESTIONING?

Active listening means the visible behaviors you exhibit to show the speaker that you are listening. An often-neglected aspect of questioning skills is the trainer's ability to listen actively to the answers provided by learners. How you listen is critical because it is the best way for you to recognize if your question was understood, if the participant understands what he or she has learned, and if corrective action is necessary.

Active listening is used when learners are transmitting a message—as well as feelings— to the trainer. When learners feel that you have been listening carefully to them, they realize that their comments or responses are valued and respected. That contributes to a positive learning climate.

Use Exhibit 8–4 to assess your own active listening skills. The tool in this exhibit focuses on the key elements that contribute to active listening. These elements will be explored in the next section.

Exhibit 8–4
Active listening skills assessment tool.

Directions: Rate yourself on the following questions using the 1 to 5 scale. Then ask a colleague to rate you. Compare your responses to those of your colleague. The items where there are differences could represent areas to focus on to improve your active listening skills. Use the results of this assessment as a starting point to improve your active listening skills.

1. When listening to others, I make eye contact

1	2	3	4	5
Never	*Rarely*	*Occasionally*	*Usually*	*Always*

2. When listening to others, I lean forward

1	2	3	4	5
Never	*Rarely*	*Occasionally*	*Usually*	*Always*

3. After listening to others, I correctly paraphrase what they said

1	2	3	4	5
Never	*Rarely*	*Occasionally*	*Usually*	*Always*

4. While listening to others, I think about how to respond

1	2	3	4	5
Never	*Rarely*	*Occasionally*	*Usually*	*Always*

5. When listening to others, my mind wanders to other topics

1	2	3	4	5
Never	*Rarely*	*Occasionally*	*Usually*	*Always*

6. After listening to others, I ask clarifying questions

1	2	3	4	5
Never	*Rarely*	*Occasionally*	*Usually*	*Always*

7. When listening to others, I watch their facial expressions for cues to understanding

1	2	3	4	5
Never	*Rarely*	*Occasionally*	*Usually*	*Always*

8. When listening to others, I observe nonverbal language

1	2	3	4	5
Never	*Rarely*	*Occasionally*	*Usually*	*Always*

9. When listening to others, I am able to detect underlying feelings

1	2	3	4	5
Never	*Rarely*	*Occasionally*	*Usually*	*Always*

USING NONVERBAL BEHAVIORS TO CONVEY ACTIVE LISTENING

When two people communicate, nonverbal cues indicate how much active listening is occurring. Maintaining eye contact with someone is a powerful way to show that you are listening to them. If you were listening to learners as they respond to a question but you were also continually looking around the room or at your notes, the learners will feel that you are not listening to them. On the other hand, if you maintain direct eye contact with the speaker, it shows that you are paying close attention. Further, eye contact is useful for detecting subtle nonverbal cues from the speaker representing important feelings that are embedded in the message.

Other nonverbal behaviors can also demonstrate to the learner that you are actively listening. You can, for instance, show that you are paying attention by frequent nodding, leaning toward the speaker, or using facial expressions such as smiling or raising your eyebrows. When you offer such nonverbal acknowledgements to the learner, the learner's confidence level can be enhanced. Further, learners realize, through such cues, that you understand what they are saying. (If you do not understand, interrupt by asking, "Do you mean...?" or "What are you saying?")

PARAPHRASING TO CONFIRM LISTENING AND UNDERSTANDING

You can also demonstrate active listening skills as well as confirm your understanding by the responses you give to learners. If you make such remarks as "yes," "right," and even "uh-huh," you are showing that you are listening to the learner. In addition, an especially powerful way to confirm that you are listening is to stop the speaker periodically and provide a paraphrase. *Paraphrasing* occurs when you restate, in your own words, what the speaker has said. Paraphrasing does not involve a verbatim repetition of the words. Instead, it typically takes the form of a phrase that captures the essence of what was said. Paraphrasing demonstrates to the learner that you have listened and understood or it gives the learner an opportunity to correct any misunderstandings detected. Other active listening techniques, on the other hand, are more superficial. For example, nodding and making eye contact may convey to the speaker that you are listening, but your mind could be wandering.

Paraphrasing can be a difficult skill to master, for several reasons. First, most people have a tendency to take what is said at face value, but a speaker's body language and tone can tip off a careful listener that the person does not believe what he or she is saying. For example, a learner may nod his head in apparent agreement with an argument you are making, but his folded arms could be an indication that he really is not in agreement. It is tough to paraphrase the emotionally laden content of a message. Second, if the speaker is not clear in what he or she says, it can become difficult to capture the message. Third, when there are distractions in the background—such as other people talking—it is difficult to hear on multiple levels at once. Fourth, when someone talks for a long time and conveys complex thoughts and feelings, you may have trouble capturing it all in a simple paraphrase.

For these reasons, pay close attention to what is being said and how it is being said while simultaneously processing it for a more concise retelling. Then pause and clarify in your mind what the learner said. Once you have it pictured, you can paraphrase the key elements. If you are unsure about anything the speaker said, seek clarification before paraphrasing. You might say something like, "I wasn't clear about one point. Would you mind repeating what you said about…" to convey that you may not have fully understood what the speaker said.

VERIFYING YOUR UNDERSTANDING

Another technique to use when you paraphrase is to add a qualifying statement at the beginning. For instance, you could say, "I thought I heard you say that…" or "My understanding of what you said was…" followed by the paraphrased version of the comments. Such statements—followed by a question such as "Is this correct?" or "Was that what you said?"—convey that you are seeking affirmation about your understanding of the message. It is then up to the speaker to affirm, deny, or clarify what you said.

When you accurately paraphrase what the learner has said, you reap at least two benefits. First, the learner feels that you have genuinely listened and understood. That builds trust and mutual respect. Second, other learners benefit from a succinct restatement of what the learner had said.

LISTENING TO BOTH CONTENT AND FEELINGS

Content and feelings represent two sides of the communication coin. It is easier to listen to the content of what a speaker says than to unravel the emotional content loaded into the words. Feelings can be subtle and even imperceptible. Often, the feelings behind comments are not relevant in many training situations, such as when a learner is making a general statement or is responding to an informational question. However, some responses given by learners are emotionally loaded. For example, a learner may feel excited, confused, or angry. Whatever the source of those emotions, you must recognize, identify, and show sensitivity to the feelings that are expressed. Examine Exhibit 8–5, which provides a list of common feelings and their potential causes. Consider the feelings and their underlying causes as you deliver training and as you listen to what learners say as they answer questions or make presentations.

Exhibit 8–5	
Emotions and their potential causes.	
Emotions/Feelings	**Causes**
Frustration	Inability to understand a concept or perform a task.
Pride	Mastery of a task, successful performance, correct response.
Boredom	Already knows content, no incentive or motivation to learn, doesn't recognize relevance of training.
Excitement	Grasped a difficult concept, participated in game or activity.
Anger	Forced to attend training, doesn't agree with content.
Appreciation	Thankfulness for learning new skills.
Anxiety	Intimidated by content, classroom environment, instructor, or other learners.

RECOGNIZING FEELINGS THROUGH VERBAL AND NONVERBAL CUES

Feelings may be conveyed through nonverbal behaviors. For this reason, you should watch the person who is speaking carefully. Through facial expressions, body movements, and eye contact, the speaker expresses positive and negative feelings. For example, if a verbal response is accompanied by a smile, the learner may feel pride or confidence in the response. A frown or scowl, in contrast, could signify a lack of comprehension or self-confidence.

Feelings can also be conveyed through various verbal expressions, such as an increased rate of speech, a change in pitch, or a change in volume. Learners may feel excitement or anxiety when they begin to speak rapidly. Alternatively, learners may be feeling low self-confidence when they mumble or speak in a low volume.

Determining the exact feelings associated with nonverbal and verbal behaviors is difficult. But once you are aware that there are two dimensions to all responses—content (what is said) and feelings (how the speaker feels about what he or she is saying)—you can dissect a response to identify its parts.

Think about the following vignette where a trainer is able to decipher nonverbal behavior to effectively alter the training to meet learner needs:

> Manabu was teaching a technical skills training course when he noticed that several people were either staring out the window or looking at their watches. Since they had recently taken a break, Manabu decided that the learners were probably bored. After asking a couple of questions to gauge their level of understanding, he realized that he was covering content with which they were already familiar. Manabu quickly moved on to a topic that was more complex and was able to generate increased interest and participation.

HOW CAN QUESTIONS BE REPEATED, REPHRASED, AND RESTRUCTURED?

When you listen actively, you may detect learner errors or misperceptions. When you do, you must correct them. The most common errors you may notice are incorrect answers to your questions, partial or incomplete responses, or undecipherable responses. To take corrective action in such situations, you may need to redeliver the question to the learner. When learners provide a response that is only partially correct, recognize it and build upon the partial answer through new questions or through repeating, rephrasing, or restructuring the original question. This section discusses strategies for doing this so that the goal of producing an appropriate response is achieved.

REPEATING QUESTIONS

Repeating a question involves simply restating it as it was originally delivered. That is one way you can take corrective action when learners give a poor response or are simply confused. Sometimes learners do not hear all or part of a question or do not understand it completely. In such cases, repeating the question allows them to hear it again and gives them time to rethink it and provide another response to it. When you ask questions, make it a practice to ask the question and then to repeat it immediately. This helps to ensure that everyone hears the question and gives them time, as the question is repeated, to prepare a response.

REPHRASING QUESTIONS

When learners give a poor response to one of your questions, you may find it helpful to rephrase the question. *Rephrasing a question* means repeating it with a slight variation. Rephrasing provides learners with another version of the same question that, although presented differently, has essentially the same meaning. The purpose is to guide learners toward more correct or complete responses than they provided originally. To signal the learners that a rephrased question will follow, you can say something like, "In other words…" or "Stated another way…" followed by the rephrased question.

When you prepare for delivering a training session you should practice different ways of asking the same question. Doing this provides you with an arsenal of questions from which to draw if a restatement becomes necessary. Typically you will restate questions when you detect confusion among the learners or when the responses are not correct. Doing this not only ensures that the question is heard by all learners, but also provides adequate response time.

But beware of one problem in using this technique: Learners may mistake the rephrased question for a completely different question rather than for a restatement of the same question. Because this could lead to confusion, use the technique carefully, such as asking the person who originated the question whether it was rephrased correctly. The following dialogue is an example of a repeated and rephrased question.

> **TRAINER:** *What questions do you have?*
>
> **BONNIE:** *Is there a time when using the technique is wrong?*
>
> **TRAINER:** *(Looking at Bonnie) That's a good question. (Then, turning to the group) The question that was raised is whether or not there are times when it may not be best, or even harmful, to use this technique. (Then, turning back to Bonnie) Is that what you were asking?*
>
> **BONNIE:** *Yes.*
>
> **TRAINER:** *(Turning to the group) There are several occassions when this technique should not be used...*

The trainer in this dialogue not only repeated the question but also rephrased it, elaborated on it, and checked for agreement from the originator of the question.

RESTRUCTURING QUESTIONS

To restructure a question means to alter it fundamentally to help the learners understand it. Restructuring a question may be required if you detect problems with the original question. Perhaps the question did not make sense, was incomplete, or was too complex. These problems may be detected based on the response provided by the learner or by the learner's reaction, such as bewilderment. In such cases restructuring may be needed.

A *double-barreled question*, as the name indicates, asks two or more questions embedded in one. That can cause confusion. An example of a double-barreled question is, "Do you feel that it is important for supervisors to communicate expectations for employees and reward the achievement of goals?" Such a question may cause confusion because it contains two completely different questions. One question relates to communicating expectations and a second question relates to rewarding goal achievement. Breaking it into two distinct questions makes this question clearer.

Another type of question that can lead to problems is the *leading question*. Perhaps the most famous leading question is, "When did you stop beating your wife?" That is a leading question because any answers seem to accept the underlying premise that the listener was, in fact, beating his wife at some point. Another example of a leading question that could occur in a training course is, "What is the best part of the new sales incentive program?" That is a leading question because it implies that the new program is good and also that it has only one best component. Leading questions may need restructuring because they may restrict learner thinking or lead learners to challenge your assumptions.

This section has presented strategies for repeating, rephrasing, and restructuring a question following an inaccurate or inappropriate response provided by a learner or a poorly asked question by the trainer. The purpose of these techniques is to present learners with a new or revised question that is more likely to result in a correct response. Since inaccurate responses are potentially embarrassing to learners it is paramount that you repeat, rephrase, or restructure the question without causing distress or humiliation. Handling incorrect responses in a way that does not lead to embarrassment or punishment creates a supportive learning environment. As mentioned earlier, when learners answer incorrectly, you can provide positive feedback on their effort. Doing this also contributes to a supportive environment in which learners feel comfortable and where learning can take place.

HOW SHOULD YOU PROVIDE TIME FOR LEARNERS TO RESPOND?

When you ask a question, provide ample time for learners to respond. The exact amount of time required varies, depending on the rate at which people can process information after a question has been posed, or the rate at which they are able to formulate responses or questions. To make sure that you have allowed sufficient time, try to identify and monitor general patterns of information processing and question development. Once you understand the patterns, you can match the allotted time accordingly.

A mistake sometimes made is not to allow sufficient response time, such as asking learners, "What questions do you have?" and then moving immediately into the next statement. A similar error is to say, "If there are no questions, we'll move on" and then proceed into the next segment without even glancing around the room. In both examples, learners are not given enough time to form questions and get up the courage to ask them. Further, it communicates to learners that you do not really want a response, making it a *rhetorical question*.

Another mistake is to allow too much time for response. A question such as "What questions do you have?" could be followed by a long period of silence as you wait for a response. Or you could wait too long for an individual learner to answer a direct question. Waiting too long puts undue pressure on people because they feel compelled to provide an answer, or to ask a question even when they do not have one. This pressure creates discomfort among the learners and makes the learning climate less conducive to openness.

USING SILENCE AFTER A QUESTION

A silence or pause after you ask a question can serve several useful purposes. As mentioned above, a common mistake is to not allow enough time for learners to answer. One strategy is to incorporate a pause or period of silence after the question has been posed so learners have adequate time to form an answer. A deliberate period of silence after a question also sends the message to an otherwise shy, quiet, or reluctant learner that a response is expected.

SUMMARY

In this chapter we examined effective questioning skills and techniques. Trainers who master this competency should be able to do the following:

- Use the different types and levels of questions effectively—including open and closed questions, overhead and direct questions, and reversed and redirected questions.

- Use direct questions appropriately.

- Use active listening skills.

- Repeat, rephrase, and restructure questions.

- Use silence and pauses after posing questions to give learners time to process information, respond, comment, and ask questions themselves.

STRATEGY LIST

Actionable Strategies to Improve Training Effectiveness:

Use Questions Effectively

❐ Use questions to assess learner understanding, identify learner preferences, encourage participation, enable reflection, and to capture and hold learner attention.

❑ Ask questions that are challenging enough to hold learner interest, but not so difficult that learners are unable to answer.

❑ Do not overuse questions or your audience may stop responding to them.

❑ Avoid forcing people to answer questions so that you do not alienate them or put them on the spot.

❑ Float several test questions and listen to the responses you receive to determine the learners' current level of comprehension.

❑ Set expectations up front that you plan to ask questions and want their participation.

❑ Only ask one question at a time to avoid confusing learners.

❑ Redirect learner questions to the entire group to encourage everyone's participation and to capitalize on the group's knowledge.

❑ Track the types and levels of the questions you ask to ensure you are maintaining a balance.

❑ Vary to whom you ask questions and how you ask them.

❑ Once you ask a question, use active listening skills to demonstrate that you sincerely care about the response. Make eye contact, lean toward the learner who is responding, nod in approval for the response, paraphrase what you hear, and assume a casual posture.

❑ Avoid using leading questions since they may restrict learner thinking or lead learners to challenge your motives.

❑ Avoid using double-barreled questions which combine two or more questions into one and confuse learners.

❑ Use silence after asking a question to provide learners with time to consider and reflect before answering. If you begin talking too quickly after asking a question, learners assume they do not have to answer questions if they wait long enough. However, don't wait too long either. This may create an uncomfortable environment for you as well as the learners.

Strategies for Using Different Types of Questions

❏ Ask a variety of open, closed, and follow-up questions to elicit different responses depending upon the level of participation you are seeking.

❏ Use closed questions to gauge participant reactions or opinions.

❏ Use open questions when you want to encourage more dialogue and participation.

❏ Instead of asking, "Does anyone have any questions?" ask, "What questions do you have?" This open versus closed question will encourage people to respond with something other than a simple yes or no.

❏ Use overhead questions when you want to elicit responses or gain the attention of the entire group.

❏ Use direct questions when you want to elicit responses or gain the attention of an individual learner.

❏ Use follow-up questions when you want to probe deeper into learner responses.

❏ Use reversed or reflective questions to clarify learner questions to the rest of the group.

❏ Use redirected questions to avoid informing learners that they have given an incorrect response by subtly redirecting the question to the rest of the group.

Levels of Questions

❏ Use different levels of questions to assess the depth of learner understanding and their readiness or confidence to provide answers.

❏ Begin by asking shallow questions and gradually move to the more difficult (deeper) questions.

CHAPTER 9

RESPONDING TO LEARNERS' NEEDS FOR CLARIFICATION OR FEEDBACK

Every learner in classroom training is an individual, which poses challenges for you because you train people in groups. When learners are actively engaged and involved in training, they send you signals to display their level of comfort and understanding. You can also expect to pick up signals from the actively involved learners who need clarification or feedback. This chapter covers the following topics:

- How to recognize learners with the need for feedback and clarification.

- How to provide prompt, timely, and specific feedback to ensure that learners are actively involved and want to participate.

- How to give feedback that is performance-based, not person-based.

The following critical incident dramatizes one trainer's experience in working with a learner who required much clarification and feedback.

Computer Phobia

" *This was during a basic computer class I was instructing—it covered everything from hardware to software, including an overview of some software packages. One student in this class was visibly nervous and upset. She could not seem to grasp anything presented. I tried to work one-on-one with her to help, but the rest of the class seemed to get frustrated from being slowed down. I asked her to work through the workbook at her own pace while I kept the class going. Then every so often I would see how she was doing and provide feedback on her progress. Most times I checked she was still lost. She just could not get it.* "

This critical incident also describes a mismatch between the course content and the learner. However, it does illustrate one learner's need for extensive clarification and feedback. It also shows the frustration you can experience when a learner struggles even after receiving a great deal of individualized attention.

From the survey we conducted, trainers regarded responding appropriately to learners' needs for clarification or feedback as critically important. Our respondents rated it of top importance (number one) of fourteen competencies for success in training delivery, which indicates the high importance trainers place on learner satisfaction.

IDENTIFYING LEARNERS WITH CLARIFICATION AND FEEDBACK NEEDS

Before you can demonstrate the competency of responding appropriately to learners' needs for clarification or feedback, you must first identify learners who have such needs. Once you recognize a need, you can then develop and deliver an appropriate response. The following critical incident provided by one trainer in our survey represents an extreme example of a learner's need for clarification or feedback that was probably quite easy for the trainer in this situation to recognize.

What a Question!

"I was conducting a public meeting for the Alaska Department of Environmental Conservation on communities improving protection of ground water (the source of drinking water). The purpose of the workshop was to teach residents about what they could do to protect ground water (as compared to waiting for the agency to do it for them). During questions and answers, one person asked, "Do I have to bring a gun into your office to get your agency to stop the industry from polluting?" I took a deep breath, relaxed and calmly answered him. The answer satisfied him. He felt he had voiced his concern, had been heard, and was answered."

Learners in need of feedback will sometimes make sarcastic comments or exaggerate, as happened here.

Lack of learner understanding is often the root cause of needs for clarification or feedback. The challenge you face as a trainer is that not all learners willingly admit that they are confused or that they do not understand. As noted in the previous chapter, however, you can sometimes pinpoint learners' lack of understanding by posing questions and then assessing how well they answer them. When learners supply incorrect or incomplete responses to your questions, you can safely assume that they are not getting it.

But assessing the way learners answer your questions is only one way to detect lack of understanding. Learners can also signal that they do not understand by the questions they ask, the comments they make, or the subtle or nonverbal cues they display.

Why Won't They Speak Up?

"My worst problem is participants with an unwillingness to express their views or ask questions. This is usually limited to the labor force at the floor level. It leaves you with frustration because you do not know if the material is understood or not. The presenter must devise a way to evaluate this situation on the spot."

Trainers like this one must be creative in finding ways to encourage participants to become involved so that their level of understanding can be assessed.

Exhibit 9–1 summarizes common signals exhibited by learners when they need clarification or feedback. Some of these signals are verbal in nature, such as questions they ask or comments they make. Other cues are nonverbal, such as puzzled facial expressions.

Exhibit 9–1
Need for clarification observation form.

Behaviors that may determine the learners' need for clarification:

Learners' *questions* may reflect a lack of understanding when they:

■ Are not related to the issue at hand.

■ Reveal that they do not see the relationships between various topics.

■ Focus on the same topics over and over.

Learner's *comments* may reflect a lack of understanding when they:

■ Are inaccurate or misdirected.

■ Are irrelevant or unrelated to the topic at hand.

■ Are few and far between.

Learners' *nonverbal behaviors* that may reflect a lack of understanding include:

■ A puzzled or awkward look.

■ Discussion with a neighbor.

■ Avoidance of eye contact (to prevent being asked questions).

■ Nervous movements and gestures.

■ Closed body posture.

RECOGNIZING VERBAL AND NONVERBAL INDICATORS

When learners do not understand the training content, they can demonstrate this through verbal cues such as questions or comments. When misdirected, inaccurate, or incomplete questions or comments are made, they may indicate a need for clarification or feedback. Sometimes learners simply are not skilled at posing questions or making comments. This difficulty is compounded in groups where individual learners may become intimidated or distracted by others. At other times, it is not a delivery problem; rather, the inappropriate, incomplete, or inaccurate comment or question reflects a lack of understanding and therefore represents a true need for feedback or clarification. The issues of how and when to respond to such questions or comments are discussed in the next section.

NONVERBAL INDICATORS OF FEEDBACK NEEDS

When learners do not understand, they may also exhibit many nonverbal behaviors indicating their need for clarification or feedback. You should tune in to the nonverbal behaviors representing learners' difficulties in understanding. These behaviors include:

- Avoidance of eye contact

- Nervous movements

- Strained facial expressions, such as furrowed brows

When you scan the training room, those not making eye contact or those deliberately attempting to avoid making eye contact may be showing you that they do not understand. Other indicators include nervous body movements or gestures. When learners do not comprehend some aspect of the content, they may experience anxiety or tension that shows itself through shifting in seats, strained facial expressions, or awkward body movements or positions. For example, a learner may be leaning back or slumping in the chair with arms folded. Other learners cleverly disguise their lack of understanding by pretending that they are busy taking notes or intently staring at their workbook. Regardless of which specific nonverbal behaviors are demonstrated, they point to a need for clarification or feedback. Therefore, become aware of such actions and be ready to take corrective action when you recognize the problem. Read the following scenario where a trainer was unable to identify that the learners in her training course were off-track.

> Holly's course in basic hydraulics started out well. Learners appeared to be engaged and seemed to know what was going on. At about 10:30 A.M., Holly began an hour-and-a-half lecture on the components of a small hydraulic engine. She felt that it went well. At noon, the learners had lunch and then came back to class to complete a hands-on lab. To Holly's astonishment, the class was totally lost. She wondered what happened during the hour-and-a-half lecture that she hadn't noticed. The learners had no idea what was going on and needed a great deal of hand holding and extra time to complete the lab.

Had the trainer in the above scenario been more attentive to non-verbal cues during the lecture, she may have noticed the glazed-over looks, staring out the window, yawning, confused expressions, and other signs of confusion or boredom. Instead of being on the lookout for such cues, she had one goal in mind—plow through the lecture and pass the information on to the learners.

DETERMINING HOW AND WHEN TO RESPOND

As we mentioned in the previous section, in order to be effective, you must attend to both verbal and nonverbal behaviors and discern any needs for clarification or feedback. This section addresses the next step that follows the identification of a need—determining how and when to respond.

TIMING OF FEEDBACK OR CLARIFICATION

When you notice that learners need clarification or feedback, you can use several approaches. One tactic is to make a mental note of the need and follow up on it later. Another strategy is to address the need immediately. The choice of your approach depends on several issues. If the feedback or clarification may cause embarrassment to the learner, delay it or move it offline. If all the learners are likely to be distracted or derailed by what you do, delay it until later. Finally, if the feedback or clarification demands a lengthy response—such as revisiting an entire content segment—delay that as well.

There are many cases, however, when delivering the feedback or providing clarification will not interrupt the flow of learning. Further, all learners may benefit from information provided to the one learner who required it. In fact, perceptive trainers recognize that one or two learners needing clarification are often the tip of the iceberg and that, in reality, many others probably have the same need. Also, feedback or clarification may be very brief and incorporated seamlessly into the delivery. In these situations it may be appropriate to provide it as soon as you determine the need exists.

VERIFYING FEEDBACK OR CLARIFICATION NEEDS

When you spot a possible need for clarification or feedback, you can take several steps to verify that the need really exists. Verification is necessary for several reasons. First, it ensures that your perception of a need was accurate. Verification also informs the individual learner and the entire group that you are shifting gears, which minimizes the potential for confusion. Finally, verification helps you pinpoint exactly what clarification or feedback need exists by offering learners an opportunity to deny or qualify their need. You can make statements such as:

- I want to clarify a point that was made. What is your understanding of...?

- Your question was somewhat confusing to me. Were you saying...?

- What I hear you saying is...Is this correct?

Statements and questions such as these give learners ample opportunity to restate or clarify their questions or comments to help you distinguish whether a need for clarification or feedback truly exists.

STRATEGIES FOR DELIVERING YOUR RESPONSE

Once you have verified a need for a response and chosen the appropriate time to deliver feedback or clarification, deliver a measured response to address the situation. At times, you may elect to use a redirected or overhead question to involve other learners rather than providing the response yourself. Consider how the trainer in the following dialogue redirects the original question toward to the entire group of learners:

TRAINER: *What questions do you have before we move on?*

SANDRA: *If I use this skill on the job, how will it affect my quality and timeliness?*

TRAINER: *That is a good question and a valid concern.* (Turning to the group) *Sandra's question relates to how this new skill will affect the quality and timeliness of your work. Who has already used this skill, and how has impacted your work?*

The nature of the response you provide depends on the specific question or issue as well as the situation at hand. In the scenario above, the trainer chose to redirect the question to the group because the issue for clarification did not focus on the knowledge deficit of the learner originating the question. It also enabled the trainer to capitalize on the expertise of those who had already used the skill in a job-related context. If the clarification need or question may cause the learner embarrassment, then opening it up to the group can be risky because other learners may call attention to the deficit, leading to further problems. On the other hand, if a positive learning climate exists, involving others can actually help the learner feel more at ease.

AVOID SPOON FEEDING

If you choose to provide the response, take care to avoid simply supplying the learner with the correct answer. If the learner is spoon fed in this manner then learning may be diminished because little thought is required. On the other hand, if you challenge the learner and facilitate self-discovery of the appropriate response, then comprehension and understanding are maximized because the learner retains ownership of the learning. However, a balance between challenging the learner to arrive at the answer and maintaining the learner's confidence must be maintained. Instead of saying, "Joyce, the correct answer is (*correct answer*)," a trainer could instead stimulate the learner's thinking by saying the following:

TRAINER: *Joyce, that's not the answer that I was looking for, but instead of me giving you the answer, let's work through this together. How did you arrive at your answer? Let's start at the beginning. Remember, the original problem was* (original problem statement). *What was the first thing you did to answer it?*

PROVIDING MATCHING NONVERBALS

Nonverbal behaviors are also a part of your response to learners' needs for clarification or feedback. Nonverbals—such as eye contact, gestures, and facial expressions—should be used to support, lead, or give emphasis to your response. When you are facilitating self-discovery with the learner, supportive and encouraging gestures—such as nodding, direct eye contact, or smiling—build learner confidence in the ability to answer correctly.

By the end of your response, you should have addressed all needs adequately. You and the learner should feel satisfied that mutual understanding has been reached.

PROVIDING PROMPT, TIMELY, AND SPECIFIC FEEDBACK

This section focuses on feedback. We begin by defining feedback and explaining its purposes. We then distinguish among several types of feedback and provide guidelines to follow when giving feedback. We emphasize strategies you can use to provide effective feedback to learners during training delivery.

FEEDBACK DEFINED

Feedback is information that is provided to learners to influence their performance. Feedback is usually delivered verbally, although it is often supported with nonverbal behaviors. Consider these examples of how a trainer gives a learner feedback following a skill practice session:

> **TRAINER:** *Pat, when you make eye contact with Rita and nod your head as she speaks, it shows you are actively listening to her.*

> **TRAINER:** *Susan, turning the valve to number 4 causes too much reduction in flow. A reading between 2 and 3 maintains a flow and allows an accurate reading to be taken.*

These examples demonstrate just how specific feedback can be when it is delivered effectively to a learner.

PURPOSES AND TYPES OF FEEDBACK

Feedback serves many purposes. One purpose is to support behaviors exhibited by the learner. That is called *positive* or *motivational feedback,* and it is given by a trainer to encourage, support, and reinforce learner behaviors. The example with Pat and Rita above exemplifies positive or motivational feedback because it encourages Pat to use nonverbal behaviors, such as nodding and eye contact, during communication.

Another purpose of feedback is to correct or improve poor performance exhibited by the learner. This is often called *corrective* or *constructive feedback*, because its purpose is to change learner behavior that does not contribute to the achievement of intended outcomes. The previous example about flow measurement exemplifies corrective feedback because the trainer explains to Susan that a reading of 4 is too restrictive whereas a measurement between 2 and 3 is acceptable.

COMPONENTS OF EFFECTIVE FEEDBACK

Feedback has the potential to rectify inappropriate learner performance or maintain and reinforce good performance. You should strive to provide learners with feedback that is effective. Such feedback has several important components, and this section discusses the most relevant and pertinent of those components.

PERSON-BASED FEEDBACK VS. PERFORMANCE-BASED FEEDBACK

Feedback should not be centered on individuals. You should, instead, direct it to learner behavior (activities) or performance (results). Consider this example of *person-based feedback*, which focuses on individuals: "Ron, you seem nervous." Person-based feedback risks making the individual feel defensive, hurt, or angry. Its impact may thus prevent the desired result. It is destructive because it may reduce individual self-confidence. Person-based feedback is harmful because it does not give the person something concrete to change. In this example, Ron would probably feel helpless to change "seeming nervous" because changing the behaviors associated with that may be unclear or complex. Exhibit 9–2 lists several person-based statements and contrasts them to behavior-based statements.

Behavior-based feedback, which focuses on what people do, is more effective than person-based feedback because it does not provoke defensiveness. *Performance-based feedback*, which focuses on the results people achieve, highlights specific areas in which learners can change. Such feedback should be described in concrete, observable terms. Consider this example of performance-based feedback: "Kwon, when you interrupted me, I lost the main point of my message." Kwon's behavior is the focus of this feedback. Feedback of this type directs attention to areas under Kwon's control to change. It can help him remember the consequences of his behavior and how it affects others. Further, Kwon is not as likely to become as defensive as he would if the feedback were person-based. An example of person-based feedback in

Exhibit 9–2	
Person-based vs. behavior-based statements.	
Person-based statements	**Behavior-based statements**
You looked bored with the discussion.	You were staring out the window and looking at your watch.
You were rude in class.	You interrupted people several times during class.
You seem angry about being here.	You abruptly walked out of class.
You didn't seem to enjoy the training.	You weren't involved with the class or your small group during the activity.

this case is "Kwon, you're rude." While those might not be the exact words that would be used in person-based feedback, it is easy to see the defensive reaction they are likely to provoke.

Remember this simple rule for giving feedback. First, state the person's name to get his or her attention. Then describe the observable behavior or performance. Finally, clarify the consequence or result of that behavior.

VAGUE VS. SPECIFIC FEEDBACK

Feedback should always be specific. Vague feedback makes people feel confused about what they did. Such confusion will make it unlikely that the learner will change his or her behavior in the case of corrective feedback, or maintain effective behavior in the case of positive feedback. An example of vague feedback is a statement such as "Good job." If you provide this feedback, learners may (or may not) have a clue about what they did to lead you to say this. Sometimes it may be clear, especially in cases when it immediately follows an obvious behavior. However, even if at the end of your segment you say something like "Scott, Good work in this last segment. Thanks," it may be unclear what it was that Scott did that was good—which reduces the probability that he will repeat the behavior.

On the other hand, when feedback is specific, the learner knows exactly what behavior was appropriate or inappropriate. In using specific feedback, for instance, you might say, "All the small groups finished the activity five minutes early. Thanks for managing your time so well and helping us to stay on schedule." This feedback is much better than telling the groups "Good job with the activity," because it communicates clearly to the learners exactly what they did that was good and the results of that behavior. When working in small groups in the future, learners will be more likely to be sensitive to time management and will be more apt to stay on schedule. Compare the examples of vague and specific feedback in Exhibit 9–3.

Exhibit 9–3 Vague vs. specific feedback.	
Vague Feedback	**Specific Feedback**
You performed well today.	You got involved with your peers and contributed your thoughts and ideas.
You adequately managed your workload.	You completed all of your activities and were prepared for all group exercises.
You really seemed to get the concepts.	You made several clarifying comments to your peers and helped them to understand.

THE RELEVANCY OF FEEDBACK

Relevancy is closely related to the difference between vague and specific feedback. When feedback is vague, it seems irrelevant to learners. There is no clear linkage between the feedback that is provided and the behavior toward which it is directed. On the other hand, when feedback is specific, it is more likely to be relevant to the learner. Such feedback is much more meaningful to the learner and has a greater chance of influencing subsequent behavior.

THE TIMING OF FEEDBACK

Timing can influence the power of feedback. Feedback is diminished when the length of time increases between the behavior and the feedback provided about it. In other words, feedback delivered at the end of a three-day workshop about a problem that happened on the morning of the first day will probably not be effective. Learners may not even recollect the behavior upon which the feedback is based. When feedback is delivered soon after the behavior or performance is demonstrated, it is more effective because immediacy exists between the behavior and the feedback. This principle holds true for both positive and corrective feedback. When you deliver feedback promptly, it is more likely to be clear to learners what they did well or poorly. There will also be a strong link between the behavior and the impact of that behavior. This strong association can increase the likelihood that the positive behavior or performance will be reinforced and the poor performance will be corrected.

FEEDBACK BALANCE

Feedback balance refers to the relative amounts of positive and corrective feedback given to learners. When learners receive either too much corrective feedback or too much positive feedback, you may see negative results. Learners become frustrated and feel inadequate when they are given too much corrective feedback. They may give up as their self-confidence diminishes. On the other hand, learners may not feel challenged if they are given too much positive feedback. Too much positive feedback may produce overconfidence, which may create a sense of reality shock when they return to the workplace. And when learners are given no feedback at all, they may grow confused and frustrated because they are unsure whether their understanding is correct. Therefore, strive for feedback balance to provide learners with appropriate guidance on how they are doing and with sufficient self-confidence to apply it.

FEEDBACK GUIDELINES

When feedback is effective, it can have a powerful impact on how learners perform. Conversely, when feedback is handled poorly, it can be highly detrimental to learning. This section presents some useful guidelines for you to consider and use when delivering feedback to learners so that it produces positive results.

One guideline to follow is to make sure that the feedback you give is always sincere. It is typically easy for learners to recognize insincere feedback. If you provide feedback that sounds shallow, learners will not believe it and may question its value or discard it completely. "Great, that's just what I'm looking for," delivered in an overly enthusiastic tone to every learner who responds, can begin to wear out its welcome quickly. Insincere feedback undermines your credibility because it raises questions about your honesty and sincerity. Another guideline to follow is to ensure that you use effective eye contact and proper voice inflection so that your feedback sounds as sincere as it should really be.

PRACTICING FEEDBACK

Giving feedback is something you can practice. It may feel awkward at first for you to provide people with effective feedback, but practicing can make it easier and a matter of habit. The following scenarios can offer you an opportunity to practice the techniques we have discussed thus far. First, read the scenario below and determine an appropriate feedback response. Then, use the practice sheet in Exhibit 9–4 to check the effectiveness of your feedback for the two situations on the next page:

Exhibit 9–4 Practice sheet for determining feedback effectiveness.		
Was the feedback...	**YES**	**NO**
Behavior-based		
Specific		
Relevant		
Timely		
Sincere		
Professional		
Did the person...		
Make eye contact		
Use appropriate voice inflection		
Speak with a positive tone		

Kishore just completed a skill practice where he correctly used a newly learned software package to set up a database for his organization. He was able to incorporate all of the features that he learned into the database.

After taking an interviewing skills training course, Pamela successfully created and implemented several interviews in an effort to hire a new administrative assistant. She demonstrated all of the interviewing techniques that were relevant to her situation.

Feedback should be delivered in a clear and concise manner so that the message is more likely to be received as it was intended. When a message is not clear the learner may become confused. Confusing feedback can jeopardize understanding and can lead learners to feel defensive and frustrated.

DELIVERING FEEDBACK EFFECTIVELY

When you provide feedback to a learner, deliver it in a relaxed yet professional manner. If you appear nervous or anxious, the message quality and effectiveness are reduced. Verbal signs—such as an increased rate of speech, laughter, or stuttering—convey nervousness. In addition, nonverbal signals, such as fidgeting or lack of eye contact, convey tension. In contrast, when feedback is delivered in a straightforward manner and you appear confident, the message is fully received by the learner because distractions arising from your anxiety will be diminished.

SEPARATING POSITIVE FROM CORRECTIVE FEEDBACK

Be sure to separate positive feedback from corrective feedback. They should not be delivered at the same time. Several problems arise when positive feedback is given at the same time as corrective feedback. Giving them together sends a mixed message, and learners are not sure what is most important. They may experience information overload by receiving too many messages at once.

Be aware that corrective feedback diminishes the impact of the positive feedback. For example, you might deliver the following feedback: "Jeroen, you effectively demonstrated your self-confidence by making eye contact with the customer as you gave a firm handshake. However, the volume of your speech was too low, causing the customer to strain to hear you." In this example, Jeroen might focus on the corrective feedback (low volume of speech) rather than on the positive feedback (eye contact). Keep positive feedback and corrective separated so that the impact of each is heightened.

CONSIDERING WHERE TO DELIVER FEEDBACK

Where feedback is delivered is a final consideration. The proximity from which feedback is delivered influences its impact. That is especially true with corrective feedback, which can be sensitive and can be a source of embarrassment to the learner. In the case of positive feedback, it is generally acceptable to deliver it in the presence of others. In fact, being recognized for effective performance can build learner self-esteem. Be aware, however, that receiving any feedback can be uncomfortable to some individuals. As a general rule, give positive feedback in public, but give corrective feedback privately and one-on-one. That minimizes the chance that the learner will be embarrassed. Two of the authors occasionally codeliver a train-the-trainer course. Participants in the program are asked to deliver several presentations during the program. After each presentation everyone provides the presenter with a round of applause. Later, one of authors provides specific feedback to the learner in a brief discussion that often takes place in the hall or some other private place.

SUMMARY

In Chapter Nine we covered the importance of responding appropriately to learners' needs for clarification or feedback. Trainers in our survey rated this competency as the single most important of the fourteen associated with instruction and training delivery. Trainers who master this competency should be able to do the following:

- Recognize learners with the need for feedback and clarification.

- Give feedback that is prompt, timely, and specific.

- Give feedback that is performance-based, not person-based.

STRATEGY LIST

Actionable Strategies to Improve Training Effectiveness:

Provide Learners with Feedback

☐ Watch for signs that learners need feedback such as incorrect responses to questions, confused looks, blank stares, avoidance of eye contact, and convoluted questions and comments.

☐ If feedback or clarification could be potentially embarrassing to a learner, either delay it for a later time so that it is not associated with the learner or provide the learner with feedback in private.

☐ If learner feedback or clarification demands a lengthy response, such as revisiting an entire segment, delay it until you can meet with the learner one-on-one and in private.

☐ Ask questions to verify when clarification or feedback is needed. The responses either will verify the need for you to clarify or will confirm understanding.

☐ Once you have identified needs for clarification and feedback, be careful not to provide the answers too quickly. This is a good opportunity to challenge the learners to reflect and discover their own understanding.

☐ Provide support and encouragement by nodding, smiling (but not laughing), and making eye contact when you are facilitating and encouraging reflection among learners.

☐ Use a variety of feedback including person-based, performance-based, positive, corrective, and behavior-based. Relying on one type of feedback diminishes its impact over time.

☐ Consider this simple formula when providing feedback: 1) state their name; 2) describe the observable behavior that you are addressing; and 3) clarify the consequence or result of the behavior in question.

☐ Provide feedback in a timely manner. The closer the feedback is to the behavior, the greater its impact.

☐ Maintain a good balance between positive and corrective feedback. Too much positive feedback can come across as insincere, while too much corrective feedback can be demotivating.

☐ Never give feedback unless it is sincere. Insincere feedback undermines your credibility because it raises questions about your honesty and integrity.

❐ Do not provide positive and corrective feedback at the same time. Learners will typically only hear the corrective.

❐ Generally, positive feedback is more effective when delivered in public while corrective feedback is more effective when delivered in private.

CHAPTER 10

PROVIDING POSITIVE REINFORCEMENT AND MOTIVATIONAL INCENTIVES

SKILLS ASSESSMENT

Take a moment to review the competency and associated performances that will be covered in this chapter. Consider your current level of proficiency in the competency as a whole as well as each performance and check the items where you feel you need to improve. As you read the chapter, concentrate on those areas most in need of development.

Competency:

▪ Provide positive reinforcement and motivational incentives.

Associated Performances:

▪ Match learning outcomes to learner and organizational needs and goals.

▪ Use introductory activities appropriate to developing learner motivation.

▪ Plan and deliberately use feedback and reinforcement during delivery.

▪ Judge the adequacy and appropriateness of motivational strategies used during training, and adjust as necessary.

This chapter focuses on feedback given to learners to motivate them. As you begin thinking about how to motivate learners in training, consider the following critical incident where motivation may have played an important role in this trainer's experience. As you read this, think about how you could have improved learner motivation in this situation:

Problems with Mandated Training

" Due to the nature of our business, a manufacturing facility, and our slow progress to incorporate some types of training into our daily schedule, most of our training at this point is OSHA-mandated and revolves around safety. The employees must attend all training on their days off. We do not have a temporary workforce that is able to cover employees for training during their regularly scheduled shift. We pay overtime and generally include a meal during the training sessions. Even so, most employees resent having to come in on their days off. They fail to see the importance of the training, viewing it as "just another hoop" they have to jump through to keep their jobs. Even the most dynamic instructor finds them a tough crowd. In addition to the whining, complaints, and derogatory comments at the training sessions, we get a fair number of employees who feel it is permissible to be inattentive and either talk or sleep through a session. We also have employees who just don't show up.

The training is mandatory, and supervisors have begun to see nonattendance as a performance issue. This has helped cure most of the attendance problem. In order to address the "boredom factor" I have been hiring more outside trainers that have the equipment and knowledge to provide hands-on training. This has been popular with most employees. Another difficult detail is that we must prove the employees are competent in any subject after receiving training. This is very hard to measure other than by written quizzes. If it would be possible to interview each employee separately on each issue, that would be the true measure of competence. Overall, I have not yet solved the boredom problem. "

Learner motivation is critical to successful training. Based on the critical incident experiences reported to us, stimulating learner motivation is especially challenging when training is mandatory. When learners are highly motivated, they participate actively in the program, expend effort, and work hard to achieve the objectives. In addition, when motivated, learners are more likely to transfer the skills and knowledge they acquired during training to the workplace. It is through transfer of training from the instructional setting (such as a classroom) to the work setting (job site) that an enviable return on the training investment is realized.

Positive feedback, as dicussed in Chapter 9, is only one way to create a climate that builds learner motivation. Other strategies can be used as well. One strategy is to emphasize the importance of the training results to the business and the learners. You can often do that most effectively during the opening remarks of a training session. Specific examples of opening activities designed to enhance motivation are provided later in the chapter. We will also discuss the competency of providing positive reinforcement and motivational incentives and cover the following topics:

- An overview of motivation, including motivational theories, models, and strategies.

- Matching outcomes to the needs and goals of learners and the organization.

- Effective uses of introductory activities.

- Strategies for incorporating positive reinforcement and negative feedback during delivery.

AN OVERVIEW OF MOTIVATION

This section defines motivation and presents the various theories and models of motivation.

DEFINING MOTIVATION

Motivation has been defined in many ways. In fact, we have found over one hundred definitions of motivation. We define *motivation* as forces that initiate and maintain behavior. Because motivation exerts a major influence on performance, it is the responsibility of those interested in improving performance to create systems whereby individual motivations can be unleashed. A *motivational system* consists of strategies intended to initiate and sustain purposeful effort and activity.

We assume that learner motivation is highly individualized because each learner possesses unique needs, goals, and attitudes. One size does not fit all, and one theory does not apply to everyone. Not all people are motivated to learn in the same ways. Key issues related to motivation—as noted in the IBSTPI Standards—are interest, curiosity, attention, and reinforcement.

Just as numerous definitions for motivation can be found, countless theories and models of motivation exist as well. These include need theories, cognitive theories, and noncognitive approaches to motivation.

MASLOW'S NEED THEORY

Abraham Maslow proposed a hierarchy of needs to explain what motivates people. The model is a useful framework for discussing needs and motivation. The five levels of Maslow's hierarchy—from lowest to highest—include physiological needs, safety needs, love needs, esteem needs, and self-actualization needs. These needs can be conceptualized in the shape of a pyramid with physiological needs at the base progressing to self-actualization needs at the apex.

Maslow believed that people must satisfy each level of need before progressing to subsequent levels. For this reason, the needs are organized in a hierarchy. The first (and basic) level includes physiological needs such as needs for food and water. When not satisfied, these needs tend to represent powerful motivational elements. Maslow believed that once physiological needs are satisfied, then the next level—safety needs—would increase in strength. The need for affection and social relationships would emerge only after physiological needs are satisfied, and the need for esteem would emerge only after affection needs are met. Self-actualization needs, at the highest level of Maslow's hierarchy, are the only ones that Maslow believed could never be completely fulfilled. People are always striving to reach their full potential or to become fully self-actualized. However, even though some people do reach their full potential, it is generally for a short period of time and most drift in and out of this state. Abraham Lincoln and Mother Teresa are held up as examples, because they were able to self-actualize to a greater degree than the average person.

APPLYING MASLOW'S NEED THEORY TO TRAINING DELIVERY

Physiological and safety needs are not typically concerns in most training situations. There are exceptions, of course. If learners perceive training to be hazardous—such as a situation in which they are asked to perform without safety equipment—then the learners may be focused more on assuring their own safety than on learning. But if learners feel their safety is protected, they will focus their attention on meeting higher-level needs on Maslow's hierarchy.

As a trainer, you will usually find learner attention directed to meeting higher-order needs, such as social, self-esteem, and self-actualization. You can help learners meet their social needs if you devote your time to group activities and provide opportunities for learners to become acquainted with each other through ice-breakers, breaks, and other techniques.

Self-esteem needs are important in training as well. When you build and maintain the self-esteem of learners through what you say and what you do, learners become more self-confident and willing to take risks to try out new approaches or ideas. You can help learners meet their self-esteem needs by giving them opportunities to feel successful and by providing praise, reinforcement, and recognition of what they do well.

Maslow readily acknowledges that self-actualization, the highest level, is rarely attained. Perhaps you can encourage learners to identify their unique definition of full potential and then help them see how learning might be a tool to help them achieve their professional as well as personal goals and aspirations. Be warned, however, that although Maslow's hierarchy of needs is useful for providing explanations and giving you, as a trainer, some clues about what to do, it is generally not supported by empirical research.

GOAL-SETTING THEORY

Goal-setting theory states that, if people are presented with clear goals to be achieved, they are more likely to achieve them. Motivation is thus a function of how clearly people know what they are to do and see a personal benefit from achieving the goal(s). In training, of course, goals are stated as training objectives.

The implications of this theory should be clear: When learners are presented with clear training objectives to be achieved, their motivation to attain those objectives is increased. Some evidence suggests that if individuals are involved in setting their own goals, their commitment to achieving those goals is also increased. Exhibit 10–1 depicts the relationship between involvement in goal setting and commitment level. In training situations, goals (objectives) also serve important purposes in focusing learner attention on desired results and implying what effort is needed to achieve those results.

APPLYING GOAL-SETTING THEORY TO TRAINING DELIVERY

To be useful in training situations, objectives must be specific rather than vague. When learners do not understand the meaning of a vague goal (objective), its usefulness is limited. But a specific goal communi-

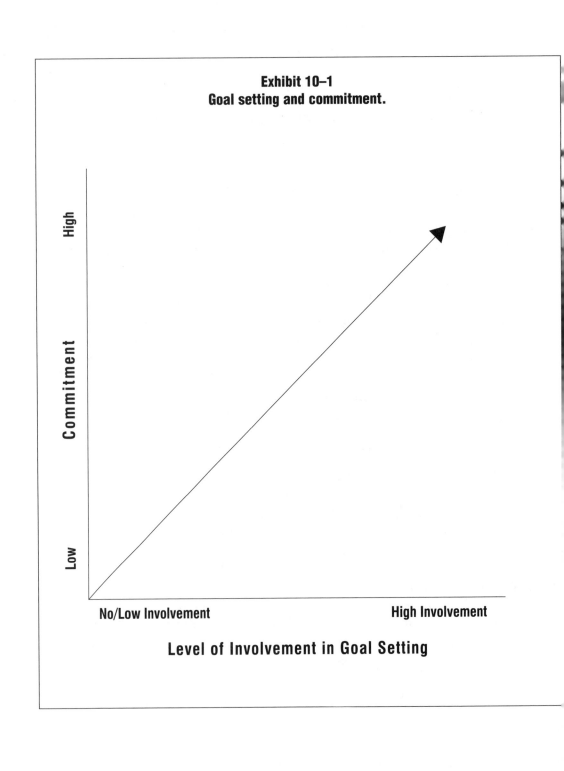

Exhibit 10–1
Goal setting and commitment.

cates to learners what they must do. For example, a vague goal is "take a good measurement," where it is unclear what is meant by a "good" measurement. In contrast, a specific goal is "using the micrometer and calibration block, measure within +/- .01 inch of the standard." This goal specifies very clearly what is to be achieved, how it is to be achieved, and to what degree.

To be effective, goals should also be sufficiently difficult to reach. When goals are too easily attainable, learners lose interest because they are not challenged. In contrast, a challenging goal focuses attention and can create a strong impetus to demonstrate achievement. Perhaps a goal of "type a report at twenty words per minute with five errors or less" is too easy for a group of learners in *Advanced Typing*, whereas "type a report at sixty-five words per minute with two errors or less" is more difficult and will challenge learners and help them to stretch their skills.

Another characteristic of an effective goal is that it can be bundled with feedback. Learners need to receive some periodic indications of how well or how much they are moving toward goal achievement. Feedback provided by you—or built in through measurable milestones so that learners can measure their own achievement—lets learners know how well they are progressing toward goal achievement. Consider a computer training course on *Microsoft Excel*, a popular spreadsheet software package, where at the end of each section there is an opportunity for learners to perform operations and work through problems related to the material covered in that section. The trainer can distribute answer keys so that learners can see for themselves how they did on the practice activities. This immediate feedback helps learners to recognize and correct errors they made or provides proof positive of a job well done.

One way to apply goal-setting theory to training is to use learning objectives presented to learners before or during training. When learners recognize the results desired from training, they are more motivated to act to achieve those goals, or encouraged to set goals for themselves before, during, and after the training session. When learners establish their own goals and expectations, they can work toward achieving results that are directly related to their work and personal objectives. Learner-established goals usually command more commitment than trainer-established goals.

In addition to goals set during the program, you can also encourage learners to establish on-the-job application goals. Such goals facilitate the transfer of training from the instructional setting (classroom) to the work setting (job site) and help learners apply what they have learned.

SOCIAL LEARNING THEORY

Social learning, proposed by Albert Bandura, is another commonly accepted and often used cognitive theory of motivation. This theory asserts that individuals can learn from others by watching them and modeling their behavior.

Behavior modeling, derived from social learning theory, is a commonly used technique for developing skills that directs learners to observe the performance of others and then model that performance. The learners may, for example, observe you perform a task and then model it. As an alternative, learners may watch a videotape of the behavior to be modeled and then model the behavior they saw on the tape.

Consider an example of how behavior modeling may be applied to supervisory training. Supervisors might be trained to coach employees by first watching you, the trainer, demonstrate coaching skills. They then practice these skills by coaching each other in role-play scenarios.

Modeling is different from imitating. Learners do not simply and mindlessly repeat or mimic the behaviors they witness. Instead, social learning theory suggests that learned behaviors are screened very carefully by the learner before deciding what aspects of the behavior should be incorporated. In the following vignette one trainer used behavior modeling during delivery.

> Leslie was delivering a training course on conflict resolution. Instead of presenting the material via lecture or having learners simply read about conflict resolution, she showed the learners a videotape of two people in a conflict situation. One of the people in the videotape demonstrated several conflict resolution techniques. After each method was demonstrated, Leslie paused the tape to discuss the technique with the group. The group then watched the demonstration again, this time watching for different aspects that were highlighted in the discussion. Leslie then divided the learners into pairs and facilitated a skill practice, enabling the learners to practice the skills they had just learned and observed.

MOTIVATIONAL STRATEGIES

A *motivational strategy* is a technique or method you use to gain learner attention, invoke effort, and build learner confidence.

KELLER'S ARCS MODEL

When properly designed, instructor guides typically incorporate activities that are designed to stimulate motivation. Your job as a training instructor, however, is to judge the effectiveness of these strategies in achieving the desired outcome. One framework developed to motivate learners was proposed by John Keller. It is commonly used during the instructional design phase of training to incorporate motivational elements into the design of the program. Keller's model is referred to as the *ARCS model*, which is an acronym for the four key elements of *Attention*, *Relevance*, *Confidence*, and *Satisfaction*. Each of these is described below.

Attention. Attention, the first component of the ARCS model, means to capture learner interest at the beginning of training and sustain that motivation throughout the course. Introductory activities you can use to achieve this purpose will be detailed in the section on using introductory activities to develop learner motivation later in this chapter.

Relevance. The focus of relevance, the second component, is to ensure that the training is applicable to the learners. When learners do not see how training will help them achieve their goals or solve their problems, they will lose the motivation to continue. This topic will be the focus of the next section in this chapter, matching learning outcomes to learner and organizational needs and goals.

Confidence. The third element of the ARCS model is confidence. Confidence deals with the perceptions that learners have about their ability to master the training content. You should attempt to achieve a balance between challenging

---

BOB PIKE

During an interview with training expert Bob Pike, we asked him, "What do you believe to be the most common problem(s) that new instructors face and what coaching advice would you have to deal with those problems?" One of his responses to this question was, "During training, learners are tuned in to two radio stations: WII-FM and MMFI-AM. WII-FM is 'what's in it for me.' If trainers can help learners identify some of the pain that they are feeling on their jobs and then give them some strategies for removing that pain, they will be much more successful. MMFI-AM is 'make me feel important about myself.' I think that a lot of trainers forget what their job is. The goal is to get learners to feel excited about what they can do, not to be intimidated by the trainer. The more confident learners are in their abilities, the more they will work to apply what they have learned and receive the benefits from that. The participant is supposed to win, not the instructor. Some trainers have the flawed belief that when the learners leave the training they should still feel that they do not know quite as much, or they are not quite as good, as 'the master.'"

learners and providing opportunities for success so that an appropriate level of confidence is developed.

Satisfaction. The final aspect of Keller's model is satisfaction. When learners are satisfied with the training, their the motivational level is likely to be high. Satisfaction can result from rewards and recognition you provide and from the feelings of satisfaction gained by learners as they demonstrate successful performance or skill mastery. How to provide feedback and reinforcement to facilitate learner satisfaction will be discussed later in this chapter.

MATCHING OUTCOMES TO LEARNER AND ORGANIZATIONAL NEEDS AND GOALS

As you begin this section, read the following critical incident and reflect on how you would handle this situation.

Loosening the Soil

" *Before training/learning can begin with adults/employees, I find that gaining their buy-in on why they are there, before telling what they will learn, is most important. Often trainees are sent to training in which they already feel competent or don't see a need to know. The time spent in "tilling" hard ground can be considerable, but will provide the environment for growth that otherwise may not happen at all.* "

Learners generally enter training with particular needs and goals. Unfortunately, as the experience above demonstrates, sometimes these needs are not readily identifiable and must be uncovered. Likewise, organizations provide sponsorship to training with the expectation that certain goals and objectives will be obtained. An important role that you, as a trainer, must play is to strike a balance between the intended outcomes of the training program and the needs and goals of the learner and the organization. When this balance is achieved, learners are motivated to participate actively and expend the effort to achieve the learning objectives.

STRATEGIES FOR CONVEYING RELEVANCE

As the discussion of the ARCS model indicated, you must help learners see how training helps them meet the needs they experience in their jobs and lives. To dramatize that point, reflect on the critical incident below, which illustrates the importance of establishing the relevance of training and the efforts made to demonstrate that relevance to learners.

Making Training Relevant

"One of the most typical problems I encounter is when participants are not interested in the material or feel they already know everything. I try to make everything seem relevant to their jobs by using specific examples, and explaining how the information I am presenting is critical for their jobs. Results have been mixed. Veteran employees will "buck the system" regardless of the relevance of the material to their jobs. Younger, new employees are easier to deal with and more eager to learn."

Learner interest can diminish rapidly if you fail to establish a clear connection between the knowledge and skills to be acquired during training and learners' needs and goals. The trainer in the critical incident above implies that there may be a difference between "veteran" and "younger, new employees." That generalization holds true in many cases, because learner interest can diminish rapidly if people do not see clear connections between what they are learning and what they need to know or do to perform or advance. In short, whether trainers like it or not, learners are always asking themselves "What's in this for me?" (a question that is often referred to as the WIIFM and is pronounced "wiff-um"). Let them know how they will benefit from the training and how it is relevant to them personally and how it will help them in their job. When learners view training as irrelevant, they question why certain topics are covered and even why they bothered to attend the training. Their interest will quickly fade as they focus their attention elsewhere.

Effective training programs stem from specific learning needs and sound instructional design. This said, it is still important for you, as the trainer, to clearly communicate the connection between the training and job performance so learners are able to recognize the relevance for themselves. Read the following critical incidents, which re-emphasize how important it is to demonstrate the benefits and usefulness of training to learners. Note especially how often this problem arises when people are required to attend training.

Don't Say "Mandatory"

"Gaining employee buy-in for mandatory training especially after-hours is a typical problem I face. I avoid the word "mandatory" and I concentrate on the benefits to the employee. I also deliver the training with a lot of enthusiasm."

Why Am I Here?

"The most typical problem is with required training and participants' perception of "this does not apply to me, why am I here?" I give examples of how the materials will be used on-the-job and how they might be used off the job. (Example: Hazardous materials training.)"

In addition to learners perceiving the training to have personal relevance, they must also see why it is important to the organization. Sometimes this is called making the business case, or establishing why training is useful to the organization. Making the business case can be viewed in several ways. First, training can be viewed as a cost because time, energy, and resources must be spent in training delivery. Training can also be viewed as a benefit because it will build knowledge and skills of use to the organization in achieving and sustaining competitive advantage.

A simple formula for determining the value of training to the organization is to subtract the costs of the training from the monetary and nonmonetary benefits derived from it. When the benefits outweigh the costs, then training is a worthwhile investment. For example, a process improvement training program for 20 learners may cost the organization $15,000. If the learners apply the training, the organization is able to save $75,000 through real improvements in the work process. In this scenario, the financial benefits outweigh the costs by $60,000. Further, intangible benefits, such as better safety, higher employee satisfaction, and better teamwork, though hard to quantify, should be considered. When these and other tangible and nontangible benefits are communicated to learners it helps them to see why training is important to the organization. That tends to increase their motivation.

The following critical incident emphasizes how important it is to show learners the relevance of training as a way to enhance their motivation. This trainer also lists several key strategies through which motivation can be stimulated further.

That's Nice, But in the Real World...

" My most typical problem is with unprepared participants who don't see the link between the education or training we provide and the "real world." As much as I can, I do the following:

- *Always provide the link even if the client says they know.*

- *Always address the underlying tones—the "elephants."*

- *Stop and involve participants in the process—don't lecture!*

- *Bring their experience into the training by using lots of small group exercises versus large group discussions where so many "check out."*

- *Facilitate learning by letting go and not controlling all experiences—it's impossible to do and you will only fail. "*

USING INTRODUCTORY ACTIVITIES TO ENHANCE LEARNER MOTIVATION

In Chapter Five, we described the importance of opening a training session effectively. Recall that we introduced six methods that you can employ as attention getters. Chapter Five also addressed the importance of creating a supportive learning climate, conveying expectations, resolving conflicting expectations, and communicating administrative details to the group of learners. We also discussed icebreakers, which are introductory activities that help learners become acquainted and that help to create a relaxed environment.

This section builds upon some of the key concepts covered in that chapter, and focuses on the impact that introductory activities can have on learner motivation. An *introductory activity* is a method used to engage learner interest or motivation. Chapter Seven discussed the use of props as a means to focus learner attention and increase understanding. Displaying a prop and discussing it during delivery is just one introductory activity you could use as a trainer. Telling a story or anecdote is another example. In fact, the techniques you can use are almost limitless.

EXAMPLES OF INTRODUCTORY ACTIVITIES

Ideally, you should have several introductory activities available and ready to use. Make sure they are easy to customize to various topics, making them more versatile. Here are some brief descriptions of introductory activities you can use:

- Have learners break into small groups and discuss their experiences with the topic at hand. Ask them to be prepared to discuss any unusual or exemplary experiences with others in the group.

- Write several topic-related, thought-provoking questions on small pieces of paper and pass them out to small groups of learners (one per group). Allow them ten to twenty minutes to answer the questions and then have them present their answers to the class.

- Give the learners assigned reading before the training course and ask them to be prepared to discuss it. During training, ask them to get with a few other people and write down any questions they may have regarding the assigned reading. Then ask them to select one question and write it on the white board or flipchart. Each question should be addressed and answered throughout the rest of the training. Alternatively, you could ask learners to identify what was most important, most enlightening, and most confusing about the reading assignment.

DETERMINING WHEN TO USE INTRODUCTORY ACTIVITIES

Introductory activities need not be exclusively used at the opening of a training program, although this does represent an appropriate time to use them. Throughout a training program the level of interest, as well as the motivation, of learners tends to wane and wax. This is a natural cycle that occurs during delivery because it is difficult to maintain peak interest at all times—especially when the training content is not inherently stimulating. For this reason, you should interject activities at appropriate times to enhance learner interest and attention. Below is a critical incident that demonstrates this approach of "mixing things up" to keep learners motivated.

Mix It Up

" On day 3 of a week-long training program, at around 2 P.M. all new hires lose their concentration from information overload. We take frequent breaks, have a light lunch that day, and I tell a few funny stories. I continue to stress why the information they're receiving is important. "

USING INTRODUCTORY ACTIVITIES TO BEGIN A NEW SEGMENT

An ideal time to use introductory activities is at the opening of a new segment of a training course. When a new part is introduced, you should focus the learners' attention so that the initial groundwork for the new part can be laid without distraction. Another prime time to use an introductory activity is immediately before a key point will be made about the subject matter of the course. Again, when learners' motivation is stimulated through an introductory activity, the likelihood that they will fully receive the message dramatically increases.

USING INTRODUCTORY ACTIVITIES AFTER BREAKS

Another opportune time for introductory activities is immediately following any break in delivery. The two main types of breaks in training are planned or scheduled breaks and unplanned breaks. Examples of planned breaks include a ten-minute formal break during a morning session or a one-hour lunch break. Often, training is designed so that such breaks occur around natural stopping points in the training. In such cases when learners return from the break they enter into a new segment of training in which some introductory activity—such as a group activity—is appropriate anyway. It is also important to understand that group energy is affected by timing and that learner energy ebbs immediately following lunch, so a group activity is ideally suited to rebuild energy before the next presentation.

On the other hand, many breaks in delivery are unplanned. For example, learners may become distracted by noise coming from another part of the facility, or a power surge that shuts down all computer systems for a time. These situations create unintended breaks or distractions in training and require you to take quick-witted action. Once the interruption has been remedied, refocus learner attention and reengage learner motivation. These moments when the learners have been distracted or have lost their focus are ideal times for introductory activities.

MANAGING GROUP DYNAMICS DURING INTRODUCTORY ACTIVITIES

Many introductory activities incorporate instructional methods requiring learners to be active participants. Examples of such methods are games and group exercises. These and many other instructional methods will be explored in detail in Chapter Eleven. For purposes of this discussion, however, we stress that it is your responsibility as a trainer to ensure that learners are comfortable participating in the activity—especially a group activity. Recall that managing group interaction was covered in Chapter Five. Related to this idea is the importance of managing group dynamics, which will also be treated in the next chapter. In short, the dynamics of the group should be appropriate to the introductory activity being used as well as the content of the training.

When group exercises are used as introductory activities, remain actively involved by circulating among the groups and ocassionally sitting in with them. When control is abdicated to the group, your role shifts to that of a facilitator. As a facilitator, monitor group processes and dynamics carefully and intervene when group members are arguing or cannot reach agreement, or when individuals are dominating small group activities. When group dynamics become dysfunctional, learners become distracted or detached and become less motivated. For example, if one person dominates the group during a group activity, others may withdraw from it and their learning will be seriously hampered. If you remain involved, however, you can identify such behavior, intervene, and take corrective action as necessary.

USING FEEDBACK AND REINFORCEMENT DURING DELIVERY

This section describes how positive and corrective feedback can be used to reinforce and motivate learners. In this way, feedback enhances learner confidence and motivation by rewarding and recognizing achievement and success.

REINFORCEMENT THEORY

The reinforcement theory of motivation, which is grounded in behaviorism, has existed for many years and was initially developed by E. L. Thorndike and John Watson in the early part of the twentieth century. It was later refined by the well-known behavioral psychologist B. F. Skinner. Reinforcement theory suggests that individuals engage in certain behaviors because of the rewards associated with them and avoid other behaviors because of the consequences associated with them. In essence, this theory asserts that behavior is a result of the actual or anticipated consequences (either positive or negative) associated with it. Reinforcement theory sometimes evokes the image of a rat in a maze or a pigeon in a cage responding to various stimuli. Still, useful aspects of reinforcement theory are applicable to training situations.

POSITIVE REINFORCEMENT

Several important concepts are related to reinforcement theory and are essential to understanding it. One such concept is *positive reinforcement,* which means pleasant, or positive, outcomes linked with a particular behavior. Such positive consequences lead to repetition of the behavior. *Extinction* is a phenomenon related to positive reinforcement, and it means that behavior tends to disappear over time when pleasant consequences are discontinued.

NEGATIVE REINFORCEMENT

Negative reinforcement and punishment are two concepts that are frequently confused. *Negative reinforcement* is simply the removal of an unpleasant stimulus that results in increased frequency of the behavior. An example of negative reinforcement is the removal of asking direct questions of learners. In this example, the target behavior is learner participation. The unpleasant activity (for some of the learners) is direct questions, which may evoke anxiety among certain individuals. The learners in this scenario are likely to become motivated to participate because they know that doing so will decrease the number of direct questions the trainer will ask.

PUNISHMENT

Punishment, on the other hand, involves the delivery of an unpleasant stimulus following undesired behavior, and is likely to cause a decrease in the behavior. If you ask two learners engaged in a side conversation to share with the group what they are discussing, you are in some ways punishing them. The intent of your action is to decrease side conversations during training, and you put the learners on the spot as a mild form of punishment.

We do not recommend that you use punishment during training except in extreme cases involving immediate safety hazards or legal issues. Punishment can have detrimental results beyond merely suppressing undesirable behaviors. It can, for instance, lead to defensiveness or build hostility when the learners feel that they are being scolded or treated like children. In addition, others who witness the punishment are likely to become irritated and turn against the trainer. On the other hand, if learners feel your punishment of, say, unruly, rude, or belligerent learners is justified, then they may appreciate and support your taking corrective action. As a rule, however, exercise caution and handle behavior problems in more subtle ways, such as discussing them one-on-one. Also, keep in mind that positive reinforcement typically has a greater impact on learner behavior than punishment during training.

STRATEGIES FOR INCORPORATING POSITIVE REINFORCEMENT DURING DELIVERY

When learners demonstrate successful performance, apply reinforcement theory. Sometimes such reinforcement can be planned and deliberately used because practice exercises or skill tests are incorporated as part of the training design. At other times, however, reinforcement will be more spontaneous and result from behavior that you feel merits positive reinforcement, such as sudden participation from an otherwise silent participant. When you provide the learner with positive reinforcement following an achievement or desired behavior, the learner's confidence level is likely to be raised, the success can be built upon, and the behavior will probably be repeated in the future. Some examples of statements of positive reinforcement appear below.

- Jeff, you answered all of the questions correctly and managed to finish on time.

- Kat, by implementing these skills into your job, you have become a model for other employees to follow.

- Trey, you inserted the correct formulas into your spreadsheet, enabling you to perform the proper calculations.

- Bonnie, the length of time you made eye contact with the customer was perfect. It was neither too brief nor so long that it became uncomfortable.

Positive reinforcement can be delivered in many ways. Positive reinforcement can be tangible, such as a small reward or prize, or it can be intangible, such as verbal praise or recognition. Below is a critical incident that relates the use of this technique, and several others, as a way to stimulate interest and motivation:

Keeping Them Interested

" *The subject matter I train is often boring and dull. I have trouble frequently trying to keep people interested and involved. I use humor and incentives such as candy and toys to liven up the sessions. I also give the participants frequent breaks throughout the session.* "

USING RECOGNITION AND FEEDBACK AS POSITIVE REINFORCEMENT

Often the most powerful forms of reinforcement are intangible. When you recognize people for a job well done or when you praise them for specific behaviors or accomplishments, their self-esteem is bolstered and they will usually repeat the behavior. Another common form of positive reinforcement is simple feedback. When people know that they performed or responded correctly, this awareness can serve as a catalyst for repeated behavior and for building confidence. The following vignette demonstrates the use of feedback as positive reinforcement.

> **TRAINER:** *Matthew, you have really been working hard to learn feedback skills. During the skill practice, I noticed that you gave Alex very specific, relevant feedback in a timely manner. The result was a positive change in Alex's behavior.*

On the other hand, when learners do not receive feedback about their performance they may become confused about whether they are on target. This confusion can lead them astray so that they do not perform correctly in the future or they are less motivated because they do not know what to make of the results of their efforts. A similar situation can arise when learners receive little or no praise or recognition for their efforts. When this happens, learners lose their motivation because they perceive their efforts to be going unnoticed.

One fortunate characteristic of some training is that feedback and positive reinforcement are often built into the training itself. For example, a person learning a new skill, such as diagnosing an engine problem, may receive feedback from training equipment set up to provide visual cues such as red and green lights to indicate incorrect and correct actions. In this manner, learners can identify for themselves when they performed successfully.

Most adult learners possess a high degree of self-awareness. They generally know whether they are learning and moving toward their goals. This internally sensed feedback works as a source of information to the learners about their performance and thus helps them to continue or discontinue behaviors leading to the desired objectives.

JUDGING THE APPROPRIATENESS OF MOTIVATIONAL STRATEGIES

As was mentioned earlier in this chapter, effective instructional design deliberately incorporates motivational strategies that you, as a trainer, can use throughout delivery. An important assumption made in this book is that such strategies were, in fact, considered and incorporated into the training course design. These motivational strategies are typically outlined in the instructor manual along with directions for best ways to use those strategies. Although these guidelines are useful in helping you to encourage learners and tap into their motivation, you must still continuously monitor and evaluate their effectiveness. This section describes several criteria and techniques by which you can assess motivational strategies to ensure that they were successfully applied during delivery.

DEVIATING FROM THE INSTRUCTOR GUIDE

Instructor guides provide structure to training and facilitate achievement of objectives. However, instructor guides are not meant to be restrictive, and you should make changes based on the situation and the needs of the group. In the case of motivational strategies, this rule applies as well. However, if strategies are not followed, there should be reasonable justification. For example, if learners are already energetic, enthusiastic, and highly motivated, then you can skip the initial activities in the instructor guide designed to stimulate enthusiasm. In other words, visibly high levels of learner motivation may be sufficient justification for eliminating an activity designed to achieve that very end.

MODIFYING MOTIVATIONAL STRATEGIES

Since each training program, group of learners, and situation is different, you may need to make major modifications in your motivational strategies to ensure effectiveness. The goal of such strategies is to stimulate and sustain appropriate amounts of interest and participation from learners. When the strategies aren't working you will need to revise or modify them. It is up to you to assess the adequacy of the strategy and make any needed adjustments. Whenever possible, make the assessments and adjustments before delivery, rather than on the spur of the moment. Regardless of when or what adjustments you make, evaluate their impact on learner interest, participation, and motivation.

IDENTIFYING INDICATORS OF LEARNER MOTIVATION

Cues as to the level of motivation may be seen in the extent of active verbal participation, the sense of excitement, and nonverbal signals, such as eye contact or leaning forward. Signs of a lack of motivation may include low levels of verbal communication and participation, avoidance of eye contact, withdrawn body posture, and distracted attention. Exhibit 10–2 lists behavior indicators that point toward high and low motivation levels. Motivation is a continuum where learners will range from high to low. The exhibit represents the two extreme positions, but learners may fluctuate along these points. Use these indicators as clues to determine the level of learner motivation that is present and take corrective action as necessary. Keep in mind that these behaviors are merely indicators of motivation and should always be verified. A learner who is not vocal or highly involved may simply be shy.

Exhibit 10–2
Indicators of high and low levels of motivation.

High Motivation	Low Motivation
Makes eye contact	Avoids eye contact
Asks questions	Uninvolved in training Does not ask questions
Contributes own experiences	Uninvolved in training Does not participate in conversation
Provides comments and insights	Uninvolved in training Does not make a contribution
Applies new skills during skill practices	Uninvolved in training

EVALUATING THE EFFECTIVENESS OF MOTIVATIONAL STRATEGIES

In addition to motivational strategies, the use of feedback and rein-forcement during delivery should be evaluated for effectiveness. Two types of feedback we have discussed are positive and corrective. The purpose of feedback is to maintain or enhance learner performance. When you provide feedback and reinforcement to learners, you should ascertain the effect. Identify whether the learners' performance has indeed improved as a result of the feedback. If not, you may need to deliver additional or revised feedback. If improvement was seen, then note this fact for possible future use.

Another method for determining the effectiveness of motivational strategies is to determine how much the learners recognize the value of the training. As mentioned early in this chapter, you should show how training will help meet individual needs and help achieve desired busi-ness results. At the conclusion of training, learners should be able to justify their participation in training in terms of the personal and orga-nizational benefits that were reaped from it, both present and future. If learners leave training believing that it was a waste of time, it indicates either a disconnect between the desired outcomes and actual program outcomes, or your inability to demonstrate the relationship between the training and the organization's or individuals' needs and goals. Either problem can be very harmful to your credibility, that of the train-ing department, and even that of the organization, because the value of the program will be called into question.

Finally, when judging the adequacy of motivational strategies, make sure that your use of rewards and incentives is useful and appro-priate. For example, if you throw candy to learners who respond cor-rectly to questions, some may be offended because they feel that you are treating them like children or animals. In other situations learners may respond favorably to such an incentive, and it may actually encourage increased levels of involvement and enthusiasm. Other problems can arise when you provide rewards and reinforcement either to a very restricted number of learners, or lavishly to all learners regardless of their behavior. You can often predict in advance what effect rewards and incentives will have on learners by considering the group, the needs of learners, the content of the training, and other characteristics.

DOCUMENTING REVISIONS

Just as all changes made before or during delivery as well as the sup-porting rationale should be documented, adjustments to the motivational strategies should also be documented. In addition to the specific modifications and accompanying justifications, supply your perceived evaluation of the results of those changes. Rationale for changes may include characteristics of a particular group, learner needs, and the training situation. The purpose of diligently recording changes is to communicate revisions and, if necessary, feed them into the design so that future offerings of the training can be improved. When adjustments to the motivational strategies are made, you and/or the instructional designers should determine whether permanent revisions to the training material should be made or if the situation was unique and changes are not necessary. Another option is to include the situation and the adjustments that were made as instructor notes that are incorporated into the material so that adjustments can be made under similar conditions in the future.

SUMMARY

In this chapter we discussed the competency of providing positive reinforcement and motivational incentives and covered the following topics:

- Summaries of several motivation theories, including need theories, cognitive theories, and noncognitive approaches.

- How to apply motivation theories during training delivery to sustain learner motivation and commitment.

- Matching outcomes to the needs and goals of learners and the organization.

- Strategies for incorporating positive and negative reinforcement during delivery.

STRATEGY LIST

Actionable Strategies to Improve Training Effectiveness:

Increase Learner Motivation

❏ Motivate learners by providing them with timely, specific feedback and recognition.

❏ Use the "What's In It For Me" (WIIFM) technique by emphasizing the importance of the training results and benefits to the business and to the learners.

❏ Involve learners in setting their own training goals to increase their commitment and motivation in achieving them.

❏ Make learning goals specific, measurable, challenging, and realistic.

❏ Use positive as well as negative reinforcement (not the same as punishment) to encourage positive behavior.

Motivational Strategies

❏ Use stories, anecdotes, icebreakers, and other introductory activities to capture learners' attention. Also, inform learners why they need to know this new information and how it will help them do their job.

❏ Provide learners with opportunities during training to successfully use the new skills to build their confidence. Emphasize how the new skills enhance their current skills and job performance.

❏ Use introductory activities when you detect that learners may be getting sleepy, tired, or generally disinterested. These activities help you generate interest by moving to a new topic and encouraging participation.

❏ Use a variety of motivational strategies to maintain impact.

❏ Monitor learners for signs of motivation (or lack of motivation) such as verbal activity, eye contact, level of participation, and a general sense of excitement or enthusiasm. Use these signs as indicators of when to employ more or different motivational strategies.

CHAPTER 11

USING TRAINING METHODS APPROPRIATELY

SKILLS ASSESSMENT

Take a moment to review the competency and associated performances that will be covered in this chapter. Consider your current level of proficiency in the competency as a whole as well as each performance and check the items where you feel you need to improve. As you read the chapter, concentrate on those areas most in need of development.

Competency:

❏ Use training methods appropriately.

Associated Performances:

❏ Implement a variety of training methods.

❏ Manage the group dynamics associated with each method.

❏ Employ training techniques appropriate to methods and training situations prescribed.

❏ Judge the appropriateness and effectiveness of methods and techniques.

A variety of *training methods* are used by trainers during delivery to facilitate learning. You may, for example, use such training methods as lectures, discussions, large or small group activities, individual activities, collaborative learning, problem-based learning, and case studies. Exhibit 11–1 briefly describes several training methods, which will be discussed more fully in this chapter. By altering the training methods

Exhibit 11–1
Training methods.

Training Method	Description
Lecture	Lecture is a unidirectional method of teaching that relies on the instructor's knowledge and ability to present that information.
Discussion	Discussion is a two-way conversation between trainer and learners or among learners. This method encourages learners to ask questions, make comments, and share their thoughts.
Group activity	A group activity is a project or exercise where learners engage in and work toward a specific outcome or produce a specific product. The trainer often acts as a facilitator by guiding, directing, and monitoring learner performance.
Individual activity	An individual activity is similar to a group activity, with the exception that learners work independently and are solely responsible for the final outcome or product.
Collaborative learning	Collaborative learning is a form of learning where learners share responsibilities and are dependent on one another in achieving a specified goal.
Problem-based learning, or action learning	Problem-based learning (sometimes called action learning) is when learning occurs through solving an actual problem and reflecting on the learnings. There usually is not one correct answer, but rather several possible outcomes.
Project-based learning	Project-based learning is when learners are presented with a project to complete. Similar to problem-based learning, the learning occurs as the project moves forward to completion.
Case study	The case study method is a form of problem-based learning. In this method, learners are presented with a real or fictitious scenario and must apply new knowledge as well as prior experience to analyze the situation and develop a solution.
Self-directed learning	During self-directed learning, the learner controls the pace, timing, sequence, and content of learning.
Learner-led learning	This method involves learners teaching one another. This could be one-on-one instruction or one learner teaching the group.
Business game	Business games are activities designed to simulate some aspect of a business. Business games may or may not be competitive, where only one learner or group of learners "wins."

you use during delivery, you can keep learners interested, activate different learning styles, and enhance comprehension and retention. There are many training methods available, and you should be proficient in using them to help meet learners' needs.

If you rely on only one training method—such as lecture—the training may be of limited value. One reason is that over-reliance on one method becomes tiresome. Another reason is that individuals learn in different ways, and using mutiple methods will increase the likelihood that learners will have been touched by at least one of these methods. A third reason is that different learners and training goals demand flexible approaches.

Varied training methods add variety, which can command attention from learners, as the trainer in the critical incident below describes:

Dozing Off

 " *The problem I face most often in teaching (delivery) is speaking to students who cannot stay awake because of already having put in too many hours at the work place. We are an off-site facility. Midnight shift is horrible to try to keep students awake for six- to eight-hour classes. I have found that at break time (ten-minute breaks every hour), if I turn on an exciting video (cops, or incredible feats, natural disasters) it wakes them up immediately.* "

This chapter reviews common training methods and offers helpful tips for using them. It covers the following topics:

- Description of the different training methods, including lectures, role playing, discussions, individual exercises, case studies, games, and debates.

- Managing group dynamics.

- Strategies for using the many different training methods.

- Making adjustments during delivery.

USING VARIOUS TRAINING METHODS

Using a variety of training methods stimulates learner interest and arouses curiosity. It also leads to increased understanding and retention. According to master presenter Bob Pike of Creative Training Techniques International, located in Minneapolis, "In our programs we use the 90/20/8 rule. No module that we teach ever runs more than ninety minutes, the pace changes every twenty minutes, and we try to involve people in the content every eight minutes. That is based on Tony Buzan's book, *Use Both Sides of Your Brain*, in which he writes that the average adult can listen with understanding for only ninety minutes, but can listen with retention for twenty minutes."[1]

The critical incident below dramatizes the importance of using different training methods.

Shake It Up!

" A common problem I have is jazzing up the slower times of training— making sure that the presentation is constantly varied to keep everyone interested. "

TRAINING METHODS AND LEARNER PARTICIPATION

One way to distinguish among training methods is by how much learner participation is required from each. Some methods—and lecture is a good example—allow learners to be passive. Other methods, such as collaborative learning groups, demand active involvement from learners. *Experiential learning* is a term associated with training methods that require active participation from learners because learning occurs in a practical project or assignment that gives learners hands-on experience with the material.

A second way to distinguish among training methods is by how much trainer control is provided by each method. Some methods—and lecture is again one of those—vest control in you, the trainer. Conversely, other methods—such as group problem-solving—shift the locus of control to learners because they become active participants in the learning process without much involvement from you.

Typically you will find that the training method recommended for a course is described in the instructor guide. The choice of method depends on the desired results and is usually determined during the instructional design phase. This section reviews training methods you can use and the important characteristics, advantages, disadvantages, and other issues associated with them.

THE LECTURE OR PRESENTATION METHOD

Lecture is a traditional training method. Many people think of it first when they think of training or any other educational experience. The word *lecture* conjures up images of a teacher presenting information while standing at the front of a classroom filled with students who are seated silently at their desks. In the lecture method, the trainer transmits information orally to an audience. Lectures are unidirectional because the trainer is the primary communicator who conveys information to the group, while the group's role is to listen. Some learners might be seen feverishly taking notes while others drift off to sleep, carry on side conversations, or become distracted with something they find more interesting than a lengthy lecture. Sometimes visual aids and media such as transparencies, chalkboards, or charts are coupled with the lecture method to enhance its effectiveness.

The lecture method has both advantages and disadvantages as a training method.

ADVANTAGES OF THE LECTURE METHOD

The primary advantage of the lecture method is that it is an efficient way to transmit a large amount of information to learners in a short time. Since the purpose of some training programs is to raise awareness or supply information, lecture can be an appropriate way to do that. For example, information about a new HR policy or an update on a new procedure or project may need to be conveyed in a lecture to disseminate information quickly. There are also occasions in training—such as introductions or summaries—where lecture may serve this purpose more efficiently than other methods.

SIVASAILAM THIAGARAJAN

In an interview we conducted with training expert Sivasailam Thiagarajan ("Thiagi") we asked him, "What do you believe to be the most common problem(s) that new instructors face and what coaching advice would you have to deal with those problems?" He responded in this way: "New instructors have a great need to 'cover' all the learning points in detail. My coaching advice to instructors is that their job is not to 'cover' the content but to 'uncover' it or to help participants 'discover' it. I recommend that they let go of their obsession with disseminating information in great detail and focus instead on helping participants experience and master the core content.

"New instructors choose their training methods in two ways: (1) the way they were taught or (2) the way they would prefer to learn. This presents some interesting problems. My advice to you is to become aware of these biases and consciously strive to use different methods. I suggest that the trainer should have at least three different methods for teaching each module of instruction."

The lecture method is also useful when training involves many learners. Information can be conveyed in a time-effective manner from trainer-as-expert to learners-as-novices. While some training methods require more time, lecture is generally a way in which information can be communicated directly and without much delay.

DRAWBACKS TO THE LECTURE METHOD

The lecture method has been a frequent target of criticism. In fact, research conducted among directors of training showed that the lecture was perceived to be among the least effective training methods.[2] One reason the lecture method is criticized is that it does not encourage learner involvement. As a consequence, learners may grow bored and distracted as they listen to it. They lack ownership in the learning process—with the result that they remember less than when they are actively engaged in it.

Nor does the lecture method adequately tap into the vast experience residing in the group. In the lecture, the trainer (who is usually a subject matter expert) is the sole source of information. That suggests that the learners have nothing of value to add and in almost all cases, nothing could be further from the truth.

STRATEGIES FOR USING THE LECTURE METHOD

The lecture method has developed a negative reputation. Many people describe it using words such as "boring," "ineffective," and "outdated." That is particularly true for a generation nurtured on the sophisticated production values of commercial television and the instant availability of vast amounts of information on the Web. They grow impatient with the slow pace of oral communication, where the spoken word is transmitted at about 150 words per minute while the average listener can listen to about 750 words per minute.

While the lecture method sometimes deserves the bad reputation it has acquired, that does not mean it is always inappropriate. Nor does it mean that lectures must be delivered in boring ways. You can use several strategies to improve the delivery of lecture. One is to combine it with other training methods. When training involves lecture with other methods such as case studies or group discussions, learner involvement improves and retention is higher. In addition, you can ask questions frequently during a lecture to enhance learner involvement. When you use questions during lecture, it becomes more interactive and in a way can transform it into a large group discussion.

SHORTEN THE TIME OF THE LECTURE

Another way to improve traditional lectures is to reduce how much time you spend on them. The *lecturette* and *mini-lecture* are terms used to describe an abbreviated lecture. The length of a lecturette may vary, but often ranges from ten to thirty minutes. A fifteen- to twenty-minute mini-lecture may be an ideal target time because it corresponds to the rule of thumb mentioned earlier that states that the delivery method should be varied about every twenty minutes to match learner attention span. The traditional lecture provides in-depth coverage of an entire subject, but the lecturette is focused and covers only one point, which is then paired with reinforcement and practice by another training method like a small group exercise.

MAKE LECTURES LIVELY

A final way to improve the traditional lecture method is to use lively presentation methods so that it does not become dull. Chapter Seven described ways you can use humor, stories, and nonverbal behaviors like gestures and facial expressions to keep the presentation lively. Use these and other presentation skills during lecture delivery to energize the topic, capture attention, and galvanize learner interest. That should improve the overall effectiveness and impact of the lecture.

INDIVIDUAL EXERCISES

The individual exercise is another training method that you may use. As the term implies, an *individual exercise* is any activity performed by individual learners. While there are many such methods, they share one characteristic in common: Learners work independently on exercises, activities, or other scenarios to master subject matter or reinforce what they have learned. Examples include assessments, reading assignments, and in-basket exercises. They are advantageous because they permit learners to work at their own pace and direction. There are, however, some disadvantages to these as well. These will be discussed in the sections that follow.

ASSESSMENTS

Assessments include inventories or questionnaires in which each learner rates himself or herself on the content or questions presented. An example of an inventory is an "ideal job inventory" where individuals respond to questions about their work and career aspirations and preferences. The result is a recommendation or profile about preferences. Questionnaires often contain rating scales on which learners rate themselves along various dimensions. An example of a questionnaire is an assessment listing various leadership competencies with corresponding proficiency rating scales. Exhibit 11–2 depicts a sample questionnaire on which learners can rate their need for development on tasks associated with the competency area of Supervision and Management.

If you used the self-assessment instrument in Exhibit 11–2 in training, you would instruct learners to rate the importance and need for development on each task. When the questionnaire is completed, learners would then multiply the columns to arrive at an overall score. The learners could then prioritize a list of developmental needs to determine priorities. The result is a developmental profile that points the learner toward areas needing improvement. Action planning is a follow-up step after the self-assessment. It helps individuals improve in areas where they perceive their skills to be weak.

Some assessments—like the one described above—allow learners to calculate their own scores. These are called *self-scoring assessments*. They may also provide additional information on how to interpret and use their scores for development and action planning. More complex instruments may involve sending the scoring sheet to an external organization to be processed and returned as a detailed report complete with narrative descriptions, charts, graphs, comparisons, recommendations, and strategies. Other instruments may also require a *full-circle or multi-rater assessment* in which many people—including subordinates, peers, immediate supervisors, customers, distributors, suppliers, and even family members—rate the individual, after which these ratings are compared to the individual's score(s) as a basis for developmental planning.

WHEN AND HOW TO USE ASSESSMENTS

Many individual assessments covering many topics are available commercially. They can be quite costly, however, which can be a constraint.

Another constraint is on when and how to use these assessments. Usually you cannot just pass them out without providing the learners thorough guidance and explanation. Generally, you need to introduce assessments to help learners understand what the purpose is, how the results will be used, how the assessment should be completed, and how much time should be allotted for completion. These issues should be spelled out in the instructor guide or administrator guide accompanying the assessment. Further, you as trainer may need guidance to field questions that come up as learners fill out the assessment. You should make yourself available to answer questions from individuals as they complete assessments.

Exhibit 11–2
Sample self-assessment.

For each task listed in the left column below, *circle an appropriate response code in the middle column to indicate* **how important** *you consider the task for success in your job.* Use the following scale for the middle column: **1 = Not important; 2 = Some importance; 3 = Important; 4 = Much importance; 5 = Very high importance.** Then *circle an appropriate response code in the right column to indicate* **how much need you have for professional development in this task area.** Use the following scale for the right column: **1 = No need; 2 = Some need; 3 = Need; 4 = Much need; 5 = Very great need.**

Supervision and Management

	Task	Importance	Need for Development
1	Supervise staff on daily basis.	1 2 3 4 5	1 2 3 4 5
2	Establish and communicate staff accountability.	1 2 3 4 5	1 2 3 4 5
3	Delegate work as necessary.	1 2 3 4 5	1 2 3 4 5
4	Support staff members in achieving their goals.	1 2 3 4 5	1 2 3 4 5
5	Provide regular feedback and counseling to staff on performance.	1 2 3 4 5	1 2 3 4 5
6	Evaluate staff performance.	1 2 3 4 5	1 2 3 4 5
7	Provide staff members with professional development and growth opportunities.	1 2 3 4 5	1 2 3 4 5
8	Promote staff.	1 2 3 4 5	1 2 3 4 5
9	Lay off or terminate staff as necessary.	1 2 3 4 5	1 2 3 4 5
10	Manage office work flow.	1 2 3 4 5	1 2 3 4 5
11	Make decisions promptly and effectively.	1 2 3 4 5	1 2 3 4 5
12	Identify/manage priorities on a daily basis.	1 2 3 4 5	1 2 3 4 5
13	Juggle multiple/conflicting priorities.	1 2 3 4 5	1 2 3 4 5
14	Serve as an exemplary role model.	1 2 3 4 5	1 2 3 4 5
15	Motivate/encourage department and staff.	1 2 3 4 5	1 2 3 4 5

Perhaps the most important aspect of individual exercises is the follow-up. When assessments are completed by learners, but are not discussed or tied in to the content of the training, learners can become confused. They may wonder why they bothered doing an assessment that was not used, or they may question its value. For this reason, you should always plan a debriefing, follow-up, or wrap-up explanation so that learners see a clear connection between the assessment and the subject matter of the training.

READING ASSIGNMENTS

Reading assignments are another form of individual exercise that you can incorporate into training. Some people learn best by reading, and at times it is a refreshing change of pace to permit learners to work independently during an otherwise trainer-led program. The reading material that learners review becomes the primary source of content for that segment and, as such, essentially replaces the trainer or subject matter expert. A distinct advantage of using reading assignments is that learners can work at their own pace and style. For example, some learners might prefer to use a highlighter or take notes while reading. Sometimes, reading assignments can be used before or after training as either a preview of the program or as reinforcement following training. They can provide much information in a short time, thereby eliminating the need for heavy reliance on lecture.

You can also insert additional reading or reference material in an appendix of the participant guide. This allows you to use this additional information during class if there is sufficient time or, if you run out of time, it can be presented to learners as an outside-of-class reading assignment. This provides a nice buffer to level out inconsistencies in the training schedule. Further, it allows interested learners to go into greater depth on the subject if they so desire.

POTENTIAL PROBLEMS WITH READING ASSIGNMENTS

There are several disadvantages to using reading assignments. One is that some learners are illiterate or semi-literate, an increasing problem in corporate America. Literacy problems may be difficult for you to detect, since many people are adept at hiding them. A second problem is that learners may not do the reading. That is particularly true with pre-work reading, where some people do not see the relevance of the assignment or do not want to take the time to read it. Learners may also lose interest if the material is not stimulating or is too voluminous.

If you elect to use a reading assignment as pre-work, be sure to include a cover letter that describes the material and provides the learner with clear directions on what to read, when they should read it, and why it is important that they read it.

IN-BASKET EXERCISES

In-basket exercises are interactive simulations in which learners analyze information, set priorities, and make decisions on issues confronting them. An in-basket, as the name implies, is usually filled with what you would find on a desk—such as reports, memos, letters, and of course, junk mail. This timed method is frequently used in leadership or management development training programs or behavioral assessment centers. An in-basket exercise places learners in a day-in-the-life situation, where they are asked to perform typical management tasks and activities. During the simulation, which can be videotaped, learners are often assessed against predetermined competencies, such as time management, problem solving, or decision making.

ADVANTAGES AND DISADVANTAGES OF IN-BASKET EXERCISES

One disadvantage of this method is that reality is difficult to duplicate in an in-basket simulation. Learners are asked to react to situations when they are unaware of critical issues that could affect their decisions—such as the organization's history, corporate culture, working relationships, or in-house politics. Other assessments, such as multi-rater assessments, may be preferable because, although they are subjective in nature, they focus on actual job performance rather than performance under contrived or artificial conditions. Sometimes learners complete an in-basket before or after training, which can save time and encourage self-directed learning. Developing effective in-basket exercises can require extensive instructional design work, time, and financial resources if the exercises are valid and reliable.

CASE STUDY OR PROBLEM-BASED LEARNING

Case studies present written or computer-based scenarios that describe an actual or fictitious problem situation. Learners must usually apply the knowledge and skills they acquired from training and prior experience to examine the case, make decisions, and propose solutions or recommendations. Although case studies may be used as individual exercises, it is more common to use them for group work. In addition to developing analysis and problem solving skills, case studies can facilitate the development of teamwork, communication, and presentation skills—especially when learners are asked to report their findings to a class.

But the case study method does have disadvantages. As is true of in-basket exercises, case studies sometimes lack realism and immediate relevance to the organizational setting. They may also be difficult for learners to comprehend when presented in written form.

One variation of the traditional written case study is the living case. A *living case* introduces an actual problem or situation occurring in the organization, and it is sometimes presented by a guest speaker who is actually experiencing the problem. Learners have the advantage of in-depth knowledge of the problem and can gather additional information about it. And solutions proposed by learners, if implemented, can lead to genuine organizational improvements.

ROLE PLAYING OR SKILL PRACTICE

Role plays, which are sometimes called *skill practices,* provide learners with the opportunity to apply new skills in a safe environment. Role plays sometimes involve the learners acting the part of other people so they can practice newly learned skills. For example, people who are soon to be promoted to supervisor may participate in role plays during a supervisory training program in which they are placed in situations where they must counsel employees for disciplinary problems, such as safety violations or excessive absenteeism. Sometimes the role play is preceded by a demonstration of the skill by the trainer, who models appropriate behaviors, thereby helping learners picture the intended outcomes before they try the skill themselves. After being introduced to the steps involved in a counseling session, learners engage in role plays with other participants playing the roles of problem employees. In this manner, an encounter with an employee is simulated in a training environment so learners can apply the skills and become confident in their ability to use them. When they are called upon to actually counsel an employee in the workplace, they are likely to be more successful than without training and practice.

STRATEGIES FOR EFFECTIVELY USING ROLE PLAYS

Since role plays mimic a real scenario and require demonstration, they increase the likelihood that training will transfer from the training site to the work site. They also give you the opportunity to supply performance-oriented feedback immediately following the role play. This feedback, coupled with subsequent opportunities to practice the skills, reinforces learning and permits learners to adjust their application based on simulated experience.

However, role plays do have disadvantages. They can be time consuming, especially if only one learner is engaged in the role play at a time while others merely observe. One way to overcome this disadvantage is to divide a group into trios and conduct simultaneous role plays. In that way, one person works as an observer for the other two who are engaged in the role play. But this method, while efficient, can lead to problems, such as managing multiple groups, handling resistance, and monitoring performance among learners. When simultaneous role plays are utilized, invest significant time in planning, communicating instructions and expectations, and preparing learners to be successful on their own. Further, circulate among the groups to monitor progress, assess performance, and provide feedback. You could also involve another trainer to increase the time and attention that can be provided to each group.

Another disadvantage of role plays is that some learners do not take them seriously or do not effectively act out their assigned roles. When this happens, the process can break down because the realism of the role play becomes severely limited. Such behavior may stem from learners feeling intimidated or foolish. These negative feelings may be exacerbated if the role play is videotaped and evaluated. When you use role plays, be sure to spend ample time preparing learners and establishing high comfort levels. Further, take time to communicate the importance of the activity and the benefits that will result from applying the new skills back on the job.

By adhering to several important guidelines, you will find that role playing is a highly effective way to transfer knowledge and skills. Exhibit 11–3 provides guidelines for making role plays more useful and for increasing their likelihood of success.

DISCUSSION METHOD

A *discussion* is usually effective in engaging learners and encouraging participation. Peer learning is one of the most direct benefits resulting from the discussion method. Discussions can involve small groups of two to eight people, or they can be structured for larger groups. Typically, discussions center around problems, questions, ideas, or issues presented to the group for consideration and verbal exploration.

**Exhibit 11–3
Guidelines for effective role-plays.**

■ Establish a casual and relaxed environment.

■ Address any concerns before the role-play begins.

■ Use real-world situations.

■ Explain the value of role-plays.

■ Clearly demonstrate expected outcomes.

■ Provide detailed instructions or directions.

■ Inform learners on how to provide effective feedback.

■ Break people into small groups rather than one large group, because people will generally feel more comfortable in smaller groups. Three people per group will enable two to participate in the role-play while one person observes and then provides feedback.

■ Allow learners to play all parts in the role-play.

■ Monitor each group, intervene when necessary, and provide feedback.

■ Debrief the whole group and address any concerns.

During the discussion, you play the role of facilitator and pose questions, encourage involvement, manage the environment, and summarize conclusions reached by the group. Be sensitive to group dynamics during discussions so that they remain focused, and be prepared to intervene when discussions deteriorate into debates or arguments, which may happen when sensitive or controversial topics are brought up. There is nothing wrong with such discussions, but you must handle them carefully to avoid hurt feelings, lasting anger, or frustrated or neglected learners. We shall have more to say about managing group dynamics later in the chapter.

DISADVANTAGES OF THE DISCUSSION METHOD

In addition to behavior problems, such as interpersonal conflict, one potential disadvantage of the discussion method is that meaningful results may not be achieved. If learners get off track or if one person dominates the discussion, then learners feel the discussion was a waste of time. This disadvantage can be overcome through effective group facilitation. Another disadvantage of discussions is that they can be quite time consuming if many people have contributions to make or when learners are verbose. Addressing those problems also requires skilled facilitation.

STRATEGIES FOR EFFECTIVELY USING THE DISCUSSION METHOD

When you want to use the discussion method, announce this intention by saying something like, "Next, we are going to have a discussion about [the topic or issue]." Doing this will convey to learners that you are shifting gears and will also communicate that they are expected to participate. In addition, you can state your expectations (such as full participation) or provide guidelines governing the discussion (such as no interruptions). One way to stimulate a discussion is to pose questions to the group that build interest or elicit opinions. For example, you could use an open question or overhead question to open a discussion about a topic. An example of this might be to ask learners, "What experiences have you had with discharging an employee?" Sometimes key discussion questions can be found in the training manual or on handouts, which allow learners simply to read the questions and begin the discussion. The discussion method is an excellent way in which new insights can be stimulated because learners can present diverse perspectives, experiences, and opinions.

To increase the chances for success in using the discussion method, it is best if you remain as neutral as possible. By interjecting strong opinions into the discussion, you may directly influence the discussion and stifle opposing opinions. That is not to say that you should avoid participation in discussions. But you should exercise caution in using your power as trainer to sway opinions or influence thinking.

A seating arrangement can also help or hinder discussions. For example, if learners are arranged in rows or if the chairs are bolted to the floor, discussion might become difficult or cumbersome. Discussion works best when chairs are arranged in a circle or with other seating arrangements that encourage learners to look at each other.

OTHER TRAINING METHODS

Many other training methods may be used during delivery. In this section we will introduce them and provide a brief description of each.

THE DEMONSTRATION METHOD

The *demonstration method* begins when you, as trainer, perform an activity or behavior while learners observe and then later perform. The demonstration can include action performed by someone other than you, such as a videotape or learner. Behavior modeling is one type of demonstration that was discussed earlier. Behavior modeling and demonstration both allow participants in training to learn through observation before performing on their own. According to the following critical incident, it is important to take precautions when selecting learners to be involved in demonstrations:

Recalling a Traumatic Moment

" *I remember an experience where I was a learner and ended up being the "butt" of an experiential learning exercise where I was belittled and bullied on behalf of the whole class's learning about a class concept. I learned a firsthand lesson to NEVER randomly use students as examples unless you get their buy-in ahead of time and make them aware of what is about to happen. It was quite traumatic.* "

GAMES AND ACTIVITIES

Games and *activities* are other training methods you can use. Games are rule-governed activities that require cooperation between members to achieve some task or goal or that pit learners against each other or another group in competition. Games can be very exciting for learners. The game is conducted to achieve training objectives, which are usually introduced before the game, and reinforced during the debriefing that follows the game. Many games exist and are widely used in training. Exhibit 11–4 is an example of a business game, which is intended to teach sales representatives about the bidding and proposal process.

Games should be carefully planned before training. However, you may choose to develop and implement on-the-spot games. Although some planning is required so that the general idea and concept of the game is known in advance, the way you play the game can be varied by situation, content, and learners. When developing training games, your creativity is important. Some trainers can formulate powerful games quickly. Others require a starting point. One recommended starting

Exhibit 11–4
Business game description.

Object of the game: To acquire business by winning a bidding process.

Board of directors: The board of directors consists of at least three trainers. Their responsibility will be to select the best proposal submitted. Selection will be based on several predetermined criteria (described below).

Teams: Five groups consisting of four people will be formed. Each member will bring a different set of skills to the table. Teams will be selected by the board of directors on the basis of skills and background. Skills and experience will be dispersed as evenly as possible throughout the teams.

Materials: All materials and tools needed to complete the bidding process will be provided. To prevent unfair advantage, additional tools should not be included. The materials will also include background information and financial data from your organization, your competitors, and the potential client. The potential client will also provide bidding process guidelines. You *must* adhere to these guidelines.

Time: The teams will have three hours to read through the information, create a plan, and write a proposal. Time management is the responsibility of each team.

Criteria for selection:
1. Adherence to the bidding process guidelines
2. Pricing
3. Quality, in terms of thoroughness, content, and readability
4. Feasibility of the project and implementation plan

The board of directors will be available at all times to answer questions. Answers will be limited to clarifying the process, however.

GOOD LUCK!

point is to begin with popular television game shows or with board games. For example, the television show *Jeopardy!* can be—and is often—used as the basis for a training game. Below are some steps for using a game based on the rules of *Jeopardy!* for reviewing and reinforcing what was learned in a one-day seminar. As such, playing the game is a good way to summarize information and encourage transfer of training. The following process provides you with a starting point for creating such a game. Many variations are possible:

- Pass out slips of paper and ask learners to write down a question on one side and the answer on the other side. (Note that additional papers can be used to collect more than one question. Also, you can prepare questions in advance, complete with categories and levels of difficulty.)

- Collect all the slips.

- Organize the learners into three teams (by counting off by threes, for example).

- Have learners get with their teams to review and discuss the key content that was covered during training.

- Next, have one learner from each of the three teams come to the front.

- Explain the rules (based on *Jeopardy!*), such as, must signal to respond, must answer in the form of a question, etc.

- Read the first questions and have learners signal to respond (for example, learners could raise their hand to respond or ring a small bell).

- Award points to the correct response and deduct points for incorrect responses (for example, first "round" points range from 100 to 500 points and second round points range from 200 to 1000).

- Keep a team score summary (on a flipchart or whiteboard).

- Rotate learners and repeat the process.

- Provide a team award to the overall "winner" of the game.

- Review areas that seemed to cause difficulty with some or all learners.

THE DEBATE

The *debate* is another method that you can use during training delivery. A debate is essentially a structured but cordial argument about a particular issue or motion. It is an effective means by which to bring out important views on a particular issue, foster teamwork, encourage public speaking skills, and energize the learners. Since the debate is a training method that is not used frequently, it also represents a change of pace that will be welcomed by many learners.

When using the debate method, first segment the training group into three teams. Ask one team to make a case for a particular position, and ask a second team to make a case against the motion. The members of the third group serve as judges to determine which side has presented the most compelling case. This can be a great way to involve learners and to raise and discuss key issues surrounding a topic.

Suppose, for purposes of an example, that you are conducting training on work teams in an organization transitioning to a self-directed work-team structure. Divide the class into three groups. Ask one group to make a convincing case that self-directed work teams *will not work*. Ask the second group to make a case that self-directed work teams *will work*. And then ask the third group to listen to each side and judge which group provided the most convincing argument. Inform everyone that the goal is to win the debate by putting forward the most convincing case. Also remind them that they have been asked to take one side or the other and that the side on which they have been asked to debate may—or may not—reflect their true opinion about the topic under debate.

After the debate teams have been formed and the issues for debate put forward, explain to the group how the debate process will be carried out. The following script suggests how you could introduce and conduct the debate.

TRAINER: *Everyone should know which team he or she is on. Keep in mind that a debate is a friendly, structured argument about a topic. The topic in this case is "self-directed work teams." One team will argue why teams will work here at (company name) and the other team will present a case as to why teams will not work.*

You will be given some time to prepare with your team. You don't want to all get up and say the same thing, so you may want to make a list of all the points you want to cover in your presentation. Then, determine who will make which points.

There are a few rules or guidelines we will follow during the debate. First, everyone must speak and, in the debate tradition, when you speak, you must stand. There is a time limit though. The maximum is three minutes per person and there is no minimum time.

When you have had some time to prepare with your team, we will come back and have a coin toss to determine which side goes first. The team that goes first will present the whole of its argument. Then, the other team will present the whole of its argument.

After both teams have presented their cases you will have some time to meet again with your team to plan a response. Not everyone is required to stand up and present in this second round, although some teams do approach it this way. Other teams appoint one or two spokespeople to present their response. There are different ways to approach the response: some teams will respond to points brought up by the opposite side; others will reinforce the points they made in round one; still others will bring up additional arguments they had not made initially.

Go ahead and take some time to prepare for the first round of the debate with your team. The "for" team can adjourn to breakout room #1, and the "against" team can use breakout room number #3. Before you leave, though, what questions do you have? (Address questions.) If the three judges can join me here in the front, I have some things to review with you.

This script gives you an idea of the instructions given to introduce a debate. Remember that learners will not conduct the debate successfully if they have not been given clear, specific directions about what to do.

Of course, many variations of these directions are possible. When you meet with the judges, the following detailed explanation can be provided about their role:

TRAINER: *Just because you are a judge does not mean that you get to take it easy! Your role, as a judge, is to make a determination* *about which team has presented the most convincing case, in your view. What I need, though, is a defensible judgment. I suggest developing some type of an evaluation scale that you will use during the debate. What I'm going to describe is just a starting point for you. You need to develop a scoring system that works for you.*

One possibility is to rate each point that is made during the debate using a 1 to 5 scale with 1 being "not very convincing" and 5 being "extremely convincing." As each person stands to deliver his or her message, you should write the person's name down and attempt to capture the main point he or she made. Then, once you have documented the point, give it a rating on the 1 to 5 scale. Scores on each point that person made could then be averaged to arrive at a score for that person. The scores for each person on the team could then be added together or averaged to reach a team score.

Just as the team members are asked to stand up and deliver a message, the same applies to you as judges. As a suggestion, since there are three of you, one person could introduce the judges. The second person could explain the scoring system that you used. The third person could render the verdict and summarize the key issues raised by each side.

You will have time to compare notes, discuss, and deliberate the results at the end of the first round and then again after the teams have given their final presentations. The judges can then compare their individual team scores to reach their verdict.

Keep in mind that the scoring system I explained is just a starting point. Think about it for a while and discuss it as a team.

Your role as trainer during the debate is a passive one—unless problems arise or clarification of the directions is required. Once the teams determine who will go first, through a coin toss, the process runs itself and you only need to provide limited guidance, such as asking team 2 to start when team 1 has finished.

Learners may find the debate both rewarding and intimidating. For this reason, be firm on the rules, but take a lighthearted, lively approach overall. Further, at the end of the debate, explain the purpose of the debate and facilitate a process in which the learners give their impressions about the process as well as the results. Make an effort to congratulate the teams for being successful, and commend the individuals for doing something that is not always easy—that is, standing up in front of their peers and making a brief presentation. Point out that everyone was successful and made excellent points.

MANAGING GROUP DYNAMICS

When you use training methods like those we have described above, take care to manage special issues associated with group dynamics that can arise. This section describes some of those issues.

ENCOURAGING LEARNER PARTICIPATION

Learner participation is one issue you should manage when using experiential learning. Participation levels vary by training method. On one end of the participation continuum, lectures and presentations place learners in a passive role. On the other end of the participation continuum, small group discussion methods place learners in an active role. You should encourage appropriate participation to match your training objectives. Related to learner participation is learner involvement. Verbal and nonverbal cues, such as active participation and open body position, can reflect how involved the learners feel in the training event.

HANDLING PROBLEMS

Sometimes problems can arise when you use any training method. Chapter Five described many learner behavior problems and ways to deal with them. Among the labels attached to specific behavior problems mentioned were the *talkers, challengers, eager beavers, latecomers, uninvolved, know-it-alls,* and *whiners.*

You may find that dysfunctional problems arise when you use various training methods. For example, during a discussion, tempers may flare. Learners may show anger because they feel strongly about a controversial issue. In such cases, diffuse the volatile situation by using skillful facilitation. One way to deal with these behavior problems is to prevent them from arising. To that end, set expectations, create guidelines, and monitor the groups to avert potential problems. Other ways to manage specific dysfunctional behaviors were discussed in Chapter Five.

SEEKING FEEDBACK ABOUT
TRAINING METHODS

You should work to create an environment in which learners can provide you with feedback about the effectiveness of the methods that you use during training delivery. If one training method was not effective—even for a small number of learners—you should know that so you can make necessary changes. Similarly, you should know when learners find a method particularly beneficial or useful. You can seek feedback by asking learners during the debriefing of an activity or on course evaluations.

THE TRAINER'S ROLE DURING GROUP-
BASED TRAINING METHODS

What should be your role as trainer during group-based training methods, such as activities or small group discussions? That is an important question. Learners are usually asked to take responsibility and act in self-directed ways during group activities. But that does not mean that you can take a break.

What should you do? Should you circulate through the group(s)? Under what conditions is this a good or bad idea? What should you be doing in those situations to be particularly effective? What is the worst thing you could do while circulating and monitoring small groups during an activity? What is the best thing you could do? The answers to these questions depend on the subject matter, the type of training method, your abilities as a trainer, and the learners' characteristics. Some benefits, problems, and strategies related to these issues are discussed below.

CIRCULATING AMONG GROUPS AND
MONITORING THEIR PROGRESS

We recommend that you circulate throughout the groups during activities and group work. Sometimes it is acceptable for you to sit with a group as they are discussing a topic. At other times, however, this may be so intrusive to learners that it brings their discussion to an abrupt halt. One way to avoid this potential problem is to announce to learners that you will be moving around during the activity. Inform participants that you will just be listening in and that they should continue their conversations. By circulating you make yourself available so that learners can ask you questions, make comments, or seek clarification as necessary. Further, by listening in on the groups, you can detect when a group is struggling, when learner behavior problems exist, or when groups get off track. In such cases it may be appropriate for you to intervene.

MONITORING THE IMPACT OF YOUR PRESENCE ON THE GROUP

Be sensitive to the impact of your presence on group interaction. If a sensitive subject is the topic under discussion—such as how participants feel about the company or their managers— your presence may limit what people are willing to say. Sometimes just the opposite is true. Sometimes it is advisable for you to actively participate with a group you are monitoring and observing. That can be done by asking questions, clarifying issues, acknowledging positive and negative points, and providing your own opinion on a subject when you are asked. Doing this can energize learners and demonstrate your interest in them and the topic. On the other hand, this behavior has the potential with some groups to shut them down, turn them off, or steer them in a different direction.

STRATEGIES FOR USING GROUP-BASED METHODS EFFECTIVELY

One way you can determine how much learner involvement is necessary is to test the waters and respond accordingly. To do that, move from low to high involvement approaches as they are described in Exhibit 11–5.

Be sure to announce to learners before a group activity that you will be circulating through the groups. When you detect problems, move to the next level of involvement to gather more information, or intervene if necessary and appropriate. To intervene, pose a clarifying question—or give additional directions—to the groups. You may also suggest a change in how a training method is used or provide additional information, instructions, or positive reinforcement to learners.

As you intervene with a group, be sure to assess the impact of what you do. For example, if you are at level one and are simply observing the group from a distance, you may detect a problem. If you then progress to level two by physically moving closer to the group, some learners may stop talking. When that happens, say something like, "I didn't intend to interrupt your discussion. When I was standing back there I thought I detected some confusion so I wanted to see if anyone needed clarification. Is everyone all right? Does anyone need clarification?" The learners can then ask for clarification if they wish to.

Exhibit 11–5.
Levels of trainer involvement during group-based training methods.

Levels of Involvement	Actions or Activities
Low Involvement	
1	Observe the group at a distance (being as inconspicuous as possible), attempting to detect dysfunctional behaviors, need for clarification, questions, or comments.
2	Observe the group from a close range, attempting to detect dysfunctional behaviors, need for clarification, questions, or comments.
3	Observe the group from a close range and make yourself "available" to one or more members of the group by establishing eye contact or demonstrating nonverbal behaviors that indicate that you are there to assist if called upon.
4	From a semidistant range, ask the group if they have any questions, comments, needs for clarification, or other assistance from you.
5	Enter the group's "air space" and ask if they have any questions, comments, needs for clarification, or other assistance from you.
6	Intervene to provide answers to questions, make comments, give clarifying statements, and provide assistance.
High Involvement	

EMPLOYING APPROPRIATE TRAINING TECHNIQUES

As we have mentioned before, decisions about key points for emphasis, sequence, timing, and choice of training methods are generally pre-scribed and organized during the instructional design phase, and are described for you in the instructor guide. The previous section of this chapter summarized many training methods you can use. In this section we discuss important strategies that you should consider to use these training methods successfully. We first describe openings and sum-maries, which are designed to introduce and conclude instructional seg-ments. We then describe transitions, which facilitate smooth and seamless movement from the closure of one sequence to the introduc-tion of the next sequence. Finally, we emphasize the importance of using various training methods to appeal to multiple individual learning styles.

OPENINGS AND SUMMARIES

When you use a new training method, introduce (or open) it in an appropriate way. Consider this example used to introduce a role play.

> **TRAINER:** *We spent the past hour discussing the different types of coaching and when each type is appropriate. To reinforce what you have learned, we are going to practice some of the key coaching skills. I want you to break into groups of three. One person will play the part of an employee, a second per-son will play the part of the coach, and a third person will observe the role play and provide feedback. After each inter-action has been conducted and feedback has been discussed, switch roles until everyone has had an opportunity to play all three roles. Each role play will take about seven to ten min-utes. Before you get started, I want to demonstrate this for you. Can I have a volunteer who would be willing to help me?*

This introduction is effective because it restated what the group had just discussed, what they are going to do, why they are going to do it, instructions on how to do it, and even provided a demonstration so learners will know exactly what they should do.

If you simply move into a new instructional sequence without proper introduction, learners can become confused. They will miss instructions or expectations because some will not realize that a new segment began. As we mentioned earlier, the opening of a training method is an excellent time to avert potential problems by making expectations and goals clear, establishing guidelines, and communicating instructions clearly. When you lay this initial groundwork, you reduce the chance that problems will arise because people know what they are supposed to do. To improve the effectiveness of your introductions or openings, you should consider the following key questions:

- What message do you need to convey in the opening?

- Will the opening inform the learners what is ahead?

- Is learner curiosity and attention aroused through the opening?

- How will you deliver the opening?

- What method(s) will you use during the opening? (For example, demonstration?)

- What verbal and nonverbal messages are appropriate, and what messages will you use?

- How will you involve learners during the opening?

- What special instructions or directions do you need to convey?

- How will you know the opening was successful?

One way to address this problem is to write out the directions for the activity, if necessary, and provide written directions to the learners. That way, they can follow along and refer to directions when, for example, they assemble in small groups and must revisit what they are to do.

The time invested and the detail covered during the introduction phase is somewhat dependent upon how much learner autonomy is associated with the training method. For example, during a lecture, little time generally needs to be spent on the introduction, while a case study may demand much time and energy.

Below is a critical incident that shows that, even when directions are provided, getting learners to follow them is sometimes easier said than done.

Why Won't They Follow the Directions?

" *I had a student trainee who was unable or unwilling to follow detailed written directions for performing a computer exercise because he didn't think it would work. This was for a task he had never seen or done but 'he knew a better way.'* "

PROVIDING SUMMARIES

Summaries bring closure to a training method. They should be positioned at the end of instructional segments, although summaries can also be provided periodically throughout delivery to help learners know where they are. Summaries incorporated during training help learners to organize and retain information efficiently. When activities are left open-ended or when the next sequence is started without proper synthesis and closure, the impact of the training method may not be realized.

DEBRIEFING ACTIVITIES

A *debriefing* is a critical—but sometimes neglected—element of training methods. The debrief occurs after learners have conducted an activity and provided their answers or solutions. Deep learning often occurs during an effective debriefing because learners can reflect on what they did in the activity and what it meant. During a debriefing, you can also determine how much learning has occurred and whether you need to provide follow-up or adjustment.

When an activity is debriefed it moves from simply a series of words or from activities of the learners to an evaluation of the learning, the process, and a distillation or synthesis of key learning points. The activity itself is simply a means to an end. The end result is the learning that resulted from the activity. At times you may confuse the training method (the means) with the outcomes desired (the ends). This is especially true in the case of games or other stimulating activities where learners have experienced an enjoyable time. If the enjoyment derived from the activity is the main focus and the learning is de-emphasized, the true value of the effort is lost. For this reason, closure of instructional sequences should provide a concise summary of the key content points. Some questions you can use during a debriefing include any or all of the following:

- What did you learn from this activity?

- How do you feel that this activity relates to our earlier discussion?

- Why do you think this activity was important?

- What would you do differently if you did this activity again, and why would you do it differently?

- What would you do the same if you did this activity again, and why would you do it the same?

- How does this activity apply to your job?

- What concerns or questions do you have regarding this activity?

- What do you think the next step should be?

- How can you use the information or skills that you learned in this activity?

To give you a clear idea about how a debriefing should be conducted, consider the following dialog between a trainer and a learner named Stephanie:

> **TRAINER:** *We role-played several scenarios using coaching skills. Before we move into the next section on "coaching to improve performance," what did you learn from this skill practice and how can you use these skills on the job?*
>
> **STEPHANIE:** *I learned that coaching skills don't come easy and that I could really use them to help develop my direct reports.*
>
> **TRAINER:** *That's interesting. What do you mean by "they don't come easy" and what do you think you could do to make it easier?*
>
> **STEPHANIE:** *I just think I need more practice. These skills just are not natural for me.*
>
> **TRAINER:** *(turning to the whole group) Stephanie brings up a good point. How can we practice these skills on the job?*

Note how the trainer in this example used summary statements to focus the debriefing and the key learning points that preceded the activity. You should also note how the trainer used open questions to stimulate thought and encourage group involvement. Clarifying questions were also used by the trainer in the debriefing to ensure that Stephanie and other learners in the group understood the key points. By asking a few questions at the end of a skill practice, this trainer successfully involved the group in brainstorming ways to practice the newly learned skills back on the job. This briefing could make the difference in whether learners apply what they learn on the job. Without the debriefing, learners are not able to consolidate the key points and see how the activity showed them the importance of what they learned.

MAKING SMOOTH TRANSITIONS

Transitions provide a bridge between the closure of one instructional segment and the introduction to the next. Transitions can also effectively link new information to content that has already been acquired by learners. When transitions are poorly done or are nonexistent, the flow of the training program can seem awkward—or can appear to run together with no discrete starting and stopping points. This confuses learners because they do not recognize when one segment ends and the next one starts, and they may be confused about how one topic relates to others.

Transitions also play a key role in linking the training subject matter to problems or situations occurring on the job. Transitions can thus provide learners with a clear understanding of how they can apply the new skills and knowledge and the benefits they will obtain by doing that. For training to be seamless, make the effort to show how one part relates to others. By paying attention to the big picture, you help learners see linkages and relationships. That also helps to enhance learner motivation.

You can use many approaches to improve the effectiveness of transitions during training delivery. The listing below provides you with key steps, guidelines, and considerations when making transitions:

- Choose the format that the transition will take (for example, a transition statement, a question, an example, or a prop).

- Ensure that the transition effectively links the closure of one segment to the introduction of the next segment.

- Make sure that the transition is discrete so that it is not confused for part of the segment just ending or the one beginning.

- Consider the clarity of the transition: Is it concise, recognizable as a transition, and understandable to the learners?

- The transition should be seamless and flow smoothly.

- Sustain or energize learner attention and curiosity by way of the transition.

- Practice the transition either alone or in front of others.

ADDING VARIETY

Training delivery is similar to following a recipe. Many ingredients must come together effectively for the training to be delivered effectively.

These ingredients include the subject matter, the situation, the needs of the organization and learners, and many others. To meet the demands that arise during delivery, you must be proficient at using different training methods. If you use the same method for all situations, then your chances of success are limited. The mere fact that each learner is unique and possesses a learning style different from others should dramatize why one size never fits all. To maximize your effectiveness, use many different training methods so that learners will feel stimulated.

MAKING ADJUSTMENTS DURING DELIVERY

Sometimes you must make adjustments to how you use training methods based on learner needs, time constraints, or other considerations. For example, if you recognize that you have fallen behind schedule by twenty minutes during a heated discussion, you need to take corrective action. You may elect to continue the discussion and shorten a future segment, or stop the discussion and transition into the next part. However you modify the delivery, some justification is warranted. But always keep the desired instructional objectives in mind, since no modification can be justified if it severely compromises the achievement of desired results.

AVOID MODIFICATIONS BASED ON PERSONAL PREFERENCES

Be sure to avoid making modifications based solely on your preferences rather than on learner, organizational, or situational requirements. This point was made in an earlier chapter, but it bears repeating. Although you may prefer one training method to others, do not use it if it serves only your preferences and does not contribute to achieving the desired training objectives. Document any changes you make. Once documented, these changes should be communicated to the instructional designers so that the modifications can be made in future offerings of the course. Often such alterations can be communicated in the evaluation report that should follow training delivery. The competency of *reporting evaluation information* will be covered in Chapter Fifteen.

SUMMARY

This chapter described many training methods, defined as techniques you can use during delivery to facilitate learning, and it offered tips for using them. It covered the following topics:

■ Description of the different training methods, including lecture, role playing, discussion, individual exercises, case studies, games, and debate.

■ Managing the group dynamics, including encouraging learner participation and handling problems.

■ Monitoring and evaluating the appropriateness and effectiveness of training methods on a continuous basis.

■ Employing effective strategies for using the different training methods.

Some training methods are more effective than others, depending on the learners and the results desired. Even when training methods are carefully selected, they must be implemented appropriately if they are to achieve the desired results.

STRATEGY LIST

Actionable Strategies to Improve Training Effectiveness:

Use Training Methods Appropriately

❏ Use a variety of training methods to stimulate interest, arouse curiosity, and promote understanding and retention.

❏ Provide an overview of activities with clear objectives and directions (preferably written).

❏ Debrief activities to tie the results and key learning back to the objective-driven content.

❏ Request feedback from learners about the training methods that you are using to identify which to continue using and which to stop using. Obtain this feedback during debrief sessions.

TYPES OF METHODS

Lecture

❏ Use lecture method to transmit a large amount of information to learners in a short period of time and with large audiences.

❏ Combine lecture with other methods such as case studies or group discussions to stimulate interest and enhance their effectiveness.

❏ Keep lecture times short. Instead, use mini-lectures.

Individual Exercises

❏ Use assessment tools to promote individual reflection.

❏ Use reading assignments with a follow-up question/answer period.

❏ Use in-basket exercises to teach analysis skills, problem solving, and priority setting.

❏ Use case studies individually or with groups. This training method can often demonstrate the complexities of interrelated variables.

Group Exercises

❏ Use games and other group activities to promote teamwork and to stimulate motivation and enthusiasm.

❏ Circulate through the groups to monitor progress without being intrusive. Inform learners in advance that you will be doing this. Tell them how and why so it is not distracting to learners.

Role Plays

❏ Use role plays to provide learners the opportunity to practice new skills in a safe environment.

❏ Combine role plays with behavior modeling to create a stronger likelihood that the newly practiced skills will transfer back to their job.

❏ Incorporate feedback into role plays.

Discussion Method

❏ Use discussions to engage learners and encourage participation.

❏ Be sensitive to group dynamics so that the discussion remains focused. Caution: Discussions are prone to tangents.

❏ Start discussions by asking questions to stimulate thinking.

❏ Arrange seating so that it is conducive to discussion and participation. Arranging seats in a U-shape or circle generally works best.

Managing Group Dynamics

❏ Remember that all learners have different comfort levels with each training method. Therefore, to encourage participation from all learners, use a variety of methods.

❏ Be proactive with learner behavior problems. Create guidelines, provide them with expectations, and monitor groups to prevent potential issues from arising.

❏ Maintain a balance between learners' input with respect to their own experiences. While having learners share their own experiences can be a great teaching tool, it can also become distracting to the other learners if the conversation goes off on a tangent or if one learner dominates.

USING MEDIA AND HARDWARE EFFECTIVELY

SKILLS ASSESSMENT

Take a moment to review the competency and associated performances that will be covered in this chapter. Consider your current level of proficiency in the competency as a whole as well as each performance and check the items where you feel you need to improve. As you read the chapter, concentrate on those areas most in need of development.

Competency:

❏ Use media effectively.

Associated Performances:

❏ Use media and hardware effectively.

❏ Troubleshoot minor hardware and other simple problems.

❏ Substitute for, add to, switch, or create media as required.

❏ Judge the effectiveness of the use of media.

Chapter Twelve focuses on media and hardware. In this chapter we will discuss four broad media categories:

- Static media, including printed material, transparencies, slides, and flipcharts.

- Dynamic media, including videotapes and audiotapes.

- Telecommunications, including video conferencing.

■ Computer-related training, including the Internet, intranet, and Web-based training.

Technology has had a major impact on training delivery. In the last several years, however, the trainers in our survey rated the competency *using media effectively* as next to last in importance—number thirteen out of fourteen competencies. While the mean importance score of the competency was still quite high, it was relatively low when compared with other delivery competencies. Perhaps these trainers did not equate media with technology, but rather with transparencies and other traditional media familiar to classroom trainers.

Although using media effectively was rated as only slightly difficult, many critical incidents reported by the trainers in our study centered around problems with media use. That was especially true when technology, such as computers, played a role in training delivery. For this reason, we discuss troubleshooting and managing contingencies in this chapter. To illustrate this point, consider the following critical incident related to a computer problem.

An Ill-Timed Computer Glitch

"This was the worst experience in my training career: I was giving a computer presentation to senior managers about the value of training in our organization. I had developed and practiced the presentation on my desktop PC. For the presentation I switched the files over to my laptop. The problem I had was getting slides with large graphics to "load" quickly— some took several minutes...seemed like hours! I could tell executives were getting restless so while the slow graphics loaded I did some tap dancing (told jokes, repeated what I already said, discussed current events, etc.). I finally gave up after the fourth or fifth one. I apologized for the delay and promised to send paper copies to them. Put mildly, I "bombed"! "

DEFINING MEDIA AND HARDWARE

Media are the means by which information is conveyed during delivery. *Hardware* is the physical equipment used during training. Generally, media and hardware are both selected in the instructional design phase, and their use is described in the instructor guide. Examples of media include intangible methods of communicating information, such as speech, as well as tangible hardware, such as videotapes and the television monitor and VCR through which the videos are delivered. Hardware thus includes everything you can touch. Media may (or may not) rely on hardware.

Both media and hardware can enhance training delivery by providing the means by which to clarify, organize, and convey the subject matter of the training. In addition, media and hardware complement trainers by extending their delivery skills, adding variety, and stimulating learner interest. As a result, media can increase learner retention.

This section summarizes the media and hardware you can use during delivery. Media can be classified as static, dynamic, telecommunications, and computer-related. We will define and give examples of each medium in this section, and we will also describe their advantages, disadvantages, associated hardware, and strategies for using them in training.

STATIC MEDIA

Static media, as the name implies, is a broad category. Static media are words or graphics that are fixed or stationary. Examples of static media include print-based training material, transparencies, slides, flipcharts, and chalkboards. Each provides a visual image on which learners can focus their attention. Each also reinforces learning before, during, or after the training course.

PRINT-BASED MATERIAL

Print-based material encompasses many types of material commonly used in training, such as participant guides, manuals, handouts, assigned reading packets, maps, graphs, and textbooks. Some organizations produce printed material in-house, whereas others outsource it.

Print-based materials can be used for self-study, but most people probably think of the print-based materials used in classroom training first. Print-based material used for self-study typically contains the subject matter and methods for testing, providing self-feedback, and evaluating the training. When used in classroom training, print-based material complements, supports, or reinforces the trainer. For example, during a training program you might distribute a handout that provides the instructions for an activity. Thus, the handout supports the activity.

MAKE PRINTED MATERIAL USER FRIENDLY

A common problem with print-based training material is that it is often too focused on the subject matter and not enough on the learning process. That is usually a sign of poor instructional design. One clue that this problem exists is a handout or participant guide that is filled with text—without providing learners with space to take notes. Such printed material serves more as a textbook than a learning aid to support the trainer and the learners.

Learners who encounter densely packed participant guides may grow frustrated. When you use print-based material, make sure its layout is user friendly. Exhibit 12–1 offers guidelines for evaluating the layout of the printed material. The layout is especially relevant when learners must use the material before or after the training. Many learners have a low tolerance threshold for material that is poorly formatted.

Exhibit 12–1
Guidelines for designing and evaluating print-based material.

■ Use common language.

■ Avoid jargon or acronyms.

■ Use materials that are not distracting.

■ Use white space evenly. Don't leave large sections of open space unless it has a specific purpose such as for note taking. When large sections of white space have a purpose, clearly label it.

■ Use font sizes and styles wisely but sparingly. A rule of thumb is that there should never be more than four styles per page of text.

■ Use consistency throughout the material because it can aid in learning by reducing the learning curve associated with learning to use the material.

■ Avoid making material appear cluttered.

■ Ask people for their opinion to verify its user friendliness and readability.

PRINCIPLES FOR USING PRINTED MATERIAL

When you use print-based material, follow two basic principles to ensure that what you use supports your delivery.

USE PRINTED MATERIAL AT APPROPRIATE TIMES

The first principle is to use printed material only when appropriate. Whenever you distribute printed material, learners shift their focus to it rather than keeping their attention on you. That becomes important when you are conveying important information. In such instances, either delay the distribution of the material until the important information has been communicated or else provide learners with ample time to review the material before you continue.

ENSURE PRINTED MATERIAL IS HIGH QUALITY

The second principle is to use printed material that is of high quality. When printed material is reproduced many times for use in multiple training programs, the reproduction quality deteriorates, especially when copies are made on an in-house copy machine. When learners receive low-quality printed material, they have difficulty reading it. Worse, they view it as a reflection on the credibility of the training as well as the trainer.

Of course, another problem occurs when printed material is sent outside for preparation. Vendors may return copies with pages upside down, missing, or out of sequence. Unfortunately, learners blame trainers rather than vendors for such mistakes. Be certain to implement quality control for any material used, regardless of whether or not it was created in-house or by an external vendor.

TRANSPARENCIES, SLIDES, AND COMPUTER PRESENTATIONS

Transparencies have been called overheads, overhead transparencies, foils, viewgraphs, and flimsies. A transparency is typically a page-size sheet of clear plastic on which have been printed words, graphics, or a combination of both. When used with an overhead projector unit, the image is magnified and displayed on a screen, whiteboard, or blank wall. You can use a blank transparency with a special marking pen to write information or draw images immediately before or during training.

A *slide* is similar to a transparency except that it is an image displayed on a screen using a slide projector. A series of slides can be accompanied by music or synchronized with an audiotape to provide narration. It is possible to link many slide projectors together to create sophisticated slide shows.

COMPUTER-BASED SLIDE PRESENTATIONS

One recent development in presentation options involves the use of a personal computer (PC), a projection unit, and a presentation software package. Using the PC and powerful presentation software, such as Microsoft PowerPoint, you have the ability to develop a computer-based slide presentation that can be projected on a screen using sophisticated video projection units. With the click of a mouse, or with a wireless remote control device, you can move through a flashy presentation.

Presentation packages today are capable of producing multi-color text backgrounds. Clip-art software gives developers access to millions of graphical images and permits you to integrate them into the slides for powerful visual impact. Additional features give you the ability to decide how screens and text will appear on each slide. For example, the slide can be dropped in from the top, bottom, or either side. It can be made to begin in the center of the screen and grow outward. Countless combinations are available. The developer can also determine how each slide is built. For example, if bullet points are used, each bullet can be added from any direction, by clicking the mouse or pointer. Further, many such packages allow you to build into these slides dynamic media, such as video clips, sound, three-dimensional images, and animations.

ADVANTAGES AND DISADVANTAGES

Overhead transparencies, slides, and computer presentations all share similar advantages and disadvantages.

One advantage is that they all are useful for displaying important information that supports and reinforces your delivery. Since all three project an image toward the front of the room, they focus learners' attention. When the images are interesting, they engage learners and make it more likely that they will remember what they see (and hear).

A second advantage is portability. A box of slides, a notebook of overheads, and diskettes are relatively easy to transport. This advantage breaks down, however, when you have to transport projection and support equipment—such as the overhead projector, slide projector, screen, personal computer, video projector, speakers (for high-quality sound), cables, and other devices.

Transparencies have unique advantages that are not shared by slides or computer presentations. You can write notes directly on them or on Post-it notes affixed to the edge of the transparency. You can use these notes to prompt you during your delivery. The prompts are, of course, hidden from the learners. This method can help you avoid forgetting valuable information. Another technique that you can use is to create a printed copy of the transparencies on which to write notes for use as you deliver training. You can either hold the printed copies or position them next to the projection unit so that you can glance at them as you progress through training delivery.

The time and costs required to design and develop sophisticated presentations have been slashed dramatically with the advent of the computer, software packages, color printers, and copy machines. What was once a major disadvantage of using such presentations has now become almost irrelevant, especially after the initial capital outlay for equipment and software. You may have direct access to the equipment and software necessary to produce high-quality presentations on your own. Many people now have this capability at home.

Some disadvantages exist when you use transparencies, slides, or computer presentations. One disadvantage is that your flexibility to ad lib is reduced when you rely on these tools. In slide shows and computer-generated presentations, the slide sequence is usually predetermined, and that may force you to follow a linear sequence. Deviations from this sequence can be cumbersome. Another disadvantage is that you must often turn out the lights so that learners can view projected images clearly. When plunged into darkness, learners have trouble taking notes—or staying awake.

You can use several strategies to avoid these problems. If the training facility is equipped with lights that can be dimmed, vary the lighting to allow the projected image to be viewed without placing the learners in total darkness. If you cannot dim the lights, limit how long you deliver presentations. Learners find it difficult to pay attention to a lengthy lecture presentation, even one supported by elaborate projections. If you base your entire program on overheads, slides, or computer projection, and do not use any experiential activities, learners will experience fatigue.

You may experience other problems when you use overheads, slides, and computer-generated presentations. For example, a light bulb in the overhead projector may burn out, a proper electrical outlet may not be easily accessible, or your PC may not boot up properly. If such problems arise and you have not developed a contingency plan, you may be forced to cancel or postpone the session, or keep the learners waiting while you take corrective action. For this reason, be prepared to troubleshoot problems with audiovisual equipment.

Another option, of course, is to formulate a contingency plan. That usually involves having backup media that can be substituted. For example, you can carry paper copies of your transparencies or slides so that they can be substituted if you encounter a technical problem that cannot be quickly solved.

Common guidelines for using transparencies, slides, and computer presentations are provided in Exhibit 12–2.

Exhibit 12–2
Guidelines for using overhead transparencies.

Preparing Overheads

1. Limit transparency to one main point, idea, or concept.

2. Avoid text-heavy transparencies.

3. Use bullet points with several key words per bullet (4-6 bullets per transparency).

4. Use consistent font style throughout.

5. Avoid elaborate or overly fancy font styles that are difficult to read.

6. Create transparencies using presentation software (ex. PowerPoint).

7. Add graphics to reinforce text.

8. Use color to highlight key ideas or bullet points and to stimulate interest.

Using Overheads

9. Refer to key information by pointing (use a laser pointer for increased impact).

10. Cover information and reveal it progressively, point by point.

11. Face your audience, not the screen.

12. Turn the projector off when it's not in use.

13. Do not stand in the line of projection.

14. Use multiple projectors for dramatic impact.

FLIPCHARTS, WHITEBOARDS, AND CHALKBOARDS

A *flipchart* is a large pad of paper mounted to a wall or positioned on a three- or four-legged stand. You use wide-tip colored markers to write information or draw graphics on the pages. As a page is completed, it can be torn off and affixed to a wall with masking tape, or it can be turned over and used again. 3M (maker of Post-it notes) produces Post-it flipchart pads which when removed can be easily posted on a wall without tape.

A *whiteboard*, sometimes called a *wipe board*, is a white or colored porcelain surface that is mounted to a wall or positioned on a three- or four-legged stand. You write or draw on it using erasable color marking pens. In some organizations, the walls of training rooms are made entirely of whiteboard material so that you can write large amounts of information.

A *chalkboard*, rarely seen in modern training rooms, is the fore-runner of the whiteboard. Like a whiteboard, it can be wall mounted. (Some chalkboards are also placed on rollers.) You write or draw on it with white or multi-colored chalk. Chalkboards are still widely used in school settings from elementary to university levels.

ADVANTAGES OF FLIPCHARTS

Flipcharts are advantageous because they are portable. You can transport them to off-site training locations, and you can position them at a training site so that they are visible to all learners. They can be moved to small groups for use in activities, and they can be removed when not in use.

Flipcharts are also advantageous because they can be prepared before training. Some trainers prepare high-quality flipchart presentations that include artistic renderings and elaborate designs with multiple colors. Such flipcharts, while time consuming to prepare, capture attention and can be used more than once.

You may use flipcharts or whiteboards to write information as you present. Different colors can be used too. Colors add interest and allow you to emphasize key points in different colors.

DISADVANTAGES OF FLIPCHARTS

Flipcharts have their limitations. Because they are relatively small, they are not appropriate for groups larger than fifty or groups that are spread out in a large training room. Since notes are taken on sheets, you have to remove sheets as you fill them. That can be tough to do if you are brainstorming with a group, generating much information in a short time. To deal with this problem, experienced trainers will usually leave strips of masking tape on the side of a flipchart stand so that sheets can be posted on a wall quickly. Since flipcharts are not always prepared in advance, learners are not provided with handouts containing the information on the flipchart. That means they may have to take notes.

STRATEGIES FOR USING FLIPCHARTS, WHITEBOARDS, AND CHALKBOARDS EFFECTIVELY

Exhibit 12–3 shows examples of both an effective and an ineffective flipchart. Note that in the effective flipchart the title is clear and lets people know the topic of the discussion at a glance. Also, key points are captured succinctly in bulleted items that are clear, simple, related to the topic, and error free.

But when you read the ineffective flipchart, you see no title. That may create confusion about the topic being discussed. Note also that the flipchart is crammed with text, which means that learners will have difficulty reading it. The ineffective flipchart also contains several spelling errors that do not build confidence in the professionalism of the trainer. The effective flipchart will clearly have a more powerful impact during training delivery.

Some of the guidelines applicable to transparencies, slides, and computer presentations are also relevant to flipcharts, whiteboards, or chalkboards. In addition, be aware that when you write on these surfaces you will usually turn your back on the audience. Avoiding this awkward body position, which can be distracting to learners, is difficult if not impossible with whiteboards and chalkboards. When your back is to the learners, you also lose eye contact. In the case of flipcharts, however, you are able to stand to the side of the flipchart so learners can see what you are writing.

The effectiveness of flipcharts, whiteboards, and chalkboards also depends on how clearly you write. Write large enough and legibly enough that all learners can see what you have written. Avoid spelling mistakes since they will be exacerbated when written in large print. Another rule of thumb is to limit how much information you write. Be selective. Use bullet points. This will also shorten the time required for writing. Also, since learners often attempt to copy what is written into their notes, you will make it easier for them when you are succinct.

Exhibit 12–4 shows a summary list of "dos" and "don'ts" of using flipcharts during training delivery.

Exhibit 12–3
Examples of effective and ineffective flipcharts.

Effective Flipchart:

SERVICE EXCELLENCE

- Quality

- Flexibility

- Responsive to needs

- Exceed expectations

Ineffective Flipchart:

What we must do as a company is always give the customer what they want. When we do this we will retain them and get more busness thus achieving a profit, which will put money in every-one's pockets. To do this we must all pull together as an excellent team.

Exhibit 12–4
Dos and don'ts of using flipcharts

Do…

- Position the flipchart stand so that it is visible to all learners.

- Use large tip markers so that writing is visible.

- Use different colored markers to add visual stimulation and to highlight key information.

- Use alternate colors to group similar items.

- Prepare flipcharts in advance whenever possible.

- Write legibly.

- Check for spelling.

- Use flipcharts to capture important comments provided by learners (such as during brainstorming).

- When soliciting information from learners, write a bullet point to signal that a comment is expected.

- Stand to the side of the flipchart stand so learners can see.

- Post used flipcharts around the room so they are visible and can be referred to later.

- Have masking tape available for posting used flipcharts (tear off small pieces of tape and stick them to the stand for easy access).

- Use key words or phrases instead of full sentences (bullet points).

- Highlight important points by circling, underlining, or using a different color.

- Reveal items by progressively uncovering each item.

- Incorporate computer generated or prepared graphics, photographs, or other images.

- Add a title to the flipchart.

- Skip every other page to avoid "bleeding."

- Write notes in pencil for cues (invisible to learners, visible to trainer).

- Insert tabs on flipcharts so pages can be located quickly.

- Stick to main thoughts and eliminate "fluff."

- Turn to a clean sheet when finished (so focus can be shifted).

- Use multiple flipcharts (to present more information, combine thoughts, add visual stimulation).

Don't…

- Position the flipchart stand so that some learners cannot see.

- Expose a prepared flipchart too early (this can be distracting).

- Use small tip markers or pens so writing is not visible.

- Use light colored markers (such as yellow).

- Use a single color throughout (black).

- Write too much on one page (make too many points on a single flipchart).

- Write too small.

- Attempt to use a flipchart where it is not appropriate (to reproduce a complex graphic).

- Turn your back to the learners.

- Shuffle through flipcharts searching for items.

- Overuse flipcharts by writing on them too often (loses effect for some audiences).

- Leave a flipchart visible when finished (may be distracting to learners).

DYNAMIC MEDIA

Unlike static media, which rely on fixed images, dynamic media are active, showing a series of images, activities, or information. The focus of this section is on videotape and audiotape—two frequently used forms of dynamic media.

VIDEOTAPE

Videotapes have become very popular in training delivery. One study published in *Training* magazine in October 1996 revealed that videos were used in training by 79 percent of the participating organizations. That makes them a top media choice. Videos are frequently used to support classroom training. They convey information through presentation or lecture, by presenting situations that learners address later in the program, or by providing examples of effective or ineffective behavior for modeling purposes.

While home videos are relatively inexpensive to produce with home camcorders, the quality and usefulness of such videos remains questionable for training purposes. (However, even home video has undergone a revolution and is rapidly improving in quality. Digital video and digital sound can now be recorded at home, edited using readily available software, and placed on the Web or on CD-ROM.)

Many firms offer professional video production services. Consequently, customized video production can be outsourced. Professional video production, however, requires a substantial financial investment. Alternatively, many publishing and video companies offer off-the-shelf videos on many popular training topics, which can be purchased and used in training delivery. Some companies allow customers to rent training videos at reduced rates. Videotapes can be used in training sessions or can be made available for learners to view at home for self-study purposes or as follow-up to training.

STRATEGIES FOR USING VIDEOS DURING TRAINING

Videotapes are often effective for capturing learner attention. For example, using short clips from actual movie videos that have been purchased can provide Hollywood-style excitement. However, videos should be selected to achieve a specific purpose—such as to reinforce a point, open a segment, or convey content. Videos used for entertainment only have questionable value because trainers using them may be accused of wasting time and money.

Videos can serve other purposes than to provide information or support key points.

For instance, you can tape learners' performance during a program and use that for training purposes. Imagine you are offering a training program on presentation skills. You could videotape learners' in-class presentations. By viewing this tape later—either individually or in groups—learners can see and learn from their own performance.

Taping learners should be done carefully, however. Knowing that a camera is running can add stress and discomfort for some people, which can influence their performances. You can create a safe training climate for learners and prepare them in advance by communicating expectations, use of the tape, and expected benefits. When this is done, videos can be highly instructive.

Although some trainers use the time while a videotape is being shown to attend to other business, that practice is not recommended. Leaving the room could send a message to the learners that the tape is not important. We recommend that you watch the video attentively and take notes to reemphasize its importance. At the same time you can monitor how much attention is being paid by the learners.

Additionally, unanticipated problems may arise when videotapes are used. While the following critical incident is probably not typical, it does demonstrate a potential problem that you could face.

Fast Forward

" I was showing a film one class period when I was called away for about fifteen to twenty minutes. After I returned to the class, I noticed that the film finished much sooner than expected. My class of apprentices had fast-forwarded the video while I was gone, skipping about twenty minutes of the tape. "

This critical incident dramatizes the behavior problems that you may experience with some learners. Recall that dealing with such problems was addressed in Chapter Five. However, the incident also reinforces why you should remain while a videotape is shown. Do not take advantage of this opportunity to grade projects, listen to your voice-mail, check your e-mail, or do anything that might take you away from the video. Exhibit 12–5 provides guidelines for you to consider when using videotapes. The exhibit is divided into three sections: what to do when introducing the video, what to do while the video is played, and what to do after the video is shown.

AUDIOTAPES

Audiotapes are not as difficult or expensive for the amateur to produce as videos. However, high-quality audiotapes are difficult to prepare. They should probably be left to professionals who possess high-quality studio recording equipment and access to professional "voices"—such as actors or actresses.

In many cases you do not need to customize audio. You can purchase professional audiotapes on many topics from firms that sell off-the-shelf audiotapes on many popular training topics. Many book publishers also produce "audio-books" or "books on tape," which are read by the author or a professional speaker; short segments of such audiotapes can be integrated into your training delivery to enhance learner understanding. In addition, music recordings on tape—and free audio files on the Web—can be incorporated during your training delivery. The lyrics of a particular song may have relevance to training and may therefore enhance the impact of your delivery. Audiotape versions of leadership and personal development programs, such as *The Seven Habits of Highly Effective People* by Stephen Covey, are also commercially available. Learners can listen to such tapes before or after classroom training for preview or for follow-up purposes to reinforce learning.

ADVANTAGES AND DISADVANTAGES OF AUDIOTAPES

Audiotapes can be useful in seizing the attention of learners for a short time, if only because they are a novelty to many learners. Audiotapes may be a refreshing change from the visual imagery on which so much training delivery depends. Another advantage of audiotapes is that they can be used before or after training by individual learners for self-study or follow-up. That reinforces the subject matter of the training, improving the chance for transfer of training from the classroom to the work site.

But audiotapes do have a key disadvantage: The learners' attention may wander after a while. (Recall that learners can listen faster than most people can speak.) Another potential disadvantage is that the sound system needed to listen to high-quality audiotapes may not

Exhibit 12–5
Introducing, playing, and concluding a videotape.

When Introducing a Videotape...

■ Ensure the tape is cued to proper starting place (forward past copyright statements, advertisements, and other superfluous material).

■ Make sure the monitor is positioned so that all learners can view comfortably.

■ Ensure that loud "noise" from the television is avoided when video is started (if the TV and VCR do not automatically handle this, one strategy is to press play first and then turn the television to "on").

■ Provide learners with a verbal introduction to the tape (its purpose, an overview of content, key points to pay attention to, how the content relates to the training).

■ Dim lights or turn lights off prior to starting the videotape (ensure that learners can still take notes and see their material when lights are turned off).

■ Adjust volume so learners can hear comfortably (including learners at a distance).

During the Playing of a Videotape...

■ Watch the videotape (to demonstrate your interest in the content and to serve as a role model).

■ Take notes during the video (again to demonstrate interest and to provide a model for learners).

■ Make adjustments as necessary (to the lighting, sound levels, position of the monitor, "tracking" of the video).

■ Observe learners (to gauge comprehension, interest, and attention levels).

■ Pause the tape as appropriate (to reinforce key points, ask questions, stimulate interest, interject comments).

■ Be careful when leaving the room (may convey a lack of interest or lack of importance to the learners, behavior problems may arise, exiting and reentry may distract learners' attention from the video).

When Concluding a Videotape...

■ Position yourself near the VCR so that the tape can be stopped at the appropriate moment.

■ Avoid loud "noise" from the television when the tape is stopped (if not handled automatically, one strategy is to turn the television to "off" and then stop the tape).

■ Turn the lights back on or remove the dimmer (may be helpful to warn learners to shield their eyes).

■ Conduct a debrief session with learners (to reinforce key points, provide clarification, ask and answer questions).

■ Provide a seamless transition into next training delivery segment.

be readily available at a training site. While you can play audiotapes on small tape recorders or "boom boxes," you risk having poor sound quality that will make it difficult for the learners to hear.

STRATEGIES FOR EFFECTIVELY USING AUDIOTAPES

Exhibit 12–6 provides useful guidelines for using audiotapes in training delivery. These guidelines focus on the hardware and on the training delivery strategy needed to make the use of an audiotape successful.

TELECOMMUNICATIONS

The world of telecommunications has opened up new delivery media for transmitting training to multiple locations over great distances simultaneously. Telecommunication generally involves linking multiple sites through advanced technology such as satellite, compressed video, or cable television. Many universities, businesses, and other organizations have the hardware necessary to deliver training via these methods. According to the Web site for The National Technological University, over fifty major universities are currently linked with more than a thousand work locations. The purpose is to deliver training and educational programs to managers, engineers, and other technical professionals by way of satellite telecommunication and compressed digital video (CDV) technology. Total 1997-98 enrollment in the 500-plus academic courses offered by NTU equaled 22,000 hours of instruction. Even more staggering was the enrollment exceeding 100,000 participants for the Advanced Technology and Management Programs (ATMP), which are noncredit short courses.

ADVANTAGES AND DISADVANTAGES OF TELECOMMUNICATIONS

For many organizations, training delivered by telecommunication—which is sometimes one part of a vast umbrella term called *distance education*—yields several advantages. Cost reductions in travel expenses for trainers and learners alike are a chief attraction of delivering training in this way. Training delivered by telecommunications also minimizes or eliminates geographic barriers by permitting multiple remote-site locations (including international sites) to receive training simultaneously.

However, no media are appropriate for all uses. That is true of training delivered by telecommunications. One major disadvantage is the high initial start-up costs required to purchase quality telecommu-

Exhibit 12–6
Guidelines for incorporating audiotapes into training delivery.

■ Consider the purpose of the audiotape—how will it enhance learning?

■ Select or create an audiotape that will achieve the intended purpose.

■ Do not use a tape that is too long or too short.

■ If necessary, only use part of a tape—so it is not too long and so that only the important parts are covered.

■ Check the volume setting in advance—to ensure that it is neither too loud nor too low.

■ Make sure the tape is cued-up properly so that long delays are not present.

■ Distribute supplementary material—if available (ex. a worksheet, notes page, summary of key points, or diagrams).

■ Introduce the audiotape effectively—explain the purpose to learners, what they should expect, and key points to attend to.

■ Monitor the learners during the playing of the tape—watch for attention levels, interest, and nonverbal signs of level of understanding.

■ If appropriate, pause the tape—to check for learner understanding, ask questions of the learners, highlight key points just made or upcoming points, and to reactivate interest during long-running tapes.

■ Conclude the audiotape effectively—be in position to shut the tape off soon after completion, be prepared to move seamlessly into the next segment.

■ Debrief the audiotape or move into the next segment—summarize key points, hold a debriefing session, and determine level of learner understanding.

nications equipment. A second major disadvantage is the high cost of the equipment, which can become obsolete in a short priod of time. These problems are especially acute for small organizations with limited resources.

Many organizations, however, already have this technology in place for use with executive teleconferences and other purposes. In these cases, telecommunications access needs only to be refocused for training delivery. Of course, it often helps to have technical specialists available to assist with training and to troubleshoot the technical glitches that may occur during delivery and that fall outside the experience of many training and development practitioners.

Another possible disadvantage of training delivered by telecommunications is the impact that it may have on interactions between you and your learners. With the exception of learners at your site, other learners' interactions with you may be limited to watching you present over a television monitor or listening to you over a phone line with speaker phone. One way to address this problem is to train and station facilitators on remote sites so that learners feel that they are receiving more individualized attention. Facilitators can also lead activities, answer questions, and build relationships with learners.

Videoconferencing and other telecommunication-based training are best used to convey information to many people simultaneously at relatively low costs. For example, if the subject matter of the training is intended to provide information to learners about a new sexual harassment prevention policy, then videoconferencing can be effective in communicating information across broad distances quickly and efficiently. In such cases, the purposes are only to provide information and raise awareness, and the training consists of one-way communication with limited interaction between trainer and learners. To improve the effectiveness of this process it may be useful to provide learners with clearly organized material in advance so they know why the training is being conducted and what they are expected to learn from it. Supplementary material reinforces key points made by the trainer, and can also be taken back to the job and used.

Videoconferencing is not as effective for training that requires much learner involvement. The technology can be cumbersome and time consuming, requiring you to pay as much attention to camera positions and sound quality as you do to subject matter or delivery. Further, if learners at the remote sites have questions, problems, or want to make comments, you may find that difficult to detect. Trainers also find that videoconferencing can be difficult in monitoring group interaction and encouraging participation at the remote locations. This problem is compounded as the number of remote locations increases.

Videoconferencing also does not live up to the expectations of many learners, who expect broadcast quality commercial television with elegant simultaneous editing capabilities—and find instead compressed video characterized by blurry images and mismatches between images and sounds. Worse yet, sound-activated cameras may pose momentary distractions because a cough at one site may cue the camera to switch there automatically—only to see a confused learner who is unsure why he or she is suddenly spotlighted.

Advances in telecommunications technology have alleviated some problems and will no doubt mitigate the effects of others in time. For example, many videoconferencing systems are now equipped with movable cameras that allow room wide scans, zoom-in and out capabilities, and memorized settings that zero in on the speaker. Other systems allow you to view several remote sites through multiple monitors or multiple image boxes displayed simultaneously on a single screen. Two-way camera control is another feature that facilitates the process by allowing either the trainer at the central site or the learners at an off-site to control camera movement and operation.

In your role as a trainer, you must find creative ways to strike a balance between the cost effectiveness of the technology with the human need for interpersonal and social interaction. Many trainers who deliver by telecommunication-based training need special preparation to ensure that they know what to do when technical problems occur, how to organize training materials so that they are structured in ways that will work for telecommunications-based delivery, and how to manage discussion among multiple sites. They may also need special preparation on how to combine telecommunications-based methods so that, for instance, videoconferencing can be paired with electronic mail, faxes, Web-based delivery, audio teleconferencing, and other telecommunications-based methods.

In the near future, as digital video on the desktop improves, trainers may find themselves delivering from their desktops to remote sites. That is already possible but it, too, will require creative delivery methods and mastery of multiple technical issues.

COMPUTER-RELATED TRAINING

In recent years, rapid technological advances have dramatically increased training delivery involving computers. Several key trends have facilitated the common use of computer-related training. Cost-conscious managers, particularly those in lean-staffed organizations, have sought ways to hold down travel expenses—and the opportunity costs linked to lost work time as learners participate in off-site training—so that geographically dispersed learners can be trained efficiently. As desktop computers have increased in power and decreased in price, learner-directed and learner-paced individualized training have become a reality with computer-related instruction. The training methods that will be covered in this section are computer-aided instruction, computer-based training, and Internet-based training. Since some computer-based training methods are intended to replace the traditional delivery of training in classrooms, you should become familiar with these advances. Further, you can look for ways to position such methods so they augment classroom-based delivery.

COMPUTER-AIDED INSTRUCTION AND COMPUTER-BASED TRAINING

Computer-aided instruction (CAI) involves a software program that resides on a personal computer, on a diskette, or on a CD-ROM. It is delivered entirely by the computer-based medium, or it is combined with other media—such as a learner workbook. Most computer-aided instruction in use today incorporates powerful multimedia capabilities, which add graphics, sound, video, and text for a highly interactive and visually stimulating learning experience. The jury is still out on whether CAI is as effective as traditional classroom delivery. The topics available from training software vendors vary widely and range from technical training (such as word processing training) to nontechnical topics (such as management and supervision or interviewing and selection skills).

A major benefit of CAI is the self-directed nature of many products that are available. Learners using such programs can work at their own pace and timeframe. Further, many CAI programs come equipped with a unique branching feature that permits learners to pursue individualized directions based on their goals and learning needs. Organizations using such computer-based learning technologies often do so with the specific intent of reducing costs. For example, a training department could distribute a CD-ROM–based training program across geographic borders in a cost-effective, highly efficient manner. But a distinct disadvantage of computer-aided instruction is the loss of direct interpersonal interaction between learners and trainer(s) and between one learner and other learners. Some trainers have confronted this problem

We asked training gurus Sivasailam Thiagarajan ("Thiagi") and Bob Pike, "How do you see technology (Web-based training, computer-based training, etc.) impacting stand-up delivery?" Thiagi's response was, "I believe that face-to-face instruction and technology-based training can co-exist. It's not a case of 'either-or' but of 'both-and.' I strongly urge trainers to combine and integrate technology during, before, and after the instructional session. For example, I have used CBT to provide trainees with baseline competencies before my face-to-face training session. I use a computer simulation in the midst of my presentation (using an LCD projector) to provide some critical practice. I have used my web site as a follow-up location for additional information and enrichment activities."

Bob Pike's response to our question about the impact of technology on training delivery was, "I think there is still a fatal flaw in the way the technology is sometimes viewed. In the past twenty years look at all the technological advances that have come out, from videos, to CD's, to the Internet. You still have to ask, 'How do people learn best?' Many people are computer-phobic. Even with Generation X, 20 percent don't own or even want to use a computer and only about one in five do more than play games. There is a tendency to hold up any new technology as 'The Solution.' One of the things I've been asking groups lately is 'How many of you have purchased software for your own use, attempted to use it, but put it aside?' Usually, many people raise their hands. Then I ask them if they would prefer to have someone sit next to them to help them identify the five or six things they want to do with the software and have the person teach them how to do this. Everyone raises their hand on that one, and that's really coaching.

"There's also a new thing called 'Shovelware,' which is basically taking a classroom training program and shoveling it onto the Web. Interacting with a computer is not the same as interacting with people. If there are not ways built in for people to interact, then they're not going to do it. I think technology is not The Solution, but it is part of the solution. People learn from each other and want to interact with others and with the trainer. Think about when people dial a call center. A lot of people will press '0' so they can talk to a person. People would prefer to ask a question how they want to ask it and just talk to people rather than typing questions in, worrying about phrasing it a certain way for the search engine and things like that. Another example is e-ticketing. I was just in the airport the other day and there was an e-ticket machine there. People could get 1,000 bonus miles by using the machine and there was no waiting line. Yet there were fifteen people standing in line at the counter. Most adults are not like kids. They won't just go up to the machine, try to use it, and risk looking stupid. Some places have even started putting a person next to the e-ticket machine, I guess to help people use the technology and to give it the human touch.

"I see benefit in using technology before, during, and after training. Before training, people can get information about the course, prework, and so forth. During training, technology can be used as a way to break things up or used as activities. After training, technology can be used for electronic performance support back on the job. The other thing to remember is that technology is only going to be useful if people are familiar enough with it to use it."

by combining CAI with other media and instructional methods in a bid to harness the advantages of many media but reduce the impact of the disadvantages as well.

INTRANET- AND INTERNET-BASED TRAINING

The world of computers is replete with terminology, jargon, and acronyms. This book is not a primer on intranet, Internet, or Web-based training delivery. Nor is it a computer primer. Our aim is simply to describe the value of these media and discuss their impact on classroom training delivery.

A good place to begin any discussion of intranet and Internet-based training is with some key definitions. The Internet, according to *Que's Computer User's Dictionary,* is "a system of linked computer networks, worldwide in scope, that facilitates data communication services such as remote login, file transfer, electronic mail, and distributed newsgroups." An *intranet* is a privately owned network that possesses many Internet features but that has limited access and safeguards. Many corporations own intranets, which are accessed and utilized by their employees for training and other purposes. The *Random House Personal Computer Dictionary* defines World Wide Web (WWW) as "a system of Internet servers that support specially formatted documents...in a language called HTML (hypertext markup language) that supports links to other documents, as well as graphics, audio, and video files." Many organizations and individuals now have fully functioning Web sites. People can visit and use them for many purposes, including electronic commerce, customer service, or information downloads.

The equipment necessary to access and use the Internet is widely available at relatively low costs. The primary items needed for use include a personal computer (PC), a modem, which allows the Internet to be accessed via phone lines (or a cable hookup for even faster access), communication software, and an Internet service provider, which are widely available at a flat monthly rate or based on hourly usage. Once established, you can access the Internet to browse the WWW, log on to Web sites, perform information searches, send and receive electronic mail (e-mail), and engage in many other activities.

One powerful use of the Internet and WWW is the ability to perform searches. Search engines allow users to enter simple to complex search criteria on virtually any topic. Yahoo (www.yahoo.com) and Excite (www.excite.com) are two popular Internet search engines. When a search is finished, the engine displays a list of successful matches, called "hits," which correspond to the user's criteria. Sometimes search engines will return hundreds of thousands and even millions of hits, but only a small number represent information that will be of use to you. For example, a recent search performed on Yahoo using the term "training delivery" yielded 243,289 hits. Since not all hits are relevant, it may be too daunting to sort through all of the sites. Therefore, it is better to use more specific search criteria when searching the Web. Many search engines also provide tips for more effective searches.

Metasearch engines permit you to search across many search engines. This ability is sometimes important, since not all sites on the Web are listed on all search engines.

Intranet- and Internet-based training use the Internet or an internal corporate intranet for training purposes. There are five levels of Internet training.[1] At the lowest level is *general communication* through tools such as electronic mail and electronic conferencing. Level two is *online reference*, which uses the Internet to create a virtual library containing links to relevant information. When organizations move to level three, they enter the world of *testing, assessment, and surveys* conducted via the Internet. This use allows individuals to access such instruments online and the technology tabulates the data, produces reports, and distributes them to participants. Level four is the *distribution of computer-based training*. Learners can access entire training programs or discrete modules in a just-in-time manner at their desktops. The fifth and most sophisticated level is the *delivery of multimedia over the Internet*. This method facilitates real-time access to training that is highly interactive and multimedia-based.

As organizations progress to higher levels of Internet-based training effectiveness, the benefits they can reap from it increase. However, the costs also become higher, which is one drawback for many firms with limited budgets. On the positive side, the rapidly advancing high technology industry continually produces increasing sophistication at decreasing costs. This trend should make the Web more accessible and affordable to all users in time. Many leading-edge organizations have powerful Intranet capability, which they believe, results in numerous benefits—including better communication, information sharing, knowledge management, and improved profitability. Today, many desktop personal computers (PC's) are equipped with video capability that permits two-way video and audio transmission by the Internet, thus opening additional technology frontiers such as real-time face-to-face consulting and real-time coaching.

TRANSITIONING TRADITIONAL TRAINING TO WEB-BASED TRAINING

A framework has been created by Pamela Loughner and Douglas Harvey that you can use to help determine what elements of existing training programs can be transitioned to the Web.[2] Traditional training methods are paired with different types of Web-based technologies. Training methods included in this framework are demonstrations, discussions, games, presentations, role plays, simulations, and tutorials. The five Web-based technologies included in their framework and the training methods they can deliver include the following:

- *Asynchronous text communication.* E-mail, listservs, and newsgroups are examples of asynchronous text communication. In this type of communication, you and your participants can send and receive messages at different times. This technology is useful for delivering case studies, conducting discussions, and even enacting role plays. A key advantage of this type of communication is that it allows learners to participate at different times—which can be quite important for global training—and facilitates the development of responses by learners that are more carefully thought through.

- *Synchronous text communication.* Chat rooms are examples of synchronous text communication. If you use this kind of communication for training delivery, you and your participants can communicate in real time. This technology can be used to deliver case studies, discussions, and role plays. Because synchronous text communication occurs in real time, it is more spontaneous than asynchronous text communication.

- *Web pages.* Web pages are typically what you think of when you hear the term World Wide Web. Web pages have text and graphics and are linked to other Web pages to create a Web site through the use of HTML. This technology can be used to deliver case studies, demonstrations, presentations, and tutorials.

- *Web-based media delivery.* Along with text and graphics, Web pages can also be designed to deliver video or audio clips. Web-based media delivery can deliver case studies, demonstrations, presentations, and tutorials.

- *Web-based interactive multimedia.* Even more sophisticated than Web pages that deliver video and audio are Web pages designed to include an interactive component. The interactive component allows the trainee to practice the desired skill and receive immediate feedback. This technology is most appropriate for delivering interactive demonstrations, games, role plays, and simulations.

■ *Web-based conferencing.* Web-based conferencing systems allow individuals to see and hear each other in real time in two-way audio and video conferencing systems. This type of environment most closely resembles you and your participants working together in a classroom, permitting you to incorporate many methods you might otherwise use in a traditional classroom. They include demonstrations, discussions and debates, presentations, and role plays.

OTHER HARDWARE

Other types of hardware that can be used in training delivery include simulators and production equipment or machinery.

SIMULATORS

A *simulator* is a device that replicates the experiences or conditions of an actual job. A flight simulator used by airline pilots is one example of a simulator used for training purposes. A second example is a simulator used to train automotive techniques. The simulator might, for instance, take the form of the front end of a vehicle mounted on a stand and wired for training use. A third example is a simulator of the control room of a nuclear power plant.

Although expensive to develop, maintain, and use, simulators provide realistic substitutions for on-the-job training that is conducted on the learner's actual work site. An obvious benefit of a simulator is that it eliminates or reduces the safety risks that would be associated with, for example, landing an aircraft filled with passengers. Simulators provide a way to give learners simulated hands-on experience. The U.S. military is probably best known for state-of-the-art simulators, with vast amounts of financial and intellectual capital readily available.

PRODUCTION EQUIPMENT OR MACHINERY

Production equipment or machinery is another type of hardware that can be used for training. This hardware is most frequently used for on-the-job training (OJT) or vestibule training (sometimes called near-the-job training, or NJT). OJT is conducted on the learner's work site. NJT is conducted in close proximity to the learner's work site, such as next to an assembly line. Training conducted using actual equipment or machinery is even more advantageous than using a simulator because the trainee learns important skills and knowledge in the context of the actual job.

When learners use production equipment in the work setting for training, it can reduce production, lead to quality problems, and create safety problems because inexperienced workers in training are not as productive as trained operators. For example, when a new employee learning to operate a stamping press learns tasks by taking the controls, the result is likely to be slower production with an increased amount of rejected material—even when the training is conducted under the watchful eye of a more skilled worker. On other types of equipment, the negative results may be avoidable with planning and scheduling. For example, new employees learning how to operate forklifts could be trained during a slow work period, or off shift to practice the new skills in a safe area.

Sometimes other problems may arise when certain equipment is used. The following critical incident relates a harrowing experience that emphasizes how challenging it can be for trainers to deliver training involving equipment.

The Claustrophobic Learner

"*I was conducting training for participants of a radiological emergency response team. One of the participants became hysterical during a field exercise and did not alert us during the precourse briefing that she was claustrophobic. Part of the field exercise involved donning respiratory equipment to wear during a hazardous material response drill. The trouble began when the participant put the facemask of the respirator over her face. This person was extremely difficult to deal with and seemed to become "irrational" following the initial trauma of the claustrophobia. The other instructors and course director (three individuals) took over the rest of the exercise with the remaining course participants. I (a female) took the "victim" to a nearby medical facility, where they could check her blood pressure, pulse, respiratory problem, etc. They recommended that she discontinue her participation in the course (a five-day course) and she was advised to return home.*"

Although situations like this incident are difficult or impossible to predict, you must take what steps you can to prepare for such unforeseen circumstances. In cases like this one, trainers need to demonstrate flexibility, level-headedness, and an action-orientation to handle such a crisis situation effectively.

ADDITIONAL STRATEGIES FOR USING MEDIA AND HARDWARE

We offered some general guidelines for using specific media in the previous section. This section extends that discussion by providing some general strategies for using media effectively during training delivery.

COMMON SENSE AND COMMON PRACTICE

In general, any hardware or equipment that you use during training delivery should be operated in compliance with the practices recommended by the vendor or manufacturer. Often, purchased hardware comes with operating documentation and sometimes product training or support. For example, operating documents frequently accompany less sophisticated hardware, such as overhead transparency projectors. However, extensive training and customer support material frequently accompany complex equipment such as a simulator. The best advice is to use common sense and follow recommended operating practices and procedures supplied by the vendor or manufacturer. Guidelines available through documentation can be useful for continuing training. For example, the steps for cleaning a whiteboard on which permanent marker was accidentally used may be found in a users' guide that came with the purchase of the whiteboard. (By the way, rubbing alcohol or soft drinks will sometimes work effectively to erase permanent markings from a whiteboard.)

SAFETY CONSIDERATIONS

When hardware and equipment are used in training, follow the safety precautions provided by the vendor or manufacturer and always operate the equipment in a safe manner. Problems can arise from various sources For instance, when projection systems or computers are used during training, the power cords coupled with dimmed lights can easily trip a person. Scour and evaluate the training environment for possible safety hazards before the training occurs. Further, a qualified and certified safety professional—preferably with knowledge or experience with the Occupational Safety and Health Administration (OSHA) regulations—can assist with a formal or informal safety audit to identify potential problems at your training site. Finally, early in a training program, be sure to emphasize the importance of safety and alert learners to any potential dangers they may face during training to increase their awareness and reduce the chance of accidents.

Many potential safety problems arise when on-the-job training is conducted or incorporated into classroom training. Generally, everyone involved should adhere to all work site safety procedures. For example, if hard hats and steel-tipped shoes are required safety gear for workers in a steel plant, then these should be required by learners visiting a work site for training purposes. Make sure to review safety rules and potential safety problems with learners before they enter potentially hazardous situations. In Chapter Three we suggested distributing a small safety card as a way to alert learners to safety issues and procedures.

TROUBLESHOOTING MINOR HARDWARE PROBLEMS

When you use hardware during training delivery, you may have to play the role on occasion of troubleshooter or technician to take corrective action. Sometimes even the simplest problem can delay or halt training delivery. For example, if the light bulb in the overhead goes off, you may be left in the dark—in more ways than one—about what to do. In situations like this, you must troubleshoot the problem to determine its cause. A light bulb could go off for many reasons—not just the most obvious (a burned out bulb). To mention just a few, the building could have lost power, the cord could have been inadvertently disconnected, or a fuse could have blown. Once you have pinpointed the cause, take immediate action yourself or call a technician, if one is available.

Your dependence on technical assistance increases as the hardware and media you use become more sophisticated. Frequently, however, you may be capable of troubleshooting and correcting the problem without calling upon others. This is where contingency planning, which will be discussed later in this section, becomes important.

When minor hardware problems occur, avoid delays. For instance, your spending too much time replacing the light bulb in an overhead projector will place you behind schedule and make the learners restless. When minor hardware problems cause unplanned stoppages in your training course, do not neglect the learners. Estimate how long it will take to correct the problem. Once you have an idea, either take a short break, or give the learners an activity that will keep them occupied while you troubleshoot the problem and solve it. You can use activities from the participant guide or you could create an activity on the spot to give the learners useful work while you tend to the unplanned problem. Explain what you are doing and your plan so that learners understand why you departed from the agenda.

CONTINGENCY PLANNING

At times it may be impossible for you to solve a problem stemming from a hardware malfunction or breakdown. For this reason, you should formulate a contingency plan before training delivery so that you have alternate ways to deliver the training material. A *contingency plan* usually means a backup strategy to replace an original training delivery plan.

To emphasize how important contingency planning can be and how trainers deal with unplanned hardware problems, consider the following critical incidents.

From High Tech to Low Tech

"*I was utilizing PC's for a training class and the training database was not accessible. My inclination was to cancel the class without the hands-on availability to the database. Instead I had students write the transaction code formats, so when we were able to bring the database back online, the input could be done from their own notes. Learning was reinforced by their writing and then typing to see the desired results.*"

Capitalizing on Technical Problems

"*I was doing Internet marketing and legacy data management seminars in New York and I had equipment problems all day. I couldn't maintain ISP connectivity for showing real life examples. So, I told stories and gave the audience the up-take Web sites to visit on their own. I used it as a follow-up take-home test. Also, that afternoon my projector decided to intermittently flash even-numbered PowerPoint slides. No problem with the odd-numbered slides! I shut off the projector, went straight to the demo, and used the slide projector handouts as reference. I turned it into a discussion of the learners' data problems and how to specifically solve them. Worked great!*"

Those Pesky PC's

" *When delivering computer system training, it is very frustrating to have PC problems or the server go down. At that point, I just switch over to "theory" and "what ifs" in our business until the system is back up.* "

The cost of failure and the complexity of the hardware are two important issues you should consider when deciding whether a contingency plan is necessary. The relationship between them is illustrated in Exhibit 12–7.

The cost of failure involves more than financial consequences. In fact, nonfinancial consequences and risks can actually outweigh them. For example, if training involves many people who traveled to the training site from around the world, or if the chief executive officer (CEO) of the company is attending the training, the stakes increase significantly. In terms of complexity, when intricate, technical, and sophisticated hardware is used during training, the likelihood of malfunctions, breakdowns, and problems tends to increase. When the stakes are high or the equipment is complex, you are faced with a situation when one or more well-formulated contingency plans are necessary.

CREATING CONTINGENCY PLANS

To develop a contingency plan, you need only think through a "What if?" scenario with the major hardware and other potential problem areas. Ask and answer the question "What if X happens?" If X in this case is the overhead projector failing, answer the question by making sure that a spare light bulb will be kept in close proximity to the training site. Then ask, "What if the problem persists?" A backup plan to solve that problem would be to store a spare overhead projector unit nearby. Additional contingency plans for that situation include having extra markers or other supplies, a spare flipchart pad, transparencies of the computer-based presentation, handouts of the transparencies, or back-up hardware. Use the planning worksheets appearing in Exhibits 12–8 and 12–9 to develop contingency plans.

Even with careful preparation, contingency planning, and other precautionary measures, problems may still arise in training delivery. The critical incident below demonstrates the "touchy" nature of various media and hardware that trainers use and dramatizes the negative consequences that can be created by such glitches.

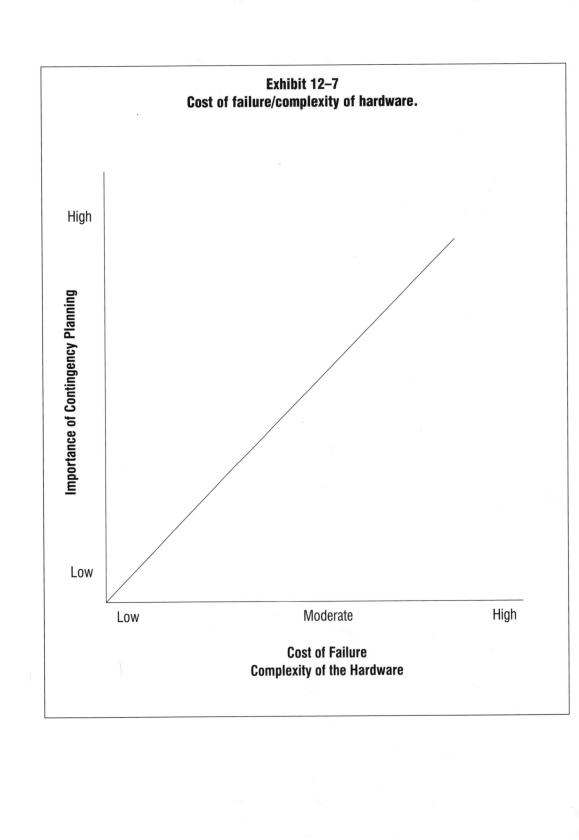

Exhibit 12–7
Cost of failure/complexity of hardware.

Exhibit 12–8
Contingency planning worksheet #1.

What technology are you using?	What could potentially go wrong?

Clearly state your contingency plan:

If the problem persists, what will you do?

List several names and phone numbers of people you can call for support.

What technology are you using?	What could potentially go wrong?

Clearly state your contingency plan:

If the problem persists, what will you do?

List several names and phone numbers of people you can call for support.

What technology are you using?	What could potentially go wrong?

Clearly state your contingency plan:

If the problem persists, what will you do?

List several names and phone numbers of people you can call for support.

Exhibit 12–9
Contingency planning worksheet #2.

Equipment	Supplies Needed	Back-up plan	Supplies Needed
The following is an example:			
Overhead projector	*Markers* *Transparencies* *Extra light bulb*	*Flipchart*	*Markers* *Tape* *Easel* *Wall brackets*

Crash and Burn

"My worst training experience involved setting up and controlling a training environment for demonstration and hands-on exercises. We were doing an extended training program in the southern sales division. The vice president of the division had been pushing countertop shipping and wanted a demonstration of how easy it was to use as part of the training program for location sales managers. We spent several hours developing a demonstration and setting up demo data on the database. An hour before the training was due to start all the data and programs were tested and confirmed. After a strong sales pitch we went into the demonstration only to have the environment blow up in our faces. The computer department had modified the required programs and new versions were moved into the training environment during the hours that separated our last test from the demonstration. Needless to say, the program was a complete failure.

We contacted the computer department, had the old version of the program moved back to the training environment and re-ran the demo. Despite all our efforts the end result was that all managers present were convinced that the system would not work. This experience reinforced for me the critical nature of your training environment and the importance of a positive training experience on the audience."

Of course, unexpected problems can bedevil trainers even without equipment or hardware malfunctions. One of the authors, for instance, was scheduled to conduct training when his wife was expecting a baby. On the night before a training session—too late for a cancellation—his wife delivered the baby at 5 A.M. Three hours later, the author dragged into the training site and provided a full day of training. One participant said at break, "You look terrible. What happened?" After hearing the story and realizing that three hours was too short notice to cancel training when the organization had invested a small fortune in participant travel costs, the learners became unusually cooperative. Had the author had a contingency plan for a backup presenter, of course, the problem could have been solved in a better way.

SUMMARY

This chapter focused on using media and hardware effectively. We defined the terms and reviewed the advantages, disadvantages, and uses of various media, including:

- Static media

- Dynamic media

- Telecommunications

- Computer-related training

We emphasized that media and hardware selection depends on the training objectives to be achieved. Some media support some training objectives better than others. Media should also be seamlessly incorporated into training delivery, supporting rather than supplanting it.

STRATEGY LIST

Actionable Strategies to Improve Training Effectiveness:

USE MEDIA EFFECTIVELY

Print

❑ Use printed material only when appropriate. Remember that when you distribute material, the learners' attention will transfer from you to the material.

❑ Use only high-quality printed material. Low-quality material is a reflection on the credibility of you and the training. Keep electronic copies of print material on hand.

Transparencies, Slides, and Computer Presentations

❑ Stand in the back of the training room to test the clarity of the presentation.

❑ Identify the best lighting adjustment before training to ensure that all learners can see the presentation. It is preferable to be in a room where the lighting can be dimmed.

❑ Keep additional light bulbs for overhead projectors and power packs for computers handy to troubleshoot problems.

Flipcharts and whiteboards

❑ Use dark colored markers when writing on flipcharts and transparencies. Avoid red and yellow because they can be difficult to see from a distance.

❑ Keep additional supplies close at hand such as masking tape and additional markers.

❑ When working on a whiteboard, BE CERTAIN you are using an erasable marker.

❑ Write clearly and legibly with no spelling errors.

❑ Write important information in pencil on the flipchart page as notes for you.

Videotape

❑ Adjust the lighting so that learners can see the video but are not totally in the dark to enable them to take notes if necessary. Also, total darkness can cause learners to become sleepy.

Audiotapes

❑ Present only short clips of audiotape. Because audiotapes only touch on one sense (hearing), learners may become distracted or bored.

Telecommunications

❑ Always have a contingency plan when using any type of technology. Caution: Do not allow your training to be entirely dependent upon one form of technology. Carry some kind of back up to plan for a technological failure.

❑ Avoid replacing training with technology. While using technology can be exciting and can enhance your presentations, remember that people learn from each other and want to interact with one another as well as the trainer.

❏ Practice using your media in advance to identify potential problems, breakdowns, or troubleshooting needs before the training occurs.

Computer-Aided Instruction and Computer-Based Training

❏ Keep in mind that many adults may not want to use computers during training. They may not know how to use one and therefore feel intimidated or embarrassed. It is important to identify this in advance.

❏ When using the Web, plan for download time. Web pages may download quickly one day, but other days it may take much longer than expected.

CHAPTER 13

EVALUATING LEARNER PERFORMANCE

SKILLS ASSESSMENT

Take a moment to review the competency and associated performances that will be covered in this chapter. Consider your current level of proficiency in the competency as a whole as well as each performance and check the items where you feel you need to improve. As you read the chapter, concentrate on those areas most in need of development.

Competency:

❑ Evaluate learner performance.

Associated Performances:

❑ Monitor learner progress during training.

❑ Administer tests and instruments.

❑ Evaluate attainment of end-of-course objectives.

❑ Judge the adequacy of evaluation.

Evaluating learner performance was rated by trainers in our survey as the single most difficult to demonstrate competency of the fourteen training delivery competencies. There are many possible reasons for that rating, though trainers in our study were not asked to elaborate. Perhaps they perceived this competency as difficult because evaluation methods are not typically embedded in the design of training courses or in on-the-job follow-up strategies. Perhaps they perceived this competency as difficult because it is not always easy to measure human behavior. Although the reasons for the trainers' rating in our study are not clear, this chapter provides some practical strategies for evaluating learners' performance.

This chapter covers the following topics:

- Training evaluation and the key issues associated with it.

- Donald Kirkpatrick's four levels of training evaluation.

- Strategies for monitoring and evaluating learner performance during training and comparing performance to training objectives.

- Guidelines for judging the adequacy of evaluation.

The Evaluation Dilemma

" My most typical problem is evaluation of skills. Evaluation is subjective and is most difficult when the individual's skills are borderline. Classroom training and testing are comparatively easy. Tests can be written and corrected and the results speak for themselves. "

As you read this chapter, think about how you evaluate learner performance and what approaches you could use to improve the evaluation of learner performance.

DEFINING TRAINING EVALUATION

Training evaluation is the process of assessing the results or outcomes of training. In short, training evaluation determines the value of training. It loops back to training needs assessment to determine how much and how well the training that was delivered solved the identified performance problems linked to knowledge or skill deficiencies. The basic question is, did the training meet the identified training needs?

KEY ISSUES IN TRAINING EVALUATION

This section summarizes key issues in training evaluation. It provides important definitions that provide a foundation for understanding how and why training should be evaluated.

TRAINING OBJECTIVES: ONE BASIS FOR EVALUATION

Effective training begins with *training objectives*—sometimes called *instructional objectives*—that succinctly state the results desired from training. Training is not conducted as an end in itself, nor to comply with government requirements, nor to protect the employer from lawsuits or grievances, nor to give employees a vacation away from the job, nor for its entertainment value. Instead, the purpose is to achieve the training objectives. By meeting the training objectives, learners also meet needs.

Training design typically specifies and documents terminal objectives and enabling objectives. *Terminal objectives* are the end-of-course objectives. They represent what the learners will know, do, or feel upon training completion. Terminal objectives are usually listed at the front of the participant guide. They usually complete a sentence such as this: "At the end of this training, learners will..." followed by a list of the knowledge, skills, or attitudes to be learned. For example, an objective for a computer course in word processing might be:

At the end of this training, learners will be able to:

- Open an existing document.

- Make changes to a document and save it.

- Create a new document.

- Create a filing system for documents.

Enabling objectives contribute to achieving terminal objectives. They are probably most important in lengthy training programs where each session of many contributes to achieving the terminal objectives. Enabling objectives are sometimes listed at the opening of each part, unit, or lesson of a training program and usually complete a sentence stem such as this: "At the end of this module (or section), learners will be able to..." followed by the enabling objectives or module outcomes. Unlike terminal objectives, enabling objectives are sometimes described by the trainer at the opening of the part and appear on overheads. An example of enabling objectives for the computer course described above might be:

At the end of this module, learners will be able to:

- Create new paragraphs in a document.

- Change the font style and size.

■ Indent by using the tab key.

■ Create a table in the text.

These objectives are more specific to a smaller section of the training than the terminal objective that describes the end result.

THE COMPONENTS OF TRAINING OBJECTIVES

According to Robert Mager, whose pioneering work in the training field led many organizations to adopt instructional objectives, objectives are comprised of three elements: performance, criterion, and condition.

The *performance* is the observable behavior a learner will be able to demonstrate upon completion of training. It is usually associated with action words, such as "list," "describe," "define," or "demonstrate."

The *criterion* is the way this behavior will be measured and provides the key to evaluating the attainment of the objective. Typically, the criterion focuses on accuracy, quality, quantity, time, or customer satisfaction. The purpose of a criterion is to provide an objective way to measure learner performance. "With 100 percent accuracy," "with fewer than two errors per page," and "in no more than ten seconds" are sample criterion statements.

Finally, the *condition* is a statement that clarifies the circumstances under which the learner will demonstrate the behavior. The condition includes the physical situation and the resources the learners will have at their disposal. "Using a pocket calculator," "given an overhead transparency," and "when approached by a customer" are all descriptions of conditions that could be used during training. In most training that is conducted, at least two of the three components of a training objective should be present or implied.

An important assumption is that objectives were, in fact, specified in the design. This provides the basis for demonstrating the competency covered in this chapter. Exhibit 13–1 is a job aid that can help you to identify the three elements of a training objective. A sample objective is provided, and the job aid identifies the three components. You can use this worksheet to assist you in writing training objectives or in evaluating objectives that you have been given.

OTHER BASES FOR DATA COLLECTION AND TRAINING EVALUATION

In addition to measuring how much or how well the training objectives are achieved, you can also evaluate many other aspects of train-

Exhibit 13–1 Objective components.		
Performance (action to be taken)	**Criteria** (to what degree?)	**Conditions** (under what circumstances?)
The following is an example: After reading the provided material and participating in the class discussion, the learners will be able to list all five steps involved in the decision-making process.		
List the steps in the decision-making process	All five (denotes 100%)	After reading the material and participating in the class discussion
Objective:		
Performance	Criteria	Conditions
Objective:		
Performance	Criteria	Conditions
Objective:		
Performance	Criteria	Conditions
Objective:		
Performance	Criteria	Conditions
Objective:		
Performance	Criteria	Conditions

ing. For instance, you can ask learners to conduct self-evaluations to assess their own performance in training or their ability to apply what they learned in training. Self-evaluations or self-reports are frequently used in training and involve asking learners about their perceptions regarding these issues. Of course, the issues of honesty and accuracy are prime limitations to this method. However, a clear advantage is that learners are often in the best position to evaluate their own performance.

Your own formal and informal evaluation of learner participation can be used to make improvements during your training delivery. It can also be folded into planning efforts for subsequent training sessions.

MEASUREMENT METHODS AND TOOLS

In many organizations, instructional designers prepare ways of evaluating learner performance by designing and developing training, and it remains only for you (the trainer) to use what they have created. For example, they may have prepared tests based on training objectives. They may have also created other evaluation tools to measure other aspects of training. You can use measurement tools throughout training, not limiting them only to the end of the program. In addition, knowledge, skills, or attitudes can be evaluated before training through pretesting to determine what learners already know, do, or feel before they enter training. Alternatively, measurement tools can be used after training to determine what the learners retained or applied on their jobs.

Many different methods may be used to evaluate or measure training. Some are summarized briefly below.

WRITTEN TESTS

The paper and pencil written test is a commonly used evaluation tool. It is a simple form of testing. Written tests consist of one or more of the following formats: short answers, essays, multiple-choice questions, fill-in-the-blank questions, and true or false questions. These items represent both open and closed (forced choice) responses. *Closed response test items* require a yes/no or quantifiable answer. *Open response test items* allow learners to give amplified or essay-type answers.

DIRECT OBSERVATION

Direct observation is another method of training evaluation. Although observation skills will be discussed in the next section, you can find that observation guidelines are helpful for structuring and focusing this type of evaluation. When you use direct observation, you watch what learners are doing. Observations can be *structured* and focused on watching for evidence of specific behaviors—such as counting how many times someone raises a hand to participate. As an alternative, during *unstructured* observations you simply observe the process of a group to get a sense, as a participant observer, what is happening in the group.

THE INTERVIEW

The *interview* is a conversation. Like direct observation, interviews may be structured or unstructured. A *structured interview* uses a series of predetermined questions. The interviewer varies little in what he or she asks so that results can be compared across many participants. An *unstructured interview* varies questions according to the people interviewed, focusing on what individuals mean by what they say. An unstructured interview can go in many directions and allows follow-up and probing. A structured interview, on the other hand, follows a predetermined pattern or set of questions designed to gather specific information.

Suppose you wanted to evaluate how well learners perceived they were learning about interpersonal skills in a training class. You could develop a list of questions about the course and use the same questions with everyone. That would be a structured interview.

But suppose you informally asked participants over break what they thought about the course. That would be a form of unstructured interview. If a participant said, "I find it boring," you might ask follow-up questions, such as "Why is that?" or "How do you think we could make it more interesting?" These follow-up questions are called *probes*, and they are meant to uncover information. Although this type of interview is unstructured, you can still prepare for it. When you know what you are going to ask to initiate a conversation, try to anticipate some of the responses and generate a few follow-up, probing questions to get at a deeper level of information and understanding.

THE SURVEY QUESTIONNAIRE

The survey questionnaire is similar to an interview except that questions are posed in written form. Like direct observation and interviews, survey questionnaires may be structured or unstructured. A *structured survey questionnaire* uses the same series of written questions consistently with many people. Structured questionnaires often used closed-ended questions and forced response items. An *unstructured survey questionnaire* is more open-ended and encourages people to write essay answers to open-ended questions, such as "How will you apply the skills covered during class in your job?"

Most organizations use survey questionnaires to assess learner perceptions about the course at its conclusion. These are called *reaction evaluations*.

Many issues come to the surface and must be addressed if the survey methodology is used. How will it be administered? Should it be anonymous? Should the entire population or a sample be surveyed? How will the response rate be boosted? These and other questions complicate the use of the survey questionnaire as an evaluation method. However, this method is highly flexible, and many options are possible to tailor surveys to the situation.

THE PERFORMANCE TEST

A *performance test* evaluates training by having the learners "show you what they can do." Unlike a paper-and-pencil test, a performance test requires a demonstration. For instance, an automotive mechanic who learned how to troubleshoot a problem with an automobile engine might be asked to troubleshoot an engine simulator. That is a performance test. Generally, a checklist of steps or an observation form is used to record and evaluate the learner as he or she performs.

OTHER FORMS OF EVALUATION

Evaluations can also be conducted in other ways. They include focus groups, attitude surveys, performance appraisals, assessment centers, and performance or work records.

Focus groups are similar to small group interviews. Learners are called together and asked questions about the training they received. Most focus groups are short —lasting an hour or so—and are tightly organized to answer a few (one to three) questions. Of course, variations on that format are possible.

Attitude surveys measure learner likes and dislikes. They are appropriate when learners are being taught values, cultural awareness, or diversity issues. For example, learners might be asked to respond (on a scale of 1 to 5, where 1 = strongly disagree and 5 = strongly agree) to a statement such as "I believe that diverse groups, including men, women, and people of different races, are generally more creative than homogeneous groups composed of all men, all women, or all members of one race." Learner responses would be tabulated after and/or before training to assess how much attitudes had changed as a result of training.

Performance appraisals focus on how well individuals meet their work or job responsibilities. When training is job-related—as it should be—supervisors or others may assess individuals by how well they applied the training received off-the-job.

Assessment centers are organized work simulations in which individuals are given a series of work-related tasks. Their performance in carrying out those tasks is observed and rated by trained assessors.

PERFORMANCE OR WORK RECORDS

A *performance record* or a *work record* is a document containing information about actual on-the-job performance. Such documents are used as part of an employee's actual job to record measures of quality, quantity, speed, cost, or accuracy. Such records can be used to determine whether a change in performance has occurred as a result of training. For example, quality records can be examined before and after training to determine whether a change occurred in reject rates or customer complaints after quality improvement training was conducted. Or, production records can be examined to see if productivity increased following training on new equipment operation. Of course, evaluators who use such data must realize that changes in performance can stem from many causes, not just training. In other words, linking training directly to performance is often difficult—if not impossible—without an expensive, time-consuming experimental design that attempts to control all variables. Often the best you can do is list the assumptions you made and state that training may have contributed to the change in performance.

In summary, the evaluation methods described above are commonly used. How each method is used can vary widely. What method you choose to use and how you actually use it are often determined before training is delivered. Your role as a trainer is usually to implement the evaluation methods chosen by instructional designers.

KIRKPATRICK'S FOUR LEVELS OF EVALUATION

Many evaluation models exist in the training and development field. However, Donald Kirkpatrick invented one training evaluation framework that has been widely adopted in corporate America. Kirkpatrick's training evaluation framework identifies four levels at which training can be evaluated, and it is useful for thinking about training evaluation. Further, each measurement method described above can be applied in one or more of the four levels.

KIRKPATRICK'S LEVEL ONE EVALUATION: REACTIONS

Level One of Kirkpatrick's hierarchy focuses on the participants' reactions to the training. It measures learner satisfaction level with the training event and all issues associated with it—including the instructor, the food, the facilities, the training material, and much more. The most commonly used way to measure reactions is the end-of-course evaluation questionnaire, sometimes called a "smile sheet" because early versions incorporated smiley faces into the measurement scale. The end-of-course reaction sheet remains the most widely used way that organizations evaluate training. Exhibit 13–2 provides an example of an end-of-course reaction sheet. Reaction evaluation is important because it is a measure of customer satisfaction with the training. A word of caution is that the responses provided on end-of-course evaluations may be more closely correlated with the trainer's sense of humor or the size of the donuts. In other words, the halo effect caused by some the nontraining components of the program may influence the evaluation responses.

KIRKPATRICK'S LEVEL TWO EVALUATION: LEARNING

Level Two of Kirkpatrick's hierarchy focuses on learning. Learning can take the form of knowledge, skill, or attitude acquisition. Knowledge is usually measured by paper-and-pencil tests. Skill is usually measured by performance tests. Attitudes are measured by attitude surveys. Of course, many methods described in the previous section can also be adapted to measure learning—for instance, interviews and survey questionnaires can be adapted to measure knowledge acquisition or even attitudinal change. Exhibit 13–3 provides an example of Level Two evaluation.

KIRKPATRICK'S LEVEL THREE EVALUATION: BEHAVIOR CHANGE

Level Three of Kirkpatrick's hierarchy focuses on behavior change. It thus moves beyond what people know, do, or feel in the classroom and evaluates on-the-job behavior change. When learners complete a program and return to their jobs, Level Three evaluation evaluates how much or how well they applied what they learned.

If the purpose of training was simply to provide information, evidence of how that information is applied on the job may be difficult to measure without administering a paper-and-pencil test on the job (or over the Web). But if training builds skills, you can measure how well those skills were

Exhibit 13–2
Level One: End-of-course reaction evaluation form.

Directions: *Please circle the most appropriate response and add any comments below.*

1. I got a lot out of the training.

1 Completely disagree	2	3 Somewhat agree	4	5 Emphatically agree

2. The instructor helped me to learn.

1 Completely disagree	2	3 Somewhat agree	4	5 Emphatically agree

3. I will use these new skills back on the job.

1 Completely disagree	2	3 Somewhat agree	4	5 Emphatically agree

4. The facilities were conducive to learning.

1 Completely disagree	2	3 Somewhat agree	4	5 Emphatically agree

5. The materials were clear and easy to use.

1 Completely disagree	2	3 Somewhat agree	4	5 Emphatically agree

6. The media/technology positively added to the training.

1 Completely disagree	2	3 Somewhat agree	4	5 Emphatically agree

7. I would advise my friends and colleagues to take this training.

1 Completely disagree	2	3 Somewhat agree	4	5 Emphatically agree

Additional Comments:

Exhibit 13–3
Level Two: Sample knowledge test.

1. What does DOS stand for?

a) Disk Off System

b) Don't Operate System

c) Disk Operating System

2. When using an Excel spreadsheet, what is the first character in any formula?

a) @

b) ~

c) =

d) ^

3. What is the file extension for a Word file?

a) .xls

b) .wrd

c) .doc

d) .dos

4. List the five steps involved in opening a new file.

   1.

   2.

   3.

   4.

   5.

applied by observation, by conducting interviews and surveys with others who can judge the learners' application, or by examining work records.

Exhibit 13–4 gives you an example of a form to monitor performance during an observation. This form can be modified to meet your needs to evaluate learner performance change on the job.

KIRKPATRICK'S LEVEL FOUR EVALUATION: RESULTS

Level Four of Kirkpatrick's hierarchy focuses on the results, or impact, of training. It answers this question: How much did training influence organizational results? Of course, *results* are defined in bottom-line measures such as productivity, profitability, return on equity, return on investment, improved safety, and many other desired outcomes.

Level Four is least used but frequently requested by stakeholders such as line managers and senior executives. It is least frequently used because it is the most difficult, time-consuming, and expensive to do well—and to satisfy skeptical managers that training made a difference. When training is evaluated at Level Four, you must attempt to show the direct connection between training and improvements in sales, profitability, market share, quality, customer service, or other bottom-line measures. Senior executives use such measures to make important business decisions.

One key to evaluating at Level Four is that an agreed-upon baseline measure must exist by which to provide a point of comparison. Without that, no compelling way exists to determine whether the training made a difference.

The first step in conducting a Level Four evaluation is to determine what is going to be tracked. Some issues you can monitor to determine the impact that training may have include scrap/rework reduction, quality improvement, time savings, revenue growth, increased production, and other bottom-line performance measures. Examine, for example, the revenue figures from a sales team over a six-month period:

April	$15m
May	$16.5m
June	$14.3m
July	$23m
August	$25m
September	$24m

Exhibit 13–4
Level Three: On-the-job behavior observation form.

New skills to be performed	Was it performed correctly? How?	How could it have been improved? Any additional concerns (safety, timeliness, etc.)
Example: Changing a tire	• The car was elevated properly by using the car jack. • The flat tire was removed correctly and safely. • The new tire was put on the car and tightly secured. • The car was lowered and the jack removed.	Could have organized tools better. By the end, the tools were scattered and could have easily been lost on a busy highway.

In this case, a new sales methodology was introduced and training was delivered in June and July. You can see the jump in sales growth between June and July.

You should be warned that making the cause and effect connections between training and bottom-line results may draw criticism from some skeptics. They may point to other variables, such as economic conditions, industry consolidation, or new technology, as possible explanations of the change. As you enter the realm of Level Four evaluation, you are cautioned to provide evidence rather than proof, mention assumptions you made, and highlight other variables that may have influenced results.

ADDITIONAL CONSIDERATIONS IN TRAINING EVALUATION

Not all evaluation information must come from methods described in this section. Sometimes managers want information about the training or the learners that was not part of the evaluation system planned during the training design phase. A manager may, for instance, request return on investment (ROI) information after the training has been delivered. When that happens, you must (of course) do as requested to satisfy your client.

But it may be difficult, time-consuming, and expensive to develop rigorous ROI information after the training is delivered. One reason is that no agreement may exist about how well learners performed (and what results they achieved) before the training. Another reason is that, if training is given in response to an executive mandate, no training need may have existed—in which case training did not produce measurable benefits.

WAYS TO MONITOR LEARNER PERFORMANCE DURING TRAINING

Throughout training delivery you should have ample opportunity to observe and evaluate learner performance. Some opportunities may be built into the training through the original design. Other opportunities will be more informal in nature. You can, for instance, see how well learners answer questions. Performance observation during training delivery can focus on individuals or groups. But to be effective, these evaluations should be based on predetermined performance criteria or standards. This section discusses observation skills and presents useful strategies and guidelines for monitoring learner performance during training. We will also discuss less formal evaluation methods.

OBSERVATION SKILLS

When you attempt to monitor learner performance, observation skills are critically important. Observation requires more than casually watching learners. It means attending to overt learner behaviors, and (less frequently) ascertaining covert thought processes or feelings underlying those behaviors.

To be most effective, observations should be structured. In this sense, structured means that you know what you are looking for before you start looking for it. You can do that by creating check sheets, rating scales, observation guides, and other instruments to count the frequency or evaluate the quality of behaviors. One of the authors, for example, has led a presentation skills training workshop. Part of the program involves the learners making a five-minute presentation in front of the entire group. A check sheet is used by the instructor and other evaluators to check off key behaviors, such as eye contact, use of transparencies, and gestures, which should be incorporated into the presentation. The check sheets make it easy both to observe the participant and to quickly and accurately capture information as it is demonstrated.

Often, observations are conducted in an unstructured manner and then organized and evaluated. Using this skill effectively, however, can be difficult. For this reason, we highly recommend using instruments to plan what behaviors you will look for. Such instruments should be valid and reliable so that the resulting data is understandable and defensible.

COMMUNICATING OBSERVATION GUIDELINES TO LEARNERS

Clearly document and communicate the basis for your observation to learners. When you do that, learners will have clear expectations about what will be measured, how it will be measured, and how their behaviors will be evaluated. For example, a learner may be observed performing a psychomotor skill such as starting a pump. After the training has been delivered, the learner must perform the task while you observe and evaluate. You could use a checklist with each task step and associated measurement criteria as an evaluation tool to structure what you observe. As the learner performs each step, you check it off—or make notes about how well the learner performed each task or what problems he or she encountered. Evaluation tools of this kind can be most effective for conducting multiple observations—such as before training to establish a measurable baseline and after training to measure learner skill application. You can also conduct follow-up observations to evaluate the learner's skill on the job.

USING MULTIPLE OBSERVERS

Sometimes more than one trainer or evaluator monitors and evaluates learner performance. Using multiple raters improves the validity because many perspectives are incorporated into the rating. However, one key to that is ensuring that the raters agree on what they are watching and how they will measure it. Observers should receive training before they begin their observations to increase their level of agreement on what to watch and what to measure. This process is sometimes called *calibration*. To calibrate multiple evaluators, gather together to discuss the performance you are evaluating. Agree upon what you are looking for, and how it should be performed. Identify different levels or degrees of performance and decide as a group how each should be rated or scored. Then, determine the level of consistency among raters by evaluating against a predetermined standard and comparing the results. Differences in scoring can then be discussed and corrected so that everyone is on the same page. This will prevent each evaluator from evaluating performance differently. Without calibrating multiple evaluators, evaluation becomes highly subjective, decreasing the validity of the evaluation results.

STRATEGIES FOR EVALUATING LEARNER PERFORMANCE

When you monitor learner performance during training you will find several strategies especially useful. The previous section mentioned how important it is to establish objective criteria, so that the same or similar standards apply to all learners. Take the time to communicate these standards to learners so that everyone is aware of how they will be monitored and evaluated.

Another issue is the frequency of observations. If you observe learners only once—or for a short period—you may not have enough information to draw an accurate picture of the individual's ability. Therefore, ensure that you observe each learner more than once so each person has ample opportunity to display his or her skills. If possible, make these observations periodically throughout training delivery. This approach is fairer to learners and is more useful to you because you need not rely on a single observation to judge a learner's abilities.

One major problem with many evaluation methods is that they may be *obtrusive*, meaning that people know they are being watched. For example, if learners know you are watching their performance, they may grow uncomfortable, become distracted, or even change what they would normally do. If you use a videocamera, you may produce continuing anxiety among learners. Even written tests may cause "test anxiety" reminiscent of early educational experiences or based on concerns about what will be done with the test results.

One way to deal with this problem is to provide a thorough explanation before you conduct testing or perform observations, so that learners will know what you are measuring, why you are measuring it, what will happen to the results, who will see the results, and what actions will be taken (if any) based on the results. For example, if you are using a check sheet as a structured observation tool, the tool should be shown to learners before it is used so that they can see it, attempt to perform in ways matched to it, and ask questions about it. If you make notes on a form—such as an interview guide—be sure to tell them that you will be writing while they are speaking. The more information you can provide to learners, the more comfortable they should become with the process. (Of course, in organizations where low levels of trust exist, you may have difficulty anyway because people may not trust what you say—or trust management to follow the guidelines that you establish in good faith.)

Another way to deal with the problem of obtrusive evaluation methods is to make them as unobtrusive as possible. For example, if you use a video camera to capture learner performance, position it in an inconspicuous location. Small video cameras are now available that can be mounted on a wall or in the corner of a room, thus making them blend into the setting and become less distracting to learners. When taking notes, you can reduce learner anxiety by capturing key bullet points rather than taking copious notes.

ADMINISTERING TESTS AND INSTRUMENTS

You may be tempted to assume that you can simply pass out tests and instruments without experiencing further problems. However, be sure to plan for many contingencies to ensure that tests and other measurement instruments are used properly. When tests are administered without careful planning, learners may feel intimidated and resist the process.

AVOIDING BIAS IN TEST ADMINISTRATION

In the context of testing, *bias* refers to errors in results due to problems that are introduced. Bias can stem from many sources. How you administer a test has the potential to introduce bias. Tests can be conducted in many ways, of course, ranging from highly formal events to informal methods, such as experiential learning activities. Administering standardized tests such as the GMAT or SAT examinations involves formal administration procedures. During these tests, test takers are instructed to use a number-two pencil, told that no discussion will be permitted, given strict time limits, and provided with precise directions that are read (to ensure consistency across test sites) by the proctor.

Such directions are not usually given as formally or explicitly in training situations. As a result, bias—otherwise known as error—can be introduced into testing situations in subtle ways. For example, if you provide one learner group with detailed instructions and emphasize certain issues when administering a written, multiple-choice test but forget to do exactly the same with another group, the test results may vary widely depending on what you said. To avoid such test bias, take steps to minimize or eliminate it by planning carefully how you will administer a test. Then be consistent with all groups.

Tests and measurements developed by instructional designers often produce accompanying documentation about proper test administration procedures. Adhere to those directions closely to ensure that the test is administered as intended. As with any other changes you make during training delivery, be sure to document any special procedures you use or any changes you make, especially those that could have an impact on results.

AVOIDING BIAS THROUGH TIMING

The previous section on monitoring learner performance discussed the strategy of observing and evaluating learners on a periodic and continuous basis. The timing of testing is usually determined in the instructional design stage and spelled out in the instructor guide. The test administration time should follow the training delivery schedule so that the tests are given when planned. However, instructional designers typically give trainers some flexibility about the timing of the test.

TEST ANALYSIS AND SCORING

Procedures for analyzing and scoring tests should be planned and followed carefully and consistently. Different methods and measurement tools have different scoring procedures associated with them. For example, a multiple-choice test can generally be scored or "graded" easily by comparing the learner's responses to the answer key, which displays the correct responses. Other methods, such as interviews or essay responses, are more difficult to analyze because they are qualitative. Much has been written about how to analyze qualitative data, and you may want to review some of that literature if you give questions that yield qualitative results. A simple approach to analyzing such information is content or thematic analysis. That usually involves counting the appearance of key words or key themes appearing in open-ended responses and summarizing important findings and trends that are detected.

EVALUATING ATTAINMENT OF END-OF-COURSE OBJECTIVES

All activities and subject matter used in training should be geared, with a laser-like focus, to achieving training objectives. When learners do not achieve terminal training objectives, you may be tempted to blame the learners. However, poor performance is as much a reflection on the trainer as on the learner. Adult learning theory proposes that individuals learn in different ways, at varying rates, with different styles and preferences. Some learners may master the subject matter faster than others. Don't penalize slower learners, but be sure to measure all learners against the same performance standards.

CRITERION-REFERENCED EVALUATION

Evaluating all learners against the same measurable performance standards is called *criterion-referenced evaluation*. In criterion-referenced evaluation, all learners can be successful so long as they meet the requirements. In fact, that is the goal: All learners should master the training and receive a grade of "A" to indicate they have met or exceeded the standard. In other words, they have achieved mastery.

Criterion-reference evaluation stands in stark contrast to *norm-referenced evaluation*, in which learners are compared to each other and the results are placed on a normal distribution, as shown in Exhibit 13–5. In norm-referenced evaluation, for example, some learners are successful and receive A's, others receive B's, C's, or D's. But it is possible for the highest score to be only a 20 percent, since learners are compared to each other rather than to an absolute standard.

OBJECTIVITY

When you evaluate learner performance, minimize subjectivity. Objectivity is increased when valid instruments are used, multiple raters are introduced, and sources of information are defensible. Many commercially available tests and measurement tools come with sup-

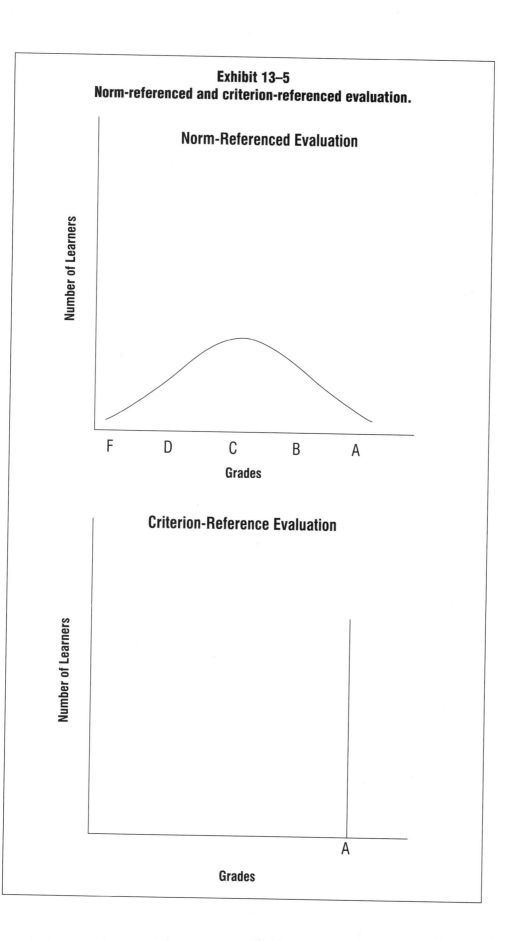

Exhibit 13–5
Norm-referenced and criterion-referenced evaluation.

Norm-Referenced Evaluation

Number of Learners

F   D   C   B   A

Grades

Criterion-Reference Evaluation

Number of Learners

A

Grades

porting validity and reliability studies. Conducting validity and reliability studies is sometimes difficult to do internally with a self-developed instrument, since sophisticated methodologies and statistical testing are required. Further, rigorous validity and reliability are not always necessary. However, evaluation judgments made about learners' performance should be as objective as possible and should be derived through defensible sources, such as test results. Some tips to help increase objectivity of evaluation are:

- Use the same tests in the same way for everyone.

- Be very careful to treat everyone exactly the same.

- Use tests and procedures that have already been established as valid and reliable.

- Use multiple data points.

- Keep your evaluation job-related and measurable.

- Periodically evaluate your processes and tests for validity concerns.

Also be aware that there may be some legal risks or implications in training. For example, if workers will be hired, promoted, transferred, terminated, or their performance evaluated in whole or part based on evaluation information obtained during training, you need to be concerned about legal defensibility. *Legal defensibility* refers to how much or how well the evaluation results will hold up in a court of law. That is why measurement instruments used for making employment decisions should be reliable and valid. Although legal counsel, statistical consulting advice, and other expert guidance are needed to ensure legal defensibility, you should be aware of the standards in the *Uniform Guidelines for Employee Selection Decisions*, published by the Equal Employment Opportunity Commission (EEOC).

AWARDS OF COMPETENCE

When learners achieve terminal training objectives, you may present them with an award or certificate to recognize their achievement, or give them a grade or a certification to indicate their success. Typically, the criteria for receiving such awards are prescribed in the instructional design phase and are specified in the instructor guide. To maintain objectivity and a sense of fairness, adhere to these guidelines. Rewards and recognition administered as a result of successful performance can have a major impact on learner motivation.

JUDGING THE ADEQUACY OF EVALUATION

Since evaluating learner performance is so important, you need to be able to judge how adequately the evaluation process was conducted. Employ measurement tools and methods as prescribed in the instructor guide, and pay close attention to how much and how well these prescriptions were consistently met. When you must modify how or when tools or methods are used for evaluation, be sure to document those changes.

One way to judge the adequacy of the evaluation is to identify how much the evaluation process interferes with learners or their activities. As we discussed, evaluation should be conducted as unobtrusively as possible. Reflect on how well that goal was achieved so that you can make future adjustments when necessary. Another way to judge the adequacy of the evaluation is to consider how objectively and consistently evaluation was conducted.

Once you judge the adequacy of the evaluation, make improvements as necessary. Making judgments about the evaluation process itself should be done on a continuing basis, and you should make adjustments as necessary.

SUMMARY

As this chapter pointed out, evaluating learner performance was rated by trainers in our survey as the single most difficult to demonstrate competency of the fourteen training delivery competencies. Nevertheless, evaluating learner performance is often a front-burner issue with top management and other stakeholders, who want to know whether training achieved its desired results and whether there was a return on the investment in it.

This chapter:

- Defined evaluation as the process of assessing the results of training and described some key issues associated with it.

- Described Donald Kirkpatrick's well-known four levels of training evaluation—reaction, learning, behavior, and results.

■ Presented ways for monitoring and evaluating learner performance during training and for comparing performance to training objectives.

■ Presented guidelines for judging the adequacy of evaluation.

STRATEGY LIST

Actionable Strategies to Improve Training Effectiveness:

Training Objectives

❑ Create clear, measurable objectives. By setting clear, measurable training objectives, you can evaluate learner performance based on how well learners met the objectives rather than other, less measurable criteria such as entertainment value.

❑ When writing or reviewing objectives, be certain to include the behavior that learners must be able to demonstrate, how the behaviors will be measured, and the conditions under which the learners must demonstrate the behaviors.

❑ Remember that even though evaluation is conducted on the back-end of training, it really is a front-end responsibility. Evaluation goals need to be created during the design phase of training (probably by an instructional designer). The trainer's responsibility is to be certain that the goals are in place and that they match the learners' needs.

Learner Evaluation Guidelines

❑ When observing performance during training, create and use checksheets of the behaviors that you are looking for.

❑ Use multiple methods for evaluating learner performance such as written tests, observation, interviews, surveys, and performance tests. Multiple methods will enable you to create a more accurate picture of the learners' skills and abilities.

❑ Use multiple observers/perspectives to improve the validity of the results. Caution: All observers should be calibrated so that they are evaluating the learners the same way.

❏ If evaluating learners through observations, try to observe in an unobtrusive manner. Some learners become anxious, preventing you from getting an accurate picture of their performance.

❏ Maintain consistency among all learners regarding instructions, timing, and analysis.

❏ Minimize subjectivity as much as possible.

❏ After the training is conducted and evaluated, judge the adequacy of the evaluation and make changes as necessary for the next training session.

CHAPTER 14

EVALUATING THE DELIVERY OF INSTRUCTION

SKILLS ASSESSMENT

Take a moment to review the competency and associated performances that will be covered in this chapter. Consider your current level of proficiency in the competency as a whole as well as each performance and check the items where you feel you need to improve. As you read the chapter, concentrate on those areas most in need of development.

Competency:

☐ Evaluate delivery of training.

Associated Performances:

☐ Evaluate the instructional design, as modified, during delivery.

☐ Evaluate a trainer's performance.

☐ Evaluate the effects of other variables—including the training environment—on learner accomplishments.

☐ Judge how well a course works for a particular group of learners in a particular situation.

As the trainer, you are the channel through which information is delivered and learning is facilitated. That is not to say that learners will be completely bewildered if they have an ineffective trainer. But, to achieve good results on a consistent basis, you need appropriate and effective delivery skills. As a trainer or instructor, you are usually the most visible source of training, and you will be blamed if any aspect of the training experience is not effective. Of course, the subject matter of the training, the quality of the training materials, organization politics, the setting in which the training is conducted, learner motivation, and countless other issues can all dramatically influence how learners and others evaluate your training delivery. You (or another qualified person) should monitor the training program during delivery to assess its quality and effectiveness based on the training objectives and predetermined performance standards. The feedback you receive can be helpful to you in achieving quality results and continuous improvement.

The following critical incident demonstrates the negative, and in this case vague, feedback that trainers sometimes receive on their evaluations about their training delivery.

Harsh Feedback

" I was substituting for another trainer and assumed one of the students had learned a specific "task sequence" and was not following it in the exercise. I explained to her a better sequence. She replied that the other trainer had taught this way. I later got the feedback from her on an evaluation that I was a "flake." "

Whether such statements are unfairly made, anything perceived as important to a learner is important to the learning process.

This chapter covers the following topics associated with evaluating the delivery of training:

- The adequacy of the instructional design as it is modified during training delivery.

- Guidelines for evaluating your own training delivery.

- Issues, such as the learning environment, that affect perceptions of how effectively training is delivered.

- Ways of judging how well a training course works for one learner group.

Taken together, these issues may point to the need to modify future training course offerings to improve delivery.

MODIFYING THE INSTRUCTIONAL DESIGN DURING TRAINING DELIVERY

As you deliver training, you are frequently confronted by difficult situations, such as a mismatch between materials and learners. Recall from Chapter Two that it is your responsibility to match the training program to the unique needs of one learner group. One way you can do that is to modify examples to make them relevant to the participants. Also recall from Chapter Five that it is your responsibility to adapt how you deliver the training to take unique learner characteristics into account. One way to do that is to modify exercises and training methods or reorganize the sequence of topics. When you note that learners are unresponsive to the training or appear bored, you must first recognize the problem and then take corrective action. To stimulate bored learners, for instance, introduce an exercise or ask thought-provoking questions.

DOCUMENTING AND JUSTIFYING CHANGES

Remember to document changes you make during training delivery so that the information can be reported to instructional designers, managers, or other trainers. In addition, always make sure that you justify your changes and do not make them arbitrarily or because they suit your preferences.

When you and others examine any changes made to the instructional design of a training course, be sure to focus on what the changes were and why they were made. To that end, start with the documentation provided by the trainer. Note special issues, such as the unique characteristics of the learners, the setting, or the subject matter. Once you understand what changes were made and why, consider how they influenced the original instructional design of the course and the achievement of training objectives.

If your modifications improve the results, then the instructional designers and others can decide whether they should become permanent changes to the training program. If not, then the outcomes of the approach can be documented for future reference.

GUIDELINES FOR EVALUATING YOUR OWN DELIVERY

Each trainer is unique, possessing different strengths and weaknesses. You must therefore evaluate yourself periodically to build on your strengths and improve on your weaknesses. The competencies outlined

BOB PIKE

We asked training expert Bob Pike, "What do you believe to be the most common problem(s) that new instructors face and what coaching advice would you have to deal with those problems?" One of his responses to this question was, "I think one common problem is that new instructors tend to have a high need for feedback on how they are doing. Not all groups will be willing or able to provide them with feedback. One trainer that I was working with said to me, 'I don't ever want to work with a nuclear power group again,' because they gave him no feedback during the program. However, at the end of the program they indicated that it was one of the best training programs they had ever attended. This new trainer wanted feedback from the beginning and throughout the program, not just at the end. This is not always going to happen naturally with certain groups. The style of some groups may be more analytical or reserved and therefore less likely to give feedback to the trainer. I think that related to this is that new trainers sometimes struggle with knowing how to get feedback from groups on how the training is going.

"Because feedback is important for trainers and not all groups provide it, one of the things I do is to build in regular reflection time. Every two-and-a-half hours or so, I ask learners to reflect for about two minutes on what are the most important ideas that have been covered, what they have learned, and what they can apply to their jobs. I have them document these on an 'action ideas' list. Then I ask them to share their ideas with others in their group for about three minutes. I then go around to the whole group and get their comments.

"There are really two types of learners. *Participative* learners learn from others in their groups. *Reflective* learners can learn alone. When many learners are at a table working in a group, they will learn from each other. Someone that is sitting there during this activity might not be able to come up with any learnings, but when they hear ideas that other people come up with they might say 'yeah, I can apply that too!' Learners tend to stimulate others and you get the piggy-back effect. Doing some of these things is a great way to give the trainer feedback about the 'take-away' value that learners are receiving from the training. It's solid evidence on how the learners are doing and therefore on how the trainer is doing as well."

in this book represent the competencies essential to effective training delivery. Evaluate your proficiency in each competency—especially those demonstrated during delivery.

PERFORMANCE APPRAISALS

If you are a full-time trainer who delivers much instruction, your performance appraisal may be influenced dramatically by how well you deliver. Performance appraisal occurs all the time. People are always making judgments about you. However, they may be formal (planned) or informal (unplanned).

FORMAL APPRAISALS

Formal performance appraisals are designed to occur on a regular basis—such as annually, semi-annually, or quarterly. Generally, the training manager or director is the person who is involved in the formal performance appraisal process for internal trainers. However, others may be involved as well. For instance, learners, other trainers, and line managers may be asked to evaluate you or participate in your evaluation. In fact, *multirater evaluations*— known as 360-degree performance evaluations—gather feedback and observations from many people to provide a more complete and accurate picture of your performance. In addition to self-ratings, the 360-degree evaluations gather data from other stakeholders, including peers, supervisors, direct reports, internal and external customers, and suppliers. Exhibit 14–1 provides a graphical representation of the 360-degree evaluation process.

First, the evaluation data are collected and a written report is produced. Then, at a scheduled time, the person who conducted the appraisal sits down with you in a private meeting to review your performance. Preferably the formal evaluation process is an extension of continual discussion and coaching between you and your manager. In other words, there should be no surprises regarding the substance of the review.

INFORMAL APPRAISALS

Appraisals are often quite informal in nature. To improve your skills you might ask a colleague to observe and critique your performance for your own developmental purposes. The informal appraisal typically does not occur with any regularity and is done as needed. Many people could be involved in an informal evaluation. For example, you could ask a peer, a colleague, your manager, or even a program participant to

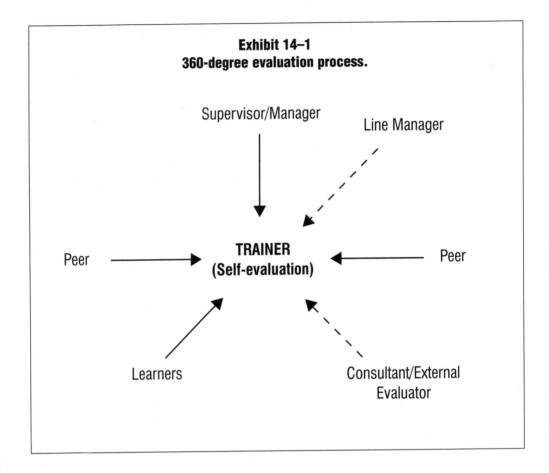

Exhibit 14–1
360-degree evaluation process.

evaluate your performance and provide you with feedback. You could also perform a self-evaluation. Regardless of who actually observes you and provides you with feedback, the purpose is to increase your awareness of your strengths and weaknesses and help you develop an action plan for your own continuous improvement.

CONTENT OF THE PERFORMANCE APPRAISAL

A common criticism of performance appraisals is that they are often vague and subjective. Too often appraisals present the evaluator with topical areas such as "Quality of Work" or "Productivity" or "Customer Focus" and then supply a rating scale to be marked with items such as "Poor," "Meeting Expectations," or "Outstanding." Such evaluations are fraught with problems. First, what "Quality of Work" means is open to broad interpretation. Five evaluators could easily come up with five different meanings for quality. Also, another problem is that descriptors on rating scales such as "Acceptable" lack specific meaning and do not tell trainers *why* they are acceptable. When individuals are presented with vague feedback, they do not know what to do to improve.

IMPROVING APPRAISALS WITH BEHAVIORALLY ANCHORED RATING SCALES

Behaviorally anchored rating scales (BARS) attempt to deal with some of the problems inherent in traditional appraisal methods. This type of rating scale replaces subjective rating statements such as "Excellent" or "Poor" with precise statements of actual behavior. We recommend that observable, measurable, or quantifiable behavior statements be used whenever possible. In this manner, those who evaluate instructor performance have clear behaviors against which to rate the person. Exhibit 14–2 provides an example of a behaviorally anchored rating scale.

The exhibit is a typical end-of-course, Level One reaction, evaluation form (recall Kirkpatrick's evaluation hierarchy discussed in Chapter 13), which has been converted into behaviorally anchored rating scales. Learners completing this evaluation at the end of a course all have the same specific indicators. In this manner each person completing the form has a similar perspective on what a rating of "5" on question two really means. In this case it would mean, "The instructor was the best instructor I have ever had." This information would be helpful for the trainer as well. If a trainer received twenty evaluation forms after a particular course and received ten scores of "1" and six "2s," he would know, unfortunately, that with the majority of this group of learners he rated somewhere between "one of the worst" and "the worst" instructors they had ever experienced. This may not represent good news for him, but it is a deeper meaning than being between "poor" and "very poor."

FORMATIVE, CONCURRENT, AND SUMMATIVE EVALUATIONS

In addition to evaluations that are formal or informal, another way you can classify types of evaluations is to distinguish between those that are formative, concurrent, or summative. A *formative evaluation* is simply one that is conducted before widespread delivery of training as a way to ensure the materials and methods will be effective. A *concurrent evaluation* is conducted as training is delivered. A *summative evaluation*, on the other hand, is administered at the end of training to measure success of the effort.

Exhibit 14–2
Sample behaviorally anchored rating scales (BARS).

1. Rate your ability to apply the knowledge and skills covered to your present job.

5	4	3	2	1
I found the content very useful and relevant. I will be able to use it every day.	The content was relevant and useful. I will use it occasionally.	The content was useful and relevant. I may or may not use it, though.	The content was not very useful or relevant to me. I will use it infrequently.	The content was definitely not useful or relevant at all. I will never use it.

2. Circle the statement that most closely fits how you feel after the workshop.

5	4	3	2	1
I will be more effective because of this workshop and will also help others to be more effective.	I will use what I learned and become more effective because of it.	I will adequately use what I learned in this workshop.	I may occasionally use what I learned in this workshop.	I will never use what I learned in this workshop.

3. Please rate the overall quality of the program.

5	4	3	2	1
This was the highest quality program I have ever attended.	This program was one of the highest quality programs I have ever attended.	This program was of average quality.	This was one of the lowest quality programs I have ever attended.	This was the lowest quality program I have ever attended.

4. What is your overall rating of the instructor?

5	4	3	2	1
The instructor was the best instructor I have ever had.	The instructor was one of the best instructors I have ever had.	The instructor was average.	The instructor was one of the worst I have ever had.	The instructor was the worst I have ever had.

FORMATIVE EVALUATION

A *formative evaluation* is usually a pilot test or a rehearsal of training. The idea is to try out a training course before it is delivered widely to a targeted audience. The goal of a formative evaluation is to ensure that the subject matter is on target and that the instructional methods work. When problems are detected, they can be corrected before training is formally rolled out. Trainers, managers, and learners from the targeted audience may participate in formative evaluation sessions to review the training and provide feedback to trainers and designers on what works and what does not work.

CONCURRENT EVALUATION

A *concurrent evaluation* is conducted at any time during delivery, but certain times are more logical for a concurrent evaluation than others. For example, if you are conducting a three-day workshop, an opportune time to carry out a concurrent evaluation is at the end of the first day. If the training is only one day in length, however, immediately after the first segment or before the first break might be an appropriate time. The concurrent evaluation serves as a "reality check" to make sure you are on track, that the learners are up to speed, and that no problems are present.

By conducting concurrent evaluations, you can identify problems during the training delivery process and make midcourse corrections. Concurrent evaluations are generally informal and encourage learners to offer their honest opinions about the training, the trainer, the environment, and other relevant program elements.

The start, stop, continue method. You can conduct concurrent evaluations to gather timely information from the learners by using one simple but effective technique called the *start, stop, continue* method. The idea is to ask learners to determine the following:

- What should the trainer START doing that he or she has not done up to that point?

- What is the trainer doing that is not effective and that he or she should STOP doing?

- What is the trainer doing that is effective and he or she should CONTINUE doing?

Learners can work independently on these questions, in small groups, or as a large group. One way you can use this method is to divide learners into small groups of three to five, and ask them to write the words *start*, *stop*, and *continue* on a blank sheet of paper. The learners discuss each area, reach consensus on their responses for each, and then report their conclusions to the larger group. When this approach is used, learners may be reluctant to deliver negative messages in front of other people, or to share this information with you. One alternative is to have the responses written on a whiteboard or flipchart. If anonymity is important, ask learners to write their comments on sheets of paper and turn them in to you.

An example of feedback that might be given for *start* is, "We only took one break in a three-hour period, we'd like to *start* having a break at least every ninety minutes." For the *stop* response, learners might suggest, "We want to hear more from you, *stop* having so much group work." An example of feedback on the *continue* part of the exercise is, "The examples from your experience are very valuable, please *continue* to provide us with real world examples." Exhibit 14–3 shows actual responses two of the authors received when they conducted a start, stop, continue activity with a group of learners one-third of the way through a graduate level course on performance analysis. Not all, but many suggestions were incorporated into the remainder of the course, improving the quality of the learning experience. When you use ideas generated through this process it helps to let learners know what changes you are making and why you are making them. It also shows that you value their opinions. Furthermore, when you incorporate some of the changes they suggest, they feel a sense of ownership and commitment.

Concurrent evaluation feedback can be useful because you can use it to gauge learner reactions to you and the program.

Using questionnaires. Another way you can conduct a concurrent evaluation is to develop a short questionnaire that learners can complete at various points during the training course. The purpose is the same as the start, stop, and continue exercise—to obtain learner feedback that can be incorporated for improvement into the remainder of the program. A sample concurrent evaluation tool appears in Exhibit 14–4.

Note that the questionnaire in this exhibit seeks opinions from learners about the program, their learning, and their views on what they can apply on the job. You can, of course, modify this questionnaire to obtain information about other issues. Questions can be written to solicit open-ended responses. You have many options to administer this tool. For instance, you could form small groups, as suggested in the directions on this particular tool, or you could ask learners to answer

Exhibit 14–3
Results from a start/stop/continue exercise.

Start

- Sharing success stories as well as "not so successful" stories, provide more examples of what works and what doesn't.

- Handing out a sample report and describe in detail before assignment is due.

- Writing a brief agenda on the board.

- Talking more about outside articles.

- Discussing topics that are supplementary to the assigned readings.

- Ordering dinner.

- Providing at least one break.

- Providing a reminder of assignments at least one week before they are due.

- Using more activities.

Stop

- Allowing discussion to get off the topic.

- Reviewing everyone's paper/assignment in class.

- Reading handouts.

Continue

- Class discussion, open environment, group interaction, conversation, encouraging participation, question/answer sessions.

- Small group activities.

- Leaving early.

- Quality lectures.

- Real world examples.

- Providing direction on projects.

- Exposure to models/methods/tools.

- Asking for feedback about class.

Exhibit 14–4
Sample concurrent questionnaire.

Directions: The purpose of this tool is to obtain your thoughts and opinions about the training up to this point. Please take a few minutes to discuss the following questions in your group. Be prepared to share your responses with the trainer and the others in the class.

1. What is your most significant learning so far?

2. What have you learned so far that you will be able to apply to your job?

3. What do you feel would make this training better?

4. What questions do you have at this point?

the questions individually in writing and turn them in to you for review. Be sure to express your appreciation to the learners for providing their comments. Generally, a simple "thanks" will suffice. You provide your clearest expression of appreciation by adopting the suggestions offered by the learners. You should also make it a point to explain to learners why some suggestions could not be acted upon. Further, describing to the learners the changes you have made based on their input will help them recognize improvements.

Using feedback gathered through concurrent evaluation. Virtually any issue could be raised during the concurrent evaluation process, and you must be prepared to hear both criticism and positive feedback. Further, some comments made by learners at this point may surprise you. Be prepared to welcome any feedback and view it as an opportunity to improve the learning experience.

Integrating concurrent evaluation into delivery has the potential to produce many desirable results. When learners are asked for their feedback they feel valued and a part of the process. They appreciate the fact that you listened to their needs and changed your approach. Finally, the rest of the training experience should be better through the use of the improvement suggestions.

SUMMATIVE EVALUATION

A *summative evaluation* is conducted after training delivery. For example, if you were conducting a three-day workshop, summative evaluation would occur at the end of the workshop. Summative evaluations are used to determine what happened as a result of training and are generally more formal than formative or concurrent evaluations. According to master presenter Doug Malouf of DTS International in Sydney, Australia, trainers should evaluate everything. He recommends that trainers "examine every presentation and ask, 'What could I do next time to make it more effective?' Have a friend give you some positive feedback so that every event is a learning event."

Level One in Donald Kirkpatrick's evaluation framework measures learner satisfaction, usually through end-of-course participant evaluations (labeled "smile sheets" because some use pictures of smiling or frowning faces). An important item contained on most end-of-course evaluations is a reference to your effectiveness as a trainer. This information is important to you because it provides feedback immediately upon program completion. Often such evaluations include an open-ended response area that allows learners to make specific comments about your effectiveness. These qualitative comments coupled with the ratings provide evaluation data that are valuable to ascertain your effectiveness.

One disadvantage of a smile sheet is that it might not provide specific information to you about what you did during delivery that was particularly effective or ineffective. When the evaluation sheet simply states "Comments," then learners are likely to respond with comments such as "Good job, Eric!" or "Yvonne was great." Such statements provide you with no specific feedback—or suggestions to improve your delivery. One way to deal with that is to pose more specific questions, such as "What did the trainer do to encourage an open learning climate?" or "What was *especially* good or bad about the way this trainer delivered this course?"

BE AWARE OF THE HALO AND HORN EFFECTS

The halo effect is one problem you may experience when people evaluate your training delivery. The *halo effect* means that people develop strongly positive feelings about a training course. As a result, they rate everything well—even when that does not apply to all components. For example, when assigning a value to the effectiveness of the trainer, learners may assign higher ratings based on something unrelated to your performance—such as the food served, the entertainment provided at night, or the jokes you told.

The opposite problem is the *horn effect,* which means that people develop strongly negative feelings about a training course. As a result, they rate everything poorly. When one of the authors gave a presentation at a conference, the handouts did not arrive on time. When they finally did, they were photocopied out of order. Also, the room was far too hot, the video projector did not work properly, and the technician did not show up to fix it until the middle of the session. Not surprisingly, the presentation ratings were very poor—even though open-ended comments at the end of a participant reaction sheet included these statements: "I felt sorry for this poor presenter. The conference staff here is *useless* and should be *fired*" and "The conference staff should be fired and the presenter given their combined salaries." But that did not change the low ratings! As a trainer, you are held responsible for the training experience in its totality, even when others are incompetent.

End-of-course evaluations provide a snapshot of your overall effectiveness as a trainer, but you should be cognizant of the limitations we have mentioned above. Consider the impact an end-of-course evaluation had on one trainer.

Kristin conducted an all-day workshop on creating Web pages. By the end of the day, all twenty-three people had created their own Web site in some form. She felt the course had gone well and was anxious to see the evaluation results. Two weeks later, the evaluation results were in. She quickly scrolled to the section about trainer performance. Twenty-two people had rated her performance on a five-point scale as either a 4 or a 5. However, one participant rated her as a 1. While the overall percentages revealed that the class was overwhelmingly satisfied with her performance, she couldn't take her eyes or mind off of the low rating. This rating tormented her to the extent that she wanted to call everyone in the class and ask them how she could have made it better, hoping to identify the one dissatisfied customer. She also did not want to teach this course ever again.

In this situation, the participant could have misunderstood the scale and recorded the wrong number, or the participant truly was not satisfied with the training. The point is, however, that Kristin's overall rating was exceedingly high and did not warrant her response. Conscientious trainers are an asset, but this trainer may have taken it a little too far. Trainers must develop thick skins and let go of negative comments such as this. In most training experiences, there will be one or two learners who are dissatisfied with some aspect of the training, so do not take it personally if they seem to take it out on you.

EVALUATION OF TRAINER COMPETENCIES

The typical smile sheet may contain only one or two rating items focused on your performance or your training delivery. But, you can seek more feedback, and use it for your own development, by expanding the evaluation sheet to focus on the fourteen delivery competencies in the IBSTPI Standards. Special emphasis can be given to the ten competencies directly related to delivery. A tool of that kind is provided in Exhibit 14–5, which contains the same competencies that we have used in this book. Each competency can be rated according to how much and how well you have demonstrated it.

An evaluation form like the one appearing in the exhibit can be used in several ways. You could perform a self-assessment by reflecting upon, and then rating, your performance in each competency area after you have delivered a training program. You could also videotape yourself delivering training, after which you and a colleague could review the videotape and rate you with the form. Of course, you should rate both the presence and the absence of the competencies. For example, if

Exhibit 14–5
Training delivery evaluation tool.

Trainer: _____ Observer: _____

Date: _____ Program: _____

Directions: The purpose of this instrument is to assess the delivery performance of a trainer. This tool can be used as a self-assessment or it can be used by another person while observing the trainer during delivery. Please rate the **effectiveness** of the trainer in each competency area. The scale is from 1 (low effectiveness) to 5 (high effectiveness). In addition, use the comment area to record specific behaviors that are demonstrated or missed, or additional comments regarding performance.

Trainer Competencies	Rate the trainer's effectiveness in each competency area					Examples/Comments:
	Low Effectiveness 1	2	3	High Effectiveness 4	5	
1. Establish and maintain credibility	1	2	3	4	5	
2. Manage the learning environment	1	2	3	4	5	
3. Demonstrate effective communication skills	1	2	3	4	5	
4. Demonstrate effective presentation skills	1	2	3	4	5	
5. Demonstrate effective questioning skills and techniques	1	2	3	4	5	
6. Respond appropriately to learners' needs for clarification or feedback	1	2	3	4	5	
7. Provide positive reinforcement and motivational incentives	1	2	3	4	5	
8. Use instructional methods appropriately	1	2	3	4	5	
9. Use media effectively	1	2	3	4	5	
10. Evaluate learner performance	1	2	3	4	5	

you ignore a learner's request for clarification or feedback, then that missed opportunity should be noted.

GIVING AND RECEIVING FEEDBACK

To be effective, feedback must be both clearly given and received. The person giving you feedback should supply specific information about how well you demonstrated the competencies. When information about the quality of your delivery has been gathered, it should be fed back to you.

USING ACTIVE LISTENING SKILLS WHEN RECEIVING FEEDBACK

Your ability to listen actively when receiving feedback is as important as the clarity of the feedback you receive. Apply these skills: Lean forward to show that you are paying close attention, use effective eye contact, nod occasionally to show your interest, paraphrase what you hear, and direct attention to body language as well as spoken word. You should feel free to ask questions or seek clarification if you are uncertain about the feedback you received.

PROFESSIONAL DEVELOPMENT ACTION PLANNING

To improve your effectiveness continuously, you must plan for your professional development. This process can range from the structured to the unstructured. Exhibit 14–6 displays a professional development planning tool that you can use. These worksheets were specifically designed to help you improve your delivery competencies.

Professional development planning can help you establish a long-term strategy for your own performance improvement. The intent is to uncover specific developmental needs and then to formulate a concrete plan for converting weaknesses into strengths. Step One is to conduct a self-assessment about your performance on each of the fourteen delivery competencies. Once you have completed this step, move on to Section I to review your developmental needs. In this section, multiply the importance ratings by the need for development for each competency. The result is a developmental priority.

Section II asks you to review the list of developmental priorities and select what you believe are your three greatest needs, those with the highest priority ratings. Transfer these items to the worksheet and analyze them to determine their key components.

Section III moves from assessment and analysis into professional development action planning. In this section, formulate an action plan to develop your skills in the key areas needing improvement. As is mentioned on the instrument itself, the intention is that you will identify learning and development experiences in which you can engage on a self-directed basis. The questions that follow on the guide are designed to help you identify key resources you will need—and barriers you expect to face—as you implement your developmental action plan.

Exhibit 14–6
Trainer professional development assessment and action planning worksheets.
Self-assessment instrument.

Directions: This instrument contains the 14 trainer competencies. Please rate the **importance** of each item to your current job as trainer as well as your **need for development** in each. The scales are from 1 (low importance/low need for development) to 5 (high importance/ high need for development).

Trainer Competencies	How *Important* is this competency to your current job?					How much *Need for Development* do you have in this competency?				
	Low Importance 1	2	3	High Importance 4	5	Low Need 1	2	3	4	High Need 5
1. Analyze course material and learner information	1	2	3	4	5	1	2	3	4	5
2. Assure preparation of the instructional site	1	2	3	4	5	1	2	3	4	5
3. Establish and maintain instructor credibility	1	2	3	4	5	1	2	3	4	5
4. Manage the learning environment	1	2	3	4	5	1	2	3	4	5
5. Demonstrate effective communication skills	1	2	3	4	5	1	2	3	4	5

Exhibit 14–6										
Self-Assessment Instrument (continued)										
6. Demonstrate effective presentation skills	1	2	3	4	5	1	2	3	4	5
7. Demonstrate effective questioning skills and techniques	1	2	3	4	5	1	2	3	4	5
8. Respond appropriately to learners' needs for clarification or feedback	1	2	3	4	5	1	2	3	4	5
9. Provide positive reinforcement and motivational incentives	1	2	3	4	5	1	2	3	4	5
10. Use instructional methods appropriately	1	2	3	4	5	1	2	3	4	5
11. Use media effectively	1	2	3	4	5	1	2	3	4	5
12. Evaluate learner performance	1	2	3	4	5	1	2	3	4	5
13. Evaluate delivery of instruction	1	2	3	4	5	1	2	3	4	5
14. Report evaluation information	1	2	3	4	5	1	2	3	4	5

ISSUES AFFECTING PERCEPTIONS OF EFFECTIVE DELIVERY

While the effectiveness of your delivery is arguably the most important issue influencing your success as a trainer, other issues are also important. Reflect on these issues and evaluate how much they may impact learner accomplishments and the overall quality of the training. This section covers several important issues that influence your success but that are not directly related to your performance in training delivery.

(Exhibit 14–6 continued)
SECTION I: REVIEWING YOUR DEVELOPMENT NEEDS

Section I of the report asks you to transfer the scores from the self-assessment instrument. Each competency has two corresponding numbers with it. The first number represents the importance of the competency and the second number represents your need for development. To calculate your developmental priority, simply multiply the importance × need for development. The higher the number, the higher the need for development in that area.

Take some time to review and reflect on your development priorities. When you have reviewed the items below, move on to *Section II*.

Trainer Competencies	Need for Development × Importance	Development Priority:
1. Analyze course material and learner information	_____ × _____ =	_____
2. Assure preparation of the instructional site	_____ × _____ =	_____
3. Establish and maintain instructor credibility	_____ × _____ =	_____
4. Manage the learning environment	_____ × _____ =	_____
5. Demonstrate effective communication skills	_____ × _____ =	_____
6. Demonstrate effective presentation skills	_____ × _____ =	_____
7. Demonstrate effective questioning skills and techniques	_____ × _____ =	_____
8. Respond appropriately to learners' needs for clarification or feedback	_____ × _____ =	_____
9. Provide positive reinforcement and motivational incentives	_____ × _____ =	_____
10. Use instructional methods appropriately	_____ × _____ =	_____
11. Use media effectively	_____ × _____ =	_____
12. Evaluate learner performance	_____ × _____ =	_____
13. Evaluate delivery of instruction	_____ × _____ =	_____
14. Report evaluation information	_____ × _____ =	_____

(Exhibit 14–6 continued)
SECTION II: IDENTIFYING TOP THREE DEVELOPMENT NEEDS

The purpose of *Section II* is to identify your top developmental needs and reflect on the key aspects of those needs. This will be used to develop your Action Plan.

Step 1: First, return to *Section I* and circle your three highest developmental priorities (based on the three highest numbers in the column labeled "Development Priority"). In the space below, write the top three development priorities that you identified in *Section I*.

⇨ Highest Development Need #1 (write here):

⇨ Highest Development Need #2 (write here):

⇨ Highest Development Need #3 (write here):

Step 2: Once you have written your top three development priorities in the spaces above, spend some time reflecting on each of these items. The following questions might help you in your critical reflection: (1) Do you believe this actually represents an important development priority for you? Why or why not? (2) What is the nature of this development priority? (3) What are some of the key aspects of the priority?

Step 3: Now, in the space below, list the specific actions, behaviors, skills, and performances that make up this development priority. This will help you to focus in on key aspects that you believe are critical to the competency.

⇨ Key Aspects of Development Priority #1 (list below):

⇨ Key Aspects of Development Priority #2 (list below):

⇨ Key Aspects of Development Priority #3 (list below):

(Exhibit 14–6 continued)
SECTION III: PROFESSIONAL DEVELOPMENT ACTION PLANNING

The purpose of *Section III* is to create a strategy for developing skill and proficiency in your priorities identified from Section II. This Action Plan represents specific self-directed learning activities that you will engage in. This form is written generically so that it can be duplicated and used for additional future action planning.

1. Development Priority (write here):

2. What key development activities will best help you to develop skills and proficiency in this Development Priority? (list below):

3. When do you expect to begin and complete each of the development activities listed above? (write specific dates next to the activities above, if possible):

4. What key resources will you need to engage in each of the development activities listed above? (include financial resources, people, and other resources you will need):

5. What barriers do you expect to encounter? How do you plan to prevent or handle each barrier you encounter? (list below):

6. How will you know that you have been successful in your development efforts? What will success look like? (explain below):

CHANGES TO THE PHYSICAL ENVIRONMENT

The physical environment influences learner perceptions of your performance as a trainer. At times it may be necessary for you to change the physical arrangements of the training facility. For example, chair or desk positions may have to be modified to accommodate more learners than were expected, or the room configuration may need to be changed. When you make such changes, be sure to evaluate the impact. Sometimes changing the physical arrangements can negatively influence the learning climate. Learning can be impeded, for instance, when you move chairs and desks closer together or change the room layout. If too many learners are crowded into a small room, they may face many distractions. If the room configuration is changed from a horseshoe shape to rows, learning again might be impeded because learners must turn to have face-to-face interactions with other learners.

When changes to the physical arrangements are necessary, recognize them and initiate those changes when possible, but be sure that you have justifiable reasons for doing so. Document these reasons and then ask the learners how well they feel the physical arrangements support the learning climate. You can also simply look at the learners: Do they appear to be too crowded? Are some learners unable to see the front of the room? What impact does a change have on learner interactions with each other or with you? Ultimately, determining how much the changes enhance or impede learning is key in judging whether the changes were justifiable.

CHANGES IN SEQUENCE OR SCHEDULE

The training schedule and the sequence of topics can influence perceptions of your performance as a trainer. The delivery schedule is usually outlined in the instructor guide, which should clearly describe the sequence of activities, instructional methods, and breaks. But there will be many occasions when you have to make modifications to the schedule. For example, you may be conducting a small group discussion raised by learners when the schedule calls for a reinforcing activity. Similar to changes to the physical arrangements, justify and document changes to the delivery sequence. Perhaps, in your judgment, conducting a small group discussion about the relevant topic will help learners relate a concept to a work situation and facilitate transfer of training from the classroom to the workplace. In addition to the intended impact, the actual impact of this change in sequence should be evaluated to determine its effect on learning.

SITUATIONAL ADJUSTMENTS VS. DESIGN REVISIONS

Changes to the physical arrangements, changes to the sequence or schedule of the training, and other adjustments that are made during delivery may represent modifications that are unique to the situation at hand or they may reflect design changes. When adjustments are situational they are typically incorporated to meet the peculiarities of a unique learning group. Such changes, while important to recognize and document for future purposes, do not necessarily reflect major design revisions. As was mentioned previously, these changes do require detailed justification.

Some changes, however, have implications that go beyond slight modifications made to meet the requirements of a specific situation. Major adjustments could necessitate fundamental changes to the instructional design of the training course. These changes must be distinguished from situational changes, perhaps with the assistance of instructional designers. If required, the need for the changes should be verified and then incorporated by instructional designers so that future offerings of the program reflect the modifications.

JUDGING HOW WELL A TRAINING COURSE WORKS

When a training program is complete, take steps to judge course effectiveness. Consider many issues, such as the characteristics of the group of learners and the situation. Among other issues, consider how appropriate the training is to meet learner needs and how appropriate the training methods proved to be during delivery. Finally, identify barriers to the transfer of training from the training setting to the work setting.

JUDGING THE APPROPRIATENESS OF TRAINING

A well-designed training program should have clearly defined objectives that are directly related to training needs. But recognize that learners also enter training situations with unique needs. If delivered correctly, the training should meet the needs of individual learners while also achieving the training objectives. Early in a training course identify learner needs and expectations. Throughout delivery, facilitate learner progress toward achieving the objectives. Then judge the effectiveness of the training based on how well both goals were met. When learners' needs are not met or when the objectives are not attained, then you cannot consider the training program as successful.

JUDGING THE TRAINING METHODS

How well did the training methods used during delivery contribute to achieving the training objectives? Reflect on how well each method you used contributed to learner achievement. Of course, you can also ask the learners how well they felt the training methods contributed to achieving the training objectives. You can do that informally, for example, by asking learners about the method immediately after you used it. Consider the following dialogue to see how you might do that:

TRAINER:	*Lisa, what did you think about working in teams?*
LISA:	*At first it was a little awkward because no one knew what to do. After we assigned the different roles you described, everyone was fine and did their job.*
TRAINER:	*Did working with the team help you personally learn the content?*
LISA:	*Definitely. It helped me to see a broader range of ideas. We were also able to develop better strategies and recommendations because we were able to capitalize on so many backgrounds and experiences.*
TRAINER:	*Would you like to see more teamwork used during training?*
LISA:	*Sure. I think it is a good way to learn. All of my team members enjoyed it and felt like they got a lot from it. Although, if we work on teams frequently, I would like the opportunity to move around, change people, and switch roles. I think that will further help us to utilize different backgrounds and experiences.*
TRAINER:	*Lisa, thanks for your input. It helps me to know what learners like and dislike.*

Of course, if you want more formal feedback, you could always prepare a short questionnaire for learners to complete. Such a questionnaire could contain rating scales or an open-ended section for comments. You could administer that at the end of the course—or at the end of one part of a course.

IDENTIFYING BARRIERS TO TRANSFER

The transfer of training from classroom to workplace is an increasingly important issue in the training and development field. When learners complete a training program and return to their jobs, they often do not apply what they learned in the classroom. It is estimated that less than 10 percent of training transfers from the training site to the work site.

For now, think about your role in training delivery in helping to encourage transfer of training. As you deliver training, help learners identify the obstacles they might encounter on the job that could prevent them from using what they learned in training. Obstacles might include lack of time to practice, a supervisor who does not support the training, or no opportunities to use the skills. Once the barriers have been identified, help learners formulate ways of surmounting those roadblocks. Many strategies can be used by you, the learner, and the learner's manager before, during, and after training to improve transfer of training. When those barriers have been identified, document and communicate them to appropriate people—such as top managers and learners' supervisors—through the evaluation report. Chapter Sixteen has an entire section on strategies for improving the transfer of training.

SUMMARY

This chapter examined the following issues associated with evaluating the delivery of training:

- How to consider the adequacy of the instructional design as it is modified during training delivery.

- What are the guidelines for evaluating your own training delivery.

- What affects the perceptions of how effectively training is delivered.

- How to judge how well a training course worked for a group of learners.

STRATEGY LIST

Actionable Strategies to Improve Training Effectiveness:

Evaluate the Effectiveness of Training

☐ Modify training to meet learner needs by altering exercises, changing training methods, and reorganizing the sequence of topics.

☐ Document any changes you make and explain these changes to the instructional designers.

☐ Ask your co-workers to sit in on your training and provide you with feedback about your training skills. You may want to create a checklist of behaviors that you want them to review and comment on.

☐ Ask learners to take a few minutes to reflect on the training and create a list (about 2 to 3 items) of the aspects of the content and the style of the course that they liked and why, as well as what could be improved.

☐ Videotape yourself training and watch it at a later time to see yourself in action. Reflect on how you can build on your strengths and improve your areas of weakness.

☐ Use the end-of-course evaluation to generate ideas for making training better. Instead of using a 5 to 7 point subjective scale, attach behavioral anchors to the scale so that you can generate specific, measurable feedback.

☐ Keep in mind that most forms of trainer/training evaluation are subjective. Therefore, it will be important for you to look at the overall picture and watch for trends rather than get bogged down with feedback from one source.

☐ Remember that you as a trainer will be evaluated on everything from the cleanliness of the facilities to the friendliness of the training staff. Seeking feedback on all aspects of the training can help you to identify how tweaking small, non–training delivery components can make a huge difference for your overall evaluation.

CHAPTER 15

REPORTING EVALUATION INFORMATION

SKILLS ASSESSMENT

Take a moment to review the competency and associated performances that will be covered in this chapter. Consider your current level of proficiency in the competency as a whole as well as each performance and check the items where you feel you need to improve. As you read the chapter, concentrate on those areas most in need of development.

Competency:

❏ Report evaluation information.

Associated Performances:

❏ Prepare to report post-course summary and evaluation information.

❏ Report evaluation and end-of-course information.

❏ Recommend revisions and changes to existing materials and provide suggestions for new programs and activities.

❏ Report information about learning and physical environments.

❏ Judge the adequacy, appropriateness, and timeliness of reports given to instructional designers and appropriate management.

After training delivery, you have the responsibility to convey evaluation data to your stakeholders. You can communicate this information by a report or a briefing that documents the training-related issues you have evaluated. The evaluation reports you make, as a trainer, will usually contain your key observations made during delivery and your recommendations about course-related changes that need to be made.

This chapter covers the following topics:

- Planning an evaluation reporting strategy.

- Matching the evaluation information with the intended audience, including the primary stakeholders who have an interest in receiving that information.

- Designing, producing, and distributing the training evaluation report.

- Considering the timing of reports, recommendations for revisions, and legal implications.

This chapter will help you to avoid situations like the following critical incident.

Keep It Short and Simple (KISS)

" *I was asked by my supervisor (director of training and education) to create an evaluation report that would be sent to our vice president. I worked on the report for three straight days and developed what I thought was a great looking report. It was twelve pages—lots of detail. I sent it to the VP by the end of the week. About two weeks later, I got it back in company mail. He wrote on the first page with red pen, 'What do I need to know this for? Why is this information in here? This is too long—rewrite it and get it back to me. Make it one page.'* "

The trainers participating in our survey did not rate the competency reporting evaluation information as very important. In fact, they rated it as the least important of the fourteen delivery competencies. However, even as the lowest ranked competency, it was still rated with a mean importance score that fell almost midway between "important" and "very important." Perhaps this competency was rated as relatively low in importance because it was viewed as not directly related to training delivery. *Reporting evaluation information* does take place after the more visible role of training delivery is complete.

PLANNING AN EVALUATION REPORTING STRATEGY

Training can be evaluated for many reasons and purposes. We discussed Donald Kirkpatrick's four levels of evaluation framework in an earlier chapter, and each level implied reasons to evaluate training—including measuring reactions, learning, behavior change, and results. We also identified three overarching reasons for evaluation. The first reason is that evaluation helps to justify the existence of the training department, showing the unique value added by the training function to the organization. The second reason for evaluation is to make a "go" or "no go" decision regarding continuation of a training program in the future. If training does not produce desired changes or if the cost of training outweighs its benefits, then perhaps the program should be modified or discontinued. On the other hand, if the evaluation shows that the value of the program is high, then its continuation is justified. The third reason for evaluation is to gather information to make program improvements. If training objectives were not achieved during a program, then perhaps the design or delivery methods should be changed to help learners meet training objectives in future offerings. In addition to these three broad reasons for training evaluation, this chapter covers a fourth reason for training evaluation: to meet the unique needs of different audiences.

KEY PLANNING CONSIDERATIONS

When you plan an evaluation reporting strategy and develop the report itself, keep several considerations in mind. First, identify the audience that is interested in receiving the evaluation information. Exhibit 15–1 identifies people representing a potential audience and some reasons for their interest.

We are assuming that each audience identified in this exhibit has reasons for wanting to receive training evaluation results. If not, then a report should probably not be sent. Most likely, different audiences want different evaluation information. For example, instructional designers want to know what changes were made during delivery and why those changes were made. On the other hand, managers who sent people to training want to know what the learners can do differently upon program completion and how those changes will influence job performance and results. They may also want to know what new skills they should support and encourage among learners. We'll have more to say about determining evaluation needs of various stakeholders later in the chapter.

Exhibit 15–1
Potential recipients and uses/purposes of evaluation-report.

Audience	Use/Purpose
Line manager/supervisor	The learner's supervisor may want this information for several reasons including selection and promotion, further development, career pathing, or to facilitate transfer and monitor the progress of the new skills.
Learners	Learners would want this information so that they can assess their own skill level to monitor future development in key areas.
Training manager/director	Training managers can use this information to provide trainers and instructional designers with feedback.
Upper management	Upper management may want this information so that they can assess the skill level of their workforce.
Human resources	Human resources may want this information so that they can assist with career pathing, look for skill deficiencies, and monitor overall training performance.

PREDICTING HOW DIFFERENT AUDIENCES WILL USE THE INFORMATION

You should also forecast how evaluation information will be used by each audience. By clearly understanding the intended use of the evaluation report, you are better equipped to tell people what they want to know so they can make informed decisions. For example, instructional designers may make permanent changes to a training course based on the evaluation report. Managers may send more people to future program offerings if they value the benefits received. Training managers may change facilities or make equipment or material purchasing decisions based on evaluation results. You may also decide to make changes to how you deliver the course based on an evaluation report.

CONSIDERING THE SCOPE AND FORMALITY OF THE REPORT

Once you have considered the audience that will read the report and their reasons for wanting it, you are positioned to make decisions about the scope and formality of the evaluation report. *Scope* refers to how much the report covers. Is it about one course or many? One offering of a course or all offerings given in a year? *Formality* refers to the organization of the report. A report can be organized in many ways—from a simple bulleted list of key points to a multi-page document with substantial supporting detail. In corporate cultures that are informal, an informal evaluation report may be appropriate. Such limited scope evaluations are concise and focus only on key findings. They may even be handwritten or presented orally as a brief overview during a management or staff meeting. In more formal corporate cultures an evaluation report may have to be more comprehensive and well documented.

TAILORING EVALUATION REPORTS TO THE INTENDED AUDIENCE

Who will receive the report? That is an important question, since the intended audience influences what information the report should contain. For example, instructional designers may require nothing more than a simple e-mail message to document key changes made during delivery. In contrast, the chief financial officer (CFO) may want a detailed analysis with an executive summary, raw data, charts, graphs, recommendations, conclusions, and other relevant information. A common sense strategy you can use to ensure reports are tailored appropriately is to ask the target recipients what format they prefer. Alternatively, you can ask a key informant, such as the Vice President of Human Resources, for recommendations on what format a report going to the President should take. An *informant* is someone who may have important insight into key preferences or needs of the report recipient. For example, knowing that a particular person likes to see a one-page executive summary or pie charts can save you time and effort.

CONSIDERING TIME AND RESOURCES

How much time and what kind of resources are available to prepare the evaluation report are important considerations. Large organizations, such as Motorola University, have entire training evaluation departments or teams of people charged with conducting evaluation activities. In other organizations one trainer may be responsible for conducting evaluations and reporting results. Comprehensive, broad-scope evaluations require a significant time investment and resource commitment. Some organizations elect to conduct evaluations and report results only for selected training programs, such as a new program being introduced for the first time, a high profile program where many people have an interest in the outcomes, or a program whose value or viability is under suspicion.

DETERMINING HOW MUCH EVALUATION DATA TO COLLECT

How much information the stakeholders require in the evaluation report is another issue warranting consideration. For example, some organizations collect Level One data through end-of-course smile sheets for all or most of the training courses they conduct. They may collect Level Two (learning) data on many training programs, and Level Three (on-the-job behavior change) data on some programs. However, they may collect Level Four (results or impact) data only on a few key programs or on no programs at all. In this way they strike a balance between available resources and evaluation activities. We recommend that time and cost estimates be made so that key decision makers are aware of the costs associated with undertaking training evaluation initiatives.

CONSIDERING THE REPORT FORMAT

Some trainers develop and use a standardized report for all evaluations. Others customize reports to meet the needs of specific clients. A standardized report can reduce the time needed to produce it. A customized report is useful, however, because it can effectively link the data contained in it with specific audience needs.

REMEMBERING THE K.I.S.S. PRINCIPLE

A good rule of thumb when producing an evaluation report is the "KISS" principle—which means *Keep It Short and Simple.* Match the language and format to the preferences of your targeted audience. Few managers have the time or patience to search for the information they need to make decisions. Likewise, business people are usually not impressed with academic jargon where the message gets buried in descriptions of the methodologies that were employed or of how the evaluation was conducted. An executive summary should provide your readers with everything they want to know to make informed decisions. Again, we recommend that you ask the intended recipient or a key informant so that you know exactly what length is expected.

OBJECTIVITY

Objectivity is a major concern that arises in discussions about training evaluation. A trainer conducting an evaluation of his or her own training course is akin to an accountant auditing his or her own books. The results are suspect because the objectivity is open to question. There can be a temptation to alter results, ignore them completely, or cast them in a favorable light. That should not be surprising—especially if a trainer's performance appraisal or job depends on the report outcomes.

This ethical dilemma can be difficult to reconcile. Involving neutral people during the evaluation can minimize the appearance of bias. Of course, the issue also depends somewhat on the corporate culture. If the organization values continuous improvement, then openness is more likely to be welcomed.

STRATEGIES FOR MINIMIZING SUBJECTIVITY

Try to make training evaluation as objective as possible. One way to do that is to acknowledge the assumptions and limitations of the evaluation process. A second way is to establish an audit procedure by which the results of evaluation are double-checked for accuracy. Another way is to use third parties, such as external consultants or teams from other departments, to conduct evaluation and report results. These strategies can help to reduce the chance, or at least the appearance, of subjectivity.

MATCHING EVALUATION INFORMATION WITH APPROPRIATE AUDIENCES

Many individual audiences have interest in training evaluation information, but each audience has specific needs for this information. Attempt to match the evaluation information to the needs of each audience receiving the report. Focus your attention on how well the report meets the information and decision-making needs of each audience.

DETERMINING EVALUATION NEEDS OF VARIOUS STAKEHOLDERS

Potential audiences for an evaluation report include learners, line managers or supervisors, training managers, instructional designers, other trainers, senior managers, and customers. The information needed by each group can vary widely. Exhibit 15–2 contains a list of potential evaluation information needs and offers a starting point for you to use in thinking about what evaluation information to supply and to whom.

Exhibit 15–2
Evaluation information potentially required by various stakeholders.

Stakeholder	Evaluation Information Potentially Required
Learners	■ Performance information ■ Test results ■ Comparisons with other learners or with standards ■ Other?
Management or supervisors	■ New skills or knowledge acquired by learners ■ Transfer of training barriers ■ Learner performance/accomplishments ■ Expected benefits/payoff ■ Attendance information ■ Other?
Training managers	■ Facility information ■ Food service ■ Participant satisfaction ■ Suggested improvements ■ Trainer performance ■ Other?
Instructional designers	■ Adjustments made during delivery (methods, sequence, material, etc.) ■ Achievement of objectives ■ Problems experienced ■ Other?
Other trainers	■ Participant satisfaction ■ Barriers to transfer of training ■ Strategies for overcoming barriers ■ Changes made during delivery ■ Problems encountered during delivery ■ Instructional design considerations ■ Other?
Top management	■ Bottom-line impact of training (in terms of cost, quality, productivity, performance improvement) ■ Alignment of training with organizational mission, vision, and strategy ■ Other?
Customers	■ Benefits they should expect to receive (e.g., better quality, service, reduced costs, etc.) ■ Other?
Other Stakeholders?	

First identify stakeholder requests for evaluation information and forecast who might find value in it. Then, determine the needs of each person or group.

DESIGNING, PRODUCING, AND DISTRIBUTING THE REPORT

Many methods are available for reporting and presenting evaluation information. The form you use depends on the purpose of the report, the audience, the resources required, and the resources available. Generally when people think of an evaluation report, they think of a written document. However, you can also make an oral presentation to report end-of-course evaluation information. Such presentations can be made during a staff or management meeting or in a one-on-one session with appropriate stakeholders. Combining an oral report with visual aids or delivering it through a presentation software package can help to enhance the image and professionalism of the report and presentation.

In addition to written and oral reports, evaluation information can be conveyed via other methods. For example, centrally located bulletin boards, newsletters, or other company publications are effective ways to communicate evaluation information. In this era of high technology, e-mail, electronic bulletin boards, or listservs are still other means by which you can reach many people efficiently to communicate evaluation information and present reports.

FORMAT OF THE EVALUATION REPORT

When you produce an evaluation report, take into account several format considerations. First, use appropriate grammar, syntax, vocabulary, and language. If an evaluation report is written, it should flow smoothly and be easy to read. If you make an oral presentation, it should be clear, understandable, and engaging. Follow the advice given in Chapter Seven about delivering reports. Reports should always be professional since they are a reflection on your credibility and that of the training department. A carelessly assembled report containing typographical errors, inconsistencies, or inaccurate information can be damaging to your credibility. Seek a balance between brevity and thoroughness.

If your report is presented in written form, organize it as follows:

1. *Cover page*: This provides the title of the report, the date, the company name, and your contact information.

2. *Table of Contents*: This provides titles of all sections and sub-sections, with page numbers.

3. *Executive Summary*: This is a one- to two-page summary of the report that is aimed at busy senior managers who want to skim a short summary and get all the key facts.

4. *Evaluation Report*: This section provides specific and detailed information about the training and the learner's performance. It contains a brief background description of the training, the purpose of the evaluation study, key questions answered by the study, any assumptions or limitations on the study, the methods used to carry out the evaluation, and the results.

5. *Conclusions and Recommendations*: This section draws conclusions from the evaluation results and offers recommendations for improving the training, if necessary.

CONTENTS OF THE EVALUATION REPORT

Organize your evaluation report to suit the needs of your audience. If you are addressing different audiences, prepare separate reports that will answer the questions likely to weigh on the minds of each group. If you write a single report for all audiences, you risk overwhelming each audience with unnecessary information. The likely result is that nobody will read it.

Be sure to include in any report such information as:

- The needs that the training was intended to meet.
- The training objectives for the course.
- Results of end-of-course reaction surveys, if they were administered.
- Results of tests taken by learners in aggregate or individual form, if tests were administered.
- Results of on-the-job follow-up studies to assess transfer of training to the job, if they have been conducted.
- Impact or training outcome study results, if they have been conducted.

Report any unexpected occurrences during delivery, such as a spontaneous discussion focused on an important topic. This information could represent important details about which other trainers should know. Outcomes achieved through the training should also be documented. Include both positive and negative outcomes. Chapter 14 discussed barriers that can impede the transfer of training from the classroom to the worksite. Document such barriers and convey them through the evaluation report. You may want to include your recommendations on strategies for overcoming those barriers as well. Also include the appropriateness of the trainer to the delivery assignment. This information might be useful to training managers who match trainers to appropriate programs so that they can balance and optimize their strengths, experiences, and capabilities.

Use the checklist provided in Exhibit 15–3 when writing a formal evaluation report to help you remember important issues that should be included.

OTHER KEY CONSIDERATIONS

We have covered many important issues related to reporting post-training evaluation information. Three additional considerations are the timing of the report, recommendations for revisions and new programs, and legal implications.

TIMING

If stakeholders plan to use the report to make decisions, then timing is critical. Deliver the information to stakeholders so that they have ample time to digest the information, ask follow-up questions, and make informed decisions. Likewise, evaluation data for some stakeholders can be viewed as feedback to them. Learners, for example, may receive information about their performance on tests or skill demonstrations administered during training. As we discussed in Chapter Eight, feedback should be provided in a timely manner so that it is useful to those receiving it.

You and evaluators should establish schedules and deadlines for reporting evaluation information to stakeholders. These schedules and deadlines become another criterion by which you can judge the effectiveness of the evaluation report. Establishing time frames is also useful for project management and planning purposes to ensure that the reports are delivered in a timely fashion.

RECOMMENDATIONS FOR REVISIONS AND NEW PROGRAMS

As we explained earlier in this chapter, make it a point in your evaluation report to pass on information about recommended changes to

Exhibit 15–3
Checklist for writing a formal evaluation report.

Does the Report Contain?	Yes (✔)	No (✔)	Remarks
1. A Management Digest or Summary. Does this explain briefly:			
A. Why the report was requested?	( )	( )	
B. What program was evaluated?	( )	( )	
C. What the program hopes to achieve (i.e., outcomes)?	( )	( )	
D. How the program is conducted?	( )	( )	
E. Who requested the evaluation?	( )	( )	
F. When the evaluation was conducted (i.e., over what time period)?	( )	( )	
G. How the evaluation was conducted?	( )	( )	
H. Who conducted the evaluation?	( )	( )	
I. What were the major results or findings of the evaluation?	( )	( )	
2. A Background Section. Does this explain briefly:			
A. Why the program is being conducted?	( )	( )	
B. What needs the program is intended to meet?	( )	( )	
C. How the program is delivered?	( )	( )	
D. Where the program is delivered?	( )	( )	
E. Special problems confronting the program?	( )	( )	
F. Who offers the program?	( )	( )	

Exhibit 15–3 (continued)
Checklist for writing a formal evaluation report.

Does the Report Contain?	Yes (✔)	No (✔)	Remarks
3. An Evaluation Section. Does this explain briefly:			
A. What, specifically, was to be evaluated?	( )	( )	
B. How the matter for evaluation was delineated?	( )	( )	
C. Relevant criteria, if appropriate?	( )	( )	
D. The research design used?	( )	( )	
E. Any limitations on results as a consequence of the design?	( )	( )	
F. Major assumptions made in the evaluation?	( )	( )	
G. What data-collection method was selected?	( )	( )	
H. Why the data-collection method was selected?	( )	( )	
I. How data were collected?	( )	( )	
J. How data were organized?	( )	( )	
K. How data were analyzed?	( )	( )	
4. A Findings Section. Does this explain:			
A. Progam Results?	( )	( )	
1. In terms of participant reactions?	( )	( )	
2. In terms of learning?	( )	( )	
3. In terms of productivity increases?	( )	( )	
B. Differences between results and criteria?	( )	( )	
C. Dollar values of improvements less program costs?	( )	( )	

Source: Rothwell, W. J., and Sredl, H. J. (1992). *The ASTD Reference Guide to Professional Human Resource Development Roles and Competencies, Volume II* (2ⁿᵈ ed.). Amherst, Mass: HRD Press. 800-822-2801 (Checklist for Writing a Formal Evaluation Report), pp. 446–448.

appropriate people. Among other things, report information about program administration. For example, training managers need to know about problems during delivery that were attributable to the facility, food, other services, program material, logistics, and room arrangement. Communicate positive aspects as well. If a new catering service is used and learners comment positively about the quality of the food, pass that information along.

Your views, good and bad, should be conveyed to instructional designers, other trainers, and managers as appropriate. For instance, if you detected a problem with the wording of directions for a training activity, provide that feedback to instructional designers. All changes you made during delivery should also be communicated. If more than one trainer is involved in delivering a program, their independent and collective views should be expressed.

LEGALLY DEFENSIBLE INFORMATION

Training evaluation information can be used in making human resource decisions such as hiring, promoting, dismissing, disciplining, compensating, or rewarding individuals. Since such decisions have legal ramifications, be sure that the evaluation information used for these purposes is as accurate and defensible as possible. As an example, assume that three learners attended an assessment center experience and underwent a day of simulated interactions, in-basket activities, and interviews. These were all evaluated, and the results were compiled in comprehensive evaluation reports based on the participants' performance. This report was then used to make a decision about promoting one person. The legal implications are obvious. If one candidate is chosen for promotion over the two others based on the assessment center results, the others could (if members of protected groups) file lawsuits against the organization to charge unfair discrimination. They may feel that they are more skilled and qualified than the other person and that the assessment center process was flawed and did not reflect their true abilities. Such situations can place you and your organization in legal jeopardy. For this reason, any information contained in an evaluation report should be supported, especially if used for legally charged decision-making.

One way to better ensure that evaluation data is legally defensible is to make it specific and quantifiable whenever possible. Establish evaluation criteria in advance, through a rigorous methodology, so that you can evaluate actual learner performance against these criteria objectively. This generally occurs during the instructional design phase when tests are prepared. For example, you may place tick marks on a check sheet whenever targeted behaviors are demonstrated. Another way to improve the validity of such evaluations is to introduce multiple raters so that different viewpoints can be used to reduce rater error. Information presented in an evaluation report should be complete and contain the conclusions that are drawn from the data.

SUMMARY

The trainers participating in our survey did not rate the competency reporting evaluation information as very important. However, reporting evaluation information provides a feedback loop to stakeholders to demonstrate the value added from training. This chapter covered the following topics:

- Post-course evaluation and the reporting of training evaluation information.

- Matching the evaluation information with the primary stakeholders who have an interest in receiving that information.

- Strategies for designing, producing, and distributing training evaluation reports.

- Key considerations in preparing evaluation reports, including timing and legal implications.

STRATEGY LIST

Actionable Strategies to Improve Training Effectiveness:

Reporting Evaluation Information

❐ When reporting training evaluation information, always create reports with your audience in mind. Different audiences will require different information.

❐ When writing a training evaluation report, keep in mind what the audience intends to do with it. This should influence the scope and formality of the report.

❐ When writing the report, remember the KISS method. That is, *Keep It Short and Simple.* Include only information that is relevant to the audience.

❐ Minimize subjectivity with reporting evaluation information by establishing an audit procedure by which the results of the evaluation are double-checked for accuracy.

❐ Make certain that the intended audiences receive the training evaluation report in a timely manner for decision-making purposes.

❐ Remember to include both positive and negative aspects of the training evaluation information.

CHAPTER 16

INTERNATIONAL TRAINING, COTRAINING, AND TRANSFER OF TRAINING

SKILLS ASSESSMENT

To this point, *The Complete Guide to Training Delivery: A Competency-Based Approach* has focused on the fourteen competencies needed for effective training delivery as they were identified in the IBSTPI Standards. The competencies provide a logical framework for organizing this book—and building your skills as a trainer. However, the following important topics on training delivery have not been addressed previously in sufficient depth, and are covered in this chapter.

- Training delivery in international settings.

- Cotraining.

- Ensuring the transfer of training.

First, the expansion of the global economy, the rise of the multinational organization, and the collapse of geographic boundaries have opened the door to international training opportunities. You may be asked to travel to distant lands to deliver training, or, even if you stay in the United States, you may find yourself in training rooms with learners of diverse cultures and backgrounds.

Second, you may also find yourself in situations where you must deliver training with another trainer. These cotraining situations can be rewarding, but they can also pose unique challenges. If you are accustomed to working alone, you may face some new challenges when delivering training with another person. Although many of the competencies discussed throughout this book apply in cotraining situations, this chapter describes special strategies for success when multiple trainers are involved in delivery.

Third and finally, this chapter emphasizes some key points about transfer of training from the classroom to the workplace as one important measure of training success. We discuss transfer of training in detail and offer some strategies for ways to improve it.

TRAINING IN INTERNATIONAL SETTINGS

Delivering training internationally can be highly rewarding and exhilarating. It can number among the most memorable experiences you will have as a trainer, though you may be surprised at the differences you will encounter. This section of the chapter reviews important issues related to international experiences and offers strategies for improving your success when you deliver training internationally.

CULTURAL DIFFERENCES

Cultural differences have the potential to create misunderstandings, barriers, and problems for you as a trainer in international situations. The term *culture* refers to the value systems, norms of behavior, and beliefs held by a particular group of people. Exhibit 16–1 shows a list of common cultural characteristics.

The people comprising a culture may represent a nation, a region, a locality or community, an organization, a group, or even a family. Culture is important because it influences how people, events, and situations are interpreted. It is a filter that affects perception. Culture also influences behaviors in which people engage. Cultural norms represent implicit or explicit rules that let people know what practices are acceptable and unacceptable.

Differences in culture are not exclusive to international settings. Consider some differences between the people in the states of Maine and Alabama, or the differences between organizations like Microsoft and IBM. Generally speaking, however, international cultural differences are often more pronounced than differences among localities or organizations. To cite several additional examples, consider the variations in handshakes from country to country. In America and Germany, for instance, a firm handshake is the norm. In the Middle East and Asia, on the other hand, a firm handshake could be offensive because a gentle handshake is the accepted practice. The "thumbs up" sign, the "V" sign for "victory" (or "peace"), and the "OK" gesture are commonly used in the United States, but they can be deeply offensive in some cultures.

Exhibit 16–1
Common cultural characteristics.

1. Common geographic origin

2. Migratory status

3. Race

4. Language or dialect

5. Religious faith

6. Ties that transcend kinship, neighborhood, and community boundaries

7. Shared traditions, values, and symbols

8. Literature, folklore, music

9. Food preferences

10. Settlement and employment patterns

11. Special interests in regard to politics

12. Institutions that specifically serve and maintain the group

13. An internal perception of distinctness

14. An external perception of distinctness

Source: Reprinted by permission of the publisher from *Harvard Encyclopedia of American Ethnic Groups*, edited by Thernstrom, Orlov, and Handlin. Cambridge, Mass: The Belknap Press/Harvard University Press. Copyright © 1980 by the President and Fellows of Havard College.

Some of the strategies we suggest later in the chapter can help you to raise your consciousness of the issues and take steps to prevent disaster.

PROBLEMS THAT MAY ARISE

While many delivery problems stem from cultural differences, perhaps even more difficulties arise from inadequate planning or logistics. This section highlights some of the potential difficulties and offers useful strategies for making international experiences successful.

PERCEPTION OF THE TRAINER

How you are perceived as a trainer can vary dramatically across cultures and can influence learner behavior significantly. For example, many

Asian, European, and South American cultures view trainers, like teachers or professors, as authority figures. Learners are reluctant to question the trainer. The lecture method, widely used in many educational settings in other nations, is expected. Information flows in one direction—from trainer to learner. That does not mean that learners are incapable of participation; rather, they have been socialized from long educational experience to be passive learners. In contrast, learners in Western cultures are willing (and sometimes eager) to question and even directly challenge trainers' authority, credibility, and expertise.

A similar issue can arise when learners are unwilling to express concerns or share information with someone who is not part of their culture. A willingness to celebrate diversity, while a value prized in the United States, is not appreciated in some international settings—where thinly veiled racial, ethnic, or sexual prejudices may be the norm. For this reason, do not be surprised in some international settings if a long silence follows your questions or your requests for learner opinions.

PERCEPTION OF TIME

Time has special meaning in international settings. For instance, expectations about starting times can vary. In one culture the norm is to arrive early and start on time, while in others being late is acceptable or perhaps common practice. The perception of time in an Eastern culture may also differ from Western standards. A "long time" in Asia may equate to centuries, whereas a "long time" in America may mean last week or yesterday. One reason for such differences is that, in reality, the focus in some cultures is not on time but on building and maintaining relationships. Western society emphasizes speedy and effective task completion and de-emphasizes relationships. These differences can create problems for you when you attempt to manage starting and ending times and monitor the length of breaks.

FACILITIES AND EQUIPMENT

In some international settings, especially in developing nations, inadequate facilities or equipment can be a problem. Interestingly, as evidenced by the large number of critical incidents provided by trainers in our study, this is a large problem area in the United States as well. In international environments, you may find that many modern conveniences taken for granted in the United States may be missing or inadequate elsewhere. You may also experience unique problems (by U.S. standards) related to temperature control, lighting, and seating due to antiquated buildings and inoperable machinery.

One of the authors engaged in a training assignment during the hot season in a South American country. He found that the training room air conditioner was ill equipped to cool the large room and its forty participants. As a result, the training room was so hot and humid that everyone experienced discomfort. The learners from that country seemed to find that situation to be quite typical, and it turned out to be more of a burden for the trainer.

In addition to temperature problems, trainers in international settings may experience electrical shortages, power losses, and even blackouts. Insufficient lighting and excessive noise from adjacent rooms may be common. Trainers working in developing nations may find themselves in even worse environments—such as huts with dirt floors and leaking thatch roofs, and without electricity, running water, or bathrooms.

Equipment and supplies may also be inadequate in some international settings. Chalkboards may be much more prevalent than flipcharts and whiteboards. Transparency projectors considered antique by U.S. standards may be state-of-the-art in other countries, while computer-based projection units may be rare or nonexistent. Further, a blank wall may serve as a projection screen to display images. Quality copies for handouts may be difficult to obtain, and access to the World Wide Web may be a dream due to unreliable phone systems.

The best advice is to take no physical facility issue for granted, especially if you are organizing training remotely, by phone or e-mail. Be explicit in the requirements, and be persistent in finding out whether those requirements can be met. If not, arrange as best you can for contingencies. We should note that if you have the opportunity to deliver training at an international facility of a U.S. multinational corporation, you may be pleasantly surprised at the high quality of the facility and the adherence to U.S. standards.

LANGUAGE BARRIERS

When you deliver training in the English language, you may find that your participants speak English only as a second language. While some learners may be proficient in English, others may struggle with common words or phrases—not to mention technical jargon. You can ask learners who are more proficient in the language to help those with limited proficiency, or you can use a bilingual participant or other person available to clarify and interpret what you say.

In other situations, you may need to deliver training in another language. That obviously requires language fluency as well as subject matter expertise. Keep in mind that even years of language courses may be insufficient to prepare you to deliver training in another language.

Language problems can also surface in printed materials. Learners may struggle with words or phrases that they have difficulty translating (some learners may be unwilling to admit that they have these problems). One clue that there is a language problem is when learners pull out their well-worn dictionaries. Printed material may be in English or in the native language, or in a combination of the two languages. You could also deliver training orally in English, and provide printed material in the native language for reinforcement and future reference.

ADJUSTMENT DIFFICULTIES

If you are involved in international training delivery, you may encounter many additional problems in working, living, and traveling abroad. Jet lag is a common problem when training starts the day after a sixteen- or twenty-hour overseas flight. When jet lag is severe, it can include upset stomach, sleep deprivation, insomnia, depression, and disorientation. Other adjustment problems may include electrical appliances that do not function, problems with water, safety concerns, your digestive system resisting or rejecting food, and general feelings of homesickness. Any of these problems can affect how well you deliver training.

STRATEGIES FOR EFFECTIVE INTERNATIONAL TRAINING

The first and foremost rule when engaged in international or intercultural training delivery is "Do not ignore cultural differences!" The key is determining what differences are important, and then deciding how to deal with them.

Sylvia Odenwald, author of *Global Training,* cites MCI international trainer Joyce Rogers, who provides the following advice to global trainers:

You need to be concerned with:

- Perceptions—How people see the world.

- Assumptions—Underlying beliefs/values.

- Expectations—That things will be a certain way.

Solicit help from people who have effectively trained in other cultures:

- Have them create appropriate case studies.

- Have them write critical incidents.

- Have them help train the trainers.

Some required qualities for the trainers of global trainers:

- Do not have an axe to grind.
- Do not pontificate.
- Do not share war stories.
- Demonstrate acculturation.
- Are reflective.
- Are observant.
- Are introspective.
- Are able to adjust.
- Select a peer as a mentor.
- Are quiet and observant, then tailor the training.
- Maintain a moderate rate of speech when training in trainees' second language.
- Find a local to be the translator of language and culture—someone who can step out of the trainee role and become the interpreter.
- Train in the native language if possible—it helps empathy.
- Use the written word and art graphics wherever possible.
- Keep everything open for discussion.

TRANSLATORS

If you hire a translator to assist with training delivery, make sure that the translator knows not just the languages used but also the subject matter. A poor translation will only confuse learners. The translator's or interpreter's qualifications, background, and experience should be verified through careful screening before he or she is hired to help with the training.

Simultaneous translation is one form of translation that can be used in training delivery. The trainer speaks in English and the translator simultaneously converts the message into the native language. Typically, the translator uses a microphone to convey the translated message to the learners, who wear special receiver headsets. This method is quite effective because it allows real time communication. If participants wish to ask you questions, they speak into a hand-held microphone while you wear the headphones and listen to the translation in English. Simultaneous translation is preferable to other methods that only provide for one-way communication between you and the learners.

Simultaneous translation is not without problems, however. One major issue for inexperienced trainers is the distraction created by translation. The translator's voice creates "noise" that may sound like a side conversation, which requires an initial adjustment period before you are able to tune it out. One solution may be to make the translator sit behind a special box or shield in order to block out as much of the noise as possible.

Pacing is important for translation as well. If you are nervous and speak too rapidly, it may be difficult for the translator to maintain an appropriate pace. That can lead the learners to believe you are rushing through the material and that the material is less important. It may also cause the quality of the translation to suffer because words are missed or the translator cannot keep up. One of the authors recalls his first experience using simultaneous translation. It was about fifteen minutes into the training before he made eye contact with the translator, who was stationed in the back. The author quickly realized that he must have been speaking at breakneck speed for the entire fifteen minutes because the translator was red-faced, sweating, and frantically signaling him to slow down.

Although you should deliberately speak slowly and steadily, you may, however, use vocal changes and tone variations. Just be sure that the rate of speech is manageable for the translator. If you maintain regular eye contact with the translator, the translator can signal you if you are speaking too quickly or when she encounters other problems. When the translator is located in the back of the training room, she has a unique vantage point and can detect learner confusion or questions. In that case, be sure to establish a system of nonverbal communication, such as hand signals, in advance. A signal of breaking an invisible stick, for example, can signal you that the translator would like to take a break soon.

You may find the equipment needed for simultaneous translation to be restrictive. In most situations in which an on-the-spot translator is working with you, you must use a microphone, receiver headsets, and participant microphones. Movement and flexibility becomes easier when the microphones and headphones are wireless rather than fixed to the podium or microphone stands. Remember to wear the headset when participants make comments or ask questions so that none of the translation is missed. Whenever possible you should participate in a practice session to familiarize yourself with the equipment and how it is used. That also provides an opportunity for you and the translator to practice how you will work together.

CULTURAL INFORMANTS

A *cultural informant* is a person who has in-depth experience and/or expertise about a particular nation or culture. Often the informant is a member of the target culture with fluency in your language. This person may be a cotrainer, the translator, a participant, or some other person involved with the training (such as the client or sponsor). The informant can play many roles during delivery and can be highly beneficial to you.

Informants can help you before delivery by explaining the characteristics of the group and key barriers you may encounter. By arranging a meeting with the informant before training, you can ask questions and get detailed information about the group and its cultural norms. Informants can also help you make any necessary adjustments to solve these problems. By helping you to feel comfortable, explaining certain norms and differences, and providing specific recommendations, such as what and where to eat or avoid eating, an informant makes an international experience more enjoyable. The informant can also serve as a guide and host for you inside and outside of the training environment. Most trainers involved in international training seize opportunities to sightsee and immerse themselves in the new unfamiliar culture.

Cultural informants can prove highly useful to you during delivery as well. Sometimes the participants may have questions or issues that you are ill equipped to answer. Those questions may require specialized or culture-specific knowledge, such as questions about local customs or country-specific legal issues about which you may be uninformed. At these times, cultural informants can assist you by providing insight or even answering the learners' questions directly.

PLANNING AND PREPARATION

Most problems experienced during international training delivery can be avoided through proper planning and preparation. It is often the small forgotten details that result in minor aggravations and sometimes flare into major catastrophes. Some details relate to issues outside of training delivery, such as not packing appropriately for the weather conditions or forgetting an important phone number or credit card.

These inconveniences can indirectly affect delivery because they may cause you to lose your focus on the delivery. Forgetting necessary material, supplies, or equipment may be errors that are difficult to overcome in an international location where resources may be in short supply.

DEALING WITH BLUNDERS

Even with thorough planning and preparation, errors can still arise during delivery. Some blunders may involve making a cultural faux pas, such as using inappropriate gesture or nonverbal action. Others may result from forgetting material or from your own disorganization.

When you make mistakes, as we all do, recognize the error. Often the translator, the informant, or even the learners can let you know what happened if it is not apparent to you. Early in the process, you might admit that you could make inadvertent errors and that you welcome helpful feedback. Once errors are recognized, you can apologize. But be sure you do not make the same blunder twice.

We have found that learners recognize that international trainers are not out to insult them intentionally. They are willing to overlook errors as long as the same ones are not repeatedly made. Another strategy that is helpful in establishing rapport with learners is to learn at least a few phrases in their language. When you learn a few simple phrases—whether it's "buenos dias" (good morning, in Spanish), "she she" (thank you, in Chinese), or "yassas" (hello and goodbye, in Greek)—learners will appreciate your interest in their culture and will usually be eager to assist.

RESOURCES FOR INTERNATIONAL TRAINING

Many resources are available to you if you plan to be involved in international training. Although these resources do not always apply directly to training, they can be helpful in gaining insight into unfamiliar cultures.

PROFESSIONAL SOCIETIES AND ORGANIZATIONS

The American Society for Training and Development (ASTD) has many resources available that can be helpful for international training. ASTD has members in over 100 countries and has an International Visitor's Center for those visiting the United States from an international location. ASTD also has an Information Center that can perform searches on international topics. The annual ASTD international conference typically attracts over 7,000 people from eighty nations. This provides global trainers with great opportunities to network with peers, make contacts at the global level, and obtain expert advice and insight from international members. In addition, ASTD also has forums, committees, and subgroups dedicated to global training and human resource development. ASTD produces many useful publications, which will be described later in this section.

The International Federation of Training and Development Organizations (IFTDO), with members in over fifty countries, also has many resources that can help you if you face an international assignment. Some resources you can find on their Web site include a Global Registry, which is a database containing contact information for many international consulting firms, organizations, training vendors, and other associations related to the training and development field. Another section of the Web site contains on-line articles written by domestic and international authors about topics of relevance to global trainers. A *World Human Resource Directory*, which lists member organizations, is also available to members of IFTDO.

PUBLICATIONS

The American Society for Training and Development publishes the practitioner magazine *Training & Development,* and the scholarly journal *Human Resource Development Quarterly*, both of which frequently contain articles about various topics related to global training and development. Another practitioner publication, *Training* magazine, contains pertinent articles as well.

The International Society for Performance Improvement produces *Performance Improvement* and *Performance Improvement Quarterly,* two publications that frequently contain articles on international training topics. In fact, the March 1999 issue of *Performance Improvement* was dedicated to international and cross-cultural issues.

Blackwell's of England, a well-known international publisher, also publishes the scholarly *International Journal of Training and Development*. One author of this book is the U.S. editor of that journal. That journal is the only true international research journal dealing with training, with editors in Europe, the United States, and Asia. As the name suggests, all articles in the journal have an international focus.

INTERNET RESOURCES

In addition to the Web sites for organizations like ISPI, ASTD, and IFTDO mentioned above, the Internet provides much information about international training. Basic searches on any of the common engines, such as Yahoo (http://www.yahoo.com) and Excite (http://www.excite.com) will yield numerous "hits." Although many references generated during an Internet search may be irrelevant, others can lead you to organizations, articles, Web sites, and other resources related to global training. The volume of training-related information available on-line is baffling and expanding exponentially.

Discussion groups are another valuable Internet-based resource for those wishing to learn more about international training. TRDEV-L is an example of a listserv dedicated to training and human resource development professionals. On a daily basis, subscribers to this free service receive a digest of e-mail postings that discuss training and related topics. Individuals can post questions to the discussion list and receive answers from the subscribers. There are over 6,000 subscribers from more than fifty countries. Also available on the TRDEV-L Web site is an archive of discussion summaries.

OTHER RESOURCES

One general purpose resource that you may find useful is a country profile service. *Country Profiles and Background Notes* is a U.S. government publication available through the Superintendent of Documents. Additionally, embassies and consulates sometimes make information available upon request to interested parties. Videotapes and films about global travel and work are also available commercially or in public libraries. The book *Global Training* by Sylvia Odenwald has an appendix of additional training resources you might find useful. Your local public library may carry many resources on international travel and tourism in general and perhaps even on international training topics. Finally, local colleges and universities may offer extensive assistance to those who inquire. Language departments often have short courses— and more traditional semester-long courses—you can take. Further, scholars, researchers, teachers, and other experts may be located through colleges and universities and may be excellent sources of information, as are students from other countries.

COTRAINING

Cotraining refers to situations in which several trainers collaborate to deliver instruction. Different people may work with you in cotraining situations, including a peer who is in the same position as you; a subject-matter expert (SME) with specialized content knowledge; an assistant who works in a subordinate role; or a guest speaker or guests on a panel. This section covers some of the cotraining formats that may be used. We also address problems that can arise when multiple trainers are used as well as strategies for solving such problem situations. Finally, we discuss how to work with subject matter experts.

FORMATS FOR COTRAINING

Several combinations can be used when multiple trainers will deliver training. This section describes lead trainers (sometimes called a master) working with an assistant, rotating trainers, and simultaneous training. Each delivery format is viable, depending on the training situation. Each is presented according to complexity and potential for problems beginning with the least complex.

LEAD TRAINER WITH AN ASSISTANT

In this arrangement, one trainer takes the lead during training delivery, and the helper serves in a supportive role. Assistant trainers are often useful when small groups, activities, or role-play training methods are used. These methods require the trainer to monitor the groups closely and intervene when necessary. An assistant can monitor or intervene with groups so that the lead trainer can focus attention on the program.

A particularly appropriate time to pair up trainers is during train-the-trainer experiences. An assistant working with a lead trainer can ensure one-on-one coaching to certify that the assistant is competent to lead future training sessions. For example, an assistant trainer new to the field or the program can be coached through delivery, with the lead trainer serving as a role model. Sometimes the assistant trainer assumes primary responsibilities under the close supervision of the lead trainer. This is akin to an abbreviated mentoring experience and can be highly beneficial when combined with formal or informal assessment, feedback, coaching, and development planning on training delivery competencies.

In the most basic arrangement, the assistant simply functions as a "pair of hands" for the lead trainer, changing transparencies, advancing the slide projector, distributing hand-outs, and carrying out other low-level tasks. This is especially valuable when the trainer is physically unable to perform these tasks or when a large audience is involved. Also, when precise coordination is necessary, such as during a timed or choreographed presentation, the success of the trainer depends in large part on the skill of the assistant.

ROTATING TRAINERS

Rotating trainers is an arrangement that relies on multiple trainers—but only one trainer delivers at a time. Unlike the use of an assistant who is subordinate to the lead trainer, rotating trainers are generally at the same level. While one trainer delivers, the other trainer is offline—observing, taking notes, or preparing for the next segment. At some point the next trainer delivers while the first person assumes a secondary role. This rotating format does not really differ from a single trainer delivering training. However, the two trainers must manage their transitions and plan to avoid inconsistencies—or, worse, contradictions. Further, each trainer should reinforce the subject matter without redundancy.

SIMULTANEOUS COTRAINING

Simultaneous cotraining is the most complex arrangement, and therefore the most prone to difficulty. Two or more trainers—typically peers on the organization chart—deliver training simultaneously. Although they do not speak at the same time, they do coordinate and synchronize delivery. They jointly deliver content, ask questions, and provide feedback. Two (or more) trainers are thus at the front of the classroom at the same time.

If you should participate in delivering simultaneous cotraining, try to work with those with whom you are well acquainted and who possess complementary personalities. Two trainers may have quite different styles but may still complement each other. If you rehearse your sessions and choreograph them well, simultaneous cotraining can be dramatically more powerful than one trainer working individually.

Some training topics are more conducive than others to simultaneous cotraining. If the program is highly structured—such as a course in fluid mechanics for engineers—simultaneous cotraining might cause more problems than it solves, as learners struggle to master difficult subject matter and the rapid-fire delivery that characterizes simultaneous cotraining. On the other hand, a course in interpersonal relationship building or interpersonal skills would benefit from simultaneous cotraining. The reason? Courses that depend on interpersonal interaction are made more powerful when multiple trainers deliver, field questions, and work individually with learners. Further, the professional trainers can model the new behaviors for learners and demonstrate these new skills before learners try them.

The biggest problems that can occur with simultaneous training typically stem from personality conflicts. One trainer trying to dominate the delivery, or working at cross-purposes with the cotrainer, can create major problems. Learners quickly pick up on contradictions and any conflicts between the trainers.

POTENTIAL BENEFITS OF COTRAINING

When multiple trainers are used effectively, the potential benefits can be tremendous.

COTRAINING ADDS VARIETY

Variety is a clear benefit. Two (or more) trainers can create a highly stimulating experience for learners. Synergy can result from the dynamic interplay between trainers. Cotraining helps to heighten the interest level among participants because the different styles and personalities of the trainers help to stimulate curiosity and hold attention.

COTRAINING CREATES A SUPPORT SYSTEM

When trainers combine forces for delivery, they form a natural support system. If one trainer is faced with a difficult question, a stubborn learner, or a hostile group, the other trainer may be able to intervene. If one trainer does not know the answer to a question, the other can seamlessly jump in and assist.

Take a simple example. Marie, a nursing trainer, draws a blank when a learner poses a question. Bill, a cotrainer in the program, recognizes that and interjects by stating, "Marie, if I may, I think one way of answering that question is (*explanation*)." By doing that, Bill subtly moves the focus from Marie to himself. It allows Marie time to recover while Bill provides the answer.

Trainers can also support each other by reinforcing points made by the cotrainer. For example, Abby might say something like, "I want to re-emphasize the point that Katie made earlier. This concept applies here as well because (*explanation*)." That strengthens the point made by Katie and facilitates learner understanding.

COTRAINING PREVENTS FATIGUE

People who have never led classroom training think that it looks easy. But, in fact, it can be very tiring for the trainer. It is tough for trainers to stay energetic—especially during many days of training. (Experienced trainers describe that this way: "It is tough to tap dance for a very long time.") Of course, the trainer's energy level is important because the learners' level of enthusiasm and energy is often directly related to that of the trainer. By redistributing the burden of staying alert and energetic, cotraining prevents fatigue and provides the basis for a sustained high energy level in a training course.

TIPS FOR IMPROVING THE EFFECTIVENESS OF COTRAINING

To this point we have presented some potential problems and potential benefits of using multiple trainers. This section offers four tips to minimize the problems and maximize the benefits derived from cotraining:

1. Plan for cotraining.

2. Balance the rotation among trainers.

3. Practice delivery.

4. Hold a debriefing session after training.

TIP 1: PLAN FOR COTRAINING

Planning is always important for effective training delivery. However, its importance is magnified when multiple trainers deliver a course. You must effectively plan your delivery sequence, division of course material, and other technical issues. You must also plan to integrate effectively your delivery styles and process issues. (*Process issues* include "who does what when," as in: "Will you describe fire evacuation procedures at the start of the course, or should I do that?")

In considering division of labor, consider your respective strengths and weaknesses. One trainer may know the subject matter of one part of the course better than the other. Another trainer may know how to run a game, simulation, or activity better than the other. Such stylistic differences, strengths, and weaknesses provide clues to how the work should be subdivided.

Also give some forethought to how you will handle expected problems that may come up. For instance, suppose the course is an introduction to a new employee performance appraisal system that will be used by the company. It might be expected that the learners in the course would complain about how low company salaries are. (Many people associate wage and salary with performance appraisal.) By anticipating that complaint, the trainers can discuss it in advance of delivery and formulate a plan for how they will handle it.

TIP 2: BALANCE THE ROTATION AMONG TRAINERS

Learners will notice if one trainer does all the talking and the other one just stands there silently. At some point, the learners will say, "Why do we have two trainers? That seems like a waste." Equally bad is two trainers talking at the same time—or contradicting each other. The learners will say, "Those trainers never talked to each other to work out these differences before the course, and now we do not know what to think." To avoid these criticisms, plan for your cotraining and make sure that the workload is balanced. How it should be balanced depends on the sequencing of the subject matter and your relative strengths and weaknesses.

TIP 3: PRACTICE DELIVERY

The old saying that "practice makes perfect" applies to cotraining. Just as actors and actresses must rehearse how they will perform, so must trainers practice how they will deliver. Practice is particularly important for cotrainers, who need to organize what they will do, how they will do it, and when they will do it. Points of disagreement among trainers will usually surface during practice, and can be worked out before you stand before a group.

During practice sessions, focus attention on your transitions. How will you shift from one trainer to another? Awkward, lengthy, or disjointed transitions will only confuse and distract learners. Practice helps make these transitions smooth and seamless. One strategy for making transitions is for the first trainer to introduce what the second trainer will be covering. The following dialogue demonstrates this technique:

TRAINER ONE (ROSE): *"…So, we've covered five strategies that you can use for greeting customers. Next, Alma will take you through an exercise so you can practice these methods."*

TRAINER TWO (ALMA): *"Thanks, Rose. Let's first get into groups of three so we can practice some of the methods that Rose covered."*

A second strategy for making transitions, similar to the one described above, is for the second trainer to summarize what the first trainer covered. This method is dramatized in the dialogue below:

TRAINER ONE
(JULIA, turning
to Norie): *"Now I'm going to pass the torch to Norie for the next segment."*

TRAINER TWO
(NORIE): *"Just to recap what Julia covered. She started out by describing the process for recognizing account discrepancies. Recall that she covered…"*

You may object that you do not have enough time to practice. And, to be sure, practice can be time-consuming, difficult to arrange in busy schedules, and even expensive if trainers are geographically separated. But it is worthwhile to do because it results in more effective training delivery.

TIP 4: HOLD A DEBRIEFING SESSION AFTER TRAINING

Our final tip on how to maximize the benefits of cotraining is to hold a debriefing session after training. You and your cotrainer should get together long enough to reflect on what happened. What worked particularly well in the course? What needs to be improved? How could your interaction have been better? By answering these questions, you and your cotrainer can pinpoint changes needed in future course offerings or improvements needed in how you work together in delivery. The debriefing is also a good time to surface concerns, frustrations, and problems. For example, if an introverted trainer felt like her cotrainer was making fun of her during delivery, she can provide her colleague with feedback about that during a debriefing meeting. Such problems must be worked out, especially if trainers plan to cotrain in the future.

WORKING WITH SUBJECT MATTER EXPERTS (SMEs)

A *subject matter expert* (SME) possesses much knowledge, skill, or ability in a special area. Subject matter expertise stems from education, experience, and other credentials that give individuals credibility when discussing a topic in their field. For instance, a Ph.D. in engineering with twenty years of engineering experience and a hundred published articles is a subject matter expert in his or her special area of engineering.

SMEs are often involved in the instructional design phase of training. They usually work closely with instructional designers—who are called *instructional design experts* (IDEs) to distinguish them from the

SMEs—to prepare rigorous training. IDEs tap the knowledge of SMEs to create well-designed training. Similarly, SMEs work closely with trainers to deliver the material.

SMEs play a valuable role in training. Unfortunately, subject matter expertise does not translate directly into training delivery skill. In short, an expert in a subject may not know how to prepare training materials or deliver the subject matter to learners. In fact, many problems stem from assigning SMEs to deliver training without properly preparing them. While SMEs can field questions from learners requiring broad or deep knowledge of the subject matter, they are not always effective public speakers or facilitators. Nevertheless, SMEs are sometimes called upon to deliver training on their own. This can be a recipe for disaster, as the following critical incident demonstrates:

The Runaway SME

"*Twice during the course of a year, part of my job is to arrange environmental health and safety training for the 350 employees at our manufacturing site. Each session lasts approximately four hours, during which several mini-sessions are held on various OSHA-mandated topics. Generally I train on one subject and recruit other plant employees to train on the remainder of the subjects offered during that session. It has been difficult to get plant employees who have enough expertise and are willing to stand up in front of other employees in a classroom situation, despite receiving overtime pay and a bonus.*

At one session, I had to resort to using an employee who, although knowledgeable in his field, was considered a "character." Unfortunately, due to parallel schedules, I was unable to attend his class. I heard it was hilarious, awful, gross, ridiculous, etc. from the various comments I received. The session was on "electricity for nonqualified employees." Apparently, at one point in the presentation, the instructor described himself quite graphically as standing nude straddling the bathtub and toilet and fixing a bathroom fixture. I think it even got worse from there. The management was singularly displeased with this individual and questioned my sanity in having him instruct at the session.

Since that time, I have managed to recruit a fairly stable number of employees who have expertise, organization skills, presentation skills, and are willing to prepare a "dry run" of their class so that it can be critiqued by myself, the other instructor and our division trainers. The division trainer and I conduct a "train the trainer" class and make our skills available to this group. The comments from both employees and management have indicated to me that this new "system" is providing much better training and instructors."

When SMEs are involved in training delivery, they should either first cotrain with someone who is an excellent public speaker or facilitator, or receive a train-the-trainer course in how to deliver instruction. Often a formal or informal qualification process—such as the one described in the critical incident above—can be used. Many organizations offer train-the-trainer programs designed to help SMEs build their training delivery competencies. This approach ensures that learners will receive the full benefit of the SME's unique knowledge while also being encouraged to learn.

TRANSFER OF LEARNING

Transfer of learning refers to how much or how well the new knowledge, skills, and attitudes acquired during training actually result in on-the-job behavior change. Changes in behavior and performance equate to learning transfer.

What Happens after They Leave?

" *The biggest problem I face is keeping the training alive after students go through the program. It is essential for everyone to practice and use the skills ASAP after the training program. I get approximately 60 percent of all students to complete at least one follow-up project. This number should be higher.* "

Getting people to practice on the job what they learned in training is, of course, one approach to encourage transfer of learning. However, note that the trainer in the critical incident above is unable to get learners to do that. That probably means that the learners are not encouraged to change their on-the-job behavior by their supervisors.

THE IMPORTANCE OF TRANSFER OF LEARNING

Transfer of learning is important for many reasons. First, learning is useless unless it is applied. Unless learners apply what they learned, the organization wastes time, money, and effort on training. For example, workers attend a workshop on creative problem solving in which they learn and practice a five-step approach to problem solving. But if they never use this problem-solving model after training, then its value is negligible. Similarly, if workers receive training on a popular software package and then have no occasion to use it until two years later—after two more releases of the software in updated versions—then it is not worthwhile.

In contrast, effective training is directly and immediately applicable to the job. Training should be designed with job application in mind. During training delivery, encourage transfer of training, reinforce its importance, identify the barriers that learners perceive will hinder their on-the-job application of what they learn, and help learners—and management—knock down those barriers. If you fail to do that, then the training is usually a waste.

WHEN TRANSFER OF LEARNING SHOULD BE MEASURED

When should you measure the transfer of learning? The answer to that question depends on several issues. Without doubt, the type of training dictates the time frame required for determining transfer. Technical training and on-the-job training, on the one hand, should usually be immediately applicable and should therefore lend itself to immediate measurement of transfer. Interpersonal skills training and cultural awareness training, on the other hand, are usually not immediately applicable, and some time may be required before measurement of transfer is appropriate or possible. For this training, you should generally wait about three to twelve months before measuring on-the-job transfer of learning.

HOW CAN TRANSFER OF LEARNING BE MEASURED?

You can measure learning transfer in many ways. The method you choose depends on how much time, money, and

BOB PIKE

One question we asked training guru Bob Pike during an interview was this: "What is the most fulfilling or enjoyable aspect of training delivery for you?" He responded, "The best feedback I ever received was after a five-day training program. At the end someone came up to me and said, 'I didn't see anything here that I can't already do.' Someone was surprised when that didn't bother me. My reaction was 'Great, that's the goal!' I love to have people who can hardly wait to get back and increase their impact and hearing from them thirty, sixty, or ninety days later that they applied what they learned.

"Just last week I was the keynote speaker at an ASTD chapter in Arizona. The Board wanted to take me to dinner after the meeting. One member showed up to dinner with a copy of my book that she received in one of my programs back in 1987. She then proceeded to say, 'here are some things I'm still doing differently that I learned in the program.' She had tape flags on pages to reference key things."

effort you can spend on it, what kind of information you want, and how valid you wish the results to be. Another issue relates to the leverage you have to influence learning transfer outside of the classroom. This section describes several ways you can measure transfer of learning.

DIRECT OBSERVATION METHODS

One way to measure transfer of learning is by direct observation of learners at some point after training. The observer may be the trainer, the supervisor, or some external evaluator. The observer sets out to determine how much or how well learners have applied on the job what they learned in training. For example, if customer sales representatives attended training to learn a new sales tactic, then they could be observed to see how often and how well they are using the new tactic. Through this method the observer can determine level of transfer by looking for evidence, or lack of evidence, of the target behaviors. If you are unable to be heavily involved in determining transfer outside of the classroom, perhaps you can work with others—such as managers or the participants themselves—to coach them and help them apply this method.

Problems associated with observation methods. Potential problems exist with direct observation. One problem is that observation can seem intrusive to the person under observation, and that in turn can exert a negative influence on performance and results. For example, a customer service representative under observation may grow nervous because she knows she is being watched, and she may not apply the new sales tactic as effectively as she would under normal circumstances.

Another problem is that observation only works when people have an opportunity to apply what they have learned in training. If the customer services representative is observed during a period when she does not need to use the new sales tactic she has learned, then changes on the job will not be observed.

A third problem is that observation can be expensive. It can be costly in financial resources, time, and effort. When supervisors have to spend a lot of time in the observation process, the cost can increase dramatically.

A fourth and final problem is that some training simply does not lend itself to observation. When learners were taught a new technical procedure or work process, their performance can be observed easily in most cases. But if they were taught ways of handling interpersonal issues, their behavior may be more difficult to detect through observation.

Strategies for using direct observation effectively. Use several strategies to improve the effectiveness of direct observation. First, develop a structured approach to observation. For example, create a checklist or worksheet to organize and give structure to the observation. Use the sample checklist appearing in Exhibit 16–2 to measure how well behaviors have transferred to the job. Second, ensure consistency in your observations. Using a checklist as shown in the exhibit allows different people to observe with consistency.

Exhibit 16–2 **Sample observation checklist.**			
Skills Covered in Training	**Application on the Job**	**Proficiency or Competence** **1=Low** **2=Moderate** **3=High**	**Comments**
1. Take patient's temperature	Yes	3	*Explained purpose. Friendly with patient. Answered questions.*
2. Take patient's blood pressure	Yes	3	
3. Take patient's pulse reading	No	1	*Skipped this completely.*
4. Take blood sample	Yes	2	*Had difficulty locating vein.*
5. Take urine sample	Yes	1	*Did not explain purpose of sample, amount of urine needed, or location of restroom.*

LEARNER SELF-ASSESSMENTS

Learner self-assessments are another effective and relatively inexpensive way you can measure transfer of learning. Learner self-assessments usually work well because learners are ideally positioned to determine how much and how well they have applied what they have learned to their jobs. The Transfer of Training Evaluation Model, which will be described later, uses anonymous learner self-assessments to gather information about transfer.

Self-assessments often involve questionnaires completed by learners. Such questionnaires pose key questions, which may be open-ended or closed-ended, and are designed to gather relevant information about how much or how well course content has been applied to the job. Self-assessments are usually formatted in paper-and-pencil formats, but emerging technology, such as Web-based or computer-based survey programs, offers exciting new possibilities for gathering questionnaire data. Questionnaires are completed by learners and returned to the evaluator either with or without individuals' names.

INTERVIEWS AND FOCUS GROUPS

Alternative methods for collecting transfer information include one-on-one interviews and focus group sessions. The format of interviews or focus groups may be highly structured with specific questions, or open-ended and more like discussions or conversations. An example of an open-ended question that you could pose to a focus group or during an interview is, "What skill or skills learned in training have you been able to apply since returning to your job?" A sample closed-ended question that could be asked is, "Have you applied the technique of *lead-time reduction* learned in the Continuous Improvement workshop?" These formats allow you to ask specific information, probe, clarify, and engage in dynamic interactions with the learners. An example of a follow-up question that you could use to probe is, "Doug, you mentioned that you were able to apply listening skills to your job. Could you be more specific as to which of the listening skills you have used?" A follow-up question that might be coupled with the closed-ended question mentioned above is, "George, you indicated that you have applied the technique of *lead-time reduction*. How exactly did you use it?"

Disadvantages of using interviews and focus groups. Interviews and focus groups are often more costly to evaluate than questionnaires due to the time and resources that are required. Costs mount quickly when much information must be interpreted. With interviews and focus groups, and in many cases with self-assessments, the results are often qualitative. The person evaluating such information may take notes, videotape, or tape-record the discussions. When these techniques are used, it can be daunting to transcribe recordings and analyze the information in order to identify key themes or trends.

Another disadvantage of using self-assessments, interviews, and focus groups is that anonymity is usually lost, which may lead to biased results or inaccurate information. Perhaps people believe some responses will result in pay raises or promotion—or perhaps they simply want to please the person conducting the evaluation.

THE TRANSFER OF TRAINING EVALUATION MODEL

In 1995 the Waste Isolation Division of Westinghouse Electric Corporation, working in partnership with the United States Department of Energy (DOE), published an executive summary describing a model called the Transfer of Training Evaluation Model (TOTEM). This report detailed the analysis, design, development, implementation, and evaluation of the TOTEM. The purpose of the TOTEM was to provide an efficient method for determining the effectiveness of objectives-driven classroom training. Specifically, this is accomplished through anonymous post-training surveys of trainees. You can implement or help your organization incorporate this method of training transfer evaluation as a way to determine rates of transfer for courses that are delivered. You can use the results to pinpoint potential problem areas and to make necessary improvements to course design and delivery, thereby improving transfer rates.

During the development of the transfer evaluation model, many criteria were established by the Organizational Development (OD) section of the Waste Isolation Division. OD determined that it needed a transfer of training evaluation approach that met the following conditions. It must:

- Provide an overall transfer of training rate from the classroom to the job for any given course.

- Provide transfer of training rates from the classroom to the job for all major content areas of any given course.

- Provide instructional staff with clear, concise feedback for systematically improving transfer of training rates for: (1) content areas that need more instruction; (2) content areas that need less instruction; and (3) content areas that should be left alone.

- Be user friendly (to instructional staff, administrative staff, and management users), easy to use and interpret, and readily computerized.

- Be budget friendly—inexpensive to use.

- Ensure valid results by: (1) determining whether the trainees possessed the skills and knowledge *before* taking the class; (2) minimizing defensiveness and organizationally desirable responses; and (3) maximizing honest and frank feedback.

The OD staff reviewed thirteen models. Exhibit 16–3 summarizes the results of this review. These findings provide you with a snapshot of what many of the transfer models measure and do not measure. Unfortunately, the authors of the report did not provide the names of the models they reviewed.

Exhibit 16–3
Sample: Percentage of training transfer
models that met each WID criterion.

Percentage	Criteria
77%	Provides an overall transfer of training rate from the classroom to the job for any given course
38%	Provides transfer of training rates from the classroom to the job for all major content areas of any given course
38%	Provides instructional staff with clear, concise feedback for systematically improving transfer of training rates: 1) content areas that need more instruction; 2) content areas that need less instruction; 3) content areas that should be left alone
15%	Is user (instructional staff, administrative staff, and management) friendly—easy to use and interpret, readily computerized
15%	Is budget friendly—inexpensive to use
0%	Ensures valid results: 1) determines if the trainees possessed the skills and knowledge *before* taking the class; 2) minimizes defensive and organizationally desirable responses; 3) maximizes honest and frank feedback

Source: TOTEM, Transfer of Training Evaluation Model (Carlsbad, N. Mex.: Waste Isolation Division, Westinghouse Electric Company, 1995).

After the unacceptable results of the review of current models, the organization decided to develop an internal model, which eventually became TOTEM. The TOTEM focuses on trainee responses to three fundamental questions concerning each course-enabling objective:

1. Before the class, could you perform xxxx (where xxxx = the enabling objective restated)?

2. Can you currently perform xxxx?

3. How often are you applying your knowledge of xxxx on the job?

The TOTEM was field-tested by the Waste Isolation Division (WID) with a Business English training program, a five-day, forty-hour course, containing forty-three enabling objectives. Exhibit 16–4 displays an example of the questions that were included in the field test of the transfer model.

Exhibit 16–4
Sample TOTEM question set.

1a. Before taking BUS-100, could you identify   Y   N
proper agreement between a subject and a verb?

1b. Can you currently identify proper agreement   Y   N
between a subject and a verb?
If you answered N [NO], skip to question 2a

1c. How often are you applying your knowledge of   **0 1 2 3 4 5**
subject-verb agreement in your job?

1d. *If your answer to 1c was 0 [Never], please explain why:* _____

Source: TOTEM, Transfer of Training Evaluation Model (Carlsbad, N. Mex.: Waste Isolation Division, Westinghouse Electric Company, 1995).

The report notes that the basic logic of TOTEM was that *transfer of training occurred only if the trainee's response on a given objective would be as follows*:

		a.	is	*N,*
		b.	is	*Y,*
and		c.	is	$>/= 1$

OD staff members went beyond that to develop interpretation scales to give meaning to an overall transfer of training rate. Exhibit 16–5 shows the TOTEM Interpretation Scales that were created.

The executive summary report notes that the field test results provided the trainer of the Business English training course with concise feedback for revising course content to further improve the transfer of training. The TOTEM appears to be a highly valuable tool. The model not only helps to determine the current level of transfer of training for a particular course but it drives improvement efforts to increase transfer through specific corrective actions that trainers and instructional designers can take.

BARRIERS TO THE TRANSFER OF LEARNING

There are many possible barriers to the transfer of learning. Sometimes training is simply poorly designed or delivered. For example, perhaps vague objectives were written or the wrong person attended training at the wrong time. On the other hand, sometimes effectively designed and delivered training still does not result in transfer of skills back to the workplace. When transfer of learning does not occur, it could be attributable to many impediments that face learners as they complete training and return to the workplace. For this reason, identify potential barriers and work to overcome them whenever possible.

Consider four key potential barriers to transfer of learning:

- The learner's supervisor may not allow use of the new skills or will not provide the tools necessary for using the new skills.

- The learner may not remember how to perform them.

- The corporate culture may not support application.

- It may simply be easier to "do it the old way."

Many barriers fall outside of the trainer's control. For example, the learner's supervisor or management is chiefly responsible for reinforcement on the job. Awareness of the key role of the supervisor or manager in transfer was strikingly reinforced in the survey we conducted of trainers. When asked to share the most typical problems they faced on a regular basis, many trainers specifically mentioned lack of management support, buy-in, or reinforcement of the training. On pages 446 and 447 are seven critical incidents provided by trainers in our survey that relate pointedly to this issue:

Exhibit 16–5
Sample TOTEM interpretation scales.

Course Transfer of Training Rate
(average of all enabling objective transfer of training rates)

0–33%	LOW – All objectives with UNACCEPTABLE rate(s) **must** be revised before the course can be offered again
34–66%	MEDIUM – All objectives with UNACCEPTABLE rate(s) **should** be revised before the course can be offered again
>/= 67%	HIGH – No revision is required

Transfer of Training Rate by Objective
(For a given objective, number of N, Y, and >/= 1 responses to
questions a, b, and c divided by the total number of responses)

>/= 50%	ACCEPTABLE
0–49%	UNACCEPTABLE

Prior Knowledge Rate by Objective
(For a given objective, number of Y responses to question a
divided by the total number of responses)

0–66%	ACCEPTABLE
>/=67%	UNACCEPTABLE – Investigate reducing the amount of time spent on the objective

Incomprehension Rate by Objective
(For a given objective, number of responses with N for both
questions a and b divided by the total number of responses)

0–33%	ACCEPTABLE
>/=34%	UNACCEPTABLE – Investigate increasing the amount of time spent on the objective

Training/Job Disconnect Rate by Objective
(For a given objective, number of responses with N, Y, and O
for questions a, b, and c divided by the total number of responses)

0–33%	ACCEPTABLE
>/= 34%	UNACCEPTABLE

Source: TOTEM, Transfer of Training Evaluation Model (Carlsbad, N. Mex.: Waste Isolation Division, Westinghouse Electric Company, 1995).

Where's Our Support?

" *The most typical problem I face on a regular basis is lack of management support. Either they don't allow the employees to schedule time for training or don't allow them to use their new skills.* "

Where's the Commitment?

" *Lack of enthusiasm for the topic. This and the lack of commitment from management are the largest and most typical problems that an instructor/trainer in my field experiences.* "

No Follow-up

" *Follow-up is a problem I encounter after the delivery: not enough resources, and supervisors don't take it on as a part of their job.* "

Lack of Support and Resources

" *We take our reps into the field with makeshift offices. Two problems arise: One, all materials are usually not present, and two, sales managers who accompany the training department on the road do not always support all the training ideas.* "

No Upper Management Support

" *My most typical problem is not in my classroom. It is in the lack of support from executives and management. Support to create an effective classroom, to create the needed classes, in getting management to believe and the staff to participate.* "

No Management Accountability

" Management support when participant returns to work. I try to follow up with a letter to the manager stressing the importance of the course, time invested, etc. "

Is There Buy-In?

" We are a trade association for fifty member companies. My biggest problem is training follow-up. I don't have the opportunity to see if people are able and willing to use the skills we discuss during the session. I also never get a chance to speak to the attendees' supervisor or manager before the training, to get his/her buy-in, so I don't know how much support the trainee gets upon returning to work and attempting to implement the behaviors we have covered. "

STRATEGIES FOR ENCOURAGING TRANSFER OF LEARNING

You and others can take many actions to increase the likelihood that learning will transfer from the training room to the workplace. In 1992, transfer of learning experts Mary Broad and John Newstrom developed a matrix to show what different stakeholders can do at different times to improve transfer of learning. Their model is divided into three key time frames: before training, during training, and after training. They also identified three key people involved in the transfer process: the manager, the trainer, and the learner. These six variables form a 3 x 3 matrix and represent an excellent way of viewing—and discussing with others—the transfer of learning process. Broad and Newstrom identify key action steps for each group during each time period to boost transfer of learning. There are more than one hundred excellent strategies for managing transfer of learning listed in Exhibit 16–6. Some of these are common sense and will be easy for you to incorporate into your routine. Also, we suggest that you review your current training programs and processes to determine what transfer strategies are already in place and how they might be improved or enhanced.

Since the focus of this book is on training delivery skills and the role of the trainer, those readers who are trainers should concentrate on the strategies that they can use before, during, and after training to

Exhibit 16–6
Strategies for managing transfer of learning.

Training Stage	Performed by	Action	
Before	Manager	M/B.1	Build transfer of training into supervisory performance standards.
		M/B.2	Collect baseline performance data.
		M/B.3	Involve supervisors and trainees in needs analysis procedures.
		M/B.4	Provide orientations for supervisors.
		M/B.5	Involve trainees in program planning.
		M/B.6	Brief trainees on the importance of the training and on course objectives, content, process, and application to the job.
		M/B.7	Review instructional content and materials.
		M/B.8	Provide supervisory coaching skills.
		M/8.9	Provide time to complete precourse assignments.
		M/B.10	Offer rewards and promotional preference to trainees who demonstrate new behaviors.
		M/B.11	Select trainees carefully.
		M/B.12	Arrange conferences with prior trainees.
		M/B.13	Send co-workers to training together.
		M/B.14	Provide a positive training environment (timing, location, facilities).
		M/B.15	Plan to participate in training sessions.
		M/B.16	Encourage trainee attendance at all sessions.
		M/B.17	Develop a supervisor/trainee contract.
	Trainer	TR/B.1	Align the HRD program with the organization's strategic plan.
		TR/8.2	Involve managers and trainees.
		TR/B.3	Systematically design instruction.
		TR/8.4	Provide practice opportunities.
		TR/8.5	Develop trainee readiness.
		TR/8.6	Design a peer coaching component for the program and its follow-up activities.
	Trainee	TE/B.1	Provide input into program planning.
		TE/B.2	Actively explore training options.
		TE/B.3	Participate in advance activities.
During	Manager	M/D.1	Prevent interruptions.
		M/D.2	Transfer work assignments to others.

Exhibit 16–6 (continued)
Strategies for managing transfer of learning

		M/D.3	Communicate supervisory/managerial support for the program.
		M/D.4	Monitor attendance and attention to training.
		M/D.5	Recognize trainee participation.
		M/D.6	Participate in transfer action planning.
		M/D.7	Review information on employees in training.
		M/D.8	Plan assessment of transfer of new skills to the job.
	Trainer	TR/D.1	Develop application-oriented objectives.
		TR/D.2	Manage the unlearning process.
		TR/D.3	Answer the "WIIFW" question.
		TR/D.4	Provide realistic work-related tasks.
		TR/D.5	Provide visualization experiences.
		TR/D.6	Give individualized feedback.
		TR/D.7	Provide job performance aids.
		TR/D.8	Provide "Ideas and Applications" notebooks.
		TR/D.9	Create opportunities for support groups.
		TR/D.10	Help trainees prepare group action plan.
		TR/D.11	Have trainees create individual action plans.
		TR/D.12	Design and conduct relapse prevention sessions. (See Chapter 8)
		TR/D.13	Help trainees negotiate a contract for change with their supervisors.
	Trainee	TE/D.1	Link with a buddy.
		TE/D.2	Maintain an "Ideas and Applications" notebook.
		TE/D.3	Participate actively.
		TE/D.4	Form support groups.
		TE/D.5	Plan for applications.
		TE/D.6	Anticipate relapse.
		TE/D.7	Create behavioral contracts.
Following	Manager	M/F.1	Plan trainees' reentry.
		M/F.2	Psychologically support transfer.
		M/F.3	Provide a "reality check."
		M/F.4	Provide opportunities to practice new skills.
		M/F.5	Have trainees participate in transfer-related decisions.

Exhibit 16–6 (continued)
Strategies for managing transfer of learning.

	M/F.6	Reduce job pressures initially.
	M/F.7	Debrief the trainer.
	M/F.8	Give positive reinforcement.
	M/F.9	Provide role models.
	M/F.10	Schedule trainee briefings for co-workers.
	M/F.11	Set mutual expectations for improvement.
	M/F.12	Arrange practice (refresher) sessions.
	M/F.13	Provide and support the use of job aids.
	M/F.14	Support trainee reunions.
	M/F.15	Publicize successes.
	M/F.16	Give promotional preference.
Trainer	TR/F.1	Apply the Pygmalion Effect.
	TR/F.2	Provide follow-up support.
	TR/F.3	Conduct evaluation surveys and provide feedback.
	TR/F.4	Develop and administer recognition systems.
	TR/F.5	Provide refresher/problem-solving sessions.
Trainee	TE/F.1	Practice self-management.
	TE/F.2	Review training content and learned skill.
	TE/F.3	Develop a mentoring relationship.
	TE/F.4	Maintain contact with training buddies.

Source: From *Transfer of Training* by Mary L. Broad and John W. Newstrom.
Copyright © 1992 by M. L. Broad and J. W. Newstrom
Reprinted by permission of Perseus Books Publishers, a member of Persus Books, L.L.C.

improve transfer. For example, one transfer strategy that trainers can apply *before* training is to develop trainee readiness. Ask yourself how you can develop trainee readiness. One suggestion is to develop a letter that is sent to learners in advance of the program welcoming them, setting some initial expectations, asking them to begin thinking about issues, and building their enthusiasm about the topic. One example of a transfer strategy, shown in Exhibit 16–6, that you can implement *during* training is to provide learners with small spiral-bound notepads as "ideas and applications" notebooks. You can inform them that the purpose of the notebook is to capture significant insights they have as they go through the program. Tell them that they will be given ample time throughout to reflect on what they have learned and plan ways they can apply the ideas to their specific work situations.

An example of a transfer strategy that you, as a trainer, can apply *following* delivery is to develop and administer recognition systems (see Exhibit 16–6). A *recognition system* could be as simple as sending the attendees a letter signed by the president of the company that thanks them for attending. The letter could include a reminder of the key objectives and content covered in the program and encouragement to apply what was learned.

Below is a critical incident that relates a technique called the "parking lot" as a way to defer issues that require management involvement:

Beyond the Scope of Training

" *The most typical problem in my line of training (sales) is the audience identifying an obstacle to their performance which cannot be overcome or resolved within a training session (such as management doesn't give us the necessary tools—laptop). I use the parking lot as a way of regaining control of the conversation. By introducing the parking lot at the beginning of class as a place to post "issues which are out of our control" I can defer to the parking lot as the place you post the issue. I inform the group that all info will be compiled and given to the appropriate person(s) to increase awareness at the appropriate level of obstacles to performance.* "

In addition to developing strategies they can use, communicate with learners and managers about the importance of transfer of learning and suggest ways they can increase it. For example, one way learners can boost transfer is through active participation. At the beginning of a session you can explain the impact that participation can have on comprehension and transfer and encourage learners to become involved in the learning process. You can also work with managers. One strategy offered by Broad and Newstrom in Exhibit 16–6 that managers can incorporate *before* training is to encourage learner attendance. You can work with managers to convey the importance of attendance, the impact that managers can have on attendance, and the effect that this will have later on transfer. The following critical incident relates to attendance and management support.

The Impact of Low Attendance

" The new-hire training program I designed is two weeks in length. However, I rarely get all participants for the full two weeks. Obstacles are participant availability, training room availability, my availability due to lack of notice by department, and management's view of training (training is not a necessity). I cover as much of the agenda as possible—sometimes skipping evaluations or exercises since I'd rather they receive the information and then they can practice on the job. Worst case, I cover major topics (I've had to do it in two days). Results: they are unprepared and supervisors have to spend their time finishing the training. "

Transfer of learning is likely to remain an important topic in the training field. As was seen in this section, many issues influence how much training transfers from classroom to workplace. Many barriers to transfer can be removed when they are recognized and corrective action is taken to address them. When learning is transferred from the classroom to the workplace, the chances of real performance improvement increase substantially. These positive changes, in turn, enhance your credibility as a trainer, and that of your entire training department.

SUMMARY

Although this chapter, unlike others in this book, was not focused on one of the fourteen competencies needed for effective training delivery, it did provide useful information on important topics about training delivery that were not addressed in detail elsewhere.

The chapter examined the following topics:

- Training delivery in international settings. A global economy has led to global training needs, and trainers must be equipped to deliver in other countries and cultures.

- Cotraining. Growing complexity in many subject matter areas sometimes requires multiple trainers to work together, and trainers must know how to deliver training with another trainer.

■ Ensuring the transfer of learning. Effective training delivery will be wasted if it is not transferred from the classroom to the workplace. This chapter discussed strategies and models for the effective transfer of learning and offered ideas about how to increase it.

STRATEGY LIST

Actionable Strategies to Improve Training Effectiveness:

International Training

❏ Be aware of cultural differences. What may seem like an innocent term, gesture, or concept may be offensive to some cultures.

❏ Identify in advance which training methods are culturally expected and accepted by the learners.

❏ Overprepare for international training. Check materials, facilities, learner needs and requests, and any other aspect of training that has potential to be problematic.

❏ If you are traveling overseas, allow yourself an extra day or two to adjust to the time change.

❏ If you are using a translator, practice in advance.

Cotraining

❏ Before training occurs, identify who is the lead trainer for each segment of training.

❏ Cotrain with someone who has a complementary personality and skill set.

❏ Practice cotraining with your partner in advance so that your presentation is clear, smooth, and seamless.

Transfer of learning

❏ Since transfer of learning is the overarching goal of training, identify in advance how you plan to evaluate whether or not the newly learned skills have transferred back to the job. Also encourage learners and their managers to do the same.

☐ Educate managers on how to create a work environment that is conducive to the learners' transferring the newly acquired skills to their jobs. Emphasize the importance of providing learners with the tools and other resources necessary to transfer the training.

☐ Be certain that the training objectives are meeting learner needs.

☐ Send a follow-up letter to the learners and their managers reminding them of the importance of the course and the resources invested in it.

☐ Prep the learners before the training occurs. Provide them with expectations, objectives, prework, and some questions to start thinking about.

☐ Provide learners with a note pad to write down ideas, thoughts, ah-ha's, and applications as they occur during training.

APPENDIX A

RESEARCH STUDY

INTRODUCTION, PURPOSE, AND RESEARCH QUESTIONS

During the summer and fall of 1998, in an effort to supplement the research base upon which *The Complete Guide to Training Delivery: A Competency-Based Approach* rests, we conducted a survey of training professionals. The purpose of the study was to obtain practitioners' perceptions about the importance and difficulty of each of the fourteen delivery competencies. Another purpose was to gather critical incidents of worst and most typical problems encountered by trainers during delivery. We felt that this would verify and extend the initial work by the International Board of Standards for Training, Performance, and Instruction (IBSTPI), a task that to date has not been undertaken. Further, we believed that the study, especially the critical incident component, would add rich texture to the book and further ground the concepts and techniques being discussed in practical, real-world experiences of those involved in training delivery.

After obtaining permission from IBSTPI to use the instructor competencies in our study, we developed four research questions and later designed the survey around these questions. These questions are shown below:

1. How important are the fourteen competencies perceived to be by trainers in the real world?

2. How difficult to use do trainers perceive each of the fourteen competencies to be?

3. What are some examples of the most difficult training delivery situations encountered by trainers?

4. What are some examples of the most common training delivery situations encountered by trainers?

POPULATION AND SAMPLING

We wanted to survey training delivery practitioners. For this reason we turned to the membership database of the American Society for Training and Development (ASTD), the largest professional organization for the training and development profession with over 70,000 members worldwide. To target people involved in training delivery we extracted names from the ASTD Web site (http:\\www.astd.org) and performed searches using the job title of "trainer" in an effort to focus on people who were actually involved in training delivery. A final list of 500 names of trainers with their contact addresses was generated. The survey methodology section of this appendix describes the process that was used.

In an attempt to further verify that respondents were indeed directly involved in training delivery, several screening questions were posed on the questionnaire itself. Those who were not classified as being involved in training delivery were eliminated from further analysis.

The sampling strategy that we used was not intended to be random and therefore the results cannot be generalized to a larger population. Our intention was to reach actual training delivery practitioners and obtain their perceptions regarding the training delivery competencies and critical incident delivery experiences they have had.

SURVEY QUESTIONNAIRE, METHODOLOGY, AND DATA ANALYSIS

Survey questionnaire. We developed a paper-based questionnaire and administered it to gather trainers' perceptions. The instrument contained five sections. Section I contains the two screening questions mentioned earlier. The purpose of the questions in Section I was to eliminate nontrainers from further analysis and to determine the level of involvement of respondents in training delivery.

The purpose of Section II was to obtain trainers' perceptions about the *importance* of each of the training delivery competencies. The competencies were listed and respondents were asked to rate the importance of each, using a five-point scale (1 = Not Important through 5 = Extremely Important to effective training delivery).

The same fourteen delivery competencies were displayed in Section III. In this section trainers were asked to rate the *difficulty* of demonstrating each of the competencies. Again a five-point scale was used (1 = Not Difficult through 5 = Extremely Difficult).

Section IV contained the two critical incident questions. The *critical incident technique* is a means by which to gather typical and worst-case scenarios and identify training and nontraining needs. Respondents were asked to describe, in detail, their worst experience related to the delivery of training. The goal of this question was to garner those training "nightmares" or "horror stories" that trainers have experienced. About a half page of blank space was provided, with the suggestion to add paper as necessary. Respondents were then asked to describe the most typical problem faced on a regular basis during the delivery of training.

The purpose of Section V of the questionnaire was to collect background information on survey participants. Basic demographic questions, such as job title and level of education, were posed.

Survey methodology. As was mentioned, a total of 500 names were extracted from the ASTD database. A cover letter and questionnaire were sent to each of the people in the survey. The cover letter described the purpose of the survey as well as its voluntary and confidential nature. Included with the cover letter and questionnaire was a postage-paid return envelope. The letter and questionnaire were carefully and professionally developed and designed so as to increase response rate. Further, the importance and intended use of the survey were conveyed, as was the user-friendly process.

During the first week of August 1998, the survey packet was mailed to the 500 trainers on our list. Participants were asked, in the cover letter, to return the completed questionnaire by August 21, 1998. Due to time and budget limitations, no follow-up postcard, mailings, or phone calls were conducted. An identification number was placed on the last page of the questionnaire for tracking purposes. As completed questionnaires or undeliverable mailings were returned the identification number was crossed off the master list of names. The researchers received no phone calls although the invitation to call with questions had been extended.

Data analysis. The two software packages used to perform the statistical analysis were Statistical Package for the Social Sciences (SPSS) and Microsoft Excel. Most of the analysis involved basic descriptive statistics, such as mean, standard deviation, frequencies, and cross-tabs. Our intent was to paint a picture of those training practitioners who chose to respond to our survey. Our purpose was not to attempt to generalize to some larger population.

STUDY RESULTS

Response rate. A total of 5 questionnaires were returned to the researchers by the United States Postal Service as undeliverable (generally due to the person moving locations, an inaccuracy in the database, or some other error). A total of 120 responses were received through the single mailing. This represents an adjusted response rate of 24 percent (adjusting for the letters that were undeliverable). Of the 120 usable questionnaires that were received, 13 were eliminated from analysis due to a response of "No" on the first screening question, which asked about involvement in training delivery. This left a total of 107 questionnaires that could be subjected to data analysis.

PROFILE OF RESPONDENTS

The responses to the background questions that were asked at the end of the questionnaire provide a picture of the group of people who participated in this study.

Job title. A question on the questionnaire allowed respondents to provide an open-ended job title. There was extremely wide variation among the responses that were received. However, some clear patterns did emerge. Although the exact title varied, a total of sixty respondents could be classified under the position title of "trainer." Some of the titles that fell under this category included training and development specialist, instructor, trainer/presenter, facilitator/trainer, technical trainer, electrical/safety trainer, national trainer, field trainer, nuclear trainer, and many others. In addition, sixteen respondents had the words "supervisor," "manager," or "director" in their title. Beyond that the responses varied from performance consultant to CEO, with few similar responses.

Type of training. One of the questions asked trainers what type of training they delivered most often. This open-ended question, again, resulted in numerous and varied responses. A total of forty-four respondents can be classified as involved in "technical/software/computer" training. The other categories with multiple responses include "supervisory/management/leadership training and development" with eleven respondents, "sales/customer service training" with seven, and "safety training" with seven. Again, a wide variation of exact responses within these categories existed. In addition to these categories the other responses included topics as diverse as "petroleum equipment," "new hire," and "GMP training." Another interesting point about the responses that were provided in this section was that a significant number of trainers listed multiple training topics. For example, one person listed "sales, customer service, and human resources" for this question. In fact, over fifteen people listed multiple topics that were focused on seemingly different areas.

Work setting. Another question asked respondents to select a response that described their work setting. Exhibit A–1 shows the responses to this question. Over one-quarter of the respondents chose the "other" category for their answer. In examining the open-ended work settings that were listed, it appears that a substantial number listed what could be classified as "service organizations." Some of these included retail, legal, travel company, and sales organization. The responses varied widely and few patterns emerged with the exception of "software development company," which appeared several times.

Exhibit A–1
Work setting of trainers in study.

Work Setting	Frequency	Percent
Academic/Educational Institution	3	3.0
Consulting/Contracting Services	11	10.9
Government/Military	2	2.0
Manufacturing Organization	21	20.8
Service Organization	27	26.7
Financial Services	11	10.9
Other	26	25.7

Note: n=102

Size of organization. The size of the respondents' organizations ranged from one person to 600,000. For this reason, we selected six size ranges by which to describe the results. These are displayed in tabular form in Exhibit A–2.

Exhibit A–2
Size of organization of trainers in study.

Number of Employees in Entire Organization	Frequency	Percent
5 or fewer	7	7.3
6 to 100	9	9.4
101 to 1,000	33	34.4
1,001 to 5,000	25	26.0
5,001 to 20,000	12	12.5
more than 20,000	10	10.4
Note: n=96		

Educational attainment. We asked trainers to state their highest level of education completed. More trainers (55.9 percent) selected "four years of college/Bachelor's" than any other category. Exhibit A–3 displays a summary of the responses to this question.

Exhibit A–3
Educational attainment of trainers in study.

Highest Level of Education Completed	Frequency	Percent
High School Diploma or less	4	3.9
2 Years of College/Associate degree	12	11.8
4 Years of College/Bachelor degree	57	55.9
Master's	25	24.5
Doctorate	3	2.9
Other	1	1.0
Note: n=102		

Gender. There was a fairly even response among men and women with eight more women responding than men. Of the 102 responses, 55 responses (53.9 percent) were completed by women and 47 (46.1 percent) were provided by men.

Years of experience. Participants were asked to write, to the nearest year, the number of years they had been involved in the delivery of training. The answers ranged from 1 year to 31 years. The mean number of years among the 101 respondents was 7.85, and the standard deviation was 6.73.

Involvement in training delivery. As was mentioned earlier, we passed several screening questions by which those who were not involved in training delivery were filtered from further analysis. The responses provided to these questions helped to gain a general picture of involvement in training delivery as well as the percentage of time spent in delivery. Of the 107 people who responded to this question, 37 stated that they were involved in training delivery on a part-time basis (34.6 percent), and 70 individuals stated that they were involved full-time in delivery (65.4 percent).

In terms of the estimated percentage of time they spent in training delivery, Exhibit A–4 shows the breakdown between respondents involved on a part-time and full-time basis.

Exhibit A–4			
Percentage of time spent in training delivery.			
Proportion of Time	*n*	*Mean*	*S.D.*
Those involved full-time	66	55.30%	24.04%
Those involved part-time	36	27.36%	18.95%
Overall (part- and full-time)	102	45.44%	26.02%

Importance ratings. Each respondent was asked to rate each of the fourteen training delivery competencies using a five-point scale (1 = Not Important to 5 = Extremely Important). Exhibit A–5 shows the mean importance ratings arranged in descending order.

As can be seen in Exhibit A–5, the highest rated competency (most important) was "respond appropriately to learners' needs for clarification or feedback" (mean = 4.65). The least important competency was "report evaluation information" (mean = 3.42). A score of 3.0 on the rating scale represented "important." Note that all of the competencies were rated higher than 3.0, with the lowest being 3.42, indicating that trainers perceived all of the competencies to be important to training delivery.

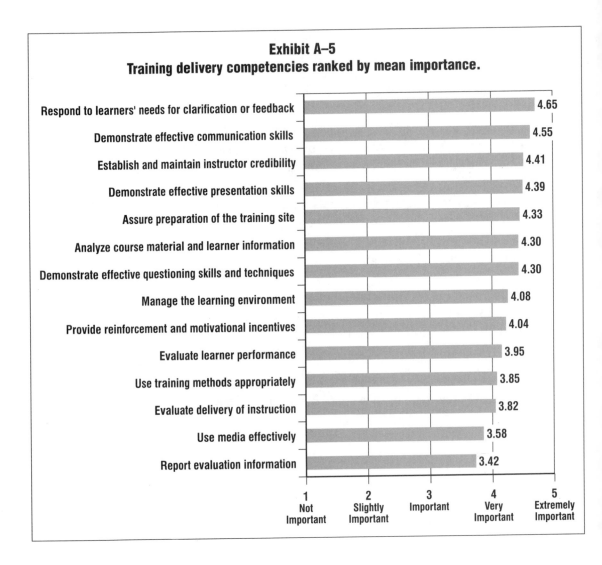

Exhibit A–5
Training delivery competencies ranked by mean importance.

Competency	Mean
Respond to learners' needs for clarification or feedback	4.65
Demonstrate effective communication skills	4.55
Establish and maintain instructor credibility	4.41
Demonstrate effective presentation skills	4.39
Assure preparation of the training site	4.33
Analyze course material and learner information	4.30
Demonstrate effective questioning skills and techniques	4.30
Manage the learning environment	4.08
Provide reinforcement and motivational incentives	4.04
Evaluate learner performance	3.95
Use training methods appropriately	3.85
Evaluate delivery of instruction	3.82
Use media effectively	3.58
Report evaluation information	3.42

1 Not Important   2 Slightly Important   3 Important   4 Very Important   5 Extremely Important

We compared the importance ratings placed by males and females on the delivery competencies. The most important competency among male respondents was "assure preparation of the training site" (mean = 4.96), which is very close to "extremely important." Among female respondents, however, this competency was rated number eleven in importance (mean = 3.89). For females the most important competency was "respond appropriately to learners' needs for clarification or feedback" (mean = 4.71). The rest of the responses were fairly consistent for males and females.

Difficulty ratings. In Section III of the survey questionnaire, trainers were asked to rate the difficulty of demonstrating each of the competencies. The results of this question are shown graphically in Exhibit A–6.

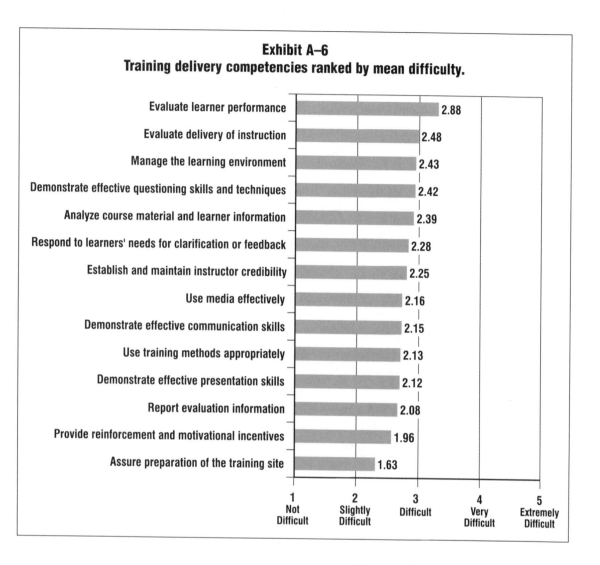

Exhibit A–6
Training delivery competencies ranked by mean difficulty.

Competency	Mean
Evaluate learner performance	2.88
Evaluate delivery of instruction	2.48
Manage the learning environment	2.43
Demonstrate effective questioning skills and techniques	2.42
Analyze course material and learner information	2.39
Respond to learners' needs for clarification or feedback	2.28
Establish and maintain instructor credibility	2.25
Use media effectively	2.16
Demonstrate effective communication skills	2.15
Use training methods appropriately	2.13
Demonstrate effective presentation skills	2.12
Report evaluation information	2.08
Provide reinforcement and motivational incentives	1.96
Assure preparation of the training site	1.63

Scale: 1 Not Difficult · 2 Slightly Difficult · 3 Difficult · 4 Very Difficult · 5 Extremely Difficult

Again, a five-point scale was used to determine the degree of difficulty (1 = Not Difficult to 5 = Extremely Difficult). The most difficult competency, according to trainers, was "evaluate learner performance" (mean = 2.88). The least difficult competency was "assure preparation of the training site" (mean = 1.63). For the most part, there was a large degree of consistency between males and females.

Critical incidents. Trainers were asked to provide critical incidents representing their worst training delivery experiences as well as their most typical problems experienced during delivery. Of the 107 respondents, 65 people provided critical incidents for worst experiences and 81 people provided them for typical delivery problems. The result was a total of 146 critical incidents. Some relayed lengthy stories with colorful detail, while others wrote only a sentence or two.

Many of these critical incidents have been integrated into the text in an effort to provide real examples of problems faced by trainers during delivery. The remaining critical incidents are shown in Appendix B and are presented verbatim in two sections: the worst experiences related to training delivery, and the most typical problems faced on a regular basis.

CONCLUSIONS

Several conclusions can be drawn from the results of the survey we undertook. One important finding was that all fourteen competencies were perceived as being important. Recall that the lowest rated item received a mean score of 3.42, which is almost the midpoint between "important" and "very important." Further, nine of the fourteen competencies were rated between 4.0 ("very important") and 5.0 ("extremely important"). In a cursory review of the training and development literature, we could not identify any verification research on the original IBST-PI competency study. Therefore, this study represents an initial verification of the fourteen competencies among training practitioners. All indications point to the belief that the competency list developed by IBSTPI is, indeed, important to delivery effectiveness.

No attempt was made by the authors to extend the original competency study by asking respondents to alter or add to the list of delivery competencies. However, it is possible to infer from the critical incidents that several additional competencies may be important to success before, during, and after delivery. The issue of lack of management support, for example, suggests that "organizational savvy" or the "ability to partner with managers" is an important but overlooked competency. That said, we do acknowledge that the IBSTPI competency study set out to identify only competencies that are important to training *delivery*. However, the critical incidents suggest that some external issues, such as the extent of management support, may have an indirect and perhaps even a direct impact on training delivery.

CRITICAL INCIDENT EXERCISE

We collected a number of critical incident experiences from training practitioners as part of our study. Many of these can be found throughout the chapters of *The Complete Guide to Training Delivery: A Competency-Based Approach.* These critical incidents are real-life experiences—told in the words of the trainers themselves—related to training delivery. The following exercise is based on the critical incidents that we did not use in the chapters.

Directions: Working alone or with others, read the critical incidents described in Parts I and II. Then, think about and discuss what you would do in these situations. Try to apply some of the principles and ideas covered in this book. There are no right or wrong answers. In some cases, trainers provided the steps they took when confronted with the problem. In these cases, consider: Do you agree or disagree with the trainer's action? Why? What are some potential consequences of the trainer's action? Also, as you develop your response, try to predict the potential outcomes of that action. In other words: What might happen (positive or negative) as a result of your approach to the situation?

PART I

The following critical incidents were provided by trainers in our study in response to the following statement: "Please describe the *worst experience* you have had related to the delivery of training."

" *When people leave your training halfway and you don't even notice it (leaving for being upset or unsatisfied). You never know what happens down the road and what the effects can be.* "

" *I traveled to Texas to train/install/set up a construction company with an accounting software package. I set up our standard software for accounts receivable invoicing. The customer was not happy with the procedures or the printed end result. My boss wouldn't listen to me and I had to rework the project three more times before I could force a conference call between the two parties. My customer told me off because our salesperson had promised the accounts receivable invoicing could be exactly the way it was in the previous software package. It took us two days to complete the project once my boss finally understood what we needed to do, but the customer was put off for a month in the meantime while my boss wouldn't listen to my evaluation of the situation.* "

" *During a dealer training class, I had two competitive dealers arguing with each other and almost coming to blows. I suggested an immediate class break and asked both parties to leave the training. The entire class was happy the two individuals were gone.* "

" *Equipment failure—the system went down. Trying to find examples from live accounts that pertain to the training material. Trying to find accounts that do not have a lot of exceptions to show to trainees.* "

" *On the first day of class, I realized that several participants did not complete the prework. The program requires the use of the feedback from the prework throughout the program, so we had to cancel it on the day of the program.* "

" *Losing a class. I taught a topic that was not wanted by the students. The classes were rowdy and sometimes openly hostile (topic related to job changes). I listened to complaints and let them vent a bit. I explained why we are changing (to keep jobs), and then proceeded with the material. This works in most cases.* "

" My worst experience was in being new to classroom training and unschooled in how to prepare, how to evaluate, how to ask questions, and many more. I went to class myself, got some methods on how to judge and evaluate myself, and just kept on teaching. The results were that I still "sweat" when I open up a new course (day one). The rest of it is much smoother now. "

" I had to train thirty mechanics on six OSHA-related topics during the employees' lunch hour. I had one participant complain that the training was stupid and that the company should be able to do something better. He did not understand that the time restrictions were created by the company, not by me, the trainer. I pointed out that he received a free lunch, got paid for it, and also was given an outline/manual of all the information covered. I also guaranteed him that any information or individual training he would want would be made available to him in the future. "

" Cliques forming in class, including several trainees plus one leader. Resolution: reassignment of environment, confront those not accepting realignment, establish control (ultimatum). "

" European execs—sexual harassment training. I had to restructure the entire course on the spot. My premise of "matter of respect" had to be replaced with "matter of culture" and U.S. law. I believe I learned more from this session than they did. "

" I was teaching a computer class for a client and needed Widows 95. The client did not have Windows 95 installed on the computers in the classroom, only Windows 3.1. Also, the client did not have an overhead projector as was promised. "

" There is not an individual or specific experience that stands out for me. However, without question my lack of preparation for training presentations has resulted in negative experiences. This also seems to be management's most disregarded need in planning. "

" *The "old timers"—people who have been employed by the organization for fifteen to twenty years who are afraid of change—or afraid of sharing knowledge for fear of displacement (insecurity).* "

" *I went to a meeting in Dallas and they were to provide a slide projector for my presentation. Although they had one, it was not functional and I had to talk about products that they could not see on slides. The district manager apologized profusely for not testing the projector. I always check equipment the night before.* "

" *Worst experience—Management had a hidden agenda for providing diversity training. Participants came in with huge chips on their shoulders, angry and vengeful. The session started as a disaster. Management provided no support, and did not prepare people in advance or frame the purpose for the education experience. I stopped the session halfway through, threw out the agenda, and addressed, through facilitation techniques and affinity diagrams, the "elephant" in the middle of the room! Everyone was hesitant at first then let it all go. The learning and findings from the affinity diagramming we applied to diversity, human interaction, and how important respect is in the workplace. Key point—as a facilitator, you must address the "elephants" and be willing to change horses in the middle of the stream to get results.* "

PART II

The following critical incidents were provided by trainers in our survey study in response to the following statement: "Please describe the *most typical problem* you face on a regular basis related to the delivery of training."

" *Attendance. Absenteeism from training classes in my region runs at almost 50 percent each month.* "

"From a client's perspective, it is nearly impossible to evaluate the return on investment (ROI) of the training."

"Hardware users who are not prepared to learn or change old way of doing things."

"I cannot be an expert on every topic in our business. I have difficulty working with the appropriate supervisors to get a project ready for presentation. They are not involved enough."

"The most difficult/typical problem I face is the bad attitude. I train in the soft skills area and very often my students feel that they do not need this type of training. It is a waste of time to them. You really can't ignore it because it (the attitude) can become disruptive. I allow the student to vent, understand where they are coming from, and then bring the rest of the class in. This way I'm not telling the student you have a bad attitude, I'm understanding. The class is giving the student direction. The class is very helpful if you engage them."

"Taking the time to analyze who your learner is. Looking critically at the needs of your learners is rarely done thoroughly enough."

"Customer does not know how to evaluate their own needs. I often have to assess their environment, procedures, methods, and hierarchy and then provide solution/options. This muddles consulting and training."

"People talking to each other during the instruction. People not paying attention."

" *Working with new employees who do not have basic computer skills. This affects them because even though we provide a service, the equipment is like a computer. They have a difficult time understanding the equipment and using the computer programs. We handle this by giving a lot of positive feedback regarding their skills as we train—more so than normal. The results are either they master it or when they get on the floor by themselves, they freeze and become too nervous to properly do their job. They are too afraid to learn something new.* "

" *Preassessment identification of students' capabilities prior to attending the course.* "

" *My most typical problem is to be asked to make a proposal based on the objectives and outcomes of training. Once the proposal is delivered, especially in manufacturing environments, it's "we want the same quality for less money and delivered in less time/fewer hours." I generally redo the proposal and trim the objectives to the time, not to the outcomes. At times, this really affects my attitude because you know the effectiveness of the course is severely affected by contact-time with the trainer.* "

" *Delivery of material in a pace that meets the needs of all the different adult learning styles.* "

" *Problems: late arrival of participants, no shows, substitution of participants, side bar discussions, participants challenging the direction of the organization, fatigue/attention span of participants. Solutions: close class at 9 A.M., charge back to departments, discussion with dealer manager and department manager. Side bar conversations: stand by people talking and ask if there are any questions by parties talking. People who challenge: suggest further discussion one to one. Fatigue: give breaks and get participants to stand up, ask questions, make sure class is a media mix.* "

" *Students are unsure of what to expect and many times feel ill equipped to be in a classroom all day. Their attention span is usually shorter than we would like it to be.* "

" *Class participants want to tell you what management did to them.* "

" *When I train newly hired sales representatives, they are often distracted because of all the other things going on (or not happening). For example, HR is behind on paper work, so they do not have the paycheck system set up yet. Or, they do not have even the basic materials they need to go out and work (like business cards and samples). My problem is getting reps to focus on learning.* "

" *Encouraging feedback while keeping that one person under control.* "

" *Participants come to class and feel pushed to be there and don't see the value.* "

" *People who don't want to be there or don't accept any personal responsibility to learn. They need to be spoon-fed rather than doing some learning (via online help) on their own.* "

" *My most typical problem I face on a regular basis is an individual coming to a seminar looking for a different approach, on a completely different subject. This is a marketing problem, not a training problem. If the individual stays through the seminar, they usually find it informative, if not applicable.* "

" *Have a series of exercises students must complete. Each is independent of the others but students generally ask, "Which one should I do first?" I suggest they review all exercises and begin the one they feel most knowledgeable, comfortable, or at ease with first.* "

" *Involvement of participants.* "

" *Avoiding 'data dump.'* "

" *The more I learn about training, the more ways I come up with to approach it. These ways take time. My most typical problem is that I am not given enough time to train some things in the manner I would like. I handle this by deciding how important it is to the goal, and address it with management if it is important enough to impact results.* "

" *My most typical problem is the training data environment. The training department shared the computer department's testing database but had no control of data renewals or program versions. This made it very difficult to set up training examples for demonstration and hands on exercises. The problems were controlled partially by continued communication between the computer department and training to keep changes to a necessary minimum during training. The ultimate solution would have been to build a separate training database. The importance of training material to the overall impression of training has on the trainee has finally been recognized and we are building a separate training database as part of our ERP implementation project.* "

" *Attendance is the problem (tardy/absence). Clear rule from Day 1. Result — Abide or attrition.* "

"Delivering a lot of information in a short amount of time."

"Last minute cancellation and no shows."

"Attendees fail to show up for training that is dependent on class interaction (i.e. teamwork, communication, internal consulting), leaving so few participants that they do not get full benefit from idea exchange among participants.

"Not enough equipment, or materials not showing up."

"Too much information, not enough time. Management says two-hour classes but to do a good job, they should be longer. So, I poll classes to determine what's important to them, provide lots of reference, step-by-step instruction which can be used in their office, offer more classes with very specific topics to cover (chunk information—example: mail merging)."

" People are happy to have reference material. They especially like step-by-step instructions, having a specific topic, etc. so they can pick/choose classes."

"Getting people to class."

"Since I'm the only trainer and we have three shifts 8 to 1, 1 to 5:30, and 5:30 to 10, there are times when we need all three shifts to be trained, so I have to see which shifts have the most need and then have to ask the new hires if they can attend the training other than their original shift that they were hired for."

"The pace of instruction in the classroom. With varying degrees of competency large blocks of time are set aside to accommodate the slowest learner. In general we have always allowed the time and had faster learners do extra work. However, they rarely need the practice."

"Unwilling participants are required to attend training."

"Seek to understand. The most typical problem is the different level of experience, motivation, and knowledge/understanding of the material. I generally handle this through assessments, pre-work, and criteria for attendance, but it doesn't always work."

"Power outage. The worst training experience I had occurred when the power went out in a hotel during classroom instruction, and after the power came on the supervisor of the group started an area meeting."

"Balancing the environment. The most typical problem I face is the poor performance of the facility in providing a quality learning environment, such as proper lights, heat, air quality. Feng Shui (Chinese art of placement)."

"I was asked to deliver a message on which I am not totally sold."

ANNOTATED
RESOURCE GUIDE

PROFESSIONAL ORGANIZATIONS RELATED TO TRAINING DELIVERY

A great number of resources are available for people involved in the training and development field. They are useful for introducing the new practitioner to the profession and for maintaining and enhancing the skills of experienced professionals. This section covers four professional organizations that are related to training delivery and include the American Society for Training and Development (ASTD), the International Society for Performance Improvement (ISPI), Toastmasters International, and the International Board of Standards for Training, Performance, and Instruction (IBSTPI). There are many other resources that could be listed, but these were chosen to provide readers with a brief overview of several well-established and highly regarded organizations. In addition to this introduction to resources, references are made throughout this book to Internet sites, workshops, discussion groups, and organizations that represent additional sources that can assist new as well as experienced trainers.

THE AMERICAN SOCIETY FOR TRAINING AND DEVELOPMENT (ASTD)

The largest professional organization related to the training and development field is the American Society for Training and Development (ASTD). ASTD's Web site can be found at http://www.astd.org/, and it contains a wealth of information about the organization as well as general information about the training and development field. ASTD has over 70,000 members worldwide representing more than 100 countries. Trainers can become national members as well as chapter members in one of the local chapters of ASTD that can be found in many cities throughout the United States.

The international conference and exhibition typically attracts over 7,000 people from 80 countries. The ASTD conference is held annually in the spring in large cities such as Washington, D.C. (1997), San Francisco (1998), Atlanta (1999), and Dallas (2000). This professional society also has forums, committees, and sub-groups dedicated to a variety of training and human resource development topics such as sales and marketing, learning organizations, and technical skills training. There are currently a total of forty-seven forums. Forum members participate on committees, receive a quarterly newsletter, and discuss current issues with peers.

ASTD also produces a number of useful publications. *Training & Development* is a magazine for practitioners and *Human Resource Development Quarterly* is a refereed journal that is more scholarly and academic in nature. Contact information for the American Society for Training and Development is shown below:

> 1640 King Street, Box 1443
> Alexandria, Virginia 22313-2043, USA
> Phone: (703) 683-8100 Fax: (703) 683-8103

THE INTERNATIONAL SOCIETY FOR PERFORMANCE IMPROVEMENT (ISPI)

The International Society for Performance Improvement (ISPI) is a smaller, but complementary organization to ASTD. The focus of ISPI is more on performance improvement, but many members of this group are training professionals. Topics of interest to those involved in training can be found in ISPI's two primary publications, *Performance Improvement* and *Performance Improvement Quarterly.* The Web site for ISPI is located at http://www.ispi.org/. Similar to ASTD, this organization also holds an annual conference and exposition. The Job Bank which can be reached through a hot link on the Web site displays hundreds of jobs related to training, instructional design, and performance improvement. Contact information for ISPI is shown below:

> 1300 L Street, N.W., #1250
> Washington, D.C. 20005
> Telephone: (202) 408-7969
> Fax: (202) 408-7972

Toastmasters International

Toastmasters International (http://www.toastmasters.org/) is an organization that helps trainers as well as nontrainers to improve their communication and presentation skills. Local Toastmasters clubs meet on a regular basis, such as weekly or monthly, and offer members the opportunity to give presentations and receive feedback on their performance from other members. Presentations that members give may be prepared in advance or may be impromptu and spontaneous in nature. Toastmasters International boasts over 8,500 clubs throughout 60 countries worldwide. Contact information for Toastmasters is shown below:

Mailing Address:
Toastmasters International
P.O. Box 9052
Mission Viejo, CA 92690
Phone: (949) 858-8255

Street Address:
Toastmasters International
23182 Arroyo Vista
Rancho Santa Margarita, CA
 92688

The International Board of Standards for Training, Performance, and Instruction

The International Board of Standards for Training, Performance, and Instruction (IBSTPI) was founded as a not-for-profit corporation in 1984. Its mission is to improve individual and organizational performance by articulating and promoting the integrity of professional practice through research, development, definition of competencies, and education; stretching the boundaries of the field through exploration, promotion, and integration of new ideas, research, and practices from other disciplines.

The Board grew from the work of the Joint Certification Task Force, which was composed of the Association for Educational Communications and Technology (AECT) and the National Society for Performance and Instruction (NSPI, now the International Society for Performance Improvement, ISPI). Created in 1977, the Joint Task Force included over thirty professional practitioners and academics with expertise in various facets of training, performance, and instruction. The task force developed the initial set of competencies for the instructional design professional and created a prototype assessment procedure. Also, during this period, members of the task force spoke at professional meetings and published articles on professional competence and certification.

The task force reorganized itself in 1983 to avoid conflicts of interest with its parent organizations. This action was taken with the approval and encouragement of the Boards of Directors of NSPI, AECT, and the Division of Instructional Development within AECT.

The Board, a group of fifteen professionals, considers itself a service organization to practitioners, consumers, educators, researchers, and vendors in the training and performance improvement field. The Board is responsible, in part, for the establishment and maintenance of ethical and best practice standards for professionals who serve as managers, designers, or trainers in the general professional field of performance improvement for individuals and organizations. The Board is also responsible, in part, for the preservation of the origins and history of the ethics and professional practice while inviting and encouraging the best of future practice.

They achieve these outcomes in several ways. Each board member serves as an exemplar of professional practice and the ethics of the profession. They serve as public advocates of the profession in speaking engagements, seminars, workshops, and other public discussions. The Board seeks to portray professional practice as a set of agreed upon competencies for the various functions of the profession. The Board publishes ideal standard competencies for trainers, designers, and managers who work in the profession of performance improvement. One intent of the board is to have these standards adopted and used by a wider array of public and private organizations. The Board also arranges to update and revise the standards of practice so they are more applicable across time and place.

The Board also publishes documents which intend to capture and preserve the essence of the origins and history of the profession so that young professionals will have a clean, clear image of best professional practice and ethical conduct. To date, IBSTPI has developed and disseminated competencies for instructional designers and developers, instructors, and training managers.

The Board invites, encourages and, in part, invents future professional practice for individual and organizational performance improvement. This is achieved by the ongoing review of historical and contemporary literature, discussion of current trends, and the attempt to imagine what the future should be.

The International Board of Standards for Training, Performance, and Instruction is about the business of promoting the definition, organization, codification, and use of the professional, disciplined craft of individual and collective performance improvement. To that end, it serves as a historian, recorder, exemplar, public advocate, and inventor of the craft.

Note: This description was provided by the International Board of Standards for Training, Performance, and Instruction and is used with its permission. Copyright © 1999 International Board of Standards for Training Performance and Instruction. IBSTPI Web Site: http://www. ibstpi.org/index.html.

BOOKS

A number of important texts were mentioned or referenced in the chapters of this book. Some focus on effective training delivery skills, but many concentrate on areas that are important to training, but were not a primary focus of this book. They are listed as resources that you can consult to learn more about these topics.

HUMAN PERFORMANCE IMPROVEMENT

Rothwell, William J. (Ed.) *ASTD Models for Human Performance Improvement: Roles, Competencies, and Outputs.* Alexandria, VA: The American Society for Training and Development, 1998. This 101-page paperback book presents the results of a competency study that was undertaken with the intent of identifying important competencies related to human performance improvement (HPI). Many training professionals in recent years have attempted to broaden their roles beyond training. This book presents a number of important models, concepts, competency definitions, self-assessment tools, and other means by which to deepen your understanding of HPI.

Robinson, D. G., and J. C. Robinson. *Performance Consulting: Moving Beyond Training.* San Francisco: Berrett-Koehler, 1995. Performance Consulting is a term that is synonymous with human performance improvement. This text provides readers with strategies for partnering with clients and engaging in performance consulting. A number of practical tools, interview guides, and case situations are provided.

INSTRUCTIONAL DESIGN

Rothwell, William J., and H. C. Kazanas. *Mastering the Instructional Design Process* (2nd ed.). San Francisco: Jossey-Bass, 1998. This is an outstanding text for trainers who are interested in learning more about instructional systems design (ISD), which is the backbone of effective training. This book is organized around the instructional design competencies identified by the International Board of Standards for Training, Performance, and Instruction.

Performance-Based Training

Robinson, D. G., and J. C. Robinson. *Training for Impact: How to Link Training to Business Needs and Measure the Results*. San Francisco: Jossey-Bass, 1989. This excellent text will help readers connect their efforts with the organization's strategy. The focus is on engaging in training that makes a difference or leads to results as opposed to training for activity.

Training Evaluation

Kirkpatrick, D. L. *Evaluating Training Programs: The Four Levels*. San Francisco: Berrett-Koehler, 1994. This text brings together Donald Kirkpatrick's extensive work on training evaluation into a guide that covers his four levels framework. Some fundamentals of effective training and development are also included.

Training Transfer

Broad, M. L., and J. W. Newstrom. *Transfer of Training: Action-Packed Strategies to Ensure High Payoff from Training Investments*. Reading, MA: Addison-Wesley, 1992. This book is an excellent resource for deepening your understanding of the process of training transfer (transferring learning from the training setting to the job). It identifies barriers to transfer and provides numerous practical strategies for encouraging training transfer.

International Training

Odenwald, S. B. *Global Training: How to Design a Program for the Multinational Corporation*. Alexandria, VA: The American Society for Training and Development, 1993. This text provides an overview of training and development in international settings. It addresses key strategic issues and provides practical guidelines for designing and implementing an effective global training program.

Magazines and Journals

Training & Development—practitioner-oriented magazine published monthly by the American Society for Training & Development, Inc., 1640 King Street, Alexandria, VA 22313; 703.683.8100. National ASTD members receive *T&D* as part of their membership dues.

Training—practitioner-oriented magazine published monthly by Lakewood Publications, 50 South Ninth Street, Minneapolis, MN 55402; 612.333.0471.

Performance Improvement—practitioner publication that is published monthly except for combined May/June and November/December issues by the International Society for Performance Improvement, 1300 L Street, N.W., Suite 1250, Washington, DC 20005; 202.408.7969. National ISPI members receive *PI* as part of their membership dues.

Performance Improvement Quarterly—scholarly journal published four times per year by the Learning Systems Institute in cooperation with the International Society for Performance Improvement, 1300 L Street, N.W., Suite 1250, Washington, DC 20005; 202.408.7969.

Human Resource Development Quarterly—scholarly journal published quarterly by Jossey-Bass Publishers, 350 Sansome Street, San Francisco, CA 94104-1342, and sponsored by the American Society for Training and Development and the Academy of Human Resource Development.

International Journal of Training and Development—scholarly journal with international focus that is published four times per year in March, June, September, and December by Blackwell Publishers Limited, 108 Cowley Road, Oxford OX4 1JF, UK, and 350 Main Street, Malden, MA 02148, USA.

TRAINING FIRMS

There are literally thousands of small and large firms that provide a wide variety of training products and services. This section highlights several firms that were mentioned in our book.

CREATIVE TRAINING TECHNIQUES INTERNATIONAL, INC.

> 7620 West 78th Street
> Minneapolis, MN 55439-2518
> Phone: 800-383-9210
> Fax: 612-829-0260
> http://www.cttbobpike.com/

Bob Pike's Creative Training Techniques International, Inc., offers a wealth of resources to help trainers improve their delivery effectiveness and move toward participant-centered training. Offers both public seminars and in-house customized train-the-trainer programs. Web site offers free articles, surveys, and product information.

DALE CARNEGIE TRAINING

> 1475 Franklin Avenue
> Garden City, NY 11530
> Phone: 800-231-5800
> http://www.dale-carnegie.com/

Dale Carnegie Training offers a variety of public speaking seminars at locations across the country and internationally.

DEVELOPMENT DIMENSIONS INTERNATIONAL

> 1225 Washington Pike
> Bridgeville, PA 15017
> Phone: 800-933-4463
> Fax: 412-257-0614
> http://www.ddi.com/

DDI provides comptency- and behavior-based human resource slutions. They specialize in selction, assessments, and training and development.

MANAGEMENT CONCEPTS, INC.

> 8230 Leesburg Pike, Suite 800
> Vienna, VA 22182
> Phone: 703-790-9595
> Fax: 703-790-1371
> http://www.managementconcepts.com/

For more than a quarter of a centurry, Management Concepts has provided training, consulting, and publishing for the mind at work.

MEREX CORPORATION

> 1270 East Broadway Road, Suite 103
> Tempe, AZ 85282
> Phone: 800-383-5636
> http://www.merexcorp.com

Merex Corporation provides workplace education training and consulting services such as needs assessment, adult basic skills training (reading and math), peer training, and writing skills training to companies across the nation. Free newsletter and learning styles inventory available on the Web site.

WORKSHOPS BY THIAGI, INC.

> 4423 E. Trailridge Rd.
> Bloomington, IN 47408-9633
> Phone: 800-996-7725
> http://www.thiagi.com/

Dr. Sivasailam "Thiagi" Thiagarajan is the president of this consulting firm. Provides a wide variety of training and performance improvement products and services including games, exercises, and other interactive activities. Many interesting materials and "freebies" on the Web site.

TRAINER CERTIFICATION RESOURCES
THE CHAUNCEY GROUP INTERNATIONAL

> 664 Rosedale Road
> Princeton, NJ 08540
> Phone: 609-720-6500
> http://www.chauncey.com/

This subsidiary of Educational Testing Service (ETS) offers trainer certification. The Certified Technical Trainer (CTT) certification includes a multiple choice exam and a performance video.

INTERNET RESOURCES
TRDEV-L DISCUSSION GROUP

Discussion groups are another valuable Internet-based resource for those wishing to learn more about international training. TRDEV-L is an example of a listserv dedicated to training and human resource development professionals (see http://train.ed.psu.edu/trdev-l/). This moderated (edited) discussion group is housed at Penn State University in the Department of Workforce Education and Development and is owned by Dr. David Passmore. On a daily basis, subscribers to this free service receive a digest of e-mail postings that discuss training and related topics. Individuals can post questions to the discussion list and receive answers from other subscribers. There are over 6,000 subscribers from more than 50 countries. Also available on the TRDEV-L Web site is an archive of discussion summaries.

THE NATIONAL TECHNOLOGICAL UNIVERSITY

Web site: http://www.ntu.edu. Offers both academic and professional development programming via distance education. Over 1,400 graduate level courses and more than 500 professional development seminars on a variety of topics delivered by satellite and over the Internet.

RESOURCES FOR INTERNATIONAL TRAINING

Chapter Sixteen discussed several important resources that are available for you to learn more about international training matters. This section highlights some of the items that were discussed in that chapter.

THE AMERICAN SOCIETY FOR TRAINING AND DEVELOPMENT (ASTD)

Web site: http://www.astd.org/. Members representing over 100 countries. An International Visitor's Center for those visiting the United States from an international location. ASTD also has an Information Center that can perform searches on international topics. The annual ASTD international conference typically attracts over 7,000 people from 80 nations. ASTD has forums, committees, and sub-groups dedicated to global training and human resource development.

THE INTERNATIONAL FEDERATION OF TRAINING AND DEVELOPMENT ORGANIZATIONS (IFTDO)

Web site: http://www.iftdo.org/index.htm. Members represent over 50 countries. Resources available on their Web site include a Global Registry, which is a database containing contact information for many international consulting firms, organizations, training vendors, and other associations related to the training and development field. On-line articles written by domestic and international authors about topics of relevance to global trainers. A World Human Resource Directory, which lists member organizations, is also available to members of IFTDO.

COUNTRY PROFILES AND BACKGROUND NOTES

One general purpose resource that you may find useful is a country profile service. *Country Profiles and Background Notes* is available through the Superintendent of Documents at the following address: United States Government Printing Office, Washington, DC 20402-9324 (phone: 202-783-3238).

EMBASSIES AND CONSULATES

Embassies and consulates sometimes make information available upon request to interested parties.

ENDNOTES

CHAPTER 1

1. *News & Notes: The Newsletter of the International Society for Performance Improvement* (July 1998): 7.

2. D. P. McMurrer, M. E. Van Buren, and W. H. Woodwell, "The 2000 ASTD State of the Industry Report" (American Society for Training and Development, 2000).

CHAPTER 2

1. D. J. Abernathy, "Presentation Tips From the Pros," *Training & Development* 53 (1999): 19–26.

CHAPTER 3

1. D. J. Abernathy, "Presentation Tips From the Pros," *Training & Development* 53 (1999): 19–26.

2. H. Forcinio, "Education, Training and Development Prepares Ford for Future," *Corporate University Review* 6 (1998): 18–30.

CHAPTER 4

1. D. J. Abernathy, "Presentation Tips From the Pros," *Training & Development* 53 (1999): 19–26.

CHAPTER 5

1. B. Tuckman and M. A. Jenson, "Stages of Small Group Development Revisited," *Group and Organizational Studies* (1977): 419–427.

2. Irving L. Janis, *Groupthink,* 2nd ed. (Boston: Houghton Mifflin, 1982), pp. 7–9.

3. B. Latane, K. Williams, and S. Harkins, "Many Hands Make Light the Work: The Causes and Consequences of Social Loafing," *Journal of Personality and Social Psychology* 37 (1979): 822–832.

CHAPTER 6

1. P. Ekman and W. V. Friesen, "Hand Movements," *Journal of Communication* 22 (1972): 353–374.

2. P. Ekman and W. V. Friesen, *Unmasking the Face* (Englewood Cliffs, NJ: Prentice-Hall, 1975).

3. E. T. Hall, *The Hidden Dimension* (Garden City, NY: Doubleday, 1966).

4. D. J. Abernathy, "Presentation Tips From the Pros," *Training & Development* 53 (1999): 19–26.

CHAPTER 7

1. D. J. Abernathy, "Presentation Tips From the Pros," *Training & Development* 53 (1999): 19–26.

CHAPTER 8

1. D. J. Abernathy, "Presentation Tips From the Pros," *Training & Development* 53 (1999): 19–26.

2. Ibid.

CHAPTER 10

1. J. Keller, "Motivational Systems," in I. H. Stolovitch and E. Keeps (Eds.), *Handbook of Human Performance Technology* (San Francisco: Jossey-Bass, 1992).

CHAPTER 11

1. D. J. Abernathy, "Presentation Tips From the Pros," *Training & Development* 53 (1999): 19–26.

2. S. J. Carroll, F. T. Paine, and J. J. Ivancevich, "The Relative Effectiveness of Training Methods—Expert Opinion and Research," *Personnel Psychology* 25 (1972): 495–510.

CHAPTER 12

1. K. Kruse, "Tech Talk: Five Levels of Internet-Based Training," *Training & Development* 51 (1997): 60–61.

2. P. Loughner and D. Harvey, "Making the Transition: A Framework of Web-Based Training Methods." Paper presented at the annual meeting of the Association for Educational Communications and Technology, Houston, TX, 1999.

CHAPTER 13

1. D. L. Kirkpatrick, *Evaluating Training Programs: The Four Levels* (San Francisco: Barrett-Koehler, 1994).

CHAPTER 16

1. S. B. Odenwald, *Global Training* (Alexandria, VA: The American Society for Training and Development, 1993).

ABOUT THE AUTHORS

Stephen B. King, Ph.D., is Executive Director of Leadership and Management Development with Management Concepts, Inc., head-quartered in Vienna, Virginia. He is an adjunct professor at Johns Hopkins University in the graduate program in Human Resources and Organization Development and works with the Research and Enterprise Solutions Department of the American Society for Training and Development (ASTD). He has published articles in magazines and journals such as *Training & Development, Performance Improvement,* and *Occupational Education Forum* and has presented at the interna-tional conferences of the ASTD and the International Society for Performance Improvement (ISPI), Linkage, Inc., and the American Association of Community Colleges (AACC).

Marsha King, Ph.D., is Senior Management Development Consultant with Capital One Financial. She is a frequent speaker on topics includ-ing human performance improvement, knowledge management, and technology-based learning environments. She has published articles on the transfer of training, human performance improvement interven-tions, and competency-based assessment. She is also an adjunct pro-fessor at Johns Hopkins University in the graduate program in Human Resources and Organization Development and is a Certified Technical Trainer (CTT).

William J. Rothwell, Ph.D., is Professor of Human Resource Development in the Department of Adult Education, Instructional Systems, and Workforce Education and Development in the College of Education on the University Park Campus of The Pennsylvania State

University. He also serves as Director of Penn State's Institute for Research in Training and Development. He was previously Assistant Vice President and Management Development Director for The Franklin Life Insurance Company in Springfield, Illinois, and Training Director for the Illinois Office of Auditor General. He has worked full-time in human resource management and employee training and development from 1979 to the present. He thus combines real-world experience with academic and consulting experience. He is the President of Rothwell & Associates, a private consulting firm that numbers over 32 multinational corporations on its client list.

INDEX

491